VALUE ADDED TAX

International Practice and Problems

Alan A. Tait

International Monetary Fund
Washington, D.C. • 1988

© 1988 International Monetary Fund

The quotation on page 304 from "Banana Republics" is
reprinted with permission; composed by Steve Goodman/
Steve Burgh/Jim Rothermel; © 1976 Big Ears Music
(ASCAP)/Red Pajamas Music (ASCAP); administered
by Bug.

Charts and cover: IMF Graphics Section

Library of Congress Cataloging-in-Publication Data

Tait, Alan A.
  Value-added tax.

  Bibilography: p.
  Includes index.
  1. Value-added tax. I. Title.
HJ5711.T36   1988   336.2'714   88-13135
ISBN 1-55775-012-2

Price: US$29.50

Contents

Part II: Effects of VAT

Part III: VAT Administration and Compliance

Tables

The following symbols have been used in this book:

... or — to indicate that the figure is zero or insignificant or that the data are unavailable or unknown;

— between years or months (e.g., 1987–88 or January–June) to indicate the years or months covered, including the beginning and ending years or months;

/ between years (e.g., 1987/88) to indicate a crop or fiscal (financial) year.

"Billion" means a thousand million.

National currencies have been converted into U.S. dollars at exchange rates prevailing in January 1988.

It should be noted that the term "country" used in this book does not in all cases refer to a territorial entity that is a state as understood by international law and practice. The term also covers some territorial entities that are not states, but for which statistical data are maintained and provided internationally on a separate, independent basis.

Preface

Academics are commonly interested in the more theoretical issues of taxation. Administrators must implement legislation and are worried about the nuts and bolts of taxation. Politicians, ideally, try to ensure that academic ideas are married to practicality to best serve the needs of the country and their constituents.

Not often do studies try to meet all three needs. Those that come the nearest are the tax reform studies and government commissions that deal with particular taxes or tax systems. The 1984 U.S. tax reform or the Canadian Tax Reform of 1987 (*Lower Rates, Fairer System*) are good recent examples. However, these deal with the problems of a particular country and sometimes lack a broader international perspective. In practice, there can be a significant gap between rhetoric (for example, about equity) and application (for example, actual evasion).

This study tries to examine a single tax, looking at problems and options in theory and their different impacts, while keeping an eye firmly on the ball of practical implementation. The interests of both administrators and taxpayers are considered. At the same time, arguments are advanced for and against alternative policies that might inform politicians or administrators considering changes. As the value-added tax is now used in Europe, Latin America, Africa, Asia, and the Pacific, examples have been taken from a wide variety of systems (as the index shows); the problems of administering a VAT in Asia and Europe are similar, and yet they can be very different; but each region can learn from the other, and this study tries to illustrate problems and solutions by international examples. These examples are obviously not exhaustive but illustrate different ways to tackle particular issues.

I would like to think this study could emphasize to university faculty and students how important are the practical details of tax implementation and, yet, I hope it is written in a sufficiently plain way (at least in parts) to be read by anyone with an interest in taxation. It has been suggested that economists should improve their knowledge of "institutional details, . . . legal processes and reasoning, and political awareness and savvy" (Nelson (1987, p. 86)). I trust this book is a move in the right direction. It cannot attempt to match the highly detailed legal analysis of, say, European Community law on the VAT, nor does it deal with minutiae of each VAT system—although sometimes detailed examples do illuminate particular problems. In many ways, it is a broad brush treatment with special detailing where issues have not been widely discussed before (such as VAT staffing, audit, evasion, enforcement, and penalties). In other chapters (for example, the chapter on computers), technical jargon has been largely sidestepped to highlight options and decisions encountered in many countries.

This book was not written at the behest of the IMF (which is not responsible for the text); however, the Fiscal Affairs Department of the Fund has worked on VATs in many countries and the writings and views of my colleagues, both staff and consultants, are scattered through this study. It may be invidious to mention any staff member by name, but special note should be made of consultants Gordon Cox, Sol Dubroof, Seamus Duignan, and André Vinck, who taught me much about how VAT works (and does not work); also the referees, who by tradition remain anonymous, but whose trenchant comments added greatly to the text. Librarians Judith Crillo, Young-ja Kim, Yvonne Liem, and Anne Salda kept pushing references to me. Esha Ray provided careful and tactful editorial advice and Ella H. Wright prepared the index. Finally, Mary C. Riegel and Carmelita O. Eugenio battled with me and a changeover of word processing systems to produce a manuscript and no one, not even myself, is more relieved to see this book completed.

PART I

Structure of VAT

CHAPTER 1

Why a Value-Added Tax?

The latest innovation is the value-added tax. Its emergence in France illustrates the process by which a sort of continuing ferment of improvisation now and then gives rise to an invention of the first order.

—CARL S. SHOUP,"Taxation in France," *National Tax Journal*, Vol. 8, December 1955, p. 328

The rise of the value-added tax (VAT) is an unparalleled tax phenomenon. The history of taxation reveals no other tax that has swept the world in some thirty years, from theory to practice, and has carried along with it academics who were once dismissive and countries that once rejected it. It is no longer a tax associated solely with the European Community (EC). Every continent now uses the VAT, and each year sees new countries introducing it. Various similes come to mind; VAT may be thought of as the Mata Hari of the tax world—many are tempted, many succumb, some tremble on the brink, while others leave only to return, eventually the attraction appears irresistible. This book has a modest intent. It tries to illustrate how different countries have tackled the problems of VAT that are common to most. It debates the major issues and discusses preferred solutions. The book is divided into three main sections: the practice and problems of VAT in terms of VAT's structure (Part I), effects (Part II), and administration, including taxpayer compliance (Part III).

In this opening chapter there are three main parts. First, a brief account of the different ways a tax can be levied on value added. Second, an examination of the reasons why countries decide to switch to a VAT. Finally, a most important consideration, why some countries have decided (for the time being?) not to adopt a VAT.

VAT in Theory

Four Basic Forms[1]

Value added is the value that a producer (whether a manufacturer, distributor, advertising agent, hairdresser, farmer, race horse trainer, or circus owner) adds to his raw materials or purchases (other than labor) before selling the new or improved product or service. That is, the inputs (the raw materials, transport, rent, advertising, and so on) are bought, people are paid wages to work on these inputs and, when the final good or service is sold, some profit is left. So value added can be looked at from the additive side (wages plus profits) or from the subtractive side (output minus inputs).

Value added = wages + profits = output − input.

If we wish to levy a tax rate (t) on this value added, there are four basic forms that can produce an identical result:

(1) t (wages + profits): the additive-direct or accounts method;

(2) t (wages) + t (profits): the additive-indirect method, so called because value added itself is not calculated but only the tax liability on the components of value added;

(3) t (output − input): the subtractive-direct (also an accounts) method, sometimes called the business transfer tax; and

(4) t (output) − t (input): the subtractive-indirect (the invoice or credit) method and the original EC model.

Direct Versus Indirect Methods

Given that there are four possible ways of levying a VAT, why has only one (method 4, above) been popular? Most taxes are levied by first calculating the tax base (income, sales, wealth, property values, and so on) and then applying a tax rate to that value. The same method might be thought sensible for a VAT. The value added should be calculated directly (methods 1 or 3, above) and the tax rate applied. In practice, the method used (number 4) never actually calculates the

---

[1]There are numerous ways to present the theory of VAT. This is the bare bones of the debate. The literature is replete with somewhat tedious arithmetical examples of how the VAT works and it is not intended to repeat them here. For a clear version, see United States, Department of the Treasury (1984, Vol. 3, Chap. 2) and for a more comprehensive treatment, see McLure (1987b, Chap. 3).

value added; instead, the tax rate is applied to a component of value added (output and inputs) and the resultant tax liabilities are subtracted to get the final net tax payable. This is sometimes called the "indirect" way to assess the tax on value added.

Why should an indirect method of tax calculation be used for VAT when the alternative seems so much more straightforward? There are four principal reasons. The most important consideration is that the invoice method (number 4) attaches the tax liability to the *transaction*, making it legally and technically far superior to other forms. As will be explained in later chapters, the invoice becomes the crucial evidence for the transaction and for the tax liability.

Second, as discussed in Chapter 13, the invoice method creates a good audit trail. Experience in countries such as Benin and Mauritania that use method 3—what in French is called the *base sur base* method—suggests that without the invoice for each transaction problems emerge, first, in ensuring that inputs are deducted only when tax is paid and, second, when inputs exceed taxable sales. This same method has been described, in Canada, as not leaving a good audit trail and as practically eroding the revenue base despite "the Calvinistic nature of the Canadian populace."[2]

Third, to use methods 1 and 2, which are accounts based, profits need to be identified. As company accounts do not usually divide sales by different product categories coinciding with different sales tax rates, and as they certainly never divide inputs by differential tax liabilities, it is clear at once that the only VAT that could be levied on an additive basis would be a single rate VAT. If a multiple rate VAT is wanted, it rules out using methods 1 and 2.

Finally, the easiest way to calculate a VAT, using the subtractive method, appears to be the calculation of the value added (output minus input) and then to apply the tax rate to that figure (method 3). In practice, companies do not find it convenient to calculate their value added in this way month by month, as purchases, sales, and inventories can fluctuate greatly. Firms may have to carry stocks that change, according to the type of production, the seasonality of trade, or anticipated interruptions of supplies. Again, this procedure is only practical using a single rate. In fact, calculating the direct value added is easiest through the trader's annual accounts, and so this method of deriving a VAT (in addition to methods 1 and 2) is also an "accounts method."

Thus, to date, method 4, the invoice or credit method, is the only practical one. The tax liability can be calculated week by week,

[2]Jenkins (1986, pp. 11–12).

monthly, quarterly, or annually. It is the method that allows the most up-to-date assessments and also allows more than a single rate to be used.

Capital Purchases

This brings us to another problem skated over in the initial presentation. How do we treat substantial purchases of long-lasting inputs (that is, capital goods)? According to the methods already mentioned, capital purchases would be inputs and would be deducted from any sales. This, of course, can cause huge fluctuations in tax liability as the purchase of, say, a new factory could occur in one month, and lead to negative value added in many of the succeeding months. Alternatively, using the additive method, profits are usually calculated after allowing for only a portion of the cost of a capital purchase (depreciation). Rarely do income tax authorities allow traders to expense their capital inputs (that is, treat each purchase as an immediate expense so that buying a factory becomes the same as buying an automobile or buying a meal); instead, elaborate rules are designed to allow different assets to be depreciated over different lengths of time (for example, machines over 7 years and buildings over 20 years). To make a VAT calculated under the full consumption base of the subtraction method (where all capital purchases are offset at once against sales) exactly the same as a VAT on the additive base, a different calculation of profits would have to be adopted. Depreciation would be abolished and all capital purchases would be offset at once in the accounts, thus making profits much smaller in the early years of capital purchases and much larger in later years, when the usual depreciation would not be deducted. Clearly, the profits shown for income tax purposes in the "profit and loss accounts" would differ hugely from those calculated for VAT.

This is not to say that one way is right and the other wrong—just that they produce very different results.

To the Retail Sale?

Although VAT is usually thought of as applied to all stages of production including the retail sale, this is not necessarily the case. Table 1-1 shows nine countries that do not apply the VAT at the retail stage (though two, Grenada and India, are not really using a VAT although the name is implied in their legislation). Two countries (Morocco and Peru) apply the VAT through the wholesale stage and

Table 1-1. Countries That Do Not Apply a VAT Through the Retail Sale

	VAT Applied at Level of		
	Manufacturing	Wholesale	Other
Brazil	Federal VAT		State VAT to retail sale
Colombia	X		
Côte d'Ivoire	X		
Grenada[1]	X		Differential rates on imports and domestic goods
India[1]	X		Mixture of ad valorem and specific excise rates
Indonesia	X		
Morocco	X	X	
Peru		X	
Senegal	X		

Source: See text.

[1] Not really a VAT; see section on "Tax Evolution and Efficiency," below.

the others only to the manufacturing level. It should be mentioned that some countries (for example, Kenya) employ a manufacturers sales tax that allows credit for tax paid on inputs and is, therefore, practically a single-stage VAT.

It is clear that all these less-than-complete VATs create problems. All involve a much smaller tax base than one which includes retail sales and, therefore, their tax rates must be higher to yield an equivalent revenue. A VAT to the wholesale level must define a wholesale price because traders often combine manufacturing and wholesale activities as well as wholesale and retailing activities; this leads to a complex set of rules or regulations defining "up-lifts" from factory gate prices or establishing standard discounts on retail prices. A VAT through the wholesale stage should only be considered as a temporary interim arrangement on the way to extending the VAT fully to the retail stage. It is doubtful whether the inefficiencies for both taxpayer and administration ever make it worthwhile other than as a temporary arrangement.

The VAT on manufacturing and importation is more common. It allows a developing economy to levy a buoyant tax on an ad valorem principle and accustom its traders to a credit system. Frequently, the small manufacturers are exempt and, de facto, the VAT is a tax on imports and on large, well-organized industry, especially multinationals. After a few years' experience, the manufacturing VAT can be extended to the retail level. While this is a more attractive option than the VAT to the wholesale level, it involves an even smaller tax base. However, experience gained from the more limited base and the use of credits allows the VAT to be extended to the sale of all goods and services. (Argentina, Bolivia, and Korea used a manufacturing sales tax with a credit mechanism before moving to a complete VAT.) Of course, there are still problems. In Morocco, where there are some vertically integrated firms, the VAT, although formally levied on manufacturers and wholesalers, can extend right through to the retail stage; a provision allows that an enterprise selling to a connected enterprise (that is, wholesaler to retailer) has to pay VAT on behalf of the retailer. This provision is only included to catch cases of abuse, and, where a genuine internal transfer price can be proved, it is accepted. Nevertheless, this sort of provision exemplifies the difficulties faced by systems that do not apply VAT through the retail stage.

Prices Inclusive or Exclusive of Tax?

The final possible variation in VAT is whether or not the tax rate is levied on a price inclusive or exclusive of the tax liability. A 10 percent VAT, on a price exclusive of VAT, is clear to the consumer. However, it does mean letting the purchaser know both the price before VAT is applied and the amount of tax that must be paid. Alternatively, if the tax is quoted tax inclusive, then a rate of only 9.1 percent would be needed to generate the same revenue (9.1 percent of 110 yields 10). In theory, it makes no difference which method is used; in practice, though France originally used it, only Finland and Sweden have persistently employed the tax-inclusive base.

On another pricing issue, U.S. commentators often claim incorrectly that the VAT conceals the tax burden from the consumer. Consumers in Europe can see goods priced with or without VAT; if without, they are then exposed to the shock of VAT added at the cash register. If anything, this is a much greater "tax shock" than the usual tobacco, gasoline, or liquor excise common in the United States. Any sales tax can be "concealed" from the taxpayer; this is not a criticism restricted only to VAT.

The Choice

So, in theory, we have the choice of adopting one of four basic forms of VAT, allowing capital purchases to be fully expensed or depreciated over time, and quoting the rate on a price inclusive or exclusive of tax. In practice, the choice has been much more limited.

As noted already, the methods of deriving VAT from company accounts basically require a single rate tax, or a business or trade that deals in a particularly homogeneous commodity; for example, the hotel trade (which is dealt with later). Most countries do not wish to build in this lack of flexibility to their VAT in the initial legislation (although Japan has suggested this method); so this leaves only one practical option, the subtractive-indirect method. Indeed, this is the type of VAT adopted by almost all countries to date.

However, while theory points us toward this conclusion, it was not theory that persuaded countries to adopt the invoice or credit method of calculating VAT. France, the first country to use a VAT, did not sketch the pros and cons of the different ways of levying VAT, as we have just done, and then implement it. In practice, why do countries adopt a VAT?

Why Adopt the VAT?

Countries introduce a VAT because they are dissatisfied with their existing tax structure. This dissatisfaction falls broadly into one, or possibly all, of four categories: (1) the existing sales taxes are unsatisfactory; (2) a customs union requires discriminatory border taxes to be abolished; (3) a reduction in other taxation is sought; or (4) the evolution of the tax system has not kept pace with the development of the economy.

Unsatisfactory Sales Taxes

THE CASCADE TAX

The simplest sales tax is one that takes a straightforward percentage of all business turnover. Because tax on tax occurs as a taxed product passes from manufacturer to wholesaler to retailer, this has become known as a cascade tax. The defects of this type of tax are well known[3] and have caused most countries using it to switch.[4] As Table 1-2 shows,

---

[3]Cumulative and unknowable tax liabilities, different tax liabilities depending on the degree of industrial vertical integration, difficulty in assessing the amount of cascade tax to be rebated on exports or imposed on imports, and so on; see Cnossen (1987c).

[4]As a rough rule of thumb, it is estimated that the effective rate of a cascade tax to the retail stage is approximately two and a half times the nominal rate; thus, a turnover tax of 4 percent is equivalent to a retail sales tax of 10 percent.

Table 1-2. Summary Showing Substitution of VAT for Other Taxes and Proposed Effect on Revenue

	Date VAT Introduced	Sales Taxes Mainly Replaced[1]	Designed Effect On Revenue	Other Concurrent Tax Changes
Argentina	Jan. 1975	Wholesale sales and provincial cascade turnover tax	Equal yield	Provincial tax changes
Austria	Jan. 1973	Cascade wholesale	Equal yield	Lower income tax
Belgium	Jan. 1971	Cascade wholesale	Equal yield	. . .
Bolivia	Nov. 1973	Multistage ring system	Equal yield or increase	Individuals can offset VAT against a 10 percent tax on gross income: a 1 percent cascade turnover tax retained
Brazil[2]	Jan. 1967	Cascade tax on sales and consignments	Equal yield	Changes in federal-state revenue shares; separate tax on services
Chile	Mar. 1975	Cascade turnover, manufacturers tax, and special luxury tax	Increase	Gasoline, income, and property taxes raised
Colombia	Jan. 1965	No previous sales tax	Increase	Income, property, and capital gains taxes changed
Costa Rica	Jan. 1975	Multistage ring system	Increase	Increased excises
Côte d'Ivoire	Jan. 1960	Manufacturers VAT	Equal yield	. . .
Denmark	July 1967	Wholesale	Increase	Increased excises
Dominican Rep.	Nov. 1983	No previous sales tax	Increase	Reduce reliance on customs duties
Ecuador	Aug. 1970	Turnover taxes on mining and manufacturing	Increase	Mining taxes reduced

Country	Date			
France	Jan. 1968	An earlier and less sophisticated VAT	Equal yield	Tax exemptions abolished and income tax adjustments
Germany, Fed. Rep. of	Jan. 1968	Cascade retail	Equal yield	...
Grenada	Apr. 1986	Stamp duties and taxes on services	Equal yield	Corporate and income taxes abolished and corporate cash flow tax introduced
Greece	Jan. 1987	Turnover tax, stamp duties, and special import levy	Equal yield	"Luxury tax" retained
Guatemala	Aug. 1983	Stamp duty on sales, services, and imports	...	...
Haiti	Nov. 1982	Seventy-nine excises	Equal yield	Replaced commissions, levies, and excises
Honduras	Jan. 1976	Single-stage ring system	Increase	...
Hungary	Jan. 1988	Production and turnover taxes	Increase	Massive tax and subsidy restructuring including corporate and personal income taxes
India[3]	Apr. 1985	...	...	...
Indonesia	Apr. 1985	Manufacturers ring system with eight rates	Equal yield	Reform of the income tax
Ireland	Nov. 1972	Wholesale and retail sales	Equal yield	Some tariff reductions
Israel	July 1976	Various sales	Increase	...
Italy	Jan. 1973	General and local government sales	Equal yield	...

Table 1-2 (*continued*). **Summary Showing Substitution of VAT for Other Taxes and Proposed Effect on Revenue**

	Date VAT Introduced	Sales Taxes Mainly Replaced[1]	Designed Effect On Revenue	Other Concurrent Tax Changes
Japan[4]	Apr. 1989	No sales tax	VAT would increase revenue but offset by corporate and personal tax reductions; net revenue neutral	Reduction in corporate and personal income taxes and changes in excises
Korea	July 1977	Eight sales taxes representing 40 percent of revenue	Equal yield	Changed excises
Luxembourg	Jan. 1970	Cascade wholesale	Equal yield	. . .
Madagascar	Jan. 1969	Cascade production	Increase	. . .
Mexico	Jan. 1980	Cascade production and revoked 18 selective sales taxes	Equal yield or increase	Lower border VAT of 6 percent
Morocco	Jan. 1962	Cascade production	Equal yield	Change in corporate and production taxes
Netherlands	Jan. 1969	Cascade wholesale	Equal yield	Lower income tax
New Zealand	May 1986	Wholesale tax	Yield extra revenue	Changes in personal and corporate income taxation and fiscal incentives and low income credit introduced
Nicaragua	Aug. 1978	Multistage ring system	Equal yield	Reduced customs duties
Niger	Jan. 1986	Cascade manufacturers	Yield extra revenue	Replace existing taxes on services
Norway	Jan. 1970	Sales taxes on 65 percent of consumption	Loss	Reduced income and property taxes

Country	Date	Previous tax	Revenue	Other changes
Panama	Jan. 1976	No sales tax	Increase	Stamp taxes reduced and increased excises
Peru	Jan. 1973	Cascade production and stamp tax	Increase	...
Philippines	Jan. 1988	Eight sales and stamp taxes	Increase	Restructure income taxes
Poland[4]	1989	...	...	...
Portugal	Jan. 1986	Cascade wholesale tax and other duties	Equal yield	Abolition of stamp duties and minor taxes
Senegal	Mar. 1961	Manufacturers VAT	Equal yield	...
South Africa[4]	Apr. 1989	Retail sales tax	Equal yield	Substantial review of direct and indirect taxes
Spain	Jan. 1986	Cascade production tax and 20 other sales taxes	Equal yield	
Sweden	Jan. 1969	Retail sales tax and capital goods tax	Equal yield	1 percent payroll tax to offset lost revenue
Taiwan Province of China	Apr. 1986	Cascade retail tax and stamp duty	Equal yield	Separate sales tax on financial services, night clubs, and small businesses
Thailand[4]	Jan. 1989	Business turnover tax	Equal yield	...
Turkey	Jan. 1985	Eight production taxes and other duties on goods and services	Equal yield	Ad hoc export tax rebates phased out and individuals allowed to deduct VAT as a withholding off-set against a 10 percent tax on gross income; offset diminishes as income rises

Table 1-2 (concluded). Summary Showing Substitution of VAT for Other Taxes and Proposed Effect on Revenue

	Date VAT Introduced	Sales Taxes Mainly Replaced[1]	Designed Effect On Revenue	Other Concurrent Tax Changes
United Kingdom	Apr. 1973	Multirate wholesale	Loss	Selective employment tax removed
Uruguay	Jan. 1968	Manufacturers single-stage tax and a cascade turnover tax	Equal yield	. . .

Source: Various country reports and see text.

[1] This column is as accurate as a brief summary can be: "cascade production tax" refers to a cascade tax on business turnover restricted to the production stage; "cascade wholesale tax" extends the turnover tax to include the wholesale stage; "cascade retail tax" extends the turnover tax to include the retail stage; "manufacturers," "wholesale," or "retail" taxes are single-stage taxes, some operated on a ring system, others on a credit system.

[2] Note Brazil introduced a federal VAT on interstate transactions and a state VAT on intrastate sales (ICM); however, the Federal Government determines the tax base and rates.

[3] Not actually a VAT but a federal excise (with both ad valorem and specific rates) with credit for purchases (but not for capital goods).

[4] Proposed.

most of the early users of VAT switched from various forms of cascade taxes. Indeed, it was the disadvantages of the cascade element that persuaded the French, first, to allow a credit for the tax content of purchases of raw materials against the sales tax liability and, second, to allow a credit for the tax content of capital purchases. In this way, the VAT using the invoice method developed from ways to mitigate the disadvantages of the original cascade tax. Indeed, Finland, for example, levies a sales tax at an effective rate of 19.05 percent using a credit mechanism, but does not allow the purchase value of fixed assets, fuel, and other goods consumed in the business to be deducted. In this way, Finland is still at a stage preparatory to a full VAT.

MANUFACTURER AND WHOLESALE TAXES

Not as simple as the cascade, but much fairer, is a single-stage tax levied on manufacturers, wholesalers, or retailers. However, some undesirable cascading can be found even in countries that use or have used single-stage sales taxes (Australia, Austria, Belgium, Canada, Luxembourg, Mexico, Morocco, the Netherlands, New Zealand, and the United Kingdom). Cascading occurs whenever taxable goods are produced using taxed inputs. The problem is more frequently found when the point of impact of the tax is far from the retail stage; for instance, as in a manufacturers or importers tax, since the likelihood of a manufacturer buying his inputs from another manufacturer or from an importer is much greater than buying them from a retailer. But even retail sales taxes, by including in their definition of taxable sales the sales of certain kinds of producer goods that can also be used as consumer goods, can produce cascading.[5]

The difficulties of operating a manufacturers sales tax are well exemplified by the Canadian example. Since in a manufacturers sales tax the tax liability can differ sharply according to the source of the inputs and the amount of integration between the manufacturing, wholesale, and retail stages, Canadian businesses reduced their tax liability by setting up related, but separate, distribution companies. This meant the markup of the distribution company did not enter the tax base. To combat the loss of revenue, the administration devised a set of rules (effective July 1988) that create complex uncertainties for traders.[6] Treating the symptoms rather than the disease is a classic

---

[5]See Shoup (1973, pp. 220–21).

[6]See discussion in "TPI Country Survey—Canada: Sales Tax Reform," *Tax Planning International Review* (1987).

case of the trail that leads countries away from unsatisfactory sales taxes to the VAT.

Cascading can also occur when a variety of different sales taxes are used. Some countries become dissatisfied not only with the complexity of administration but also with the complex and multiple relationship between traders and government when many taxes are used. In Korea, eight indirect taxes (a business turnover tax, a commodity tax, and taxes on textiles, petroleum, gas and electricity, travel, admissions and entertainment, and food) were replaced by the VAT and a supplementary "special consumption tax" (more or less an excise). In this way, the Government sought to simplify tax administration as each previous tax had its own rate structure (from 0.5 to 300 percent), a different tax base, and administrative procedures.[7] The tax content of exports, because of cascading, was unknown.

One way to avoid the worst[8] cascading is to allow credit for some purchases. Indeed, this has been a common way of moving (unconsciously in the case of some countries) toward a full VAT. However, sometimes countries find (for example, South Africa) that the revenue cost of giving up taxing, say, capital goods, makes it difficult to give credit, or at least, to give full credit immediately. As a result, the credit for tax is gradually and sporadically extended and the system moves toward a full VAT.

Other mechanisms to avoid cascading are in use. One that is fairly common under manufacturers or importers sales taxes is to allow manufacturers registered as taxpayers to acquire tax free, locally produced goods or imported goods used as inputs. This is the so-called ring system (Bolivia, Costa Rica, Honduras, Indonesia, and Nicaragua before the VAT; see Table 1-2) where sales between registered traders (within the ring) are tax free, but sales to unregistered taxpayers outside the ring—such as retail sales—are taxed. The main problem with this system is the weight placed on the registration number. Traders are meant to verify that they sell to or buy from only appropriately registered traders free of tax; however, such is the value of this privilege that many traders invent or abuse registration numbers and evasion can reach epidemic proportions.

The best solution, even for a manufacturers or importers sales tax, is probably a credit system similar to that in use for VAT even if it does not fully compensate for all tax paid on inputs (for example, because of exemptions). One additional advantage of this system is that at least a part of the tax is payable when the inputs are purchased, and any

[7]Choi (1984, pp. 1–6).
[8]But not all—see Hemming and Kay (1981, pp. 80–81).

subsequent action by the manufacturer to evade taxation results in a loss of only part of the tax. Tax administrators always prefer cash in the bank that taxpayers must claim back; a bird in the bush is difficult to see, never mind catching. Another advantage is that it accustoms traders to working with a tax system that depends on the invoice and on a credit for tax paid, and is halfway home to a VAT. Indeed, some Central American countries (Costa Rica, Honduras, and Nicaragua), as in France originally, have adopted a VAT almost as though by accident through moving from a ring system to a credit mechanism.

Some countries, such as Australia and New Zealand, have used single-stage wholesale taxes and found them unsatisfactory. These wholesale taxes were introduced many years ago (in 1933 for New Zealand) and exhibited many signs of their age. Numerous exemptions and multiple rates complicate the structure and erode the base of single-stage wholesale taxes. Politicians try to classify goods according to their "luxury" nature, and also attempt to exempt some goods as potential business inputs. Exemptions become based on the nature of the purchaser or the end use of the goods instead of according to the nature of the goods.[9] Retail prices are distorted because different retail markups are not taxed and it pays to adjust transfer prices to maximize the untaxed markups. Retailers carry tax-paid stocks, which affect their liquidity and which limit the ability of the wholesale tax to respond quickly as a demand management tool to changes in tax rates. Exports frequently must absorb some of the domestic wholesale tax, as is the case in Canada. This situation places exporters at a disadvantage or leads to a depreciated exchange rate. Finally, services cannot be included under the wholesale tax. For all these reasons, countries find the single-stage tax on intermediate goods unsatisfactory.

It is clear that with any sales tax, the higher the tax rate, the more incentive there is for taxpayers to evade the tax. Assuming a given need for revenue on the part of the government, the form of sales tax that provides the broadest possible base is the one that requires the lowest rate. From this point of view, either a retail sales tax or a VAT carried through the retail level has a comparative advantage over sales taxes with more limited bases.

RETAIL SALES TAX

For countries with a sophisticated tax administration and good

[9]In a classic example, New Zealand exempted motorcycles used for farm work but not for ordinary road use; the distinction is not easy in practice. On the difficulties of administering a wholesale sales tax, see Cnossen (1983, pp. 316–23).

taxpayer compliance a retail sales tax is an attractive option. The 45 U.S. state sales taxes, at rates of 4–8.25 percent, are efficient sources of revenue, raising about 20 to 60 percent of tax revenue in Vermont and Washington, respectively, with an average of 33 percent. However, even under favorable conditions, problems begin to accumulate as the tax rate rises. At 5 percent, the incentive to evade tax is probably not worth the penalties of prosecution; at 10 percent, evasion is more attractive, and at 15–20 percent, becomes extremely tempting. Only Iceland, Norway, South Africa, Sweden, and Zimbabwe have operated retail sales taxes at rates over 10 percent. Both Norway (with a retail sales tax rate of 13.64 percent) and Sweden (11.1 percent) decided to switch to a VAT even though, as countries outside the EC, they did not have to adopt it. South Africa is dissatisfied with its 12 percent retail sales tax and is exploring ways to change to a VAT. Iceland now has a retail sales tax of 25 percent, and the continuous concerns about evasion have resulted in legislation to introduce a VAT.

Zimbabwe levies retail sales taxes at 15 percent and 18 percent, yielding about a quarter of total tax revenue. This may be the most successful example of a retail sales tax levied at high rates, though there is increasing worry about evasion.[10] Nevertheless, in a relatively simple economy, there seems to have been a widespread acceptance of the tax though this may have been due, in part, to the major portion of revenue secured from a few major retailers.

Switzerland uses what can be called a retail sales tax (although basically it is a wholesale tax) and has twice rejected a VAT. Finland uses a manufacturers tax and a retail sales tax at 6 percent and 4 percent, respectively. However, "there has long been consideration of shift to a general value-added tax."[11] Finally, Paraguay levies a retail sales tax on the larger retailers and on sales to smaller retailers by manufacturers and wholesalers at rates ranging from 4 percent to 14 percent. The VAT has not been adopted in Paraguay because of fear of the additional paperwork required.

There is substantial discussion about the retail sales tax versus the VAT,[12] but the main problems of the former seem to be the following:

- The higher the rate, the more collection weight is put upon the weakest link in the chain—the retailer, especially numerous small retailers.
- All the revenue is at risk. It has been suggested that this is also

[10]Due (1983a).
[11]Due (1986b, p. 243).
[12]Due (1986a) and Cnossen (1987c).

true of VAT if the retailer successfully claims all his credit on purchases, but clearly it is more difficult to do so under the accounting requirements of VAT.

- The audit and invoice trail is poorer than under a VAT, especially for services.
- There have to be troublesome "end-use exemptions."
- Revenue is not secured at the easiest stage, that is, at the time of importation, and this can be crucial for many developing countries.

In other words, a single point retail sales tax is efficient at relatively low rates, but is increasingly difficult to administer as rates rise. This, of course, can be seen as an advantage by those who wish to restrain the capacity of the government to raise revenue through broadened sales taxes (a common refrain in the U.S. Congress). By association, a VAT that partly circumvents this disadvantage can be caricatured as a license for government profligacy.

Interestingly enough, Norway is the only country that, having changed from a retail sales tax to a VAT, has considered seriously the possibility of switching back. Many held that the VAT compliance costs were high and the opportunity for fraud greater. However, a Treasury paper[13] argued that the VAT fell more certainly on final sales than the retail sales tax, it was more secure (19 percent of the registered firms made 90 percent of the sales), it improved accounting standards, and the possible advantages of the retail sales tax in no way compensated for the transitional costs involved in moving back to a single-stage tax.

Others have also pointed out that a VAT may be less open to lobbying influences than the retail sales tax; a successful lobbying effort on the retail sales tax removes the tax from the entire industry, but lobbying under a VAT is more diffuse as there is the issue of zero rating versus exemption (see Chapter 3) and the likelihood that upstream traders will still be left with tax liabilities on inputs if the good is only exempted but not zero rated.

Special Needs of Countries in Regional Economic Groupings

The VAT was the choice of the member countries of the EC as the best way to promote neutrality and uniformity of the tax burden and to provide incentives for increased productivity and industrialization.

[13]See the discussion in Due and Brems (1986, pp. 11–12).

The recommendation of the EC Fiscal and Financial Committee that all member countries shift to the VAT form was formulated in 1962.[14] The change for the original members was finally completed in 1973, when Italy implemented the tax.[15] However, other recommendations regarding uniformity of rates and eventual adoption of the origin principle for taxation of trade within the EC have not been put into effect and indeed the EC is now firmly on the path of the destination principle (see Chapter 8 for a discussion of this issue).

Most of the countries in the Latin American regional groups—the Latin American Integration Association (LAIA, formerly known as the Latin American Free Trade Association or LAFTA) and the Andean Pact—have adopted value-added taxes. Brazil also has a federal manufacturers VAT which, like the Colombian manufacturers VAT, features a credit system to avoid cascading.[16] Although the Latin American countries in the LAIA have a long way to go before reaching the stage of tax harmonization that can be found in the EC today, it appears likely that the VAT will eventually become the harmonized form of general sales taxation in the region.[17]

The VAT can be applied either on the basis of origin or on the basis of destination—which then allows replacement of the destination principle by the origin principle when a significant degree of harmonization has been achieved. However, this is one of those textbook arguments that are always presented, yet are wildly out of touch with reality; the possibility of any free trade area adopting the origin principle of taxation must be decades away.[18] Indeed, the application of the origin principle with a VAT could be an administrative nightmare.[19]

Of course, none of these issues need preoccupy countries that do not intend to be part of a customs union. However, the VAT is the only

[14]See European Community, Commission of the European Economic Community (1963).

[15]Members joining the EC later had to introduce a VAT; Ireland (1972), the United Kingdom (1973), Portugal (1981), Spain (1986), and Greece (1987).

[16]Oddly enough, the names of the VAT differ: *impuesto al valor agregado* (Argentina, Mexico, and Uruguay); *impuesto sobre las ventas* (Colombia, Costa Rica, and Honduras); *impuesto a las transacciones mercantiles y prestación de servicios* (Ecuador); *impuesto a la transferencia de bienes corporales muebles con crédito fiscal* (Panama); and *impuesto a los bienes y servicios* (Peru). Perhaps, as in New Zealand (goods and services tax), countries thought that by calling a rose by another name, it might smell more sweetly and its thorns would be ignored?

[17]See Longo (1981).

[18]Consideration of these aspects in more detail can be found in European Community, Commission of the European Economic Community (1963, pp. 102–103).

[19]See Cnossen (1987c).

common sales tax in a customs union, other than a retail sales tax, that fulfills the obligations for tax neutrality on traded goods and services under the General Agreement on Tariffs and Trade (GATT).

A Reduction of Other Taxation or to Simply Increase Revenue?

Some countries look to a VAT not only to replace existing sales taxes but also to increase revenue (see Chile and Denmark in Table 1-2). However, some have viewed it as a new source of revenue which will enable other taxes to be reduced or abolished. Much of the debate in the United States about VAT has revolved around the possibility of replacing the corporate profits tax, reducing the rate of individual income tax, permitting property tax relief, financing social security, reducing the payroll tax, or, more generally, reducing the public sector borrowing requirement.

Until 1986, no country had used the VAT to reduce the corporate profits tax. The early British review[20] rejected VAT as a substitute for the corporate profits tax, largely on grounds that the substitution of a tax that would be passed forward for one that was not must increase prices. The increased prices would decrease the competitive position of exports, and the balance of payments on current account would deteriorate. Increased wage demands to maintain real wages would increase costs and this would further decrease the international competitive position of exports. Numerous arguments can be mounted against this exposition and it can be shown that with different assumptions, prices need not rise and profits and investment could increase.[21]

In the United States, it is claimed that the substitution of VAT, which will be fully rebated on exports, for the corporate income tax, which is not rebatable, would improve the competitiveness of U.S. industry and improve the balance of trade. This somewhat simplistic argument can be rejected.[22] Nevertheless, proposals are made for such a substitution. However, the fall in the effective rate of corporate taxation in recent years has meant this substitution is no longer such a live issue.[23]

[20]United Kingdom, *Report of the Committee on Turnover Taxation* (1964, especially Chap. 8).

[21]Tait (1972, Chap. 7).

[22]See evidence of Richard A. Musgrave in United States, Congress (1972, pp. 131–32) and Tait (1972, pp. 103–108).

[23]But C. Lowell Harriss testified to the Ways and Means Committee of the U.S. Congress on September 27, 1984 that the corporate tax should be eliminated and a VAT substituted. See United States, Congress (1984, pp. 330–37).

New Zealand also amended its corporate income tax in connection with VAT, but this was to increase the rate from 45 percent to 48 percent to align the top rate with the new top rate for personal income taxation; so the change is better seen associated with personal taxes than with sales taxes.

Increasing the revenue collected from the indirect tax base, when replacing existing sales taxes by a VAT, allows adjustments in direct taxes. Although Denmark increased revenue when the VAT was introduced in 1967, this permitted adjustments in income tax to offset, partly, any consequent change in prices. Similarly, it can be argued that top marginal rates of income tax could be reduced and the lost revenue replaced by VAT (although the switch would be regressive). A more current debate is on using VAT revenue to reduce the burden of payroll taxes to finance social security. It has been suggested that businesses in Argentina saw an advantage in a VAT, which would be rebated on exports and which might be more difficult to collect, replacing part of the payroll tax, which was not rebated, was easily assessed, and was collected quite efficiently.

In general, much of this desire to use VAT to replace other taxes flows from dissatisfaction with an increased reliance on direct taxes. As Table 1-3 shows, *every* member country of the Organization for Economic Cooperation and Development (OECD) collected a smaller proportion of its revenue from indirect taxation in 1975 than in 1965. The fall for some was as much as 42 percent (Spain) or 30 percent (Belgium). The required increase in direct taxation to offset the falling importance of indirect taxes was, as a proportion of gross domestic product (GDP), as high as 100 percent (Turkey) or 71 percent (Switzerland). Faced with such problems, some countries (Denmark, Luxembourg, and the United Kingdom) used the VAT during 1975–84 to stem the tide, halting the increase in direct taxes and transferring some of the burden to the VAT. Other countries (Italy, France, and Norway) were less successful in containing the increase in direct taxes, and some (Belgium, Ireland, and Sweden), as a percentage of GDP, combined substantial increases in both direct and indirect taxes.

The most interesting countries, however, are some of those that have not introduced a VAT. In 1965–82, Australia increased its reliance on direct taxes from 65 percent to 68 percent of total revenue; Canada, from 59 percent to 67 percent; Japan, from 74 percent to 85 percent; and Switzerland, from 69 percent to 81 percent. In each of these countries, the introduction of VAT has, to date, been debated but rejected or delayed. This may suggest that were VAT to be introduced,

Table 1-3. Taxes on Goods and Services as Percentage of Total Taxation in OECD Countries

| | 1965 | 1970 | 1975 | 1980 | 1984 | Percentage Change | | |
						1965–75	1975–84	1965–84
Australia	35	32	29	31	32	−17	10	−9
Austria	37	37	35	32	33	−5	−6	−11
Belgium	37	35	26	26	25	−30	−4	−32
Canada	41	32	32	33	33	−22	3	−20
Denmark	41	39	34	37	35	−17	3	−15
Finland	43	41	34	39	38	−21	12	−12
France	38	38	33	30	29	−13	−12	−24
Germany, Fed. Rep. of	33	32	27	27	27	−18	0	−18
Greece	52	50	48	40	43	−8	−10	−17
Ireland	53	52	47	44	45	−11	−4	−15
Italy	39	39	29	27	26	−26	−10	−33
Japan	26	22	17	16	15	−35	−12	−42
Luxembourg	25	21	21	21	24	−16	14	−4
Netherlands	29	28	24	25	25	−17	4	−14
New Zealand	28	27	24	22	27	−14	12	−4
Norway	41	43	38	35	36	−7	−5	−12
Portugal	44	45	41	45	44	−7	7	0
Spain	41	36	24	21	26	−42	8	−37
Sweden	31	28	24	24	25	−23	4	−19
Switzerland	30	27	20	20	19	−33	−5	−37
Turkey	54	49	41	29	34	−24	−17	−37
United Kingdom	33	29	25	29	30	−24	20	−9
United States	22	19	18	17	18	−18	0	−18

Source: Organization for Economic Cooperation and Development, *Revenue Statistics of OECD Member Countries, 1965–1985* (Paris, 1986), p. 94.

increasing reliance on direct taxes could be halted and switched to indirect taxes.

However, in practice, as the examples of Belgium, Ireland, and Sweden show, such an outcome is by no means automatic. Stopping the rise in the direct tax burden requires more than the introduction of a VAT. Strong political decisions are needed to prevent "bracket creep," to contain the use of proportional payroll taxes for social security, and to resist the temptation to use a buoyant VAT revenue as simply another way to increase expenditure.

Certainly, VAT as a buoyant revenue source, closely linked to increases in consumption, has become a crucial part of overall revenue for all countries using it. Indeed, many countries find that their initial revenue from the first year of VAT turns out substantially higher than forecasts based on past sales tax bases or on national income accounts. Indonesia's manufacturing level VAT, "in the first year of operation . . . managed to raise revenues about 45 percent over target . . . even in a country that has a reputation of having a weak tax administration."[24] As Tables 1-4 and 1-5 show, VAT frequently contributes 15–25 percent of central government tax revenue and 5–10 percent of GDP. The experience of countries using VAT has been all one way—upward (except for Costa Rica where the VAT was reduced from 10 percent to 8 percent within a few months of its introduction in response to public protests; also, a consolidation of rates in Peru left the standard rate of VAT at 18 percent instead of 20 percent originally). In all other countries, rates of VAT in 1988 were at least the same as they were at the introduction of VAT and were usually higher.

Tax Evolution and Efficiency

Countries are supposed to move from simple to complex tax structures and from systems that distort allocation to those that are more neutral. The easiest point of taxation for countries with a simple economic structure is at importation. Customs duties are one of the oldest forms of tax, visible and not too difficult to administer. Excises, usually with specific rates and relying on physical controls, follow. However, as trade becomes more complex, countries are pushed, as far as indirect taxes are concerned, toward introducing a truly general sales tax for its revenue buoyancy and lack of distortion.

This need not always occur. For instance, countries in the Middle East do not use general sales taxes. Numerous excises are levied and the intent may be to add commodities one by one to move toward a general sales tax, but progress has been slow. Socialist regimes in Eastern Europe use turnover taxes, sometimes employing over a thousand different tax rates. Other countries recognize that a multiplicity of ad hoc sales taxes at different rates is inefficient both administratively and economically, and they move to VAT to consolidate and modernize their tax structure (for example, Chile, Haiti, Hungary, Indonesia, Korea, and Mexico).

Usually, countries find the demand for government revenue to be such that a broad-based sales tax is desirable. Relying on selective sales taxes with narrow bases becomes increasingly distortionary. While some move through the stages of credit and ring systems, there is a

[24]Jenkins (1986, p. 11).

tide in the affairs of tax men which leads, if not to greatness, at least to generalness. As mentioned earlier, the VAT has become a fashionable tax, accounting for important shares of revenue and GDP (Tables 1-4 and 1-5). While fashion may not be the best way to develop a tax system, it is, undoubtedly, a powerful influence.

The more VAT systems there are, the more likely it is that a country, developing its indirect tax systems, will adopt a VAT. There is also some common sense in this. The more examples there are to follow, the less likelihood of mistakes. Legislation and regulations can be adopted to suit the particular contingencies of a country, but it is better to have half a dozen alternative laws and experiences to start from than none at all. The visible success of VAT in many countries in generating buoyant revenues is a selling point for other authorities looking for a modern revenue base.

Indeed, a remarkable recent development can be ascribed partly to this "fashionable" growth of VAT. The first socialist economic system to adopt VAT has been Hungary in 1988. The objective of the tax reform was to "diminish the tax burden on the business sector, to make it more uniform, and to simplify taxation and budgetary relationships."[25] This is an enormously ambitious, complex tax and price reform involving the introduction of a uniform corporate income tax, a personal income tax, and a VAT, along with reductions in corporate subsidies and reform of social security financing. It is interesting that when the authorities were examining all the possible options for a completely new sales tax, they eventually settled on the invoice or credit method of VAT; "basically, the Hungarian system will be in line with international practice."[26] From recent pronouncements, it sounds as though the Polish authorities may be following the same path arguing that their present tax system no longer fully meets the needs of the economy and that the system needs to evolve to improve efficiency.[27]

Another reform that involves a VAT to finance a gradual lowering of tax rates throughout the tax system is that recommended in the Report of the Margo Commission in South Africa.[28] However, the form of VAT suggested is unique. The tax is named the comprehensive business tax, which is an origin-based, direct-additive accounts

[25]Lukács (1987, p. 447).
[26]Lukács (1987, p. 449).
[27]Reported in the *Wall Street Journal* (New York), December 29, 1987, p. 10.
[28]South Africa, *Report of the Commission of Inquiry into the Tax Structure of the Republic of South Africa* (1987).

Table 1-4. VAT as Percentage of Total Tax Revenue, 1975–86

	1975	1976	1977	1978	1979	1980	1981	1982	1983	1984	1985	1986
Argentina	7.7	10.3	10.7	11.1	11.4	12.5	21.7	23.7	14.9	13.3	15.3	…
Austria	20.2	20.7	19.4	18.5	18.7	18.3	18.3	18.2	18.9	19.7	19.6	19.4
Belgium	16.6	18.2	17.8	18.0	16.7	17.7	18.6	17.8	17.8	17.1	15.6	…
Bolivia	5.9	5.1	6.6	7.4	7.2	5.5	4.8	6.4	6.8	5.4	…	…
Brazil	—	—	—	—	—	—	—	1.4	3.0	3.3	3.7	…
Chile	23.1	27.4	33.7	37.2	39.5	39.8	44.0	46.2	37.4	38.3	38.7	39.9
Colombia	15.4	15.7	16.5	17.8	18.9	18.8	20.6	25.5	21.2	…	…	…
Costa Rica	10.9	9.8	9.3	9.2	9.7	10.0	8.2	10.4	17.4	17.6	14.9	17.4
Côte d'Ivoire	…	…	…	…	…	10.6	…	…	…	11.7	…	…
Denmark	23.1	25.4	27.1	29.8	31.6	32.1	33.1	32.5	30.7	29.4	28.3	26.9
Ecuador	12.4	11.1	12.3	15.0	15.2	11.9	14.4	13.8	12.4	11.8	9.5	…
France	26.1	26.6	23.8	24.3	24.1	23.5	23.5	23.6	22.9	22.4	22.5	…
Germany, Fed. Rep. of	13.1	12.9	12.4	13.1	14.0	14.0	13.9	12.9	13.3	13.0	14.1	13.6
Guatemala	13.9	15.8	14.8	14.1	15.9	14.6	20.0	24.8	…	…	…	…
Haiti	…	…	…	…	1.1	6.5	0.2	0.3	10.8	12.3	17.3	17.3
Honduras	6.6	7.5	7.4	7.1	7.5	7.1	7.8	…	…	…	…	…
Indonesia	9.3	9.6	8.9	8.5	5.1	4.7	4.5	5.9	6.0	5.8	13.1	19.3
Ireland	16.3	17.4	18.8	20.9	18.2	15.6	16.2	20.1	21.9	22.2	13.1	…
Israel	16.1	19.6	23.5	29.9	25.3	25.0	25.8	27.7	28.0	30.7	31.2	…
Italy	15.2	15.8	16.5	15.0	14.5	16.2	15.9	15.4	15.7	15.9	15.3	12.5
Korea	14.1	12.4	16.9	22.6	22.5	24.9	24.5	24.6	25.1	24.4	24.0	23.6
Luxembourg	12.8	12.0	11.1	11.3	11.4	11.6	12.5	13.4	13.1	14.5	…	…
Madagascar	…	…	…	22.5	21.4	23.4	21.9	26.3	…	…	…	…
Mexico	19.2	19.4	17.7	17.1	18.2	17.3	20.8	15.5	19.7	20.9	19.1	…
Morocco	21.1	27.1	25.8	25.0	24.1	24.3	24.2	27.8	29.2	28.6	30.4	…

Country												
Netherlands	14.5	15.2	16.2	16.5	16.1	16.3	16.0	15.3	15.1	16.1	16.6	17.1
Nicaragua	13.0	12.4	12.5	11.4	8.9	10.7	12.6	10.7	10.4	9.1	11.5	10.9
Niger	...	16.3	12.3	14.8	14.0	14.5	...	...	...	...	...	...
Norway	27.2	27.0	27.3	27.2	25.3	22.9	22.0	22.7	23.3	21.9	22.2	24.0
Panama	—	—	6.7	9.4	9.3	8.9	8.9	9.1	7.4	7.6	7.8	...
Peru	29.6	32.0	30.6	30.5	32.4	...	33.3	32.1	...	20.8	17.2	11.5
Senegal	9.0	8.6	10.2	13.6	14.9	15.7	12.4	17.5	21.3	...	...	...
Sweden	18.0	16.8	17.2	19.8	20.3	19.9	20.2	20.0	19.9	18.5	20.1	20.0
Turkey	6.6	7.6	6.3	4.7	4.1	3.0	3.5	...	5.1	6.1	21.9	...
United Kingdom	10.0	9.8	9.5	10.4	11.9	16.5	14.3	15.3	15.9	16.8	17.9	17.6
Uruguay	23.8	22.8	21.2	20.8	22.2	27.0	27.6	27.8	23.5	26.3	28.9	26.7

Source: International Monetary Fund, *Government Finance Statistics Yearbook,* Vol. 11 (Washington, 1987).

Table 1-5. VAT as Percentage of GDP, 1975–86

	1975	1976	1977	1978	1979	1980	1981	1982	1983	1984	1985	1986
Argentina	0.7	1.2	1.3	1.4	1.5	1.9	3.0	3.0	2.0	..	..	..
Austria	5.9	6.0	5.8	5.9	5.9	5.8	6.0	5.8	6.0	6.4	6.2	6.1
Belgium	6.4	7.1	7.1	7.4	6.9	7.3	7.7	7.5	7.5	7.4	6.7	..
Bolivia	0.6	0.5	0.6	0.6	0.6	0.4	0.4	0.3	0.2	0.1	..	..
Brazil	—	—	—	—	..	—	—	0.3	0.6	0.5	0.6	..
Chile	5.8	6.2	7.8	8.6	9.5	10.2	11.1	10.7	8.1	8.8	8.6	8.9
Colombia	1.7	1.7	1.8	1.9	1.9	1.9	2.0	2.4	2.0	2.5	..	..
Côte d'Ivoire	..	..	..	..	..	2.2	..	..	..	2.5	..	..
Denmark	6.8	7.3	8.0	9.1	9.9	10.1	10.4	10.0	9.8	9.9	9.9	9.9
Ecuador	1.3	1.1	1.2	1.5	1.4	1.5	1.5	1.5	1.3	1.4	1.6	..
France	8.7	9.3	8.4	8.4	8.7	8.8	8.8	9.0	8.9	8.8	8.8	..
Germany, Fed. Rep. of	3.3	3.3	3.3	3.4	3.6	3.9	3.9	3.6	3.7	3.6	3.9	3.7
Guatemala	1.2	1.4	1.5	1.5	1.4	1.5	1.8	2.1	1.6	0.1	1.4	1.1
Haiti	—	—	—	0.1	0.1	0.6	—	—	1.1	1.2	1.8	1.6
Honduras	0.8	0.9	1.0	0.9	1.0	1.0	1.0	1.1	1.1	1.0	..	..
Indonesia	1.5	1.6	1.5	1.4	0.9	0.9	0.9	1.1	1.1	1.0	2.4	..
Ireland	4.6	5.5	5.6	6.1	5.3	5.0	5.4	7.1	8.1	8.4	8.0	..
Israel	6.3	9.0	10.7	12.3	10.6	9.5	10.0	11.6	11.0	10.7	13.0	..
Italy	4.1	4.5	4.9	4.6	4.6	4.7	4.7	5.0	5.4	5.4	5.1	4.7
Korea	1.9	1.9	2.5	3.5	3.5	3.9	3.8	4.0	4.2	3.9	3.8	3.8
Luxembourg	4.7	4.4	4.4	4.5	4.3	4.4	4.8	5.0	5.3	5.7	..	..
Madagascar	..	..	..	4.1	3.8	3.7	3.2	3.3	..	..	..	..
Mexico	2.2	2.2	2.2	2.3	2.5	2.6	3.0	2.3	3.2	3.1	3.0	..
Morocco	4.4	5.0	5.5	5.2	5.1	5.2	5.3	6.0	6.3	6.2	6.5	..

Netherlands	6.3	6.5	7.1	7.2	7.1	7.3	7.1	6.8	6.9	7.1	7.3	7.5
Niger	..	1.9	1.4	1.7	1.7	1.9	..	..	..	..	..	..
Norway	9.2	9.3	9.7	9.5	8.9	8.5	8.5	8.6	8.6	8.0	8.4	9.5
Panama	—	—	1.5	1.9	1.9	1.9	1.9	1.9	1.7	1.6	1.6	..
Peru	4.3	4.2	4.3	4.8	5.2	5.7	5.4	5.3	..	2.7	2.7	..
Senegal	1.6	1.6	1.8	2.7	3.0	3.4	2.5	3.4	4.0	..	..	..
Sweden	5.3	5.7	6.0	6.8	6.6	6.4	6.8	6.8	6.8	6.5	7.2	7.1
Turkey	1.2	1.5	1.2	0.9	0.7	0.5	0.6	..	0.9	0.8	3.2	..
United Kingdom	3.1	3.0	2.9	3.0	3.4	5.1	4.6	5.3	5.3	5.7	6.0	6.0
Uruguay	4.2	4.9	4.6	4.4	4.4	5.7	6.1	5.4	4.6	4.6	5.8	5.9

Source: International Monetary Fund, *Government Finance Statistics Yearbook*, Vol. 11 (Washington, 1987).

VAT (method 1 discussed above). The tax base would include salaries and wages, interest, royalties, rent, profit, and depreciation; gross investment would be subtracted but exports would be taxed. This base is, of course, equal to sales less purchases.[29] The Margo Commission Report emphasizes that the comprehensive business tax should be regarded as an income tax but is, however, a VAT. Moreover, it is a VAT that does not exempt exports (basically because of the numerous unchecked borders in Southern Africa that make border sales tax adjustments difficult). If enacted, this would have been a remarkable, and closely watched, experiment. However, the Government has rejected this recommendation and now proposes to introduce a normal accounts-based VAT in 1989.

It should be pointed out that there are at least two so-called VATs that are not VATs at all. Grenada imposed a "VAT" in 1986 at the manufacturing level at 20 percent. However, the 20 percent rate was applied to imports and to only 40 percent of the value of domestic sales. What this means in practice is that the tax is highly discriminatory on imports (20 percent), compared with domestic manufacturing (20 percent on 40 percent is equivalent to only 8 percent on total sales). This is really a tariff of 20 percent and a local manufacturing tax of 8 percent.

The so-called Indian MODVAT (modified value-added tax) is not a VAT at all, but rather a form of modified excise duty.[30] It is a manufacturing excise tax (levied at both ad valorem and specific rates) with credit allowed for excise duty and customs in a limited number of industries. It may eliminate the cascading effect of multipoint excise levies. Introduction of a full VAT in India would seem to present numerous administrative and constitutional difficulties, including the vexed question of union-state relations.[31]

A VAT—But Not Just Yet

Given the worldwide movement to adopt VAT, the examples of countries that have considered a VAT but have decided against it are particularly interesting.

Japan is an example of a country that has held out against the VAT from the original Shoup proposal in 1953 until 1986 when, finally,

[29]South Africa, *Report of the Commission of Inquiry into the Tax Structure of the Republic of South Africa* (1987, p. 347).

[30]Chakravarty (1986, pp. 41–43).

[31]See Barman and Bisonoi (1983).

proposals for a VAT were approved by the ruling party.[32] However, this proposal was also rejected by Parliament. Australia and New Zealand both flirted with VAT in the early 1980s; Australia rejected VAT and New Zealand introduced it (but the opposition party promised to repeal it). Greece was committed to change to a VAT on entering the EC in 1981 as a full member, but successive prevarications delayed the introduction until January 1987. However, no matter how sporadic the moves toward VAT, the direction of change seems irresistible. Yet this is what makes the cases of those countries that have resisted this movement so interesting. The examples of the United States, Canada, Australia, Japan, and Iceland are all informative.

United States

The first point is that the United States is fairly satisfied with its current state and local retail sales taxes. Suggestions for a VAT at the federal level immediately run into the practicality of allowing the federal government to appropriate a general sales tax, and the problem of adding or "piggybacking" the state sales taxes on to a federal VAT. This is the overwhelming consideration for evaluating the possibility of a U.S. VAT (see Chapter 8).

In addition to the problems with the retail sales tax mentioned earlier, the United States has further difficulties. The experience of the states with retail sales taxes has been at relatively low rates (the median rate for 1985 was 4.6 percent) and frequently on a limited base (29 states do not tax food and 25 exempt most services); such administrative experience does not necessarily carry across to ensure an efficiently run VAT at, say, double the rate on all goods and services and levied on all traders.

For the United States to adopt a VAT, there has to be some reason other than dissatisfaction with the existing structure. Americans have been interested in VAT for the last twenty years,[33] but to give the flavor of recent debates, we can select five reasons given for suggesting the introduction of a VAT—shown in Table 1-6, along with the commentators and the dates of debate.

In the late 1970s, Congressman Ullman, in H.R. 5665, the (unsuccessful) Tax Restructuring Act of 1979, proposed a VAT to replace

---

[32]Despite this long gestation period, one commentator said, "The bill was apparently hastily drafted." See "Japan: Sales Tax," *World Tax Report* (1987, p. 14).

[33]For the earlier period, see the discussion in McLure (1974, pp. 96–103).

Table 1-6. Summary of Some Reasons for Advocating a U.S. Value-Added Tax

Commentator	Date	Net Revenue Increase	Finance Social Security	Replace Corporate Income Tax	Replace Personal Income Tax	Finance Defense
McLure[1]	1979–82		X	X	X	
Galvin[2]	1983		X			X
Lindholm[3]	1984		X	X		
Roth[4]	1985		X	X		
Walker[5]	1986	X				
McLure[6]	1987	X				

[1]Charles E. McLure, Jr., "The Tax Restructuring Act of 1979: Time for an American Value-Added Tax?" *Public Policy* (Cambridge, Massachusetts), Vol. 28 (Summer 1980), pp. 301–22.

[2]Charles O. Galvin, "It's VAT Time Again," *Tax Notes*, Tax Analysts (Arlington, Virginia), Vol. 21 (October 24, 1983), p. 280.

[3]Richard W. Lindholm, *A New Federal Tax System* (New York: Praeger, 1984).

[4]Senator William V. Roth, Jr., *The Business Transfer Tax Act of 1985* (S. 1102, 99th Congress, 1st Session, May 8, 1985) and "The Roth Reforms" (speech to the National Press Club, Washington, February 20, 1986).

[5]See discussion in Charls E. Walker and Mark A. Bloomfield, eds., *The Consumption Tax: A Better Alternative?* papers presented at a conference sponsored by the American Council for Capital Formation—Center for Policy Research (Cambridge, Massachusetts: Ballinger Publishing Company, 1987).

[6]Charles E. McLure, Jr., *The Value-Added Tax: Key to Deficit Reduction?* (Washington: American Enterprise Institute, 1987).

part of the payroll tax ($52 billion), the personal income tax ($50 billion), and the corporate income tax ($28 billion). In the event, Congressman Ullman was defeated in the November 1980 election (perhaps not entirely disassociated with his advocacy of VAT), but his proposals continued to attract attention. But by 1981, Charles McLure was writing, "if it is decided that a federal sales tax is needed, it would probably be better to adopt a federal retail sales tax than to impose a new and unfamiliar form of sales tax, the VAT."[34]

In 1983, during the debates on the need to increase defense spending, Charles Galvin[35] suggested that a way to "market" the VAT would be to "appeal" to the American people that a 10 percent VAT on all purchases would finance defense and permit the budget to be balanced. This, of course, is really just a different way of saying that the VAT is needed to increase net revenue. He also suggested that if it were considered that tying VAT to defense might prove a political

[34]McLure (1981, pp. 156–57); see also McLure (1980a).

[35]Galvin (1983).

liability, then why not tie it to financing social security? Again, of course, enabling the budget to move toward a balance.

A much more radical proposal was put forward in 1984 by Richard Lindholm.[36] The corporate and personal income taxes and the estate taxes were to be replaced by a VAT at 15 percent and a net worth tax at 2 percent; the VAT would be the principal generator of current revenue and the net worth tax would contribute a better equity component than the present direct taxes. As far as VAT is concerned, this proposal, of course, concentrates on the nondistorting revenue buoyancy of VAT.

The 1985 proposal by Senator Roth[37] was for a business transfer tax (BTT) to be levied, using the direct-subtractive method. That is, all traders with turnover exceeding $10 million, except retailers, were to subtract inputs from outputs leaving value added (basically wages and profits) to be taxed. This VAT would be rebated on exports as is the usual invoice-subtractive VAT but, in addition, it was proposed to allow the VAT liability as a credit against the social security tax (FICA); this suggestion seriously undermines the validity of the export rebate under GATT as it transforms the VAT from a sales tax to a direct tax. Such a direct-subtractive VAT is only practical using a single rate applied universally—"Given the likelihood that pressures for exclusions and multiple rates would not be successfully withstood, it seems inadvisable to adopt a naive subtraction-method tax such as the BTT."[38]

Charls Walker[39] polled 22 former high-level government economic policymakers and found broad support to reduce the budget deficit. Two thirds supported a tax increase, and nearly all of these preferred a consumption tax. This could be a retail sales tax or a VAT but its primary aim would be to generate a net revenue increase and reduce government borrowing.

Finally, the title of Charles McLure's book, *The Value-Added Tax: Key to Deficit Reduction?* puts the emphasis squarely on the need for revenue. "Interest in the . . . VAT . . . will increase as the Gramm-Rudman-Hollings targets for deficit reduction become increasingly difficult to achieve through budget cuts."[40]

---

[36]Lindholm (1984).
[37]Senator William V. Roth, Jr., *The Business Transfer Tax Act of 1985* (S. 1102) and "The Roth Reforms," speech to the National Press Club, Washington, February 20, 1986.
[38]McLure (1987b, p. 68).
[39]See discussion in Walker and Bloomfield (1987).
[40]McLure (1987b, p. 1).

The opposition to a U.S. VAT is summed up in five points.[41]

- Liberals oppose the VAT on grounds of regressivity.
- Conservatives fear the VAT as a "money machine."
- Both liberals and conservatives worry that a VAT would be inflationary.
- State and local officials are concerned about a VAT's intrusion into their traditional preserve for raising revenue.
- Both federal and state officials fear that the VAT would be an administrative nightmare.

Against these feelings the principal thrust behind the U.S. proposals to introduce a VAT is the need to supplement federal revenue.[42] Such a tax change could also allow social security to be financed, encourage savings, and permit direct taxes to be restructured; but the main problem is that the Federal Government does not have access to the buoyant revenue of a general sales tax. (It is estimated that a general 5 percent VAT would raise $70 billion in 1988 and a VAT exempting food, housing, and medical care would raise $40 billion.)[43] What form of general sales tax is another debate, and one well illustrated by the Australian debate (the U.S. federal-state issue is mirrored in the Canadian debate, below).

Australia

The Australian wholesale tax is admitted to be administratively complex, inequitable, and inefficient.[44] The choice for Australia to generate more revenue and achieve more flexibility to reduce personal marginal income tax rates boiled down to introducing a retail sales tax or a VAT. In the event, both proved unacceptable and it was decided to extend the existing wholesale tax and introduce a separate tax on services.

The reasons Australia decided against a VAT, despite the advocacy of such bodies as the Business Council of Australia, included the following:

- The self-policing properties of VAT had been overstated.

---

[41]See "Commentary," in Bloomfield (1987, p. 174).

[42]See also United States, General Accounting Office (1986).

[43]"Congressional Reports: Estimated Revenue Effects of Options to Raise Revenue," *Tax Notes* (1987, p. 88).

[44]Morgan (1986) and Cnossen (1983).

- The administrative costs could be "unacceptably high."
- The incentive to evade tax was as high under a VAT as under a retail sales tax.
- Overstated claims for tax credit was as significant a potential loophole as were falsified invoices.
- Compliance costs were higher under a VAT.[45]
- Trade union concerns about regressivity (a 12.5 percent VAT was expected to increase prices by about 6.5 percent and there were doubts about the promised compensation for welfare benefits).

However, reading between the lines, a possibly overwhelming consideration was the much greater "lead-time" that the VAT involved. The Australian Commissioner of Taxation estimated that the *additional* lead-time needed to introduce a VAT rather than a retail sales tax could be of the order of 12 months.[46] In a country where there is a constitutional parliamentary term of three years, the time taken to examine, legislate, introduce, and get over the initial problems of a controversial new tax can become a crucial consideration. Indeed, it is interesting that political considerations, rather than economic, may have been the deciding factor in the delays in changing to VAT in countries as diverse as Australia, Canada, Cyprus, Greece, and Japan.

Canada

Rather like Australia, Canada relies on an unsatisfactory manufacturers tax that is widely thought to involve distorting cascade tax elements in exports. A 1984 survey indicated that the average effective tax rate for domestic goods was 33 percent higher than the tax on imports competing with domestic products. Successive amendments to this tax have turned it into a set of hybrid manufacturers or wholesalers tax; several broad categories of goods are taxed at the wholesale level (for example, cosmetics, automobiles, televisions and audio goods, and household chemicals). As in Australia, Canada has toyed with the idea of a VAT.[47] However, unlike Australia the main

[45]Australia, *Reform of the Australian Tax System: Draft White Paper*, Appendix 13-B, "Choice Between VAT and BBCT" (1985, pp. 129–32).

[46]Australia, *Reform of the Australian Tax System: Draft White Paper*, Appendix 13-B.17 (1985, p. 131).

[47]See a comment by Gordon Pitts, "Value Added Tax Examined," *Financial Post* (Toronto), October 27, 1984, p. 15.

difficulty has involved the federal-state issue. All but one of the 11 Canadian provinces have substantial independent retail sales taxes that they are reluctant to give up.[48] This suggested that a direct-subtractive VAT (the business transfer tax) based on company accounts might be more suitable because its effects on prices are not explicit and a retail sales tax could still be added to it. While it is true such a method might enable VAT revenues to be allocated to the states where the value added originated, this would depend on the universality of the tax and, of course, on the use of a single rate. It would also be a unique experiment watched most carefully by other major federal systems (Brazil, India, Nigeria, and the United States). The difficulty of reaching agreement with the provinces (quite apart from all the usual concerns about regressivity and price effects) has probably been the major influence restraining Canada's adoption of the VAT.

Japan

Japan has been on the brink of introducing a VAT before. In 1980, the Finance Ministry tried to introduce a VAT-style "consumption tax" and was repulsed. The 1986/87 VAT at 5 percent was not put forward as a revenue-enhancing measure, but to replace revenues lost because of reducing the top individual income tax rate from 70 percent to 50 percent and the corporate income tax rate from 53 percent to 50 percent.

There seem to be three main problems with the proposal. First, the principal opposition to the VAT appears to come from a widespread suspicion that a VAT would give the Finance Ministry a revenue buoyant tax that could greatly expand the scope of government. At present, Japan relies mainly on excises and stamp duties for its indirect tax revenue. As reported, many think that "the Finance Ministry has long been in search of additional revenue sources, particularly the VAT. . . . In the long run, we might have a European-type large-spending government."[49]

Second, although the proposed VAT had a high exemption limit of ¥ 80 million (US$627,000) and would have exempted most of the six million individual businesses, many of these small traders supply large taxable companies and would have been unable to supply a VAT registration number allowing their customers to claim the VAT as a deduction. This, it was claimed, would put them at a disadvantage.

[48]See the interesting discussion in Gillis (1986).
[49]Makino (1986, p. 4).

There seems to have been a feeling among small traders that you were damned if you did and damned if you didn't register for VAT.

Finally, the bill included the obligation of taxable enterprises to seek code numbers from their tax offices. Although designed to prevent fraud, it was perceived that the new system could easily be applied to income and corporation taxes. Such a registration system was resented and helped sentiment against the tax that introduced it.

This controversial VAT, as part of a wider tax reform package, was unable to obtain Parliamentary approval. However, another suggestion to introduce VAT may be debated during the summer of 1988.

Iceland

For the last ten years, Iceland has considered introducing a VAT.[50] It is the only country that has levied a retail sales tax sustained at over 13 percent for many years. Introduced in 1960 at 3 percent, it mounted to 11 percent by 1970, and was supplemented by an "emergency tax" and "oil tax" in 1973/74 that increased it to 13 percent. By 1986 the base retail sales tax was 20 percent, the oil tax 1.5 percent, and an "additional sales tax" 3.5 percent, making 25 percent in all. Such a rate does cause considerable concern as collection lies entirely in the hands of retailers, since registered traders import free of tax. Evasion is suspected, and exemptions of foods and many services exclude about 40 percent of total private final consumption. Administration is, of course, fairly straightforward in a country of 210,000 where 50 percent of the population lives in the capital city. Although the Federation of Icelandic Industries has supported the VAT, its introduction has been delayed for two reasons. First, trade unions have opposed it because of anticipated unfavorable effects on prices and, second, the administrative problems of monitoring the refunds has caused doubts. However, the attractions of collecting the major proportion of the sales tax at importation (typical of a small island economy) over-rode many doubts, and the proposal is to introduce the VAT at 24 percent, although delayed again from January 1988 to January 1989.

Conclusion

This brief review shows that the reasons why countries have not introduced VAT boil down to:

---

[50]Due (1986b, pp. 240–41).

- Fear about regressivity.
- Anticipated high administrative costs, especially to monitor refunds.
- Buoyant revenue permitting larger government expenditures.
- Potential evasion.
- Compliance costs.
- Effect on prices.
- Incompatibility of VAT with a traditionally strong state sales tax structure.

Each of these concerns is dealt with separately in later chapters. Overall, we have the picture of a general sales tax that has exploded from its final form in France in the late 1960s to become the dominant sales tax of the world. The theory of the VAT has been looked at many times; it is worth looking at the practice, at the problems encountered, and how the examination of such problems may improve practice.

CHAPTER 2

VAT Rates

And though each spring doe adde to love new heate,
As princes doe in times of action get
New taxes, and remit them not in peace,
No winter shall abate the springs encrease.
—JOHN DONNE, "Loves Growth"

The rate or rates at which VAT is levied is an important consideration in the operation of VAT. Table 2-1 shows the VAT rates in effect on January 1, 1988 in 44 countries. It also shows 7 countries that are actively considering a VAT (Canada, Iceland, Japan, Poland, South Africa, Thailand, and Tunisia). Fifteen countries use a single rate (ignoring the zero rate used by nearly all for exports and by some to exempt domestic purchases—see Chapter 4). The highest single rate in use is in Denmark (22 percent), and the lowest (5 percent) is in Panama (and 3 percent proposed for Japan). The principal costs of administering a single rate VAT are the same whatever the rate chosen; given the widely perceived high costs of administration and compliance (see Chapters 12 and 16), it might be considered a poor allocation of resources to levy a VAT at a low rate. For most countries, a VAT is probably not worth introducing at less than 10 percent (a point that becomes crucial in discussing a VAT in the United States). At that rate, the administrative costs as a proportion of revenue should fall to 1–2 percent. Also, at that rate, the deficiencies of the retail sales tax start to emerge more strongly (see Chapter 1), and the VAT, with its fractionated collection at importation and subsequent stages, begins to look more attractive.

The highest selective VAT rates appear in Senegal (50 percent), Italy (38 percent), Greece (36 percent), Côte d'Ivoire (35.13 percent), and Niger and Colombia (35 percent). The lowest rates—more or less

Table 2-1. Percentage VAT Rates Throughout the World

	Date VAT Introduced or Proposed	VAT Rates[1]	
		At introduction	On January 1, 1988
Argentina	Jan. 1975	**16**	9, **18**
Austria	Jan. 1973	**8,** 16	10, **20,** 32
Belgium	Jan. 1971	6, 14, **18**	1, 6, 17, **19,** 25, 33
Bolivia	Oct. 1973	5, **10,** 15	**10**
Brazil[2]	Jan. 1967	**15**	9, **11**
Brazil[3]	Jan. 1967	**15**	**17**
Canada[4]			
Chile	Mar. 1975	8, **20**	**16**[5]
Colombia	Jan. 1975	4, 6, **10**	4, 6, **10,** 15, 20, 35
Costa Rica	Jan. 1975	**10**	**8**
Côte d'Ivoire	Jan. 1960	**8**	11.11, **25,** 35.13
Denmark	July 1967	**10**	**22**
Dominican Rep.	Jan. 1983	**6**	**6**
Ecuador	July 1970	**4,** 10	**6**
France	Jan. 1968	6.4, **13.6,** 20, 25	2.1, 4, 5.5, 7, **18.6,** 33.3
Germany, Fed. Rep. of	Jan. 1968	5, **10**	7, **14**
Greece	Jan. 1987	6, **18,** 36	3, 6, **18,** 36
Guatemala	Aug. 1983	**7**	**7**
Haiti	Nov. 1982	**7**	**10**
Honduras	Jan. 1976	**3**	**5,** 6
Hungary	Jan. 1988	15, **25**	
Iceland[4]	Jan. 1989	**24**	
Indonesia	Apr. 1985	**10**	**10**
Ireland	Nov. 1972	5.26, **16.37,** 30.26	2.2, 10, **25**
Israel	July 1976	**8**	6.5, **15**
Italy	Jan. 1973	6, **12,** 18	2, 9, **18,** 38
Japan[4]		**3**	
Korea	July 1977	**10**	2, 3.5, **10**
Luxembourg	Jan. 1970	2, 4, **8**	3, 6, **12**
Madagascar	Jan. 1969	6, **12**	**15**
Mexico	Jan. 1980	**10**	6, **15,** 20
Morocco	Apr. 1986	7, 12, 14, **19,** 30	7, 12, 14, **19,** 30
Netherlands	Jan. 1969	4, **12**	6, **20**
New Zealand	May 1986	**10**	**10**
Nicaragua	Jan. 1975	**6**	**10,** 25
Niger	Jan. 1986	8, **12,** 18	15, **25,** 35
Norway	Jan. 1970	**20**	11.11, **20**
Panama	Mar. 1977	**5**	**5**
Peru	July 1976	3, **20,** 40	**18**
Philippines	Jan. 1988	**10**	
Poland[4]			
Portugal	Jan. 1986	8, **16,** 30	8, **16,** 30
Senegal	Mar. 1961–80[6]	. . .	7, **20,** 34, 50
South Africa[4]	Apr. 1989		
Spain	Jan. 1986	6, **12,** 33	6, **12,** 33

Table 2-1 (*continued*). Percentage VAT Rates Throughout the World

	Date VAT Introduced or Proposed	VAT Rates[1]	
		At introduction	On January 1, 1988
Sweden[7]	Jan. 1969	2.04, 6.38, **11.1**	3.95, 12.87, **23.46**
Taiwan Province of China	Apr. 1986	**5**	**5**, 15, 25
Thailand[4]	Jan. 1989		
Tunisia	July 1988	6, **17**, 29	
Turkey	Jan. 1985	**10**	12, **15**
United Kingdom	Apr. 1973	**10**	**15**
Uruguay	Jan. 1968	5, **14**	12, **21**

Source: Various reports.

[1]Rates shown in bold type are the so-called standard rates applied to goods and services not covered by other especially high or low rates. Most countries use a zero rate for a few goods, and Ireland, Portugal, and the United Kingdom use it extensively to ensure that substantial amounts of goods and services are free of VAT.
[2]On interstate transactions depending on region.
[3]On intrastate transactions.
[4]Proposed or under discussion.
[5]June 1988.
[6]Senegal's VAT evolved from a limited manufacturers turnover tax with credits, and no precise date of introduction is given; it has only recently been extended to include services at rates of 7, 12.5, 17, and 50 percent.
[7]Effective rates.

theoretical—are in Belgium (1 percent) and Italy and Korea (2 percent). Generally, reduced rates applied to food are levied at 5 percent or 6 percent. The highest standard rate is 25 percent in Côte d'Ivoire, Ireland, and Niger.

The experience of changing rates has been nearly all one way—upward. Only two countries, Costa Rica and Peru (and Brazil on interstate transactions) have a lower standard rate of VAT in 1988 than when VAT was introduced. Other countries have watched VAT rates climb. Some have moved from a single rate to double rates and back to a single rate again (United Kingdom), while others have made an effort to reduce the number of rates used (Italy and Belgium). The EC has proposed that countries should use only two bands of rates, a standard rate and a reduced rate—see discussion in Chapter 8, section on "Customs Unions."

There are contentious issues relating to effective VAT rates, the relationship between VAT and excises, and tax harmonization. However, the most persistent and important problems all relate to the choice of single or multiple rates and how many multiple rates.

A Single Rate or Multiple Rates?

The basic rule is simple: use as few tax rates as will satisfy the preferences of politicians. All tax administrators prefer to use a single rate of VAT (once again, ignoring the zero rate on exports). Politicians nearly always think the public will acquiesce to a VAT more easily if products consumed by lower-income households are taxed at lower rates than products consumed by the better off. The temptation is to introduce a rate lower than the standard rate, and another higher rate, thus ending up with three rates. It cannot be emphasized too strongly that both official administrative costs and traders' compliance costs rise dramatically as the number of rates multiply and nothing much is gained in terms of revenue (see Chapters 6 and 16).

To run the simplest practical VAT (one positive rate, a zero rate, and some exemptions) requires at least 9 pieces of information from each taxpayer (the value of supplies at the two rates and the value of exempt supplies, the value of purchases at the two rates, two liabilities to VAT on output, and two liabilities to VAT on inputs). A VAT with three positive rates, a zero rate, and exemptions needs at least 17 pieces of information. The Irish tax return form, using only two rates, still requires 38 entries.[1] As the number of rates increases, tax forms become much more complicated and not only the chance of error, on the part of both taxpayer and tax officials, becomes much greater but the potential for evasion rises rapidly as well.

Apart from administrative and compliance costs, there are numerous doubts about the rationale for using multiple rates at all.

(1) Multiple rates distort both consumer and producer choices.

(2) Low rates of VAT, as the Irish Commission on Taxation noted, do not "necessarily benefit the final consumer. In reality, traders [are] faced with recouping a certain amount of VAT from consumers. They [adjust] their prices in line with what the market would bear regardless of the rate of tax prescribed for individual items."[2] That is, given multiple rates, traders will juggle their prices to what the market will bear and items with low VAT rates could end up cross-subsidizing the higher-rated items.

(3) Of course, not just low-income households benefit from the lower tax rate; such differential rates are a very blunt instrument for favoring particular households. Clearly, income tax adjustments,

---

[1]Ireland, Commission on Taxation (1984, p. 63).
[2]Ireland, Commission on Taxation (1984, p. 66).

transfers, income supplements, or coupon schemes can be better targeted to help the poor.

(4) Many countries subsidize "essential" goods and services such as food, electricity, or fuel. It makes little sense to levy a special low rate VAT on an already adjusted price rather than the standard VAT rate.

(5) Favorable treatment creates dissatisfied traders and consumers who argue that their products are at the dividing line of definition; if fresh vegetables are taxed at a low rate, why not frozen vegetables, if frozen, why not canned, and so on.

(6) A glance at any of the VAT regulations defining differential categories should quickly convince any sensible person how ill advised it is to multiply rates and create the attendant problems of definition. It is not only that VAT staff time is taken up defining the various categories of goods, assessing the borderline cases, and explaining decisions to traders and public interest groups, but that, typically, these decisions require the attention of highly qualified, intelligent staff, whose decisions will stand up to debate and argument. Such a staff can be employed much more fruitfully on administering the VAT. Settling hardline definitions therefore becomes an expensive exercise.

(7) Successful arguments for lower VAT rates erode the tax base.

(8) High VAT rates typically (except for automobiles) apply to goods that account for a relatively small proportion of total consumption. The revenue at issue is small, and the administrative cost is high. Frequently, consumers avoid sumptuary rates by adjusting their consumption. Given the small segment of the population involved, the effect on distributive burden cannot be much. Excises and user charges are the best complements to VAT to levy higher taxes on a few goods (see below).

(9) Whatever multiple rates are chosen and whatever the subsequent changes, they rarely reflect genuine changes in consumer or government preferences. As Cnossen remarked, "At the beginning of 1979, music and stage performances became taxable at the general rate; admissions to zoos, pleasure fairs, and circuses, however, continued to be taxed at 4 per cent. Presumably, this change did not signify a shift in the cultural taste of the Dutch."[3]

(10) Finally, using a general equilibrium model, it has been shown that rate differentiation leads to significant reductions (about 60

[3]Cnossen (1981, p. 229).

percent for sales tax) in the welfare gains of adopting equalized tax rates.[4]

To get a new tax off the ground smoothly requires the cooperation of the traders who must bear the compliance costs (see Chapter 6). As Roger Douglas, the Minister of Finance of New Zealand, pointed out, "Traders who would be collecting GST [goods and services tax—the New Zealand VAT] had to be assured they could cope with the new tax. Simplicity for them was, in fact, one of the key reasons for setting the tax at a single rate and without exemptions. . . . I believe now this . . . was one of the principal reasons why the tax reform package was so well accepted when it was finally introduced."[5]

The arguments are overwhelming in favor of using a single rate VAT with a zero rate for exports and very few exemptions. Should multiple rates be necessary, the fewer the better.[6]

Effective Rates

A powerful additional reason against multiple rates (were one needed) is that with "any complication in rate structure . . . the pattern of uniformity flies apart completely."[7] Even with a simple single rate of 15 percent and a zero rate with some exemptions, Hemming and Kay were able to show that the effective rates on value added in the United Kingdom ranged from -24 percent (on food) to 37 percent (on leather goods and furs). Of course, these effective rates of VAT, like effective rates of protection from customs tariffs, are not apparent to the consumer or, usually, to the trader. They occur because traders are unable to claim full credit for some inputs, yet the VAT is applied to the full value of their sale. Therefore, the actual value added in that particular trade is taxed effectively at a much higher rate. (For example, a VAT of 10 percent on a restaurant meal, where inputs represent 40 percent of the final value with no credit because they are exempt, is transformed into an effective rate of over 16 percent.)

A more pedestrian point about effective rates is that only one country (Sweden) quotes its VAT rates on a price inclusive of tax, and traders in most countries have to work from tax-inclusive prices backward to calculate their VAT liability. The obvious case would be a

[4]Ballard, Shoven, and Whalley (1982, pp. 35–36).
[5]Douglas (1987, p. 210).
[6]For a further discussion see Cnossen (1982).
[7]Hemming and Kay (1981, p. 80).

10 percent VAT, quoted at $^{10}/_{110}$, requiring the trader to use either the fraction $^1/_{11}$ or 9.091 to calculate his VAT liability at 10 percent net of tax. When numerous rates or rate changes are made, some peculiar (and to some, confusing) fractions are created. If the rate is reduced from 10 percent to 8 percent, the relatively easy fraction of $^1/_{11}$ is transformed into $^2/_{27}$ or a coefficient of 7.41. The fewer such changes, and the simpler the fractions and coefficients sought, the better.

Another minor point is that some countries have altered their effective rate of tax by adjusting the value of the good charged. Sweden used this mechanism to lower the VAT on housing (effectively halving the tax rate). Tunisia proposed a 50 percent reduction in value for a range of commodities, and Grenada adjusts the base for all domestic goods to make the effective rate 8 percent (instead of 20 percent). Finland overadjusts for the value of inputs to "subsidize" essential goods. Such adjustments discriminate for or against inputs and would not be acceptable on traded goods under GATT. Moreover, the tax shown on invoices to purchasers will have to be at the effective rate to avoid overgenerous credit claims for inputs. Naturally, such adjusted bases are discriminatory, distorting, and undesirable.

VAT Rates and Excise Duties

A VAT is levied on a price inclusive of customs duties and excises. It could be levied on a price excluding both but, given that these taxes are levied early in the production process and that levying them on a base including VAT would be administratively cumbersome, it is easier to levy the VAT on the all-inclusive base and then adjust the excise rates if necessary. Usually when a VAT is started, the excise rates are adjusted so that the retail price of excisable commodities, including VAT and excises, does not change. Excises typically are levied on four traditional goods: alcohol, tobacco, petroleum products, and automobiles; two of these (alcohol and tobacco) are usually regressive and the other two contribute to progressivity. If countries wish to try to create progressivity through indirect taxes, then it is preferable, especially in developing countries, to use a few extra excises than to complicate the VAT structure (see above) by introducing multiple rates.

The range of commodities over and above the usual goods subject to excises, even in OECD countries, is remarkably large (Table 2-2). However, realistically, in terms of significant revenue, the goods that might be considered for excises to complement the VAT, aside from those already mentioned, are electricity, telecommunications, nonal-

Table 2-2. Examples of Nonsumptuary Excised Goods for Selected OECD Countries, 1981

	Belgium	Canada	Denmark	France	Germany, Fed. Rep. of	Ireland	Italy	Japan	Luxembourg	Netherlands	Norway	United Kingdom	United States (Federal)
Jewelry		AV(r)		AV(r)				AV[1]					
Matches		S(u)	S(u)	S(u)		S(u)		AV[1]				S(u)	
Playing cards		S(u)	S(u)				S(u)	S(u)			S(u)		
Watches, clocks		AV(w)						AV[1]		AV(w)		AV(w)	
Motor vehicles		AV[2]				AV(w)	S	AV[1]					S(u)[2]
Electric power			S			S		AV(r)					
Nonalcoholic beverages	S(v)		S(v)	S(v)	AV(r)			AV[1]	S(v)	S(v)	S(v)		
Tea, coffee	S(w)		S(w)	S(w)	S(w)			AV[1]	S(w)				
Candy, chocolate			S(w)								S(w)		
Perfume, cosmetics						S(u)		AV[1]			AV(w)		
Television sets								AV[1]					
Electric appliances								AV[1]	S(w)	S(w)			
Sugar	S(w)			S(w)	S(w)		S(w)	S(w)					
Light bulbs							S(w)	AV[1]	S(w)	S(w)			
Spices, cocoa				S(w)			S(w)	AV[1]					
Food oils				S(w)			S(w)						
Salt					FM								
Lamps					S(u)			AV[1]					
Tires												S(w)	S(w)
Phonograph records					AV(w)			AV[1]					
Sporting goods								AV[1]					AV(w)
Firearms							S(u)	AV[1]					AV(w)

Sources: Commission of the European Communities and individual country budget documents for 1981.

Note: AV   = ad valorem rate.
      AV(r) = ad valorem rate on retail sale.
      AV(w) = ad valorem rate on wholesale value.
      S   = specific rate.
      S(w)   = specific rate according to weight.
      S(v)   = specific rate according to volume.
      S(u)   = specific rate according to unit.
      FM   = fiscal monopoly.

[1] Part of the Japanese commodity tax.
[2] Automobile excise rate levied according to size and/or fuel efficiency.

coholic beverages, household electric appliances, records, and tapes. Each of these has some possibility of adding to progressivity. The consumption of most rises sharply with increasing household income. Certainly the extraordinary range of goods on which excises are levied, for instance, in Japan (Table 2-2), with rates from 1.6 percent on golf clubs to 7.6 percent on small television sets and 32.1 percent on small passenger automobiles,[8] is almost a classic example of the desirability of a single rate VAT to replace such distortions of consumer choice.

The advantage of using excises instead of multiple VAT rates is that the mechanisms of tax collection are kept separate. Typically, excises are collected at the manufacturing stage from a few large producers. The tax is monitored by both physical and accounting controls. Revenue is secure and easy to collect. Instead of involving VAT and its attendant complicated collection mechanism, it is better to keep the two taxes separate, VAT with its uniform rate and the clearly recognized excises levied separately on quite independently justified grounds. However, it is quite possible to use VAT audits to supplement audits for excises.

Geographical Rates

At least one Latin American country (Brazil) uses different VAT rates in different parts of the country. Mexico has a standard rate of 15 percent, but uses 6 percent in the areas bordering the United States. The arguments in favor of this are powerful. The state retail sales taxes across the border in Arizona, New Mexico, and Texas are much lower than the 15 percent standard Mexican VAT; border residents in Mexico would make all their purchases in the United States and decimate trade in the Mexican border towns.

Despite the understandable reasons for the differential rate, it creates a potential for substantial evasion. It is a fairly simple matter to make operations transacted outside the areas where the lower rate is applied appear as if they had been performed within them, especially in the case of sales to final consumers. The temptation to do so increased sharply when the original difference of 4 percent (a standard rate of 10 percent and the geographic rate of 6 percent) widened in 1983 to 9 percent (15 percent standard rate and 6 percent geographic rate). Of course, revenue is also affected as consumers living near the lower rate areas will make their purchases in favored zones.

[8]See an excellent description in Ferron (1984).

Argentina does not use rates differentiated by region for its federal VAT; however, the states are allowed to give investment incentives that rebate the VAT in full or in part. The result is that the effective rates of VAT are varied by region and indeed by activity. Of course, this erodes the federal revenue and in a way that is uncertain both in amount and in timing. Clearly, from the Federal Government's point of view, such a development is undesirable. If regional incentives are to be given, they should be given in some other way that does not endanger federal revenue.

Portugal, to try to offset the transport costs to the Azores and Madeira, uses reduced rates of 6, 12, and 21 percent (instead of 8, 16, and 30 percent). Of course, direct transport subsidies would be preferred.

Such geographic VAT rate differences cannot be recommended as a tool of regional policy or as an expansion of local democracy. Differential rates undermine the neutrality of the VAT (which is its major virtue), encourage evasion, and erode revenues.

Rate Harmonization

Countries forming a customs union and working to achieve a true internal market need to harmonize their VAT and excise rates. The EC is the only agency to have issued proposed rules on this, and even those seem optimistic to reach the harmonized rates by the desired date of 1992.[9]

The proposal is that EC members should not make any moves that would exacerbate their rate differentials and, if possible, should move toward a common number of rates and then toward the same rates. What this means, in practice, is that countries using more than three rates should reduce their rates to three, and those using one rate "be allowed to increase that number to two."[10] For instance, Belgium, with the largest number of rates in the EC, has suggested (in a Royal Commission Report of February 1987) that five rates (6, 17, 19, 25, and 33 percent) should be reduced to three (6, 20, and 25 percent).[11]

Overall, the message as far as rates are concerned is straightforward: the fewer the better, levied on full unadjusted prices, and inclusive of customs duties and excises.

[9]European Community, "Proposed Standstill on VAT and Excise Duties," reproduced in *Intertax* (February 1986, p. 45).

[10]European Community, "Proposed Standstill on VAT and Excise Duties," reproduced in *Intertax* (February 1986, p. 45).

[11]"Belgium: Income Tax Changes Ahead," *World Tax Report* (1987, p. 9).

CHAPTER 3

Exemptions and Zero Rating
Equity Arguments

Take care of the sense and the sounds will take care of themselves.
—LEWIS.CARROLL, *Alice's Adventures in Wonderland*, Chapter 9

A linguistic quirk of the VAT is that "exemption" actually means that the "exempt" trader has to pay VAT on his inputs without being able to claim any credit for this tax paid on his inputs. "Zero rating" means that a trader is fully compensated for any VAT he pays on inputs and, therefore, genuinely is exempt from VAT.

To amplify this, the exempt trader pays VAT on his purchases, but is unable to claim this input tax liability as a credit against his tax liability on sales as he cannot impose a VAT on his exempt sales. Such a trader is out of the VAT system and is treated as a final purchaser. On the other hand, a trader liable to the zero rate is liable to an actual rate of VAT, which just happens to be zero; therefore, such a zero-rated trader is wholly a part of the VAT system and makes a full return for VAT in the normal way. However, when this trader applies the tax rate to his sales, it ends up as a zero VAT liability but from this he can deduct the entire VAT liability on his inputs, generating a repayment of tax from the government. In this way, the zero-rated trader reclaims all the VAT on his inputs and bears no tax on his outputs, and the purchaser of such a trader's sales buys the good or service free of VAT.

The next two sections of this chapter look more closely at just what "exempt" and "zero rating" imply. The following section identifies the three ways in which exemptions and zero rating are justified, and the rest of the chapter discusses the treatment of goods and services related to the regressivity of VAT.

Exempt Goods and Services

All suppliers of goods and services are either taxable or exempt. However, a fundamental characteristic of exemptions in the VAT system is that they generally do not provide complete relief from the tax. All exemption does is relieve the exempt trader's value added from VAT, but all his purchases, including capital goods, are taxed. Thus, if farmers are "exempt" from VAT, they do not have to deal with the tax man, but they pay VAT on all their inputs—fertilizer, seeds, and electricity—as well as on all their capital inputs, including farm buildings and machinery.

Exempt traders need not register with the tax authorities nor keep records for VAT (but, of course, similar records should be kept for income tax). So, clearly, exemption helps simplify the administration of VAT, but introduces inequities. If exempt traders sell goods that are not necessarily final sales, but instead are used as inputs in the further production of other goods or services, then the VAT borne on the exempt trader's inputs is built into his price and forms part of the cost of any trader buying the good for further production. Even if the good produced with the exempt inputs is fully part of the VAT system, the manufacturer cannot claim a credit for the VAT on his input because it was tax exempt and, of course, no VAT element would be shown on his purchase invoice. This means that part of the value added is taxed more than once and that a tax-on-tax cascade is introduced into VAT—the very evil that VAT was designed to eliminate. The more exempt goods and traders there are (for example, in Ireland and the United Kingdom), the more probable it is that value added is taxed at different unintended (and unknown) rates. Moreover, the more exemptions there are, the more others are tempted to claim exemption for themselves, and in this way the tax base is eroded; for example, a year after introducing the VAT, Indonesia exempted from VAT all automobiles used in the taxi business. One might guess that the number of automobiles to be used as taxis might rise sharply.

From both theoretical and practical viewpoints, exemptions should be kept to a minimum, and this is exemplified by the preoccupation of the EC Commission with exemptions. In the preamble to the Second

Directive,[1] the Council of the EC expressed the conviction that granting exemptions would create difficulties. For that reason, it was most desirable to restrict the number and scope of exemptions. The Second Directive provided that for a limited period member states could, subject to consultation with the Commission and for well-defined reasons of social interest and for the benefit of the ultimate consumers, provide reduced rates of tax, or even exemptions, if the total relief did not exceed the reliefs under the previous sales tax. The actual list of EC-approved exemptions is extremely limited (basically, exports, postal services, the provision of health and education and goods related to such services, charities, cultural services, betting and gaming, the supply of land, financial services, and leasing or renting immovable property).

If, for social or economic reasons, a country wants to grant relief, a reduced rate can be employed, but not a rate so low as to fail to absorb the deductions due for the tax paid in the preceding stages. That is, the EC Council expected that even if a reduced rate was used, there would still be some positive tax liability and the state would not be involved in a net repayment to the trader (except for exporters). Perhaps it should be pointed out (but not recommended) that there is no technical problem about using the VAT mechanism to subsidize certain products; not only is a zero rate possible, there could even be a negative VAT rate and hence a subsidy.

So, in theory, zero rating should be used when the authorities really wish to ensure that a product is to be free of VAT. Using an exemption for VAT means that the tax is borne by the trader, and if that trader sells to the public, he must pass on the tax on inputs to the public in his price or cut payments to his factors of production (capital and labor). This suggests that countries that genuinely wish to pass on to the consumer the benefits of VAT-free goods and services should be allowed to use the zero rate.

In practice, however, most countries, and certainly the EC, have frowned on the use of the zero rate. Table 3-1 shows the range of exemptions available in a number of countries. As will be noticed, some, such as food, are exempted or taxed at a much lower rate, often because it is felt that the poorer households should not have to pay the VAT on such an essential good. However, unless the entire sector of agriculture is treated in a way that relieves it of the obligation to pay any VAT, then the VAT on the farmers' inputs will be absorbed into the price charged for their output, and the consumer will end up paying

---

[1]See European Community, Second Council Directive.

Table 3-1. VAT: Summary[1] Examples of Exemptions and Zero Rates

	Belgium	Denmark	France	Germany, Fed. Rep. of	Ireland	Italy	Luxembourg	Netherlands	Norway	Portugal	Spain	Sweden	Turkey	United Kingdom	Argentina	Chile	Colombia	Costa Rica	Mexico	Madagascar	Morocco	Niger	Korea	Philippines	Taiwan Prov. of China	New Zealand
Food: basic	X	X	X		Z	Z				Z			Z	Z	X	X	X	X	Z	X	X	X		X	X	
Food: processed	X	X	X	X	Z		X	X	X	X	X	X		Z		X	Z	X	X	X		X	X	X	X	
Medical services	X	X	X	X	Z	X	X	X		X	X	Z	X	X	X	X	X	X	X	X	X	X	X	X	X	
Medical drugs	X	X	X	X	Z	X	X	X		X	X	X	X	Z	X		X	X		X		X	X	X		
Educational services	X	X	X	X	X	X	X	X	X	X	X	X	X	X	X	X	X	X	X	X	X	X	X	X		
Housing purchased	X	X	X	X	Z	X	X	X	X					Z			X		X	X	X	X				X
Housing rented														X			X		X	X		X	X			
Clothing					Z																		X			
Books	Z									Z				Z									X	X		
Newspapers		Z				Z				Z		Z		Z									X			
Entertainment, sports			X	X				Z		X						X	X		X	X	X	X	X	X	X	
Museums		X	X	X	X					X	X		X			X	X	X	X	X	X	X	X	X	X	
Government sales of goods and services					X															X		X	X		X	
Financial services	X	X	X	X	X	X	X	X	X	X	X	X	X	X	X	X	X	X		X		X		X	X	
Secondhand goods			X							Z	X								X	X	X	X		X	X	
Agricultural inputs	X	X	X		Z					Z	X				X		Z	X	X	X	Z		X			
Original art	X	X	X	X		X			X	X	X	X			X		X	X		X	X		X	X	X	

Source: Various country reports.

Note: x = exemptions; z = zero rate.

[1]The symbols are only summaries; for instance, Ireland does not zero rate all clothing but only children's clothing and shoes; Mexico does not tax all financial services as it exempts agricultural and life insurance; Chile does not exempt all medical services but only those that match the officially recognized scale of charges.

the VAT, although at a lower rate than if the standard rate were levied on food. As will be discussed in more detail in Chapter 7, different countries have different ways to relieve the agricultural sector from VAT, but only the Irish and the U.K. authorities have used zero rating to relieve the entire food sector from taxation. The EC has devised the flat credit compensation, which introduces its own distortions, and the Latin American countries have, largely, attempted to exempt from VAT the principal inputs of the agricultural sector (seeds, fertilizers, and farm equipment).

Zero Rating

Zero rating, as Table 3-1 shows, is used much less extensively, although, as noted earlier, it is the only true way to ensure that goods are provided free of VAT. The first country to use the zero rate was the Netherlands. Instead of exempting exports from tax as the original official directive of the EC required, the Dutch taxed exports at the zero rate and allowed the exporter to claim as credit the entire tax paid on inputs. This is no different, except procedurally, from other EC countries that rebate their exporters for the VAT content of their exports. Both systems involve the exporter showing the VAT content of the exported good: in the Netherlands, originally as a tax credit against VAT liability at zero percent, in other countries, as a straightforward claim against the state.

Table 3-1 also shows that Ireland and the United Kingdom are two countries that have enthusiastically adopted the zero rate. In Ireland, zero-rated consumption involves about 33 percent of household consumption and, in the United Kingdom, some 35 percent, thus, of course, severely eroding the VAT base. In Belgium, Denmark, Italy, Korea, and Portugal, the zero rating is generally simply an ad hoc measure introduced in specific instances with limited objectives in mind (for example, to reduce newspaper costs); however, "in Ireland and the United Kingdom, the large-scale use of zero-rating reflects a tax policy which is being pursued for historical, political and social reasons that are not easy to dismiss."[2]

This policy does, however, involve "extraordinary borderlines between classes of goods and services. . . . Who can remember, for example, which species of hen can be sold zero-rated and which are regarded as ornamental and hence always subject to the standard rate.

---

[2] European Community, "Further Harmonization of VAT," reproduced in *Intertax* (April 1983, p. 138).

Fathom the borderline between chocolate biscuits (taxable) and choco-late-covered cakes (zero-rated). Then once you think you have it, ask yourself whether a chocolate eclair is taxable or not?"[3] Or, to give another example, "packets of mixed fruit and nuts are subject to detailed regulations and tins of mixed biscuits must contain less than 15 per cent of their weight in chocolate biscuits in order to qualify for exemption."[4]

The Community cites five arguments against the zero rate: First, the zero rates are justified exclusively under Article 28(2) of the Sixth Directive.[5] The crucial point here is that the zero rates should be used "for the benefit of the final consumer," and the interpretation the Commission puts upon this is that zero rates cannot be used for intermediate goods. This means, for instance, that the Irish and Portuguese use of the zero rate to relieve fertilizers, animal feedstuffs, and seeds from VAT are questioned by the Community; similarly, the common exemption or zero rating of such goods by Latin American governments would be questioned under the rules of the EC. The somewhat flimsy argument is that the link between the preferential tax treatment of the good (for example, fertilizer) and the advantage to the final consumer is too indirect. Similarly, the zero rating by the United Kingdom of construction, newspaper advertising, fuel and power, water, sewerage, animal feedstuffs, and safety wear has been questioned by the Commission. Second, even where the zero rate can be seen to benefit the final consumer directly, the Commission argues that the zero rates in one member state will cause consumers in other member states to claim the same benefit, and this will disrupt the Community tax base. Third, to the extent that the use of zero-rated goods and services expands, it erodes the tax base, creating distortions and requiring a higher VAT rate to be used on the taxed sectors to raise the same revenues. Fourth, the system of refunds that have to be made to taxable persons through the zero-rating system entail high administrative costs, only to compensate traders and not to raise any revenue; this churning of money is administratively wasteful and undesirable. Finally, it is claimed that even the social justification of zero rating might be better achieved by more appropriately targeted direct transfers than through the blanket provision of indulgent tax treatment.

For all these reasons, most of which can be generalized to any other

---

[3]Dickson (1985).
[4]Douglas (1987, pp. 214–15).
[5]See European Community, Sixth Council Directive.

part of the world, the Commission views zero rates as a transitional measure that is tolerated only temporarily by the Community. Moreover, any good once taxed under the European VAT cannot later be exempted; that is, the decision to tax is supposed to be irrevocable. Every five years the Council reviews the use of zero rates and makes recommendations of ways in which they might, eventually, be abolished.

Recent proposals of the Commission suggest that Belgium, Denmark, and Italy could probably abolish their existing zero rates "without undue difficulty, especially if direct financial assistance could be granted, at least on a provisional basis, in their place."[6] This, however, skates around the real problem as zero rates in these countries are of no consequence. More important, some countries get around the "prohibition" against zero rates by levying rates of 1 percent or 2 percent which, in fact, achieve much the same purpose. For the more widespread and complex problem of the use of the zero rate in the United Kingdom and Ireland, the Commission suggests a gradual narrowing of the scope of the zero rating (say, by eliminating the exemption on children's clothing and, eventually, by applying the zero rate only to unprocessed food), and the use of a low-level rate on those goods and services released from the zero rate to be taxed under the VAT. While easy to contemplate in theory, the political practicality of such a proposal does suggest that the word "transitional" may have to be interpreted in the context of a generation rather than a year or two.[7] For instance, to accelerate change, the Commission in 1987 brought a case against the United Kingdom in the European Court of Justice. In trying to extend VAT to new building, fuel and power supplied to businesses, metered water and sewerage services to industry, animal feedstuffs, and protective clothing, the Commission is arguing that the United Kingdom should apply VAT to housing but allow government (local authority) owned housing to be zero rated. This has caused an uproar in Great Britain and is seen as an attack on the rights of Parliament.[8] (See further reference in Chapter 5, section on "Construction.")

[6]European Community, "Further Harmonization of VAT," reproduced in *Intertax* (April 1983, p. 139).

[7]A U.K. all-party Treasury and Civil Service Committee recommended that the Government should resist pressure from the Commission to extend the coverage of VAT by abolishing the use of the zero rate. See *Financial Times* (London), February 27, 1985, p. 11.

[8]See Lord Denning, "Britain Must Stand By Its Zero Option," *The Times* (London), July 22, 1987, p. 12: "The Commission is getting too big for its boots, it needs taking down a bit."

Justifications for Exemptions and Zero Rating

Basically, in practice, there are three ways in which exemptions and zero rating can be justified. First, there are exemptions that may be designed to improve, rightly or wrongly, the progressivity of the VAT. Second, there are those goods and services that are in Musgrave's terminology so "meritorious" that they may deserve to be tax free. Third, some goods and services are just too difficult to tax and administratively it is common sense not to try to tax them. Some goods could be justified under all three headings; for instance, farmers are difficult to tax, the food they produce can be considered meritorious, and exemption of food may improve the progressivity of a sales tax.

If we examine the list of exemptions shown in Table 3-1, remembering that exemption actually means liability to tax, then the list cannot be justified under the headings of improving progressivity or merit. After all, we would agree that education, health, water, books, and culture might be considered meritorious and should therefore not be taxed (that is, zero rated), but the fact is that through exemptions, these goods and services do pay the VAT on the inputs and have no opportunity to reclaim it. So schools and universities, if exempt from VAT, will pay tax on the capital equipment and fuels they purchase and can hardly be said to be free from VAT. However, it is true that their own value added, which is the major portion of their final price, is not liable to VAT and, therefore, the consumer of these goods and services does benefit, but not by as much as the actual title of "exemption" might suggest. These topics will be dealt with in Chapter 4.

At the other end of the spectrum, services such as banking, finance, insurance, betting, gaming, lotteries, and legal services might be considered by many to be suitable subjects for taxation; after all, it is difficult to see why the consumption pattern of households should be skewed in favor of financial services, while clothing, food, and shelter are taxed. The reason why these services frequently are not taxed is not because they are particularly meritorious compared with other goods and services, nor because they add progressivity to the tax structure, but simply because they are too difficult to tax. These issues will be dealt with later in Chapter 5.

The position of the EC in 1985 on these matters is shown in Tables 3-2 and 3-3. On the one hand, the decision to continue exempting transactions (Table 3-2) is to be eroded over the next few years; on the other hand, the mirror image, the discretion to continue taxing (instead of exempting) is to be reduced to only two activities, public radio and television and old buildings (Table 3-3).

Table 3-2. EC Countries: Discretion to Continue Exempting Transactions

Goods and Services	Abolished from January 1, 1986	Abolished from January 1, 1988	Date of Abolition to Be Determined
Supplies by or relating to:			
Admission to sporting events		X	
Lawyers and other members of the liberal professions		X	
Agricultural machinery	X		
Greyhounds and thoroughbred horses	X		
Telecommunications made by public postal services			X
Undertakers and cremation services			X
Blind persons or workshops for the blind			X
Cemeteries etc., for the war dead			X
Veterinary surgeons		X	
Experts in connection with insurance claim assessments	X		
Water by public authorities		X	
Credit and credit guarantees	X		
Debt collection	X		
Safekeeping and management of shares, etc.	X		
New buildings and building land			X
Passenger transport			X
Commercial inland waterway vessels	X		
Some used capital goods	X		
Recuperable material and fresh waste	X		
Fueling and provisioning private boats proceeding outside the country	X		
Fueling and provisioning private aircraft	X		
Aircraft used by state institutions		X	
Transport of goods on the Rhine and the canalized Moselle	X		
Warships		X	
Gold other than gold for industrial use	X		
Travel agents for journeys made within the Community	X		

Source: Adapted from International Bureau of Fiscal Documentation, *European Taxation* (Amsterdam), Vol. 25 (May 1985), pp. 142–43.

Table 3-3. EC Countries: Discretion to Continue Taxing Transactions

Goods and Services	Abolished from January 1, 1986	Abolished from January 1, 1988	Date of Abolition to Be Determined
Supplies by or relating to:			
Parcel post	X		
Dental technicians, dental prostheses		X	
Independent groups of persons exempt from or not subject to VAT	X		
Sport or physical education made by nonprofit-making organizations	X		
Cultural supplies made by bodies governed by public law	X		
Transportation by ambulance for sick or injured persons	X		
Public radio and television bodies			X
Intermediaries relating to the negotiation of guarantees and other security and to the management of credit guarantees	X		
Intermediaries relating to transactions in transferable securities	X		
Management of investment funds	X		
Buildings that are not newly constructed			X
Goods dispatched or transported by a purchaser who is not established within the country	X		
Aircraft operated for reward on international routes	X		
Approved bodies that export aircraft as part of their humanitarian activities	X		
Travel agents or journeys outside the Community	X		

Source: Adapted from International Bureau of Fiscal Documentation, *European Taxation* (Amsterdam), Vol. 25 (May 1985), p. 142.

Goods and Services Exempt and Zero Rated for Progressivity

Equity has been used as an argument to exempt or zero rate food, housing, public transport, and even small retailers (on the rather spurious grounds that small retailers serve lower-income households and by not applying VAT to the smaller retailers the impact of VAT on the poorer sectors of the public could be reduced). It has also been used to justify taxing—and possibly taxing at a high rate—electricity and telecommunications.

The reasons why it is inefficient and probably inequitable to use exemptions from sales taxes to achieve progressivity are well known: whatever the product or service exempted, it is being used as a proxy for income, but the bias introduced will not necessarily reflect income differentials. One example will suffice: if public transport is exempted from VAT, the assumption is that low-income households use such transport. However, it could happen that affluent brokers and advertising executives might use the suburban railways and buses, construction workers might club together to drive a car to work, and a cleaning woman may prefer to take a taxi home. The distributional consequences of exempting public transport could favor the richer households and penalize the poorer. This example might be less distorting in developing country cities such as Mexico City, Karachi, or Seoul where public transport is mainly for the benefit of the poor and the better off use cars. However, it could create other distortions, such as a probable bias in favor of urban low-income households and against the rural poor (who, typically, gain little advantage from subsidized public transport). Since public transport is frequently price controlled and subsidized, it makes differential VAT rates or exemptions even more bizarre. In general, distributional issues are better served by income taxation and by carefully targeted transfers to the households it is wished to help. However, the rest of this section discusses some of the more usual issues of exemptions from VAT justified to lessen the regressivity.

Food

There is frequently a strong political inclination to exempt food or to tax it at a lower rate. Most VATs in developing countries (Table 3-1) treat food as a special case, and in the EC, Ireland and the United Kingdom zero rate food. As pointed out earlier, unless farmers are zero rated or all their inputs are zero rated, food will still bear some VAT even though "exempted" and, of course, this VAT content will be peculiarly arbitrary depending on the mix of inputs, the efficiency of different farmers, and the relative costs of distribution, to say nothing of the different household consumption patterns.

However, given that food is, in one way or another, to be taxed less heavily, there is usually an attempt to avoid a drastic erosion of the tax base by distinguishing between "necessary" or "essential" and "luxury" foods—once more as a crude proxy for household incomes. The assumption is that poorer households will be unable to afford luxury foodstuffs. Such a distinction requires the legislation to define what is an essential food and what is not. This often boils down to a distinction between processed and unprocessed food. Yet, while it is clear that eggs, vegetables, and pulses are not processed, some doubt might exist about polished rice, flour, butter, and pasteurized milk. Attempts to finesse this problem by some reference to "processes that do not change the substance or nature of the natural product" are unsatisfactory and lead to sustained battles to widen the scope of the exemption.

More generous interpretations that consider food products in their "original state" to include foodstuffs that have undergone the processes of "preparation or preservation for the market, such as freezing, drying, salting, smoking, or stripping" and that "polished and/or husked rice, corn grits and raw cane sugar shall be considered in their original state"[9] create even wider and more contentious issues for dispute.

Even if a solution is sought by listing the (few) specific foods that will not be taxed (for example, eggs, fresh fish, fresh bread, uncooked meat, and fresh vegetables), almost certainly inequity will be created. While it may seem desirable for nutrition and equity to exempt such fresh food, the reality is likely to be that factory workers and working housewives will buy canned and frozen foods and readily prepared dishes. (The author remembers a woman member of a tax commission surveying a proposed list of exempt foods and remarking quite correctly that it had clearly been drawn up by men who seldom shopped.) Nevertheless, Korea, Indonesia, and many Latin American countries such as Brazil follow this approach. But the experience is that such a list of specified foodstuffs quickly becomes a target to be expanded by all food suppliers who feel unreasonably treated. For instance, within a year or two of the introduction of the Mexican VAT, the exempt food category was extended widely and, Turkey, after the first year of the VAT, decided to zero rate agricultural products. Nevertheless, practice and theoretical work, particularly for developing countries, "suggest strongly that there is a distributive case for exempting certain basic food products."[10]

The best rule is to tax most food (possibly at a lower rate), but accept that some cannot be taxed and acquiesce in that de facto exemption. Such an exemption will probably affect precisely those foods that might be valuable to some poorer households; fruit and vegetables sold through street markets, fish and live fowl sold by farmers bringing their own produce to market, and farm gate sales. However, all

[9]Philippines, Department of Finance, National Tax Research Center (1987, p. 16).
[10]See Bird (1987, p. 1157).

food sales through recognized retail premises should be taxed except for those in direct competition with the street markets. Farm gate sales are not taxable unless they are carried on in a continuous manner and on a scale that merits treatment as a regular retail outlet. Letting such farm sales off the VAT gives some slight advantage to the farmer, but in practice the farming community, even in highly industrialized countries, may pursue more important evasions of VAT by barter agreements than the relatively minor problem of farm gate sales. Such an arrangement in developing countries, combined with the suggested treatment for agriculture (zero rating farm-specific inputs), would mean that most food consumed by lower-income households would be VAT free.

It should be pointed out that there are dangers in exempting commodities from VAT by successively exempting the inputs into the manufacture of those commodities; Costa Rica wished to exempt ice cream from VAT and exempted the makers of ice cream, who then lobbied for the exemption of those who manufactured ice cream making machines, who in turn, lobbied for the exemption of machinery and parts that were inputs to the ice cream machines. There is no logical end to this sequence until the entire economy is exempt.

Housing

Shelter is an essential part of household consumption. Again, there are usually strong political pressures to treat housing kindly. This infringes on two other problems treated elsewhere, first, the difficulty of taxing the construction industry, and second, the problem of secondhand goods (see Chapter 5).

Secondhand goods are usually associated in the general public's mind with automobiles, furniture, clothes, and antiques, but by far the most important secondhand sales are those of land and buildings. Clearly, everyone who owns land and housing before the VAT is introduced will enjoy a once and for all gain if all new additions to the housing stock are made liable to VAT and, in theory, to avoid this discrepancy, all housing could be made liable to VAT on the first sale after the introduction of VAT. This would mean that even those living in existing houses would know that when they came to sell they would be liable to VAT; but the house would only be liable to VAT once. When an invoice showing VAT paid could be produced, no further VAT liability would arise. Any additions or alterations would, of course, be liable to VAT at the time of their construction. In theory, this would mean no advantage would be gained by those lucky enough to own a house before the introduction of VAT except the appropriately dis-counted potential VAT liability on their "delayed" sale.

In practice, immovable property comes into the VAT picture in two ways: (1) as products that are supplied to individuals as consumers and (2) as a factor of production, the price of which is reflected in the price of goods and services.

From both these aspects, the construction and marketing of new buildings should come fully within the scope of VAT. However, the notion of first occupancy is generally used to determine the time at which a building becomes an object of consumption, that is, when it begins to be used by its owner or a tenant. An old residential building is excluded from the scope of VAT as being property that has already been consumed by virtue of its first occupancy. The sale of old residential property would normally be taxable only if it is sold by a developer or builder who has substantially altered or extended it, for example, by the conversion of a large private residence into a number of separate units in such a way that its original nature is completely changed.

The sale of an existing business property is not normally chargeable unless the trader selling it received a tax credit for its purchase or development. Thus, all sales of business property built before the start of VAT would be nontaxable unless there were a significant develop-ment of the property after the introduction of VAT on which VAT would in fact be borne. A sale of a business premises built after the introduction of VAT for which the owner was allowed a credit for the input tax at the time of purchase would be taxable. If, however, the premises were sold as a going concern, along with the rest of the business assets, it would in most countries be treated as not chargeable.[11]

In general, in European countries, every effort is made to ensure that the changeover to VAT does not significantly affect the price of residential property, especially in the case of housing schemes de-signed for low-income occupants, sometimes by exemption provisions in VAT, and sometimes by direct subsidy. However, in most countries, VAT is payable on the full price of a private residence built specially by contract, but the various treatments are complicated and deserve a quick review to indicate their variety and the complexity of treatments by different countries.

As Table 3-4 shows, there is a stamp duty of 7 percent on transfers of immovable property in the Federal Republic of Germany, but about

---

[11]See the discussion in Canada, *Tax Reform 1987: Sales Tax Reform* (1987, pp. 113–18).

Table 3-4. VAT: Examples of Treatment of Buildings

	New Buildings	Used Buildings
Belgium	VAT at standard 17 percent	Registration fee of 12.5 percent
Brazil	Not liable to VAT but to a separate service tax equivalent to a tax on value added	
Germany, Fed. Rep. of	Transfer tax of 7 percent; exempt by contract when rate of 14 percent applies	Transfer tax of 7 percent
Ireland	Reduced rate of 5 percent applies, plus stamp duty at 4 or 6 percent; registration tax at 10 to 17 percent	Stamp duties at 4 or 6 percent
Luxembourg	Exempt except where built by contract when rate of 12 percent applies	VAT at 6 percent (9 percent in Luxembourg City)
Mexico	Standard rate at 18 percent, but a special rate of 8 percent on low-cost housing	Not taxed
Netherlands	VAT at standard 18 percent	Separate transfer tax of 6 percent
New Zealand	VAT at the standard rate	
Sweden	VAT at standard rate on 50 percent of the value; stamp duty of 3 percent also applies	Stamp duty of 3 percent
United Kingdom	Zero rated	Stamp duty

Source: Various country reports.

80 percent of sales of residential property qualify for a lower rate for social reasons. A person who buys a plot of land on which to build a residence is charged the stamp duty at 7 percent (and no VAT), but this may be waived if a residence of limited size is to be erected within a specified period. Where an individual buys a plot of land and engages a builder to construct a residence on it, he bears stamp duty at 7 percent on the price of the land and VAT at 14 percent on the contract price for the building. On the other hand, the sale of a completed house by a speculative builder is chargeable to stamp duty at 7 percent, the only VAT borne being that on the materials used in its

construction. Similarly, if an individual, who is not associated with the building trade, buys a plot of land and himself builds a residence on it, he would bear VAT only on the materials used, as well as 7 percent stamp duty on the site. Should the individual be a builder himself, he would be charged with VAT on the full value as self-delivery.

Where a trader has an extension built to his business premises by contract, VAT is charged by the building contractor, but the trader gets an immediate credit for the tax. If a construction company erects an office block on its own site and sells it to a development company, the sale is subject to stamp duty only, but the purchaser may opt for liability to VAT, a course that would be favorable to him if it is being rented to taxable persons.

In France, a number of transactions in connection with immovable property are exempt from VAT. Some of these relate to township developments, sale of building sites for the construction of low rental apartment blocks, and so on. The rules governing these exemptions are quite complex and contain many exceptions.

A person disposing of an interest in immovable property in Ireland is liable to VAT on the disposal in the following circumstances: (1) he must own an interest in it and that interest must be for a minimum of ten years from the time of its creation; (2) he must either have developed the property himself or have been entitled to a VAT credit for the tax referable to the development or purchase of the property; and (3) the transfer by him must consist either of the disposal of his full interest or the granting of a lesser interest for a minimum period of ten years.

He is chargeable to VAT at a special low rate of 5 percent on the sale price, though it is interesting to note that originally the Irish legislation reduced this tax liability by also adjusting the value of the property (to only 30 percent of the contract price) on which the VAT was levied. The Irish have also tried to offset the impact of the VAT on young married couples by creating a grant for the first time owner-occupiers of new houses of £Ir 750.[12]

In Norway, the stamp duty on the transfer of real property is negligible. Building construction as such is not chargeable to VAT but the service element in the cost of a building under a building contract is chargeable separately from the VAT on the materials used.

Sweden is an interesting case in that, although the standard rate of VAT applies to sales of new housing, the effective rate is only half the nominal, as the tax base is adjusted and the VAT is levied on only 50 percent of the contract price.

[12]See Ireland, *Budget, 1985* (1985, p. 23).

The U.K. treatment is unusual. The grant, assignment, or surrender of any interest in or right over land, or of any license to occupy land, is exempt from VAT without credit for prior-stage tax, with a few exceptions such as holiday rentals, the right to park a vehicle, to take game, or to fell timber, and a few other items. Where a person constructs a building or has it built on contract, and he grants the freehold a lease for over 21 years to another person for the building or any part of it or its site, the transaction is zero rated. The supply of building or civil engineering work in connection with the construction, alteration, or demolition of a building is also zero rated, but repair and maintenance services are taxable. Obviously, this form of zero rating leads to major problems for the treatment of the construction industry (see Chapter 5).

Indeed, it creates subtle loopholes that absorb large amounts of administrative time and talent to anticipate and block. As one commentator noted, "the taxpayer was able to incur (with careful timing) a substantial amount of input tax attributable to future exempt supplies in a period in which he was treated as fully taxable. In this way he effectively recovered input tax relating to future exempt outputs."[13] It is better not to give taxpayers these opportunities, and the taxation of housing should be made as uniform as possible.

In Brazil, the VAT was removed from the construction industry almost immediately after introduction to avoid increasing housing costs and clashing with the Government's attempts to ameliorate the housing problem. Instead, a service tax is applied on the value added of new housing and traders are allowed to deduct the cost of purchases of materials that have borne the VAT from their turnover to calculate the base for the service tax.

In general, it should be noted, that most EC countries apply a transfer or registration tax to the sale of existing (not new) housing, which may be viewed as a tax in lieu of VAT. Also, most countries have already aligned VAT and transfer taxes; one is waived if the other is applicable.

The EC Commission is arguing in its European court case against the United Kingdom that a distinction should be drawn between privately and publicly owned housing. The United Kingdom argues that publicly owned housing is designed to meet a direct social need and can, therefore, be zero rated under the formulation permitting zero rating where spending is for social reasons. It has been commented, "the formulation of this clause is hopelessly imprecise. Spending on holidays for the poor or computers for the young could

[13]Rayney (1987, pp. 81–82).

equally be regarded as spending for social reasons."[14] Clearly, this is unsatisfactory. All housing should be taxed under VAT and governments should pay VAT even if it only means transferring income to another pocket. At least that ensures that the relative costs of government spending are assessed on an equal basis. (See further discussion in Chapter 4.) If the government wishes to subsidize housing, it can do so by a direct subsidy, debated and voted through the budget on an annual basis.

Public Transport

Article 6(1) of the Second Directive of the EC on VAT defined the provision of service as any transaction that does not constitute a "supply of goods," but Article 6(2) provided that the rules of that directive, as regards the taxation of services, had to be applied only to certain services that included "the transport and storage of goods, and ancillary services." Thus, from the start of VAT, EC member states were required to charge the transport of goods[15] but initially were not specifically required to tax the transport of passengers.

The Sixth Directive of the EC set out a uniform basis of assessment of VAT in member states. The only form of passenger transport for which exemption is authorized is the supply of transport services for sick or injured persons in vehicles specially designed for the purpose by duly authorized bodies. However, Annex F to that Directive lists passenger transport among the transactions that member states may continue to exempt during a *transitional* period, provided they had exempted it in their VAT law on the basis of the Second Directive. The final date of the transitional period would be fixed by the EC, but would not be later than that on which the charging of tax on imports and the remission of tax on exports in trade between member states are abolished.

All EC member states tax the transport of goods and all except Denmark, Ireland, and the United Kingdom tax the domestic transport of passengers. In Denmark, passenger transport is exempt for regularly scheduled services. In Ireland, the transport of passengers within the state is exempt. The exemption applies to all means of

---

[14]"A Vatman's Home," *The Times* (London), September 17, 1987, p. 17.

[15]Exceptionally, and as a temporary measure, the transport of goods on the Rhine and the canalized Moselle are exempt from VAT in France and the Federal Republic of Germany by virtue of the Mannheim-Rhine Shipping Treaty.

transport, whether by bus, train, airplane, or taxi and extends to the transport of passengers' accompanied baggage. In the United Kingdom, the transport of passengers is zero rated.

In Italy, the supply of public transport to individuals, within a town or between towns that are less than 50 kilometers apart, is exempt. Passenger transport by land, air, or waterways (including travel by taxi) is charged at the low rate of 4 percent. Similarly, in the Federal Republic of Germany, transport within a municipality or for distances less than 50 kilometers is taxed at the reduced rate of 7 percent (compared with the full rate of 14 percent). In France, the low rate of 7 percent applies to passenger transport and in Luxembourg and Spain, a low rate of 6 percent.

In general, the international transport of passengers is exempt, but some countries grant exemption only on a reciprocal basis.

In VAT systems outside Europe, transport of goods is invariably taxable, but the treatment of passenger transport varies from one country to another. In Uruguay, it is exempt, but in Chile, it is taxable. In Korea, domestic passenger transport is exempt, except for services by air, express bus, chartered bus, taxi, special automobile, or special ship. International passenger transport by air or sea is zero rated on a reciprocal basis.

For a country considering the introduction of VAT, the EC Directive provides a useful guide for the taxation of the transport of goods. This service should be chargeable, and in the case of international transport, it should take account of the distance covered in each country.

The case for charging public passenger transport is less clear, especially if the great majority of the population cannot afford to travel other than by public transport. The practical point can be made that progressivity is probably enhanced if public transport of persons is zero rated, but automobiles and gasoline are taxed heavily; use of private automobiles (and taxis—which, of course, should be liable to VAT) is usually closely correlated with income, whereas public transport, especially in developing countries, is used by lower income earners. It is true that in some industrialized conurbations, as already mentioned, there could be some perverse distributional consequences if public transport were zero rated.

In general, although it may be better to ensure that public transport pricing genuinely reflects relative costs and that subsidies are reduced or eliminated, the service may be exempted from VAT, especially in developing countries. In developed countries, passenger transport should be liable to VAT. In all countries, goods transport should be liable to VAT.

Electricity, Gas, and Telecommunications

Food, housing, and public transport have all been proposed for exemptions or zero rating on the grounds that charging them to VAT would tax lower-income households disproportionately. The opposite case is made for ensuring that electricity and telecommunications are not exempt from VAT; typically, these services are consumed in increasing amounts as household incomes rise. Usually, of course, they are provided as a government service; because they are publicly provided, it is often argued they should be exempted from VAT as taxing them would simply be a transfer from one state pocket to the other. This is not wholly true, as exempting such services from VAT would skew consumer behavior in favor of consuming such services and would lead to a misallocation of investment in favor of the public enterprises providing the services and, hence, penalize all producers.

There are two further considerations that strengthen the argument for taxing utilities. Because production is usually concentrated in few suppliers, VAT is easy to collect and cheap to administer. Second, if supplies are by public corporations, such suppliers are often tardy in transferring surplus revenues (if any) to the exchequer, and the monthly VAT collections are a magnificent tax handle to transfer speedily a portion of the turnover to the state.

In some countries (for example, Brazil), VAT is not levied on the production and distribution of electrical energy; instead, a central government "replacement" or equivalent tax is levied.[16] The problem with this is that unless the replacement tax is fully integrated with VAT, allowing businesses to claim it on inputs as an offset to their VAT liability, cascading can occur.

So, on grounds of equity, expediency, revenue, and ease of administration, electricity, gas, and telecommunications should not be exempted or zero rated under VAT.

---

[16]Guerard (1973, p. 137).

CHAPTER 4

"Merit" Goods

What I like about the Order of the Garter is that there is no damned merit about it.

—LORD MELBOURNE, quoted in *Melbourne* by David Cecil
(London: Constable and Company, 1965), p. 211

It has been argued that some goods are so "meritorious" that they should not be taxed. Conversely, it has also been persuasively argued that there are no such things as merit goods.[1] However, even the stern dictates of the EC's Sixth Directive recognize that activities in the "public interest" should be exempt, namely, postal services, hospitals, medical and dental care, education, cultural activities, and noncommercial radio and television.[2] Such services, it is implied, are in the public interest, but do not necessarily have to be provided by public bodies. Education can be offered by public and private schools; hospitals can be state owned, charity owned, or run for profit. It is the perceived merit of the service that counts, not the ownership of the agency providing the service. Frequently, all goods and services provided by the government are also lumped in with sales to be exempted on the grounds that they must be meritorious.

To understand the issues (and emotions) involved, five examples will be looked at in more detail, namely, children's clothing, medical and veterinary services, cultural activities, government purchases and sales, and nonprofit organizations.

---

[1]McLure (1968).
[2]European Community, Sixth Council Directive.

Children's Clothing

Children's clothing has been considered for exemption and zero rating in a number of countries. The justification could be couched in terms of progressivity, in that expenditure on children's clothing might form a higher proportion of low household income. However, it is difficult to sustain such an argument as rich households can have many children and spend large amounts on their clothing. Basically, the somewhat fuzzy idea behind such an argument for exemptions must be the emotional feeling that to tax children's clothing is more "immoral" than taxing old people's clothing or sick people's clothing. It really does not stand up to logic, but as the Irish Prime Minister found out when he tried to put VAT on children's shoes and lost an election, logic and politics do not necessarily go together.

Two strong points argue against any exemption for children's clothing. First, the definition of what constitutes children's clothing as distinct from small adults' clothing is almost impossible and has produced much unconscious (and perhaps conscious) humor. The image of Her Majesty's Customs and Excise inspectors pulling out their tape measures to ensure that "two-piece bikinis (that is, those with lower part having side seams of 4 inches . . . or less)" must have a design tolerance not to exceed "20 inch . . . waist-crutch-waist of lower part"[3] belongs to a cartoon rather than a Customs and Excise notice. Clearly, the detailed measurement needed and the scope for alternative interpretations must create the opportunity for evasion and a need for administrative supervision out of all proportion to the advantage gained.

Second, even if such activity could be successful, it would be in vain. Surveys show that expenditure on clothing and footwear as a proportion of total expenditure actually increases as household expenditure rises. Thus, "an even greater share of the tax foregone through zero-rating or reduced rates [on clothing] goes to the better off than in the case of food."[4] The message is clear—if you want to help a particular target group (in this case, the children of the poor), it is more efficient to aim transfer expenditures at such households than to erode the VAT base by poorly targeted exemptions or zero rating.

---

[3]United Kingdom, H.M. Customs and Excise, *Young Children's Footwear and Clothing* (1986).

[4]Ireland, *Commission on Taxation* (1984, p. 71). See also Appendix 9.

Medical and Veterinary Services

The EC's Sixth Council Directive states that "the provision of medical care in the exercise of the medical and paramedical professions" shall be exempt.[5] Of course, this requires a definition of what constitutes "medical and paramedical" care in each country, and authorities can and do differ in their definitions. An example will demonstrate a borderline decision; the British VAT authorities held that a yoga center that rented accommodations for the study and practice of yoga should not be exempt from VAT. However, on appeal the courts found that the registered charity provided services closely linked to welfare and social security work and, like old people's homes (which are exempt from VAT in the United Kingdom) supplied benefits— that did not have to be *medical* benefits—which were exempt.

The line between medical and other services can be uncertain and will differ between countries. The provision of local remedies, acupuncture, massage, spa hotels, and slimming centers can all be exempt medical services in some cultures, while in some other countries they can be taxed.

Medicines, as an extension of medical services, might be expected to be zero rated or exempt. However, again, there are problems of definition. Drugs or medicines supplied by a registered pharmacist on the order or prescription of a registered doctor can be exempted, but this transfers the responsibility to the doctor. Obviously, pharmacies sell many products that might be considered as auxiliary to medicine (such as antiseptics, disinfectants, and soaps) but that should be liable to VAT. A tough line can be taken that medicine should not be excluded from VAT:

> We do not favour the exclusion of oral medicines from taxation or, indeed, for that matter any other type of medicine. While some outlays on drugs and other medical products have to be made by most consumers, these normally account for a relatively modest portion of expenditures. However, we do accept that there are people who are compelled, by circumstances over which they have no control, to spend very considerable amounts on these products. With a general sales tax these consumers would have to bear a disproportionate share of the tax burden because of their state of health, irrespective of their financial circumstances. We believe that these people should be assisted directly by the state. We also believe that the most effective and efficient way to do this is not through the general exemption from taxation of all medicines or

[5]European Community, Sixth Council Directive, Article 13A1(c).

even certain groups of medicines which could extend into the area of unnecessary and "fringe" pharmaceuticals, but rather through direct monetary payments to the people concerned via the Department of Health or the Department of Social Welfare. Indeed such schemes are already operated by regional health boards. We, therefore, recommend that oral medicines should be charged to value-added tax.[6]

This statement exemplifies the preferred treatment, though it is recognized that politically it may be difficult to sustain. In developing countries, the incapacity of the social services to ensure that the chronic need for medicine can be met may require that a blanket exemption be given to all (registered) drugs. The variety of treatment in the EC suggests a wide difference of opinion. For instance, France, Italy, Luxembourg, and the Netherlands use a reduced rate on drugs, the United Kingdom exempts them, Ireland uses the zero rate, while other countries tax them.

Even when legislated, implementation may prove difficult. In Greece,[7] a government requirement that doctors use perforated and stamped prescription forms led to protests that "a prescription is not comparable to a grocer's receipt." Furthermore, police checks in Athens found that of 14,720 prescriptions only 607 complied with the law. Doctors threatened to fight every summons through the courts. The Finance Ministry retaliated by publishing a list stating that over 50 percent of all doctors had declared an income of under Dr 500,000 (US$3,795). The Government was accused of "wilful distortion." This is clearly a slippery slope but even if the allegations were true (whatever the truth may have been) and even if medical services were to be exempt from VAT, the doctors still should have been required to complete their accounts in such a way so as to distinguish between VAT-liable and non-VAT-liable services to facilitate assessment to income taxation.

Veterinary services cannot be considered simply as an extension of medical services, nor can they be treated solely as an input to agriculture. As they are not specific to agriculture, they cannot be zero rated unless the authorities expressly wish to do so or exempt such services from VAT. However, if such services are overwhelmingly supplied to agriculture, and farming is an important industry in the country, the authorities (as in Belgium, Ireland, Italy, and the Netherlands) may decide to treat the sale of such services to private individuals as a minor matter and exempt all veterinary services.

[6]Ireland, *Commission on Taxation* (1984, p. 71).
[7]"Greece: VAT," *World Tax Report* (1987, p. 12).

However, in a fully operational VAT, on as broad a base as possible, veterinary services would not be considered as "meritorious" as medical services. They would be taxed and, indeed, the EC Commission intends that they should be taxed. The discretion that was granted to the countries that did not tax veterinary services was only because these countries had not taxed such services previously. As Table 3-2 in Chapter 3 indicates, veterinary services are to be taxed in all of the countries. Indeed, in 1987, the EC Commission brought suit against Italy for its exemption of veterinary services (classified in Italy as medical services).

Cultural Activities

"I reach for my gun when I hear the word 'culture,'" might be the slogan for a VAT administrator. Most people will have their own idea of a cultural activity that is thought to be sufficiently meritorious to be free of VAT. However, as Table 3-1 in Chapter 3 shows, there is plenty of room for differences of opinion within the EC, and this is true worldwide. A football match can be culture to one and to another a waste of money. Within a seemingly homogeneous category, such as "theater admissions," disagreement surfaces even over what is actually shown in a theater; opera is cultural but a topless show is not (though today topless opera is not unknown and might make a difficult case for classification).

The vitriolic debate in 1984 over the attempt by the U.K. authorities to extend the VAT to books exemplifies much of the argument. Opponents argued that books were a part of the national heritage, that they were the fulcrum for education, that scholarship would suffer, that authors would be punished (and they were already being paid a pittance), that publishing profits would be cut, and that only books appealing to a "mass commercial market" would be published. Even in the darkest days of World War II, when the purchase tax was introduced, "Parliament refused to tax the printed word,"[8] and stamp duty on newspapers was removed as long ago as 1855. All true, but against this must be reckoned the impossibility of separating the wheat and the chaff: "To support the publication of possibly unreadable and at any rate largely unread works of high literary seriousness of intention, quite unnecessary financial assistance is provided for nicely illustrated books about gardens, the memoirs of statesmen, Mills &

[8]Maurice Cranston in a letter to *The Times* (London), October 3, 1984, p. 15.

Boon romances, repair manuals for the Ford Granada, Spanish phrase-books, [and] pop-up books about the intestines."[9]

One reaction to this problem is to use differential rates: "Gallic logic has produced a series of rates for printed material ranging from 4% on business magazines, 7% on books, up to 33.3% on pornography."[10] Yet, this tax on knowledge, fought so bitterly in both the United Kingdom and Ireland, stands at 22 percent in Denmark and 23.46 percent in Sweden, neither noted for their literary backwardness.

Any solution to this discussion will be subjective, but given that differential rates simply make explicit the relative subjectivity of the politician (and create massive compliance problems for booksellers and administrators—who must decide in France what is business and what is pornography). As it is difficult to justify any one particular publication more than another, and difficult to understand why food might be taxed but not books, taxation at the standard rate appears the best bet.

If the taxation of books is claimed to be a subjective decision, how much more so is the levying of VAT on works of art. The United Kingdom and France charge VAT on the difference between the selling and purchase prices (in France the difference may be set at a standard 30 percent) at 15 percent and 18.6 percent, respectively. The other member states of the EC have levied VAT at the full selling price at rates from as low as 6 percent (Belgium) and up to 35 percent (Ireland).[11] (Ireland, however, exempts artists from paying income tax on their artistic earnings.) What is "unique" is difficult to define. Portugal, in its 1987 budget law, decided that hand-woven, artist-designed tapestries should be exempt, provided that no more than eight copies are produced under the artist's supervision and that each item bears a serial number, the artist's name, and the weaver's name.[12] There is no consensus on such treatment (see Table 4-1), and indeed taxing at the standard rate has proved controversial; for instance, Belgium reduced its VAT rate on works of art from 17 percent to 6 percent in 1984. However, broadly, there seems less sympathy for lower rates of VAT on works of art than on books. Perhaps, nowadays, what constitutes a "work of art" is so uncertain that even confident VAT officials fear to tread, and the best treatment is to make no exemption and charge all such sales to VAT at the standard rate.

[9]Anthony Quinton, "VAT Brevis, Ars Longa," *Sunday Times* (London), November 4, 1984, p. 41.

[10]White (1985, p. 33).

[11]See European Community, "VAT on Works of Art—Belgium—Common EEC System," reproduced in *Intertax* (September 1984, p. 354).

[12]"Portugal: Taxation 1987," in *European Taxation* (1987, p. 267).

Table 4-1. EC Exemptions and Special Rates for Selected Cultural Activities

	Books	Admission to Entertainment	Admission to Exhibition	Sheet Music	News-papers	Theater Performances	Works of Art
Belgium	R			R	X	R	R
Denmark					X		
France	R	R	R	R		R	X
Germany, Fed. Rep. of	R	X				X	R
Ireland	R	X			R		
Italy	R						H
Luxembourg	R						
Netherlands	R				R		R
United Kingdom	Z			Z	Z		

Source: Adapted from Dennis A. Parkinson, *Value Added Tax in the EEC* (London: Graham and Trotman, 1981), pp. 207–14.

Note: R = reduced rate; X = exempt; H = higher rate than standard; and Z = zero rated.

Of course, "culture" can creep into VAT in other ways. For example, the 1984 U.K. decision to tax repairs and alterations to buildings was subsequently changed to zero rate alterations (but not repair or maintenance) of buildings listed as historically valuable and to ancient monuments and listed churches. In this way, a blanket provision was eroded on cultural grounds.

"Culture" is an emotional word that embodies the idea of merit, but what is culture to one is not culture to another. It would be far better to tax all cultural items and, through the delegates of the people in parliamentary debate, decide whether any specific activity should be a charge on the budget as an explicit, directly targeted subsidy or the recipient of, say, public commissions.

Government Purchases and Sales

Government purchases can be made tax free by allowing sales to the government to be treated like an export sale, that is, zero rated. This seems, however, a needless complication. Whether or not the government pays tax on its purchases hardly matters from a revenue view-point, as the payments on one side of the account will be balanced by collections on the other; it is merely a bookkeeping transaction. On the other hand, if sales to government are zero rated, this creates another opportunity for some evasion; traders could show sales to the government that did not actually take place, or some invoices of sales to government could be deliberately overstated. It is probably as simple a method as any to treat government purchases as a normal part of the tax structure although there are frictional costs.

Of course, persons supplying taxable goods or services to exempt persons or bodies should understand that they, as suppliers, are liable for tax on all such goods or services. So, typically, taxable goods and services supplied to government departments, local authorities, hospitals, schools, banks, insurance companies, charitable organizations, and other exempt persons are not free of tax. Liability rests with the supplier, not with the customer. Sales to government are treated as a retail sale. This means that all government departments pay VAT, and the budgetary evaluation of expenditure between one department and another reflects the differing ratios of VAT-liable goods and services to non-VAT-liable purchases (for example, personnel). This is fair and proper, as it is the way to ensure a dispassionate appraisal of the relative costs of different government departments.

The EC argues that, "States, regional and local government authorities and other bodies governed by public law shall not be considered taxable persons in respect of the activities or transactions in which they engage as public authorities, even where they collect dues, fees, contributions or payments in connection with these activities or transactions."[13] Of course, the tricky question is to define the activities in which public bodies act as public authorities, especially if their activities compete with similar business in the private sector. In the Federal Republic of Germany, for instance, land registry offices that, on occasions, acted as quantity surveyors, were not taxable because they were public authorities. The protests of professional associations persuaded the authorities that significant distortions of competition could arise and the law was changed to make the services of the Government liable to VAT from January 1, 1982.[14] This could be the judgment; that is, whether or not the exemption of public authorities

---

[13]European Community, Sixth Council Directive, Article 4(5).

[14]Described in European Community, "First Report from the Commission to the Council on the Application of the Common System of Value Added Tax," reproduced in *Intertax* (January 1984, p. 33).

will lead to "significant distortion." On the other hand, the simplest solution is to tax all such government sales.

In many developing countries, there is frequently a wish to encourage or protect government employment and this provides a continuous temptation to discriminate, using taxation in favor of the government. This in itself suggests that, so far as VAT is concerned, as many government sales of goods and services as possible should be taxed if there is any possibility that they compete with the private sector.

Supplies by nonfinancial state enterprises are an even more difficult area. If supplies by the government are made tax free, the government could be in a direct unfair competitive position vis-à-vis private suppliers. This involves the provision of varied goods and services, and the tax law might authorize that any government-owned entity be treated as a taxpayer if it performed in a regular manner the economic activity of a producer, merchant, or person rendering services (as in Belgium). The point is to ensure that government provision of services is not given an unreasonable freedom from tax compared with alternative private sector provision.

The EC's Sixth Directive states that governments (including local governments and "bodies governed by public law") shall not be considered taxable persons except "where treatment as nontaxable persons would lead to significant distortions of competition."[15]

While this may be clear, for instance, in the case of transport where state-owned buses compete with private buses, it is less clear if all the railways are state owned. In this instance, there would be no competition with any other railway, but there could be a significant tax advantage if privately owned buses and trucks were competing for passengers and freight and were taxed. The same could be said about competition between the government postal service and private parcel deliveries. Are state-owned telephones in the telephone business or in the communications business? In one case, they could be said to have no competition; in the other, there could be massive private sector competition.

In general, government trading liability to VAT should be made as wide as possible to prevent distortion of trade. About the only usual widespread government trading activity that should not be liable to VAT is the sale of postage stamps, but telephone and telecommunications should be, as should the supply of gas and electricity, the transport of goods and passengers, warehousing, trade fairs, and running staff shops, industrial canteens, and similar institutions.[16]

---

[15]European Community, Sixth Council Directive, Article 4(5).
[16]European Community, Sixth Council Directive, Annex D.

Finally, many government agencies buy buildings. These government agencies would have to pay VAT on the new buildings, but would be unable to offset this tax liability against any sale. This raises the price of such buildings to the government compared to other businesses. The government might forgo the tax on such a sale to a government agency, at the same time reducing the price paid and, apparently, reducing government expenditure. But, of course, contract prices would soon be set by the construction industry to allow for such adjustments. Probably the least messy solution is for the government to pay the VAT embodied in the cost of a building.

Overall, the best position seems to be that adopted by New Zealand. Supplies of goods and services made to the government and its departments should be taxed on the same basis as all other taxable supplies. Similarly, all supplies of goods and services made by the government and its departments should be taxed, and taxable persons may deduct this VAT in the ordinary manner. Supplies made between departments should also be taxable. The tax should apply only to the operating expenses and not to the grants and transfers administered. Departments should be entitled to deduct tax invoiced to them on purchases of supplies in the same manner as taxable traders. This treatment of government departments as suppliers of services consumed by either the public or by other government agencies ensures comparability in the treatment of private and publicly owned suppliers and facilitates greater accountability of the use of public resources. It also means that if future rate changes affect the level of private consumption expenditure in the economy, a similar effect will occur in the public sector, and the cost differentials will be reflected appropriately, thereby enabling proper judgments on efficiency and allocation between public and private sectors.

Nonprofit Organizations

There is a strong moral case for exempting charities, and the EC has a generous list of activities conducted in the public interest that can be exempt from VAT. However, many such organizations do sell goods and services in direct competition with taxed suppliers, ranging from the trivial local sales of Girl Scout cookies to major sporting events or large educational establishments.

In many countries, the identification, registration, and control of charities may be tight, while in others the definition of what constitutes a charity may be a good deal less rigorous. The basic desirable judgment by the tax authorities should include a determination that the sale of the so-called charitable goods or services are (1) not designed systematically to make a profit; (2) any profits are not distributed but are assigned to an improvement or continuance of the supply of the goods or services; (3) the management has no direct interest in gaining from the activities; and (4) the VAT-free provision of goods and services do not place private, tax-liable traders at a disadvantage.

Of course, such provisions have to be interpreted with some give and take; the sale of cakes to support a local church might be in direct competition with a local bakery, but as long as the competition is occasional, limited, and seen to benefit a specific nonprofit-making body, the sales tax commissioners are hardly likely to levy VAT; however, should a vocational school repair cars each weekend, that might establish a regularity in competition with local garages, which would render it liable to VAT. However, in any case, usually such activities will fall below the general exemption threshold.

The Canadian authorities suggest that charities should not be liable to tax if the sales are below the threshold (Can$5,000) and if substantially all the staff are volunteers; if these criteria are not met, then charities would be liable for VAT on store retail sales, food and drink in restaurants, professional theatrical and athletic events, and sale of land for personal residential use.[17]

There will always be borderline cases, especially where payments (that is, donations) are made for charity. When the promoters of a Live Aid concert in London in 1985 charged £25 for a ticket, they had intended to make clear that the charge for the concert (VAT liable) was £5 and the voluntary donation (not liable) was £20. This had not been clear in the advertisements: "To be free of VAT, a donation in addition to an admission charge must be genuinely voluntary, and advertised as such."[18] In this case, the mistake was considered genuine and a concession was allowed.

Basically, charities should be few, strictly defined, not allowed to compete other than occasionally against normal commercial undertakings, and donations to be free of VAT must be completely at the discretion of the purchaser.

In general, for all these "merit" goods and services, common sense suggests that as far as possible, they should be treated under the usual VAT regulations. If governments wish to help particular households, transfers should be made through the budget.

---

[17]Canada, *Tax Reform 1987: Sales Tax Reform* (1987, pp. 109–110).
[18]"Treatment of Donations to Charities—Live Aid," *Accountancy* (1985, p. 22).

CHAPTER 5

Difficult-to-Tax Goods and Services

Pas trop de zèle—Not too much zeal.
—CHARLES MAURICE TALLEYRAND

Apart from exemptions and zero ratings justified on the grounds that the transactions are "meritorious" or that they help equity, there is a final miscellaneous group that is considered just too difficult to tax. The implication is that if a practical way could be seen to apply the VAT, it would be levied. Some of the categories are among the most important in the economy, for example, financial services or renting and leasing movable and immovable property; others are less important but can stir strong emotions, such as gambling and secondhand goods. In theory, all such goods and services should be liable to VAT; in practice, messy solutions are found. Eight such goods and services are examined in this chapter to illustrate the problems. These are construction, leasing, financial services, services performed abroad, secondhand goods, the trade of craftsmen, betting, and racing.

The Construction Industry

Land and Buildings

The VAT is supposed to be a tax on flows. Land is a stock and transfer of that stock should not be liable to VAT. Such transfers frequently are liable to other taxes such as capital transfer taxes or stamp duties. The purchase of land is not a consumption expenditure in the usual sense since nothing is taken out of gross national product.

This broad statement is generally acceptable; however, some stocks are taxed under VAT (for example, the sale of used automobiles) and land values can involve value added. It would be quite practical to levy VAT on the change in land value between purchase and sale, although there would be some transitional problems with the initial valuation at the introduction of VAT. Moreover, as in any land taxation, the requirement that land ownership must be registered to be legally recognized makes the property transfer easily established as a point of supply, though the price at which the transaction takes place may be more difficult to ascertain. However, despite its attraction, VAT is never applied to agricultural land, and even the EC's Sixth Directive leaves it open to states whether or not to tax persons selling building land.[1]

The problem is that the treatment of land is bound up with appropriate VAT liability of the entire sector, including the development of land, building, leasing land and buildings, and rental property. Four examples illustrate the interlocked nature of the problem. First, if land were liable to VAT, the farmer could offset any VAT liability on his purchase as a credit against his output; but in many countries, farmers are exempt from VAT and could not use such an offset and, therefore, VAT could not be charged on agricultural land without creating a cascade. Second, builders who bought land and sold a house standing on that land could credit the VAT paid on any input, including the land, against the VAT liability on the house. If building is made exempt from VAT, the VAT on inputs could create a cascade. Third, unless leasing and rental were liable to VAT, the VAT on, say, land would be unfair between those who sold land and those who rented it. Finally, if land is not taxed and new building is, then values and inputs have to be assigned separately to both land and building. The complexity of the relationships suggests that either land and building should be fully liable to the VAT (as in New Zealand) or should be prorated.

In practice, no such neat alternatives are adopted. As discussed in Chapter 7, few countries tax farmers as fully taxable persons (the notable exceptions are Denmark, New Zealand, Sweden, and the United Kingdom) and even these countries do not make agricultural land liable to VAT. Most developing countries exclude farmers from the system and frequently exempt agricultural inputs from VAT; agricultural land is never liable to VAT. For buildings and the develop-

[1]European Community, Sixth Council Directive, Article 4(3).

ment of land, the practice is best examined through the treatment of the construction industry.

Construction

The construction industry presents some peculiarities that must be analyzed to select a treatment under the VAT that is as rational and feasible as possible. In the first place, the construction industry produces goods that, from an economic point of view, can be considered either for production, such as business premises, or for consumption, such as housing. Second, construction work usually involves numerous subcontractors, who operate firms of entirely different sizes and organizational characteristics. Third, some of the activities of the construction industry, for example, low-cost housing, are frequently the target for favorable treatment by governments to accomplish certain social objectives (see Chapters 3 and 4). Fourth, there are difficulties in defining what is meant by "construction," "alterations," "repairs and maintenance," and "civil engineering."

Ideally, a VAT should be neutral. If special treatment is to be given to particular forms of expenditure, for example, low-cost housing, it is better (as mentioned in the discussion on housing in Chapter 3) to accomplish it by subsidies. The VAT should not be burdened by such devices. Equally, if the authorities wish to ensure that certain forms of construction are tax free, they would have to register traders involved in these construction categories so that they can claim credit or be zero rated. Yet, it is in the nature of the construction industry that the same builder can undertake to build both low-cost and high-cost housing. It is difficult, therefore, to enforce any provision requiring a distinction between these activities because common inputs and work forces would have to be carefully allocated among projects, based not on business efficiency but on political and social definitions.

It is best to subject the construction industry to the same treatment as other industries. The purchase of new business premises should, of course, be liable to VAT as any other purchase of capital goods, that is, should entitle the buyer to claim full credit for tax paid against his current liability. On the other hand, sales of new properties that are not business premises are sales to final consumers, and this means the purchaser has to pay the entire tax.

This is broadly what the EC's Sixth Directive tries to accomplish[2]

---

[2]European Community, Sixth Council Directive, Articles 4, 13, and 28.

but, as Table 5-1 shows, some countries supplement the VAT on new buildings by fees and taxes on the transfer of existing property.

The actual treatment under various national VAT regimes is somewhat different. Some levy the full standard rate, while others exempt or even zero rate construction work, with the result that such indulgent treatment may itself create more problems than it solves.

An example is that of the U.K. authorities who wish to distinguish between actual construction including alterations (which are zero rated) and repair or maintenance work (which is liable to the normal VAT). This leads the authorities into lists of examples of each set of work,[3] which they themselves admit are "not exhaustive"; to take one example, the installation of central heating was zero rated but the replacement of existing radiators was not. Difficulties with these distinctions persuaded the British Government to change the rules in 1984, so that all construction other than the creation of a new building became liable to VAT[4] which, of course, led to further disagreements.[5] Further definitions are needed when work may include alterations, new building, and repair and maintenance ("mixed work"); some "civil" engineering is zero rated, such as outdoor recreation grounds but not the construction of a swimming pool at a private residence. Builders' hardware, such as fitted cupboards in kitchens, is zero rated but built-in units in bedrooms are liable to VAT. Such fine definitional problems, which make the job of both authorities and traders extremely difficult, are not confined to the British example.

Basically (as mentioned in Chapter 4 in the discussion of exemptions on grounds of merit), the problem arises because of the desire to treat housing or goods considered desirable on social considerations (for example, swimming pools and recreation halls) indulgently. For instance, Sweden and Ireland have dealt with this perceived need by retaining a positive rate of VAT but adjusting the value on which it is levied. In Sweden, the effective rate on a valuation of 50 percent is half the nominal rate and, originally in Ireland, a low rate of VAT was

[3]United Kingdom, H.M. Customs and Excise, *Value Added Tax: Construction Industry* (1975, pp. 4–5), and *Value Added Tax: Construction Industry: Alterations & Repairs & Maintenance* (1975).

[4]The guidance issued by Customs got into details specifying that if an existing building was razed to its foundations, the new building using the old foundations would be zero rated, as would a new building using the wall of the old previous building; however, if more walls were left, constituting a shell "even without floor or roof," VAT at the standard rate would be liable.

[5]So that repairs to ancient monuments and churches were relieved of VAT, as were buildings listed as part of the "national heritage."

Table 5-1. Application of Article 13C(a) of the EC's Sixth VAT Directive: Summary Table of the Right of Option for Taxation of the Leasing of Immovable Property

	Exercise of the Right of Option	Status of the Lessee	Prior Notification or Authorization	Period
Denmark	In respect of each premise	Not to be taken into consideration	Yes	For at least two years
France	In respect of each premise or set of premises	Taxable person (even if exempt)	Yes	Valid up to the end of the fourth year; subsequently renewable by five-year periods
Germany, Fed. Rep. of	For each transaction, at the discretion of the optant; not applicable to small traders exempt from the tax or flat rate farmers	Taxable person who will use the immovable property for his undertaking (even for exempt transactions)	No	No limit
Ireland	General	Not taken into consideration	Yes	Until termination
Luxembourg	In respect of any building or part of a building representing a separate unit which is used entirely or, in the case of mixed use, mainly by a lessee entitled to deduct input tax; the schemes for small traders and flat rate farmers are not applicable to the transactions in question	Taxable person entitled to deduct tax	Yes	No limit

| Netherlands | In respect of each item of immovable property; not applicable to small traders exempt from the tax or flat rate farmers | Not taken into consideration, lessee must agree | Yes | No limit |

Source: Derived from European Community, "First Report from the Commission to the Council on the Application of the Common System of Value Added Tax," Annex II, Table 1 (COM(83)426 final, Brussels, September 14, 1983); reproduced in *Intertax* (Deventer, Netherlands), March 1984, p. 120.

applied to only 30 percent of the contract price. This distinctive treatment for housing, of course, makes the activity attractive and creates the need for lists of definitions similar to those in the British legislation. In some developing countries (for example, Colombia) new low-income housing is exempt, which, as mentioned above, requires a definition of what constitutes housing for lower-income individuals.

Theoretically, these reductions or exemptions from VAT are available in the EC for the transitional period only. Eventually the problem should be solved when all construction work becomes liable to the full VAT, as this is the only way to levy the tax efficiently. However, given the social priorities involved, the transitional period may be long. The European Court decision of June 21, 1988 that the United Kingdom could not zero rate industrial or commercial buildings has already been partly vitiated. Landlords will be allowed to charge VAT on rents (so that approximately three quarters of those using new offices can claim it as a credit); in addition, the new liability to VAT will only be introduced gradually.

It is not only the social priority accorded to housing that is the problem. The construction industry itself is difficult to tax. Belgium found that small building companies were likely to dissolve and disappear without paying their VAT. The authorities met this problem by making the purchaser of the house liable for the VAT should the builder not pay, thereby ensuring that the purchaser would not connive with the builder to avoid VAT liability.

The speculative nature of the building trade, the frequently undercapitalized character of many builders, and the small scale of many building enterprises means that this sector is a problem in most countries and especially in developing countries. The difficulty is compounded in most countries by a perceived need of the authorities to encourage self-help in construction to help relieve the housing shortage. However, if a private citizen buys the materials and hires workmen to build his own house, he cannot claim back the VAT paid on materials since he is not registered for the VAT. It might be possible to allow a system of temporary registration for such builders, but rather than get involved in the cumbersome business of issuing temporary registration certificates (which could easily be abused), it might be better to allow private house builders to submit their invoices to their local tax office, together with an official claim form on which the invoices would be listed. Such private noncommercial "do-it-yourself" construction typically takes much longer to complete a building than usual. The private person, short of capital, may find he has considerable VAT paid on inputs and yet cannot claim credit until the house is complete. It might be sensible to allow several claims during the construction of the house to relieve the builder from tying up too much capital.

Problems of the Definition of "Supply" Leasing

Typically, construction work is paid for by installments as materials are delivered on site, cladding completed, roofs finished, and so on; where such payments are made within a contract, specifying such payments, then the time of supply is the date when payment is received by the supplier. The receipt issued by the supplier showing the input VAT paid is used to claim the credit.

The liability to VAT when renting and leasing immovable property has to be carefully specified. The EC's Sixth Directive[6] permits member states to allow taxpayers to opt for VAT if they wish when they are renting or leasing immovable property. In most countries, the retail sale of such property is liable to VAT, and the VAT on the sale of an intermediate good (for example, a factory) is credited against VAT liability. Someone who buys, say, an apartment block, and leases or rents out the accommodations, is not making a retail sale of the property but can be considered to be more akin to an element in the chain of production; the final retail sale would only come about when the property itself (and not its use) was sold. The argument is that such an entrepreneur should be allowed to opt into the VAT and deduct the VAT liability from his sales if he sees an advantage to this. Table 5-1 shows the current EC treatment; as the United Kingdom zero rates all buildings, of course, no one (until June 1988—see above) in the United Kingdom could opt for a positive rate of VAT.

The rental of business accommodations, including such services as parking, should be taxable, but the VAT charged will be allowed as a credit to the tenant, if he is a registered trader. In practice, it is inequitable to include the supply of rental of private accommodation within the VAT base. To do so places owner-occupiers of housing at an advantage compared with those who rent. The alternative way to correct this inequity would be to impute rentals to owner-occupiers, and no matter how attractive this may seem in theory, practice has shown it to be administratively difficult, inequitable, and, politically, most unattractive.

[6]European Community, Sixth Council Directive, Article 13C(a).

Hotels and Catering

Because of their close relationship, it may be convenient to consider the renting and leasing of immovable property and the treatment of hotels and catering together. Among the exemptions, specified for activities within the territory of member states of the EC, is the leasing and letting of immovable property excluding, inter alia, the provision of accommodation, as defined in the national law, in the hotel sector or in sectors with a similar function, including accommodation in holiday camps or in sites developed for use as camping sites. The term "in sectors with a function similar to hotels" is somewhat vague and capable of various interpretations. Does it, for example, cover guest houses, boarding houses, and retirement homes for senior citizens? However, the major difficult decision is where to draw the line between long-term rental accommodation (which is not to be taxed) and short-term rentals (for example, tourist stays in a hotel) that ought to be taxed. A brief review of some practices indicates the possible treatments (and pitfalls) that apply to most countries using a VAT.

In Belgium, as a general rule, the leasing and renting of immovable property is exempt from VAT. Services supplied by homes for the aged, by nurseries and kindergartens, and by institutions, whose main purpose, according to their bylaws, is the supervision, support, and education of young people, are exempt from VAT. The renting of accommodations, furnished lodgings, or camping space by or for the account of an organization or association, recognized by the Secretary for Tourism, is taxable at 6 percent (the low rate), while the supply of meals and drinks to be consumed on the premises is chargeable at the intermediate rate of 17 percent.

In Denmark, rental of immovable property is not usually taxable. However, the rental of rooms in hotels, inns, motels, and so on, the rental of rooms in establishments for periods of less than one month, and the rental of camping, parking, and advertising space, as well as other services by hotels, restaurants, caterers, and so on, are taxable. Rental of a parking space is taxable only if it is not part of the rental of a residence.

In France, VAT is not chargeable on leasing unimproved land, rural property, and empty premises. The low rate of 7 percent applies to furnished rentals of rooms, houses, and apartments, and to meals served in canteens. The intermediate rate of 18.6 percent applies to meals in hotels and to accommodations in higher-class hotels, while the top rate of 33⅓ percent applies to five star hotels.

In the Federal Republic of Germany, renting and leasing immovable property is exempt, except for hotels, camping sites, and parking spaces (where the higher rate of 14 percent applies).

In Ireland, renting immovable property is exempt from tax, except where the rental is made in the course of carrying on a hotel business —which includes guest houses, holiday hostels, holiday camps, motels, caravan parks, and camping sites. Hotel accommodation in Ireland is chargeable to VAT at 18 percent.

In Italy, the leasing or renting of real property, including appurtenances and movable goods for the furnishing of the property, is exempt. A low rate applies to the provision of food and drink in schools and through vending machines. A higher rate applies to the supply of goods and services to guests in hotels, as well as to the supply of food and drinks in premises open to the public.

In the United Kingdom, leasing immovable property is exempt unless it concerns a hotel, a boarding house, or a holiday flat, or consists of facilities for camping or parking, or falls within a few other exempted categories. Where a supply consists of the provision of accommodation in a hotel or boarding house, tax is payable on the supply for only the first four weeks. Thereafter, tax is payable only on the value of the facilities provided other than accommodation but that value must be at least 20 percent of the total (the same rules apply to VAT in New Zealand).

In Sweden, what is, in effect, a reduced rate applies to supplies by caterers. The charge is on 60 percent of the taxable base.

Similarly, hotels and tourist establishments in Morocco pay the reduced rate of 12 percent, but restaurants are liable for the standard rate of 19 percent.

In Korea, exemption applies to leasing houses and the land on which they stand, provided that the area of the land is not more than ten times the floor space of the house. Restaurants and hotels are chargeable to VAT on their supplies.

In Norway, the provision of food and drinks in hotels, restaurants, and similar establishments, as well as in trains, ships, and aircraft during inland voyages, is taxable, but the renting of hotel rooms is exempt.

In Latin American countries, the renting or leasing of immovable property is not, as a general rule, chargeable to VAT.

As mentioned earlier, Article 13C(a) of the EC's Sixth Directive provides that member states may allow taxpayers a right of option to be taxed on the renting and leasing of immovable property, and such a provision is, as described above, included in the VAT system of the various member states. The purpose of the option is to allow a property owner, who rents property for business purposes to come within the scope of VAT, if he so wishes, to be able to pass on to his tenants the advantage of a VAT credit for the prior-stage tax borne on the property.

In general, it seems the distinction between renting long-term or short-term accommodation should be restricted to a definition dependent only on time. Definitions that have to define the end use for activities such as nurseries or kindergartens (Belgium), or defining the type of business (Ireland), do not seem as satisfactory as one that uses, say, six weeks as the dividing line between taxable and nontaxable accommodation.

In the same way, renting any property for less than the specified time should be taxable; the type of property should not need to be specified. Nor should the end user (for example, catering) be part of the legislation or regulations. All catering, as a service, should be taxable, and exemptions should not be allowed for hospitals, schools, or nursing homes (as in Ireland), or vending machines (as in Italy).

Applying differential rates to different uses or users of accommodation (as in Belgium and France) or of catering (as in Italy, Morocco, Norway, and Sweden) does not make for an efficient VAT system.

It is best to use a straightforward rule that all accommodations and services are liable to VAT at the standard rate if the occupation is less than, as suggested above, six weeks. If the stay exceeds this period, only services other than the provision of accommodation (for example, laundry and meals), are subject to the tax.

Leasing Goods and Agents

Leasing

Leasing or hiring goods, instead of buying them outright, is increasingly popular (often for tax advantages quite independent of the discussions about VAT). As far as VAT is concerned, the position is clear: leasing is the provision of a service and as such the entire charge (amortization, interest, and leasing administration fee) should be liable to VAT. If a registered trader leases an aircraft, a computer, or an earth-moving equipment, say, then the full rental is liable to VAT provided the supply and consumption of the service occurs within the territory of the country concerned. Difficulties occur where the lessor and the lessee are in different countries. Many VAT acts (including those in the EC) used to focus on where the lessor had his principal fixed establishment. Thus, in the EC, if an Italian company (VAT at 18 percent) decided to sell and lease back its new computer to a leasing company elsewhere in the EC, the VAT on the rental could be anything from 12 percent (Luxembourg) to 25 percent (Ireland). This is unreasonable and the EC's Tenth Directive changed the basis of tax to the lessee's member state.[7] This means the same tax rate applies no matter where the rental company is established or where the lessee uses the equipment. This seems to be a practical solution for most VATs.

Agents

Most VAT acts recognize that, in an arrangement using an agency, the supply is made by or to the principal and not the agent. However, where the agent is registered, he should be required to charge or account for tax on his commission. This can be no trivial matter, particularly in developing countries.

Sometimes traders have tried to siphon off profits by interpolating a main agent between a manufacturer and distributors. However, whether or not the agent is acting in the name of either party, he presumably issues invoices and collects proceeds on behalf of the agency; if he acts on his own behalf, but on the instructions of and for the account of his principal, then the agent should be chargeable on the difference between his output and input tax. The agency agreements between the parties may be written or oral or may be implicit in their general relationship. However, the agent should be required to maintain sufficient records (that is, tax invoices) to enable the authorities to trace the principal on whose behalf the transaction was undertaken.

The essence of any act or regulation should be to ensure that, whatever commercial arrangements may exist, and whatever legal agreements there may be between manufacturers and main agent or main distributor, the VAT charge extends to the full selling price by the main agent or distributor. Also, his commission must be included either in the price invoiced by the manufacturer (or the main agent acting on his behalf), or must be charged separately as represented by the difference between output and input tax on the main agent's or main distributor's own VAT returns. If one party does not wish the other party to know its identity, then the agent can receive and issue invoices between them as though he were the principal and the agency situation need not be disturbed (his input tax will equal his output tax).

[7]See European Community, Tenth Council Directive.

Commodities markets (either physical or future) constitute a supply of goods; commodities brokers' services are chargeable to VAT. If the commodity trade is large and is conducted mainly on behalf of off-shore dealings, then special arrangements can be made to zero rate such transactions. This is the so-called Black Box arrangement which argues that trades between registered traders in the London commodity markets are zero rated.[8]

Financial Services

Value added in banking and insurance is no less appropriate for inclusion in the VAT base than any other service or provision of goods. Indeed, to exempt financial services from VAT excludes from taxation a sector that is often perceived as extraordinarily remunerative, has a high visibility in terms of its physical assets, and is seen as a bastion of traditional orthodoxy. This is especially so in developing countries.

As Edwards and Mayer[9] suggest, "Why should the output of banks (and other financial companies)—namely, financial services—be exempt from VAT when most other consumption goods are subject to VAT? . . . It is difficult to find any convincing reasons in tax theory for this exemption. The theory of optimal taxation would suggest that, from the point of view of economic efficiency, exemption . . . would be justified if it were a particularly close substitute for the consumption of leisure," or, in equity terms, if financial services were a higher proportion of low-income household budgets than of high-income household budgets—"neither of these conditions seems likely to hold in practice."

Full Taxation of Value Added in the Financial Sector

At present, in no country are all financial services fully taxed under VAT, although Canada and New Zealand debated the problem in detail. A determined effort was made to evaluate all the possible ways in which various forms of financial services could be brought within the VAT (referred to as the goods and services tax—GST—in New Zealand). Table 5-2 gives a schematic presentation of one publication on the debate. The basic conclusions seem to have been that while insurance might be brought under the VAT, interest is a more complex

---

[8]See Pink (1985, pp. 85–93).
[9]Edwards and Mayer (pp. 62–63).

kind of price, bundling together elements relating to the real cost of capital, the rate of inflation, and the cost of intermediation. Moreover, the great variety of ways in which intermediation can be provided and paid for[10] suggest caution before taxing. However, the financial sector in most countries is considered able to bear a tax, and where most services are taxed, to exclude financial services seems both unfair and distortionary. A discussion of a few alternatives gives a flavor of the debate.

One country, Israel, has tried a close approximation to the full taxation of financial services. In theory, this might be the preferred solution where a bold attempt is made to make the VAT as comprehensive as possible. Because the price paid by the user of the services (interest rate, policy premium, and so on) embodies both the price of the services and other considerations, it cannot be used as a basis for a VAT. Thus, the indirect calculation used in the invoice-method VAT, whereby tax is computed on the price of the good or service and tax on inputs is subtracted, cannot be used. Instead, value added has to be calculated directly, by adding wages, salaries, and profits, and applying the tax rate to this base.

Israel used this method to tax the financial sector from 1976 (when the VAT was introduced) through 1979. Since 1979, the tax on the financial sector has been designated as a separate and distinct tax and, formally, is no longer part of the VAT. Several considerations led to this change. First, since the tax cannot be invoiced to users of financial services, it cannot be taken as a credit, and thus breaks the value-added chain. Second, if financial services were part of the VAT, credit would have to be given for financial services exported, a difficult and complicated matter that might seriously erode the base; yet if it is not allowed it could discriminate seriously against the profitable trade of providing financial services overseas. Third, the calculation of the base—wages and salaries plus profits—differs sufficiently from that for the VAT itself, that it is, appropriately, considered a separate tax. Profits for purposes of this tax must be computed on a cash flow basis and not in the way they are defined for income tax; capital goods purchased are fully expensed, rather than depreciated. In the Israeli system, no credit was given for VAT on inputs, but the tax-inclusive

---

[10]Explicit charges can be made for, say, brokers' services, but if discounted values were used as well, the VAT might have to be applied to the asset as well as to the income flow generated. Establishing a margin requires a comparison of sale and purchase prices, so that the VAT is associated with the transaction value of the instrument in addition to any explicit charges in connection with the sale.

Table 5-2. Summary of VAT Options for Taxing Financial Services

Optional forms of VAT:	Forms of Financial Services			
	Financial intermediation	Trading in financial assets	Fee and commission activity	Insurance (life or other)
Full invoice credit offset	Complex; administratively extensive; lending shifts	Complex; offshore trading encouraged	Practical	Tax should not be on full premiums; offshore competition
Special tax rates	The more simple, the more nonneutral	Tax not related to value of service supplied	Likely to be arbitrary	Possible
Zero rating	Should be limited to export of services	Should be limited to exports	No reason to zero rate	No reason to zero rate
Exemption	Cascade, incentive to self-supply services	Cascade, offshore problems	Cascade, offshore problems	Cascade, perhaps offshore problems
Direct additive accounts base	Possible cascade, low cost, problems for offshore and domestic producers	Cascade possible, offshore problems	Cascade possible	Practical

Source: Adapted from Carl Bakker and Phil Chronican, *Financial Service and the GST: A Discussion Paper* (Wellington: Institute of Policy Studies, Victoria University Press, 1985), pp. 19–30.

cost of inputs was deductible in computing profits. The rate applicable in the Israeli system is the standard VAT rate.

Were other countries to adopt a system similar to the Israeli one, they would have the advantage of imposing a tax on the financial sector, similar to that imposed on other service sectors, thus improving equity, reducing distortions, and gaining revenue. The principal disadvantage is that the tax is not integrated with the regular VAT system and does not give rise to VAT credits for users of financial services. Cascading is created and the advantages of cross-checking and integrated administration is lost. Also, presumably, the financial sector may be put at a competitive disadvantage compared to overseas financial centers offering identical services.

Selective VAT Application to Some Financial Sector Services

If it is impractical to apply the VAT in full to financial services, perhaps selected services can be taxed. The country that most closely approximated such a system is France which, since 1979, taxes banks on the amount of credit outstanding against the private sector on the first working day after the end of each calendar year. The tax is separate from VAT and is at a rate of 0.21 percent. However, a bank may opt to be integrated with the VAT system, in which case the rate drops to 0.14 percent. In this latter case, the bank may take credit for VAT paid on inputs and may issue invoices to customers detailing the tax and allowing them to credit it against VAT on their sales. The system applies only to banks; insurance companies and other entities in the financial sector are not covered.

This type of partial integration of the financial sector with the VAT has been tried in other francophone countries. There are problems with selecting the bases and setting the rates, but they are not insurmountable. In Morocco, some interest on bank loans and fees are taxed under VAT at 12 percent; a similar treatment has been recommended for Tunisia.

The insurance sector could also be integrated through a tax on policy premiums. The advantages of equity would be served, and the tax credit for users of the financial services would be generated. The principal disadvantage is that only certain financial transactions are susceptible to taxation, with a consequent danger of distortion in the financial markets. In addition, the possible need to establish a once-a-year date for valuing the base, as in the French case, could give rise to seasonal manipulation and upsets in markets.

The separate taxation of insurance under VAT has also been debated.[11] The difference is explored between "pure insurance" (automobile, fire, theft, and casualty) and life or annuity insurances. For pure insurance, taxes on premiums should be accompanied by a gross-up (effectively a tax refund) of claims at the prevailing tax rate.[12] Life insurance is more complicated, because of the element of saving involved, but could still be taxed. However, both pure and life insurance VATs would involve bringing households into the VAT system as claims by households would have to be grossed-up by the current VAT rate. Taxing insurance under a separate direct-subtraction or additive method might still be easier, but would involve cascading unless business were given an imputed credit on policies or require policies held by taxable businesses to be excluded from the tax base; this involves classifying policyholders (exempt and nonexempt) and the separation of claims.

After long debate, New Zealand decided to tax only fire and general insurance premiums. The VAT at 10 percent is due on insurance company premiums, commissions, and other income (such as proceeds from the sale of damaged goods) and on the sale of fixed assets; deductions are allowed on outward reinsurance, on VAT paid on purchases (including goods purchased to settle claims), and as one eleventh of payments made in satisfaction of insurance claims.[13] Registered persons can claim as a deduction from their own VAT liability the VAT included in their invoice for payment of premiums.

The importance of allowing the VAT content of claims is exemplified in Table 5-3, which shows why the domestic insurer is not placed at a disadvantage compared with the direct placement of the business with an overseas insurer (despite the obvious belief that premiums paid offshore, not subject to VAT, will give overseas insurers an advantage). The total claim is increased by the amount of VAT from $NZ 100,000 to $NZ 110,000, and the local insurer can increase the level of cover to cater for VAT without increasing premiums because he claims a net refund from the tax authorities. The overseas insurer must pay the claim, including VAT, and will have to increase his premiums accordingly. Nonresident reinsurers will also, effectively, be placed on the same footing as their resident counterparts.[14]

Even this limited taxation of financial services runs into difficulties.

[11]Barham, Poddar, and Whalley (1987).
[12]Barham, Poddar, and Whalley (1987, pp. 172–75).
[13]New Zealand, GST Coordinating Office, *The Fire and General Insurance Industry & GST* (1986, p. 8).
[14]New Zealand, GST Coordinating Office, *The Fire and General Insurance Industry & GST* (1986, pp. 20–22).

Table 5-3. New Zealand: Position of Resident and Nonresident Insurer Before and After Introduction of VAT[1]

(In New Zealand dollars)

	Before VAT	After VAT
Nonresident insurer		
Premium	30,000	30,000
Plus VAT	—	—
Total premium	30,000	30,000
Total claim (approximately)	100,000	100,000
VAT refunded	—	—
	70,000	80,000
Resident insurer		
Premium	30,000	30,000
Plus VAT	—	3,000
Total premium	30,000	33,000
Total claim (approximately)	100,000	100,000
Net VAT refund from Inland Revenue Department	—	7,000
Net loss	70,000	70,000

Source: Adapted from New Zealand, GST Coordinating Office, *The Fire and General Insurance Industry & GST* (Wellington: Government Printer, April 1986), p. 22.
[1]Known in New Zealand as the goods and services tax (GST).

For instance, under personal accident policies, VAT is charged only on the portion of the premium for accident cover (and not on the life cover); VAT on travel insurance relates only to the policies for accident (and not life) and only for the portion of travel within New Zealand. Where brokers, reinsurers, and underwriters have income from different financial transactions, as well as insurance (and nearly all have), some apportionment scheme must be used, such as floor area occupied, time spent, or gross revenues.

The basic problem remains that financial transactions such as insurance can bundle together so many flexible instruments, payments, liabilities, and claims over long periods of time that it is difficult to assign the "risk pool" to particular taxable entities and to ensure that distortions do not arise from cross-financing.

An Alternative Tax to Exclude the Financial Sector from VAT?

The option most commonly chosen regarding financial services is to exclude them from taxation under the VAT, and sometimes to apply an alternative tax or taxes. In the EC, the Sixth Directive explicitly exempts most insurance and banking transactions from VAT, although it allows systems in which banking institutions can opt to join the VAT, as in France. Many EC countries apply alternative taxes, often derived from taxes predating the VAT. Thus, Italy applies a stamp tax to various banking transactions. Insurance transactions are usually subject to taxes on premiums paid. In the Federal Republic of Germany, the tax on premiums is basically 5 percent. In Greece, the tax is 3, 8, or 18 percent, according to the kind of insurance. In addition, Greece has a 3 percent tax on the principal of all bank loans and advances and an 8 percent tax on all bank revenues. In Italy, insurance premiums are liable to taxes of 1 percent to 15 percent, and in France from 2.4 percent to 30 percent.

Outside the EC, the range of taxes applied to financial transactions is even greater. In Korea, a tax of 0.5 percent is applied to gross receipts from interest, dividends, insurance premiums, commissions, profits accruing from foreign exchange transactions, and many other transactions.

In Argentina and Uruguay, annual taxes on the net worth of financial institutions are imposed. In most countries with the civil law tradition, including Spain, Portugal, and most of Latin America and francophone Africa, stamp taxes at varying rates apply to a wide range of transactions conducted by financial institutions (including a tax on outstanding credit). In Colombia, leasing is taxed at the standard VAT rate (10 percent) and insurance premiums are taxed at 15 percent, but life insurance is not taxed. In all the countries mentioned above that have a VAT, the financial sector is exempt from the VAT itself.

Côte d'Ivoire is a good example of a country that taxes interest charges on bank credit at an effective rate of 20 percent. Borrowers subject to VAT may offer the tax paid on interest against their VAT liability. The tax probably discriminates against unregistered importers of consumer goods and real estate investors, but as neither of these is a category necessarily to be encouraged in a developing country, this might not be a great disadvantage. A more valid criticism is that if refunds of the tax on interest against VAT charged were tardy, then entrepreneurs, especially exporters, could be harmed; however, this is an administrative problem rather than one inherent in the arrangement.

The advantages of imposing a separate tax on the financial sector may be strong. As pointed out above, there is no fully satisfactory way to impose the VAT on the sector and allow a credit for users of financial services. An exact calculation of value added in the sector, even on an annual basis, is extremely difficult. In view of these problems, little seems to be lost and much gained in terms of simplicity if the sector is exempted from VAT and a separate tax is imposed that produces a yield approximately equal to that which would be produced by application of the VAT. If the separate tax resembles a stamp tax, that is, it applies to each transaction individually, it will have the advantage of reacting rapidly to changes in the tax base. If the tax has an annual base—as in France, Israel, Korea, and Uruguay—it will not react to intra-annual changes in economic conditions, but may be able more closely to approximate the value-added base. Any substitute tax will at least increase the equity of the overall tax system by extracting from the financial sector an appropriate contribution to the treasury.

There are, however, several disadvantages to separate taxes. First, since all would tax proxy bases rather than value added itself, they may introduce distortions in financial transactions as taxpayers attempt to shift transactions to formats that avoid the tax. This sort of manipulation, where the legal format of a transaction is artificially changed to avoid taxes while the underlying economic effect is unchanged, is especially possible in the financial sector, where there are a wealth of possible ways to structure a transaction and an abundance of accountants and lawyers to arrange to do so. Second, there is the loss of cross-checking and the need for separate administration. And third, there is the need to ensure that the substitute tax be seen as causing the financial sector to bear a fair share of the fiscal burden, and to ensure that future changes in the VAT be appropriately reflected, if necessary, in the substitute tax.

Financial Sector Exclusion from the VAT

Some countries that exclude the financial sector from the VAT (for instance, the EC) do not apply any explicit alternative tax. This solution has, of course, the advantage of simplicity. It also liberates the government from the considerable political pressure that the financial sector can bring to bear, and this in practice seems to have been a major factor for many countries choosing this option. However, it can be noted that in several countries that failed to create a specific tax on the financial sector to substitute for the VAT, the reason given was often that a pre-existing tax, usually a stamp or registry tax, already imposed a burden on the sector.

General Comment on Financial Services

The disadvantages of failure to tax the financial sector are clear: loss of revenue, loss of information that would be generated by a tax, distortions in the economy, and loss of both real and perceived equity. As the Central Bank of Ireland pointed out, "banks should be subject to the *same* taxation regime—no more and no less favourable—as other non-manufacturing enterprises."[15]

However, the problems of disentangling the costs of intermediation, the sensitivity of the financial sector to fine margins, the likelihood of encouraging (untaxed) offshore provision of financial services (through international arbitrage and "laundering"), and the important role finance plays in the efficient operation of a modern economy, all argue against experimental sales tax techniques or rough and ready solutions. Trying to get to grips with banking, as one central banker (in a different context) has put it, is akin "to trying to get your hands around a piece of jelly."[16] While unsatisfactory, the exemption of financial services from VAT, and the consequent cascade effect, looks to be the best solution for the time being.

Services Performed Abroad

The practice in the EC and most other European countries with a VAT is to zero rate the following services when they are performed abroad:

- Services relating to land and buildings overseas.
- The hire of transport for use overseas.
- Services relating to goods and activities overseas.
- Work on temporarily imported goods.
- Services for procuring exports of goods.

In addition, there is generally a zero-rating facility for a group of services that are defined as "reverse charge" services. This means that a customer in, say, the United Kingdom who receives a reverse charge service from France must charge himself VAT as if he had supplied the services. The object of this complicated arrangement is to avoid a

---

[15]Ireland, Central Bank (1980, p. 60).
[16]Quoted in David Lascelles, "The Battle to Keep Tabs in the Face of Rapid Change," *Financial Times* (London), April 21, 1986, p. 15.

possible distortion of trade. If the reverse charge did not exist there would be an incentive for exempt and partially exempt persons to order services from abroad and not in their own country thus avoiding VAT and discriminating against home industries.

Reverse charge services are in fact services that are deemed to be supplied where they are received. They generally include the following:

- Transfers and assignments of copyrights, patents, licenses, trademarks, and similar rights.
- Advertising services.
- Services of consultants, engineers, consultancy bureaus, lawyers and other similar services, data processing, and a provision of information (but excluding any services) relating to land.
- Acceptance of any obligation to refrain from pursuing any business activity.
- Banking, financial, and insurance services.
- Supply of staff.
- Services rendered by one person to another in procuring for another any of the above services.

The aim of the EC and associated countries is to ensure as far as possible that VAT does not produce distortions in trade. Reverse charge services are an example of this.

Another example is the arrangement under the EC's Eighth Directive,[17] where a businessman can reclaim any VAT he incurs in another country which would have given rise to an input tax deduction had he incurred it in his own country. For instance, a German businessman visiting France on business is entitled to reclaim from the French Government the VAT he incurs on such items as hotel accommodation and rental of cars. He has to prove that he is a taxable person in Germany and produce the invoices concerned to the French authorities. This puts the German on the same footing as his French competitors.

Of course, unless such arrangements are specifically covered by a customs or a tax treaty on a reciprocal basis, businessmen will simply have to bear the costs.

---

[17]See European Community, Eighth Council Directive.

Auctioneers and Secondhand Goods

There is general agreement that used goods sold privately cannot possibly be made subject to VAT. The position is not so clear regarding registered business to unregistered person trade in secondhand goods. Excluding these goods from coverage forces vendors who sell both new and used goods to distinguish between these two categories, and this may create increased compliance costs. In addition, these vendors will be able to evade tax by reporting sales of new goods as sales of used goods. On the other hand, making business sales of secondhand goods taxable introduces discrimination against dealers vis-à-vis direct, unregistered, person-to-person sales.

It has been reported that this disadvantage has become particularly severe in some countries for goods such as automobiles, cameras, and television sets.[18] It would not be difficult for sellers, who see this as discrimination against them, to evade tax by operating through (untaxed) individuals. One possible solution, recommended by an EC Commission, would be to tax only the dealers' margins.[19]

This is the effect of the British scheme for secondhand works of art and antiques. "A registered dealer must keep a stock book . . . of all articles which he buys and intends to sell under the scheme, showing their purchase and selling prices or details of other methods of disposal. . . . When the sale takes place the amount by which the selling price exceeds the buying price is treated as a tax-inclusive margin. . . . The tax due must be entered in the dealer's stock book and record of output tax and included in his tax return to Customs and Excise."[20]

Should it happen, peradventure, that the dealer is obliged to sell the item for less than he paid, there is no VAT liability.

The same procedure could be used for the secondhand sale of other items such as automobiles, scrap, electronic equipment, and jewelry. However, such transactions are frequently made for cash and no records are kept. Perhaps simply requiring the dealers to register for VAT pulls them into the monitoring mechanism and helps reduce evasion.

The proposed harmonized EC Directive on secondhand goods[21]

---

[18]See the case of Germany in Pohmer (1981).

[19]Pohmer (1981, p. 11).

[20]United Kingdom, H.M. Customs and Excise, *Value Added Tax: Second-Hand Works of Art, Antiques and Scientific Collections* (1973, p. 5).

[21]European Community, Amended Proposed Seventh Directive, Article 4.

suggests that the taxable amount shall be either 30 percent of the selling price or the difference between the selling and buying prices; the trader must opt for one or the other system for at least a year. Secondhand automobiles, motorcycles, and boats are supposed to be treated somewhat differently; the trader who has bought a used automobile from a nontaxable person is allowed to deduct an amount of VAT calculated on the basis of the acquisition price, but the amount deductible may not exceed four fifths of the VAT due on resale.[22] This proposal was made in 1978, but has not been adopted. It has been commented, "The EEC proposals show no sympathy for the way the antiques business is run. . . . It is not uncommon to see an article sold several times in a day in open markets."[23] It is the casual, semibarter nature of such trade that makes it difficult to tax. Indeed the EC has had to withdraw this proposal "after it had been amended beyond recognition by the EC member states."[24] It is understood that a new proposal is likely to be "closely modelled on the U.K.'s current scheme."[25]

In Korea and, as a general rule, in Latin America, secondhand goods sold in the course of trade by registered traders are taxable where such goods would be taxable if new. The treatment is, however, not the same for all categories of goods.

In Uruguay, for example, sales of secondhand furniture are chargeable on the full price, while sales of secondhand automobiles are charged on 10 percent of the selling price. In the case of a trade-in, VAT is chargeable on the full selling price.

In Colombia, the only secondhand sales taxed under VAT are those of automobiles and, even then, only if sold through a dealer; the VAT is levied on the intermediaries' markup.

New Zealand, in its VAT Act, defines secondhand goods as "goods that have previously been used, or acquired for use, or held for use, by any other person."[26] This definition includes houses and buildings. Registered traders account for VAT on their sales in the usual way; however, they can claim a national input tax credit on the purchase price of the goods (at the rate appropriate to the goods when sold new). This allowance means that, in effect, only the value added by the dealer (including the real estate broker) is subject to VAT.

---

[22]European Community, Amended Proposed Seventh Directive, Article 4(2) and 4(3).
[23]Hicks (1987, p. 29).
[24]"EC: VAT," *World Tax Report* (1987, p. 12).
[25]"EC: VAT," *World Tax Report* (1987, p. 13).
[26]New Zealand, *An Act to Amend the Goods and Services Tax Act 1985* (1988, p. 7).

Apart from the sale of secondhand automobiles in Luxembourg and of a limited range of items in France, sales of secondhand goods by private individuals are not normally chargeable to VAT. Automobiles are probably the only form of movable property where collection of the tax on secondhand private sales could be enforced by requiring the purchaser to produce evidence of payment of VAT before he is allowed to register the car in his name. To protect dealers in secondhand automobiles, works of art, antiques, and collectors' items, as well as dealers in secondhand caravans and boats, from being eliminated and the secondhand market limited to private transactions, the provision of relief on the lines adopted by the United Kingdom is probably the most realistic solution. To operate it effectively, however, taxable persons must keep adequate and detailed records of their sales and purchases so that the system can be properly controlled and supervised by the tax authorities. To extend such a system to goods such as secondhand clothing or secondhand furniture would, however, entail the risk of traders' classifying as secondhand goods items of slow-moving inventory that have been on hand for an unduly long time.

Of course, many secondhand dealers may fall under the exclusion rule for small traders, but in some countries, including many developing countries, secondhand dealers are an important element in the trading community. Therefore, although the provision on the VAT liability of dealers in secondhand goods may appear trivial, it can be important. Indeed, in the EC, "the Member States are deeply divided on this point . . . some . . . wish to see a special scheme only for certain categories of goods, and not even the same categories."[27] Basically, it seems desirable to pull these dealers into the VAT registration and require them to keep stock books that can be adequately audited. The New Zealand treatment should be followed, allowing a credit to be claimed for the VAT content on the goods purchased. Such full registration allows credit to be claimed for VAT on large capital inputs (in such businesses as large secondhand bookshops or automobile dealerships).

In developing countries, including some countries where the secondhand trade is sufficiently important for government-owned shops to conduct it, governments find it impossible to levy a tax on secondhand traders, although frequently the trade is valuable and should be taxed. In any case, the revenue yield is likely to be small and the

<hr>

[27]European Community, "First Report from the Commission to the Council on the Application of the Common System of Value Added Tax," reproduced in *Intertax* (March 1984, p. 102).

administrative costs could be large. Therefore, such activities have a low priority in the overall assessment of the VAT base.

Craftsmen

Often closely allied to auctioneers and antique traders is the trade of craftsmen. Usually these specialist craftsmen, such as jewelers, bookbinders, potters, restorers of antique furniture, engravers, and carvers are exempt under the small trader's rule. They should always have the right to opt for inclusion in the full VAT. It should be noted that the rates to which these traders are liable vary greatly:

a. Federal Republic of Germany:
14% in principle;
7% for transactions in which artistic creativity predominates;

b. Belgium:
33% for jewelry, jewels, goldsmiths' and silversmiths' wares of precious metal;
25% for articles referred to above of rolled precious metal, imitation jewelry, real pearls and precious or semiprecious stones and articles consisting wholly or partly of such pearls and stones; ornaments and fancy goods used to embellish or decorate dwellings and gardens;
19% for other goods and services;

c. Denmark: 22%;

d. France:
33% for articles wholly or partly of platinum, gold or silver, pearls, precious stones and cut stones;
18.6% for the transactions referred to above, other than resales of articles in an unaltered state, carried out by craftsmen who are registered in the directory of trades and are eligible for special relief or have opted for the simplified VAT scheme; other goods and services supplied;

e. United Kingdom: 15%;

f. Ireland:
25% for goods and services;

g. Italy:
2% for services supplied by firms engaged in restoring old buildings;
9% for articles of stone and certain building materials such as tiles;
38% for precious stones and related work, pearls and related work, nonindustrial work in platinum, hand-painted porcelain articles and "Kilim" rugs;
18% for other sales and services in the craft sphere;

h. Luxembourg: 12%;

i. Netherlands:
20% for supplies of craft products and services;

6% for unmounted precious stones or pearls, cameos (made with materials of vegetable or animal origin).[28]

Such fine distinctions in definitions of trades and rates are undesirable. Basically, the craftsmen should be exempt as a small trader, taxable under the small trader rules, or fully liable.

Betting, Gaming, and Lotteries

Unless betting, gaming, lotteries, and similar activities are forced into recognizable, easily located, identified premises or locations, they will probably be semi-illegal and untaxable. However, in most countries there are betting shops, licensed bookmakers, and state-registered totalizators, as well as lotteries, casinos, and gaming arcades. Nevertheless, the borderline between legal and illegal can be affected by VAT as exemplified by the Irish taxation of gambling. A VAT of 25 percent on the betting stake so altered the odds that those placing the bets opened accounts with bookmakers in the United Kingdom— where the VAT was half the Irish rate—and improved their odds. Of course, formally the transaction was illegal but it was almost impossible to check and eventually led to a reduction in the rate of tax on betting in Ireland.

Even where the activities are identified, it is only where the state is the organizer that it is possible to levy VAT on a reliable basis. When private individuals are running the gaming tables or machines, the monitoring of income and expenses for tax purposes (for VAT or income tax for that matter) is almost impossible. The preference has to be for more simple taxes based on clearly identified characteristics, for example, the number of gaming tables or machines, the square footage of the establishment, or a license to trade.

Sometimes, gaming machine takings are liable to VAT or special charges are made to participate in a game of chance separate from the stakes risked by players; such charges are liable to VAT at the standard rate. Of course, where establishments such as casinos sell meals and drinks as well as organize the gambling, then their activities as restaurants and caterers are liable to VAT in the normal way.

---

[28]European Community, "VAT on Goods and Services Supplied by Craftsmen in the Applied Arts Sector," reproduced in *Intertax* (February 1984, pp. 79–80). (Rates updated.)

Racing

Allied to betting in some countries is the whole complex world of racing. Basically, the VAT should distinguish between horse breeders and owners who race only as a hobby or who race continuously and regularly (it is not a good idea to include profit to judge whether racing is a business or not). Trainers, jockeys, breeders, and syndicates should all be liable to VAT and registered if their turnover exceeds the threshold. Although the arrangements of this particular business can be extraordinarily tangled, involving many intercountry transactions, the basic rule is that the value added, whatever form it takes, is taxable.[29]

Overall, the rule in applying VAT to all these difficult to tax sectors seems to be that quoted from Talleyrand at the beginning of this chapter; by all means try to pull these activities within the VAT but beware of the administrative and compliance costs of too much zeal in doing so.

[29]For a straightforward treatment, see New Zealand, GST Coordinating Office, *Bloodstock and Racing Industry & GST*.

CHAPTER 6

Retailers and Other Small Traders

So, Nat'ralists observe, a Flea
Hath smaller Fleas that on him prey;
And these have smaller fleas to bite 'em,
And so proceed *ad infinitum*.
—JONATHAN SWIFT, *On Poetry: A Rhapsody*

There is no sector of economic activity where cooperation between traders and the VAT authorities is more desirable than at the retail sale. Through the operation of the tax credit mechanism, the cross-checking of both purchases and sales is theoretically feasible at all stages before the retail level. At the final sale, purchases by a retailer can be checked against the sales of the suppliers; however, no such check is feasible for retail sales themselves because the final unregistered customers (the public) are not entitled to claim any credit for the VAT on their purchases.

The possible loss of tax revenue through suppression of a portion of sales by a retailer may be greater under a VAT than under a cascade-type business tax; for each retail sale omitted from the return, the loss of VAT is at a rate of, say, 10 percent on the value added, compared with a much lower rate of, say, 4 percent on turnover to yield an equal revenue under the cascade tax.

On the other hand, the potential tax loss is less than it would be under an equivalent retail sales tax, as the VAT collected at earlier stages is not wholly at risk unless the traders fail to remit the entire VAT liability to the authorities. This is improbable, as a nil tax return would arouse suspicions at the VAT office. Of course, a nil return under a retail sales tax would do the same. Under the VAT, the traders earlier in the chain would know there is documentary evidence of the transaction; the retailer under the retail sales tax knows there is none. Revenue from VAT is at greatest risk at the retail sale. Control in some form or another over retail sales is, therefore, a crucial objective of tax authorities in countries operating a VAT.

Countries that successfully employ VAT recognize that it imposes a burden on traders who must operate it and that to make the system workable at all, it must be adapted as far as possible to suit commercial procedures. In that spirit, the tax authorities in each country consult the various trade associations, including those representing small and medium-size retailers, from the earliest announcement that a VAT is to be introduced. It is tactful for the authorities to acknowledge that they have much to learn about business practices, and the interchange of ideas can mean that the form of VAT presented to the government contains the best of the combined views of the revenue authorities and the trade organizations.

Nowhere is this more important than at the retail stage. This chapter deals with this subject in some detail because the issue is often not given the importance it deserves; yet it is crucial for VAT in developing countries and, indeed, in terms of administrative efficiency and compliance costs, it is equally important in developed economies.

Should the Retail Stage Be Included?

The retail stage can be excluded from VAT coverage without affecting the essential structure of the tax. There are examples of countries with a VAT levied only on imports and manufactures (for example, Indonesia), and some countries apply the tax at the manufacturing and wholesale stages only. There are several reasons, however, for including the retail stage within the tax net, if at all possible.

In the first place, it is best to avoid the need to differentiate between wholesalers and retailers, since the borderline definitions between them may be imprecise and many taxpayers perform both types of operations. Second, it eliminates the undesirable use of special adjustments (for example, standard markup or discount allowances) when manufacturers and wholesalers also act as retailers. Third, it removes the incentive to split firms and pushes distributional functions forward beyond the point where the tax is applicable, so that most of the value added can be attributed to the untaxed retailer. Fourth, because retail value added frequently represents such a substantial portion of total value added, including it in the tax base greatly increases the base and allows a lower tax rate to be used to collect a given revenue.

Without wishing to exaggerate the actual use of VAT audits, the most important reason for including retailers in the tax coverage is related to the cross-checking feature built into the VAT system. The link between transactions that is so relevant for tax administration ceases to operate when the last taxable transaction takes place, since the buyer at that point is not registered and, therefore, cannot possibly claim the tax paid as a credit. Thus, assuming the retail stage is included, it is retailers who more frequently resort to practices designed to evade tax, particularly if the large numbers and small volume of their operations make it difficult for the tax administrator to detect these strategies easily. However, since the retailer can claim the VAT he paid on his purchases as a credit, cross-checking becomes feasible. The inclusion of retailers also facilitates cross-checking of sales by wholesalers and limits easy misrepresentation of the retail value added. If, on the other hand, retailers are excluded, evasion is made easier (by adjusting margins between wholesale and retail activities) for a sector that represents a substantial element of the total value added in the economy, and more significant revenue losses may result. It also requires higher tax rates to derive the same revenue.

Therefore, there is a strong case to extend the VAT through the retail level, with the proviso that the smaller traders, including retailers, should be subject to some simpler treatment. This has been the preferred solution in Latin American countries. Even Peru, which used to have a VAT levied only through the wholesale stage, has recently changed its legislation and now includes retailers; and Indonesia is actively considering extending the manufacturing and wholesale VAT to include the retail stage by 1989–90.

The Retail Problem Is the Small Trader Problem

However, in some countries, especially in Latin America, it is not just the problem of the small retailer, but the case of small traders in general that should be the subject of special legislation. In the EC, the Sixth Directive follows this approach,[1] but the discussion notes that a system of exemption and graduated tax relief cannot be considered as normal within the framework of the European VAT and that the coexistence of different special national systems may hinder the re-

[1]See European Community, Sixth Council Directive.

moval of fiscal borders. The Commission's final view (December 1983) is that the exemption and flat rate schemes (see below) are needed for small traders but should be harmonized, and the exemption level should be set at a level that excludes traders that cost more to administer than the revenue they produce. For such traders, the Commission's report suggests replacing the "delivery rule" by a payment and cash receipt rule (that is, taxes accounted for on a cash receipts basis and cash payments basis).

Most countries should aim to use a common treatment for small traders in general, rather than having special schemes restricted only to retailers. Typically, in developing countries, these simplified schemes can account for over half the registered traders (for example, in Colombia, up to 70 percent use the simplified system and, in Korea, over 80 percent are "special taxpayers," whereas, in the Netherlands, only 7 percent do not have to keep accounts for VAT). Though the retail stage is the principal problem, the problems of retailers are common to most small traders and can be considered under a common heading covering all traders and not just retailing.

The Criteria for Exemptions

What criteria should be used to decide which enterprises should be exempted (or those to be given the choice to opt out)? Turnover, value added, capital assets, numbers employed, number of establishments, number of owners, and profit have all been used to identify the exemption limit. Colombia, as an extreme example, uses four criteria for a trader to use the simplified scheme: (1) he must not be a juridical person; (2) his net income must be below a specified amount (Col\$3.6 million when enacted in December 1983—the equivalent of US\$40,500); (3) his gross assets at the end of the previous year must be less than a specified figure (Col\$10 million in 1983—US\$112,650); and (4) he must not operate more then two establishments.

Some countries use three options (for example, Austria). Others require two criteria to be jointly satisfied; for instance, in Indonesia the firm must have a relatively small turnover (US\$36,000 a year) but also must have a small capital. A high value added can be associated with small capital and, regrettably, there are plenty of examples (especially in state enterprises) of high value added (wages) with little or no profit. In any case, both capital and profits are more difficult to assess and more open to flexible accounting conventions. Even using a single criterion, such as turnover, involves choosing a maximum amount. In this respect, countries differ sharply in their practices; for instance, Denmark considers a business "small" with a turnover under DKr 10,000 (US$1,576), whereas for Japan turnover under ¥ 80 million (US$627,000) is small. The easiest measure is the number of employees; perhaps this could be considered an alternative to using sales as the criterion for the craftsman type of business. However, if the number of employees is used as the only criterion, it raises the problem of defining "full-time employees" for those on occasional employment, members of family, and pieceworkers or out workers, all of which are common practices in most countries. Perhaps more important, it could discourage the employment of extra persons as the business approached the exemption limit.[2] Indeed, when tried in France, many firms with 5–15 employees disappeared from the scene —at least statistically.

Argentina has one of the most complex sets of criteria: tax liability is assessed by the combination of net capital used in the business and the numbers employed and these, in turn, determine what is called the "fiscal debit." Indeed, there is a different matrix for industrial establishments and for commercial and service undertakings. For instance, the tax to be paid with only 1 employee and net capital under ₳ 5,000 ranges from ₳ 864 for services to ₳ 2,160 for commerce; for traders employing 7 persons and up to a net capital of ₳ 25,000, services could pay a top rate of ₳ 14,964 and commerce ₳ 23,736; further, the Argentine "simplified system" allows a "fiscal credit" (trade is allowed 70 percent of the "fiscal debit," industry 45 percent, and services 25 percent) for traders with net capital under ₳ 25,000 (US$6,397) and less than 7 employees.[3]

Another example, where turnover is used as the criterion but is differentiated according to function, is Morocco. The VAT is levied on manufacturers with a turnover exceeding DH 120,000 a year (approximately US$15,000), but wholesalers are liable only if their turnover exceeds DH 3 million—US$376,000). Of course, commercial importers must always be liable for VAT on their sales of imported goods even if they are small; evasion by splitting imports to get below any exemption limit would be too easy.

Each measure has some justification, but it is clear that the most usual and the most widely accepted criterion for exemption is turnover or sales (of course, the definition of "sales" causes some problems). To exempt smaller businesses from VAT, using turnover as the

[2]Due (1984, p. 208).
[3]"Argentina: Amendments to the Value Added Tax Act," *CIAT Newsletter* (1987, pp. 5–6).

criterion, requires agreement on the definition of sales for VAT purchases (see Chapter 17).

Problems of Small Businesses

What are the distinguishing characteristics of the small trader? By
identifying these characteristics, the authorities can tailor schemes to
meet the peculiarities and problems of small businesses. Small businesses encounter problems in seven basic areas.

Records

Small traders, especially those dealing with cash sales in more or less
street market conditions, without using tills, find it difficult if not
impossible to keep records of their gross takings. One way to deal with
such traders, as discussed below, is to exempt them entirely from the
VAT. However, if the authorities want to include such traders under
the VAT, or if their sales are above the very small minimum turnover
allowed for exemption, but still below some higher turnover which
would enable them to be incorporated fully in the VAT, then a further
option is possible. Such traders usually buy their inputs from a relatively few suppliers and have a better idea of their gross purchases
than of their sales. In this situation, the authorities can create a special
scheme allowing the trader to make a return showing the cost to him,
including VAT, of the inputs in the tax period and allow a standard
markup to be applied to that total. The purchases plus the markup
represent his gross receipts and are then multiplied by the coefficient
needed to produce the figure for VAT liability on sales inclusive of the
VAT (for example, in the case of a 10 percent VAT, by $^{10}/_{110}$ or 0.091).

The markup has to be calculated according to the type of business.
For instance, in the U.K. special "Scheme C" for retailers, five
markups can be used, categorized by the trade classification of business. Under this system tobacconists, news agents, and retailers of
liquor are allowed a markup of one sixth (16.33 percent); grocers,
butchers, and bakers are allowed one fifth (20 percent); greengrocers,
sellers of radios and electrical goods, book shops, and chemists, two
fifths (40 percent); jewelers, three quarters (75 percent); and all
others, 50 percent.

The advantage of this type of markup system is that it is extremely
simple and that it requires little record keeping on the part of the
trader. It is also easy to audit selected traders' returns of their purchases from the sales of their (usually few) suppliers and, therefore,

such a scheme continues to fit into the full VAT framework. The disadvantage of the scheme to the revenue authorities is that in using the fixed markup they are usually underestimating the actual value of the sales, sometimes by quite a large amount. The loss of VAT revenue is only on the difference between the assumed and the real markup and is usually considered a minor cost outweighed by the simplicity of the scheme and the savings in administrative costs.

From the trader's point of view, the fixed markup can also be a disadvantage if his own average markup is less than the fixed one assumed for the tax calculation; in this case, the small trader could end up paying more tax than he should. Obviously, this type of arrangement should not be used for a very large business, although in the United Kingdom large retailers do use it (which suggests that the official markup may be too low or that the savings in compliance costs on the full VAT are considerable). At the same time, providing the authorities set the markup sufficiently high, the loss of revenue is likely to be small and, of course, if the markup selected is high, it will provide an incentive for traders to opt to enter the full VAT scheme and keep the proper records of their sales, rather than run the risk of being penalized under the special scheme of fixed markups.

Multiple Rates

Small traders also have problems with multiple rates of VAT. No VAT uses only one rate. Even the simplest systems use a standard rate in conjunction with a zero rate, and some single rate systems are made into multiple rate systems by allowing percentage reductions from the base invoiced sales. Many use three or four rates. The use of multiple rates greatly complicates the task of fair treatment for small traders. This emphasizes, once again, the desirability of using only a single rate and keeping the options for exemptions or zero rates to as few as possible (see Chapters 3, 4, and 5 for a discussion of the problems of selling exempt goods and services). Indeed, the U.K. example exemplifies the dangers even with a single positive rate; because the United Kingdom opted to use the zero rate for a large number of activities, it greatly complicated what ought to have been a simple VAT.

Small traders may find it difficult to keep records of gross takings and even if they can do so, they may often find it difficult if not impossible to split their sales between the sales liable to different rates of VAT. To keep a record of sales differentiated by VAT rates requires the use of separate tills for the different products or till rolls that can identify and add up the different VAT-rated products. Moreover, the person operating the cash register must be able to identify quickly the objects liable to different VATs, and the means used for such identification must not be open to easy alteration by the customer. For example, some businesses have identified groceries liable to different rates by having different colored price labels; unfortunately, customers found it easy to switch price labels in the shops and, unless the register operator is extremely knowledgeable, the evasion can succeed (indeed, the robbery can succeed—for that is what it is). Moreover, distinguishing the different tax liabilities at the cash register requires honest operators who will not be tempted to give special advantages in reward for helping the evader or even just to favor friends (by merely pressing the wrong tax key). Even descriptions of such problems reinforce the arguments against multiple rates, especially in developing economies.

The way to deal with this problem is similar to that in the previous case. The VAT liability can be derived from looking at the input cost of purchases and using the ratio of different VAT rates on purchases as the same ratio to be applied to the gross takings. Small traders will usually be able to identify the VAT content of their purchases and this can be used as the ratio for their sales. For example, if a third of the goods were zero rated, another third standard rated, and the final third luxury rated, then sales would be similarly divided into thirds.

The disadvantage to the trader is that if a higher markup is used for the lower-rated goods than for the higher-rated goods then he could pay more tax under this scheme than under the full VAT. More likely, if this assumption were reversed then the revenue could be lost to the authorities. Once more, if the assumed markups were relatively high, there would be an incentive for the small trader to eventually opt for the full scheme and keep the full records.

Another difficulty can occur if goods purchased under one rate are transformed into something sold under a different VAT rate. A classic example is meat bought for human consumption (zero rated) but sold later as pet food (standard rated). Of course, this is not just a problem for small businesses and is likely to be even greater in developing countries, where small traders frequently combine the functions of new material purchasers, manufacturers, and retailers.

Stocks

The third difficulty faced by some small traders is that stocks can play a disproportionately large role in their enterprises. If, as under the previous two proposals for special schemes, the VAT liability on output were derived from purchases, such traders could be penalized. For instance, a craftsman who purchases inputs might take a considerable time to manufacture the salable product and, moreover, might stockpile the goods for a particular time of year, for example, a tourist season or a particular festival, such as New Year. In such a case, if his VAT in any given tax period were related to his purchases with the standard markup, then his stocks would be paying a VAT for some time before he was able to recoup the VAT liability by an actual sale.

Of course, the legitimate way to meet such complaints is to allow the trader to keep accounts so that he could be a full participant in the normal VAT, whereby his tax liability on inputs could be subtracted from his (temporarily) very small sales (and he would obtain a refund or carry a credit forward to the next period). His actual tax liability on actual sales would not occur until they were made. In this way, the VAT charge on his purchased stocks would not occur. However, if small traders are to be indulged, then schemes can be created to take account of the problem. Indeed, the U.K. special schemes for retailers allow four different ways to meet this problem (Schemes E, G, H, and J). The simplest variant is to allow the trader to make a VAT return using the expected selling prices, including VAT of the inputs purchased.

As before, the more complex the rates, the more complex such schemes have to be. If there is more than one rate used, then the split of tax liability on purchases is used to split the trader's gross takings, provided this does not create any obvious anomalies—which can be left to administrative discretion under regulations.

Provision of Services

A fourth problem is that small traders can provide services either in addition to goods or as a quite separate activity. By their nature, services usually involve relatively small current purchases. Of course, when starting a business providing a service, the trader may be involved in large capital purchases; for instance, a barber will have to purchase a shop, special chairs, and equipment. However, once equipped, his current inputs are trivial. Much the same is true of many other services. This means that the special schemes to meet the problems of retailers who cannot, or will not, maintain records of sales cannot be used for services. There is no way the purchases of a hairdresser can be marked up to assess the gross takings of that trader. It is true that some services might have a closer relationship to their purchased inputs for their sales (for example, spare parts for automobile repair) but, in general, the variety and quality of services is such that the final sales cannot be associated easily with purchased inputs. Therefore, the only special treatment available for small traders providing services is the total exemption or the special schemes such as *forfait* mentioned below.

Compliance Costs

All small businesses claim that compliance costs, as a proportion of tax paid, are much higher for them than for large businesses, although it is clear that this particular complaint seems much stronger (or perhaps better documented) in Korea and the United Kingdom. In the Federal Republic of Germany, business is concerned about the burden of federal and state legislation, but VAT is seen as only part of the problem, not a particular problem in itself.

In the United Kingdom, the million smallest registered businesses (76 percent of those registered for VAT) pay only about 7 percent of total VAT revenue (1983/84), so that it is worthwhile not only for the traders but for the VAT authorities as well to simplify the costs of tax compliance for such businesses. Similarly, in Mexico, almost 90 percent of the VAT is collected from only 10 percent of the registered traders. Perhaps one lesson from European VAT complaints is that businesses prefer to deal with the same taxing authority for both VAT and income tax; complaints seem to be loudest where the authorities are different. In addition, many small traders would prefer the option to use accounts and compute their tax return on a cash rather than an accrual basis. It might reduce compliance costs if small businesses were given the option of making returns on the usual monthly, two monthly, or quarterly basis or making only two returns, or even one return a year. Also, the authorities can assist by giving small businesses, free of charge, a simple account book.

Cash Transactions

Again, small family traders frequently pay for their purchases out of the till. No record is kept of the cash transaction, and at the end of the day it may even appear that their sales are lower than actually occurred. This distorts the VAT record of both inputs and sales. The VAT legislation must forbid this practice and, of course, this is one of the major reasons why some countries have tried to oblige retailers to issue a sales invoice.

Self-Consumption

Finally, most traders, and particularly small traders, consume part of their own production or stock. These self-supplies are a taxable transaction under VAT and tax should be paid on them. It is, however, difficult to enforce charging VAT on self-supplies, and the use of fixed markups, as described above (see section on "Records") is one way of alleviating this problem. In any case, self-supplies are usually estimated at the end of the year and not as goods are withdrawn from stock.

Five Ways to Treat the Smallest Businesses

The smallest businesses can be handled in five ways:

(1) Some countries simply exempt potential taxpayers with turnovers of less than a certain amount. The VAT, of course, applies to their purchases, including those of supplies and equipment, as well as materials and articles for resale. This is, basically, the practice in most countries in the EC. (For more details see below.) Some countries in Latin America, such as Costa Rica, Honduras, Nicaragua, Panama, and, to some extent, Brazil in its state VAT, also follow this approach.

The greatest advantage of this system is that it alleviates the task of the tax administration by eliminating the smallest traders from the tax net. An important drawback is that larger firms feel discriminated against, and this may influence their attitude toward voluntary compliance. This was exemplified in the controversy over the British proposal to increase the exemption limit to £20,500, and the support for it to be increased to £100,000;[4] it was claimed that the higher the limit was raised, the more valuable the exemption became, and that therefore the more onerous it became for a trader to cross the divide from being tax exempt to taxable. This was referred to as the "poverty trap" for small business. Obviously, as soon as a small business crosses the line and becomes liable to VAT, the tax liability will reduce profits; to earn the same profits net of VAT as he did before, the trader has to have a large increase in turnover, which, of course, is unlikely. In the circumstances, small traders are likely to suppress the sales figures that take them above the limit, and larger traders feel further penalized.

(2) A second method is the use of a multiple rate system to favor

---

[4]See Samuel Brittan, "Don't Let VAT Kill Off Jobs," *Financial Times* (London), February 18, 1985, p. 13, and correspondence on February 27, 1985, p. 21.

selected small businesses. For example, in Korea, in 1983, the VAT scheme for small traders ("special taxpayers") did not use exemptions but special rates. This created effective tax rates one third to two thirds of the usual VAT taxpayer's liability, depending on the particular trade; restaurants and construction businesses appeared to be the most generously treated (Table 6-1). Needless to say, such preferential treatment has a substantial revenue cost (and a certain inequity) to cater for the special problems of small traders.

(3) A third system tries to meet this problem by making sales to small exempt firms subject to a higher rate of tax than the regular rate. Used first in Belgium, this approach was followed by Spain, Turkey, and Argentina. All businesses must register for VAT, but small taxpayers are given a special recognizable number if they qualify (correct business sector, turnover less than a certain amount, and certain other conditions) and opt to be taxed under the "equalization tax scheme." Under this system, their suppliers must collect from the small trader an approximation of the tax (called, in Belgium, the "equalization tax") that would have been levied on their sales and pay it to the treasury. The only obligation of unregistered small businesses

Table 6-1. Korea: VAT Tax Rates by Industry

	Value Added as a Percentage of Sales	Effective Tax Rates	
		General taxpayers	Special taxpayers
Agriculture, fishery, and forestry	75.11	7.51	...
Mining	48.45	4.85	1.25
Manufacturing	25.89	2.59	1.94
Electricity, gas, and piped water	8.04	...	...
Wholesale trade	11.07	1.11	...
Retail trade	9.19	0.92	1.77
Real estate	8.48	0.85	...
Construction	66.11	6.61	1.96
Restaurants	62.61	6.26	1.87
Hotels and inns	39.75	3.97	1.95
Transportation, storage, and communications	61.12	6.11	1.94
Renting and leasing	42.55	4.26	2.00
Proxy, intermediary, and consignee services	56.03	5.60	3.46
Other services	50.46	5.05	2.09
Total	28.40	2.84	1.87

Source: Korea, Ministry of Finance (Seoul, 1984).

is to keep the purchase invoices, subject to having to pay taxes on their inventory again if the invoices cannot be shown if the administration checks. Small traders under the scheme can apply for reimbursement of VAT paid on their purchases of certain investment goods.

Although technically attractive, the system is somewhat cumbersome and there are four points to be noted about this scheme: (a) It is used only for a limited range of retailers (food, some clothing and furnishing fabrics, hardware, and books and newspapers), where the markup tends to be uniform and well known. (b) It complicates the work of firms that sell to registered and unregistered taxpayers, as well as to final customers. Each one of these categories of buyers would require a different documentation and, in addition, an unregistered taxpayer would be better off not disclosing his condition since this would imply paying more tax than a final consumer. (c) It transfers the burden of tax administration to the suppliers and to some suppliers (those dealing with small traders) more than others. Indeed, some wholesalers may be unwilling to sell to such exempt traders because of the extra compliance cost involved. (d) It is worth noting that each country that has experimented with this system has either given it up or is about to do so. Turkey experimented with this system in 1985, its initial year of VAT operation, but then removed it apparently because of complaints from large businesses and wholesalers.

To be fair, the Belgian authorities consider the scheme convenient and successful; in their view, there is little fraud with the system. Should they give it up, it is more likely to be because of pressure from the EC Commission for tax harmonization rather than because of dissatisfaction with the scheme.

(4) A fourth system is the *forfait*. It is used, for example, in Argentina, Chile, Madagascar, Mexico, and Niger for very small traders.[5] It was suggested but rejected in Portugal. A *forfait* system implies an arrangement between each trader and the local tax office for determining the amount of the trader's sales. Estimates of sales under a *forfait* system are usually done on the basis of trading results for a previous year, adjusted for general factors affecting all businesses, and any factors that might have relevance only to the particular trader. The effectiveness of the system depends on the frequency and thoroughness of the periodic reviews undertaken by the tax office.

[5]Approximately 35 percent of the 29,000 registered traders are assessed under the *forfait* scheme in Madagascar and perhaps as many as 80 percent in Niger.

Thus, for a *forfait* system to be applied with a measure of equity and success, a large number of staff and strict controls are required. In most circumstances, a *forfait* system absorbs an unreasonable amount of administrative resources. It means the diversion of valuable resources to trivial and unproductive work. Another important factor to keep in mind is that often some 80 percent of those taxpayers subject to a VAT account for only about 10 percent of the total sales that would be subject to the tax. A *forfait* system involves large numbers of staff, inconveniencing many traders about often controversial assessments that yield relatively little revenue. However, some countries appear to use a *forfait* efficiently (for example, Belgium) and claim that it eases the task of administration. If used, it is perhaps best combined with the income tax assessment and not administered through the VAT.

(5) A fifth system, similar to the *forfait*, is used by Ecuador and Peru. It consists of determination of the tax base by the tax administration on the basis of whatever records the firm has and, if the latter are insufficient or unreliable, external criteria. The figures thus set remain valid until a new estimate is made by the administration. The tax rate is applied to this figure, and the taxpayers then are allowed to deduct tax paid on purchases, but only up to the limit of the nominal tax liability previously calculated. It is argued that this system, contrary to the one that provides for outright exemption of the small taxpayer, creates an incentive for the small taxpayer to request invoices from his suppliers. But the system is ill suited to detecting the need to change the original estimates and, therefore, does not function well under rapidly changing conditions, such as under inflationary situations. In addition, it tends to confer too much power on the tax inspectors, increasing the chances for corruption.

Italy has experimented allowing traders, whose revenue did not exceed Lit 780 million (US$642,000), to calculate their VAT credit against VAT on sales by using a flat rate deduction—25 percent for services, 45 percent for production of goods, 97 percent for distribution of petroleum, and 6 percent for traders and professions. This is, of course, equivalent to a turnover tax at the various rates.

Japan proposed in 1987 to have a simplified system for "smaller" enterprises, which would be allowed a uniform tax rate of 1 percent of annual sales; that is, the implicit assumption, with a 5 percent VAT rate, was that most businesses would have inputs equivalent to 80 percent of their sales.

Overall, the preferred option is to exempt the very smallest businesses and accept that some advantage may accrue to them. However, the sales that determine the exemption limit should be kept at a low level and one of the alternative methods discussed should be used for small and medium-sized traders.

Treatment of Small Enterprises in EC Countries

France, the Federal Republic of Germany, Ireland, and, to a certain extent, Italy, had earlier turnover taxes covering the retail stage and so were experienced in the handling of large numbers of small businesses. In other countries, the previous turnover taxes did not embrace the retail stage, so the changeover to VAT brought in many new taxpayers. In the United Kingdom, for instance, it involved an increase from about 75,000 taxpayers to 1,250,000. In some countries, notably Belgium and France, and to a lesser extent, the Netherlands, the application of the VAT to the retail stage carried with it delicate political overtones, and great care was taken to avoid arousing the opposition of small traders. In Denmark, the emphasis was on equal treatment for all businesses, and accordingly, it was only the persons at the very bottom of the scale who were exempted, and the exemption limit (DKr 10,000—US$1,576) remains strikingly low to this day. In other countries, however, the approach appears to have been that it would not be worth wasting valuable administrative resources on small cases and the mechanisms for dealing with small businesses were prepared with that in mind.

By April 1, 1973, the nine EC member states had adopted VAT, each with a system for small enterprises which it considered best suited to its individual circumstances. In some countries, the criterion for special treatment was based on the amount of sales, in others on the amount of tax payable. In some countries, marginal relief was given for turnover or tax liability significantly in excess of the limit of complete exemption, that is, a form of graduated exemptions. Table 6-2 summarizes the special provision for small enterprises under the various VAT systems of the EC member states.

Important features of provisions in the Sixth Directive relating to small businesses are as follows:[6]

(1) Member states may retain their existing systems of relief for small concerns. If their turnover exemption threshold was less than European Currency Units (ECU) 5,000 (US$4,283) on May 17, 1977, it could be raised to that limit. Member states that applied tax reliefs graduated according to size of turnover could neither increase the

---

[6]European Community, Sixth Council Directive, Article 24(1).

ceiling of the graduated tax relief nor allow the condition for granting it to become more favorable.

(2) Member states that had not made use of the option to provide a scheme for small enterprises could allow exemption from tax to taxable persons whose annual turnover was at the maximum equal in national currency to ECU 5,000.

(3) Member states, giving an exemption from tax where the annual turnover for exemption was ECU 5,000 or more on May 17, 1977, could also increase the annual turnover limit to maintain its value in real terms.

(4) Exempted small enterprises are not entitled to any credit for tax borne on purchases nor can they show tax on invoices issued by them. They may, however, opt for normal VAT treatment, a course they might follow if, first, most of their customers are taxable persons who would want VAT invoices for their purchases or, second, they are engaged in a regular export trade and they wished to gain the benefit of the zero rate.

No authorization has been made to raise the ceiling above ECU 5,000. Yet those countries that used a limit above ECU 5,000 *before* joining the EC have been allowed to increase their limit to maintain the value in real terms (the United Kingdom to ECU 28,000 by 1981 and Ireland from ECU 3,000 and ECU 18,000 in 1970 to ECU 15,000 and ECU 30,000, respectively, in 1981). The EC Commission, however, has noted, "Bearing in mind that an upper limit had been imposed on Member States with exemption ceilings equivalent to less than 5,000 ECU, this development flouts the principle of the Sixth Directive, which was designed to restrict any increase in exemptions."[7]

Moreover, "the broad latitude described above has led to marked divergences between Member States' administrative arrangements which should be ironed out by the end of the transitional period by means of a common simplified scheme system of exemptions. The Commission intends to draw up a fuller report on the situation in Member States."[8]

Table 6-2 describes the main features of the treatment accorded to

[7]European Community, "First Report from the Commission to the Council on the Application of the Common System of Value Added Tax," reproduced in *Intertax* (January 1984, p. 25).

[8]European Community, "First Report from the Commission to the Council on the Application of the Common System of Value Added Tax," reproduced in *Intertax* (January 1984, p. 26).

Table 6-2. Summary of Treatment of Small Firms Under VAT in Selected Countries, 1982–87

	Complete Exemption	Tax Exempt but Must Register	Simplified Schemes	*Forfait*	Reduced Rate
Europe					
Austria				Turnover under S 3.5 million (US$301,000); assets under S 900,000 (US$77,000); profit under S 195,000 (US$16,777)	Tax payable abated by deduction; if turnover is up to S 50,000, deduct 20 percent, to S 100,000, 15 percent, and to S 150,000, 10 percent
Belgium		Turnover under BF 4.5 million (US$130,000); for food and retail sales under BF 2.5 million (US$72,000); others are liable for "equalization tax" levied by suppliers	Turnover under BF 20 million (US$578,586); sales derived from purchases by markups	When markup cannot be used, labor costs and profit margins used	
Denmark	Turnover under DKr 10,000 (US$1,576)				
France		Tax liability under F 1,350 (US$242)		Turnover under F 500,000 (US$89,681) for goods and hotels, under F 150,000 (US$26,904) for services	Tax liability F 1,350–5,400 (US$242–968) partial relief

Germany, Fed. Rep. of	Turnover[1] under DM 20,000 (US$12,108)		Turnover under DM 60,000 (US$36,326) entitled to net rebate of tax on reducing scale	Turnover under DM 20,500 (US$12,411); tax liability reduced by 80 percent, DM 20,500–60,000; remaining 80 percent is reduced by 1 percent for each DM 500
Greece	Turnover under Dr 1 million (US$7,589) for goods or under Dr 250,000 (US$1,897) for services	Turnover up to ECU 10,000 (US$7,984)		
Ireland	Turnover under £Ir 30,000 (US$48,273) for goods or under £Ir 15,000 (US$24,136) for services			
Italy	Turnover under Lit 18 million (US$14,825); inputs percentage of sales, hotels 50 percent, retail sales 70 percent, artists 20 percent		Turnover under Lit 780 million (US$642,451) flat rate credits	

Table 6-2 (continued). Summary of Treatment of Small Firms Under VAT in Selected Countries, 1982–87

	Complete Exemption	Tax Exempt but Must Register	Simplified Schemes	Forfait	Reduced Rate
Luxembourg	Turnover under Lux F 200,000 (US$5,785)				Turnover Lux F 200,000–1 million (US$5,785–28,929), reduce tax liability by 1 percent of difference between Lux F 1 million and actual sales
Netherlands		Tax liability under f. 2,050 (US$1,104); customers get VAT credit			Turnover under f. 2,050–4,150 (US$1,104–2,236) partial relief
Norway	Turnover under NKr 12,000 (US$1,891)				
Portugal			Retailers with purchases under Esc 4.5 million (US$33,311)		Coefficient of 25 percent applied to VAT paid on inputs
Spain			Turnover under Ptas 50 million (US$445,354)	Number of employees, rooms, vehicles, etc., used as indicators	
Sweden	Turnover under SKr 30,000 (US$5,027)				
United Kingdom	Turnover under £20,500 (US$11,368)		Special schemes for retailers		

Africa			
Côte d'Ivoire			*Forfait*
Madagascar	Turnover under FMG 5 million (US$3,957)		*Forfait*
Western Hemisphere			
Argentina	Turnover and net worth; suppliers use special low rate not creditable if sales made to registered traders	20 × 20 matrix of capital and numbers employed combine to give tax liability	A form of *forfait*
Bolivia	Turnover under $b 200,000 (US$90,090)		
Brazil	Exemption limit set by response to indexed (OTN) figures	Each state has special schemes	*Forfait* at both federal and state level
Chile		Fixed debit corresponding to imputed sales against which VAT on inputs offset	Imputed average sales
Colombia		Turnover and gross assets; standardized "mark-down" adjustments usually cancel VAT liability	

Table 6-2 (concluded). Summary of Treatment of Small Firms Under VAT in Selected Countries, 1982–87

	Complete Exemption	Tax Exempt but Must Register	Simplified Schemes	Forfait	Reduced Rate
Costa Rica	Turnover under ₡ 300,000 (US$4,216)				
Honduras	Turnover under L 12,000 (US$6,000) for "minor taxpayers" under income tax law				
Mexico				Forfait used extensively	
Nicaragua	Turnover				
Panama	Turnover under B 18,000 (US$18,000)				
Peru	Turnover	Turnover on estimated sales US$9,000–46,000; simpler techniques for calculation option for small firms for estimated sales or regular VAT			

Asia and Pacific

Indonesia	Turnover under Rp 60 million (US$36,190) *and* capital under Rp 10 million (US$6,031)		
Japan[2]	Turnover under ¥ 80 million (US$627,000)		
Korea		"Simplified invoices"	Special low rate for appropriate cash registers
New Zealand	Turnover under $NZ 24,000 (US$15,813)		

Source: Various country reports.
[1] See text for fuller discussion.
[2] Proposed but rejected.

small businesses under the principal VAT systems. Basically, there are four main options: exemption, a simplified scheme, *forfait*, and special reduced rates. Exemption can either be complete or it can be exemption with an obligation to register. Countries such as Denmark, the Federal Republic of Germany, Ireland, Luxembourg, and the United Kingdom (and Norway and Sweden outside the EC) have a basic complete exemption based on turnover; the lowest turnover for complete exemption is that used by Denmark (US$1,576). The German exemption with a turnover of US$12,108 may be misleading as it applies to businesses with a turnover of DM 20,000 in the *preceding year* and an *expected* turnover in the current year of not more than DM 100,000 (there were 9,000 such cases in 1982, representing a VAT revenue loss of DM 2 million). Some countries such as Ireland have different turnover exemption limits to those providing goods (US$48,273) and those providing services (US$24,136) and, in fact, the EC Commission views the Irish limit as the highest in the Community. Usually such exemptions are not mandatory; the small enterprises selling to taxable persons or exporting regularly may elect to be taxable and to be full members of the VAT system.

Some countries allow an exemption for small businesses, but still require them to register (for example, France, Belgium, and the Netherlands). In the Netherlands, exempt businessmen with VAT liability below a specified (small) assessment do not have to register (and cannot pass the tax on). Other small businesses must register and can issue invoices showing VAT included, but still get tax relief in the form of a reduced tax liability.[9]

The second major category is those countries that use a simplified scheme, often in conjunction with complete exemptions. For example, all traders in Belgium must register, but below a certain limit may opt for the "equalization scheme"; in addition, there is a scheme for businesses between the limit for the equalization scheme and up to a turnover of BF 4.5 million (US$130,000) in the general food sector and BF 2.5 million in other sectors.

Germany uses a scheme to encourage compliance and reduce administrative costs. A trader whose turnover exceeds the threshold (approximately US$12,000) by no more than $300 remits to the authorities only 20 percent of the VAT collected on sales over the threshold. The percentage that must be remitted increases by a percentage point for each additional $300 of sales until a trader with sales

---

[9]See Cnossen (1981).

of approximately $36,000 is paying full VAT. While this compensates the small trader for part of his compliance costs, it does mean that the public (who pay the full VAT) are directly subsidizing these traders. The principle that taxes collected by agents should be entirely remitted to the treasury should not be easily forgone. Tax farming should not be undertaken lightly.

This description of so-called simplified schemes should include a mention of the special schemes for U.K. retailers. Though undoubtedly designed with the laudable intent of simplifying the VAT for smaller businesses, they do represent the most complicated set of "simplified" schemes. In trying to please every small trader with their individual problems, the U.K. Customs and Excise seems to have created a series of options that may well involve more work for the administrators than ease for the businessman. As explained earlier, these schemes can be of the simplest variety, but also include more complex ideas allowing traders to estimate gross takings from their purchases of inputs and can also involve adjustments for stocks. One scheme (Scheme "G") involves calculating the output tax from the value of goods received and splitting them between zero-rated and standard-rated goods according to the ratio of the inputs. However, there is a penalty built into this scheme where one eighth is added to the calculated output as an arbitrary amount to prevent abuse of this particular scheme.

Of course, as already described above, *forfait* is used in Belgium, France, and Spain (and in many non-EC countries, including Brazil, Mexico, and a number of African countries).

Finally, there are some countries—Austria, France, the Federal Republic of Germany, Luxembourg, and the Netherlands—that use special schemes with reduced rates to give some partial relief to the small trader. In a sense, this again is a somewhat arbitrary way to keep the small trader in business (on social grounds) or to compensate a small trader for the higher compliance costs he faces in operating the VAT. Presumably it is hoped such schemes will dilute the annoyance, protest, and possible evasion of such taxpayers. The EC makes proposals[10] for harmonizing these treatments. First, member states *must* offer a tax-exemption scheme (a registration threshold) for traders whose turnover does not exceed ECU 10,000 (US$12,524); an option is allowed for countries that already have a higher threshold to adopt

[10]European Community, Proposal for a Council Directive Amending Directive 77/388/EEC (1986).

one up to a maximum of ECU 35,000 (US$27,946). Second, a simplified accounting scheme should be offered (see page 137, below).

The Preferred Solution

A preferred solution is, first, not to distinguish between retailers and any other small business and, second, to divide small businesses into two categories, as described below. Those taxpayers with a turnover below a relatively small amount should be exempted from the VAT. It is not envisaged that businessmen with sales below this ceiling should be registered or required to make any returns for VAT. All traders should, however, as a minimum, be required to record and file, in a readily retrievable fashion, their purchase invoices. There should be a severe penalty for nonregistration if sales exceeded the limit and were not reported for registration.

A small trader decides whether to register or not, mainly on whether he sells to registered or nonregistered persons. In selling to nonregistered persons, the trader with a large element of his selling price represented by his own value added (labor and profits) is likely to be better off not registering. If he sells to registered persons, it comes down to a trade off between the increase in costs and the preference of his registered customers for an invoice showing VAT. Chart 6-1 shows the simple sort of decision route needed and used in New Zealand.

A new business expecting to have sales (if they can be anticipated) in excess of the limit for nonregistration would be required to register at least one month before starting business. An existing business, crossing the threshold for the first time, would have to register within one month of the end of any 12-month period for which the sales exceeded the limit unless, first, they were not more than 25 percent above the limit and, second, they were not expected to exceed the limit in the coming 12 months. Traders and providers of services, with sales between the total exemption limit and some slightly higher limit, would be entitled to use a simplified system of accounting for which an account book would be supplied free by the tax authorities together with guidance on its completion.

The purpose of having the second category of small traders is to make the transition to VAT easier for taxpayers and to help the tax administration. This is done by providing a simple notional basis for taxing small businesses above the exempt limit. It could be enacted as a temporary provision to be used by no trader for more than, say, five years without review. Under this alternative, which would apply subject to the approval of the local tax office, the tax payable for a given

Chart 6-1. Decision Chart for Small Traders

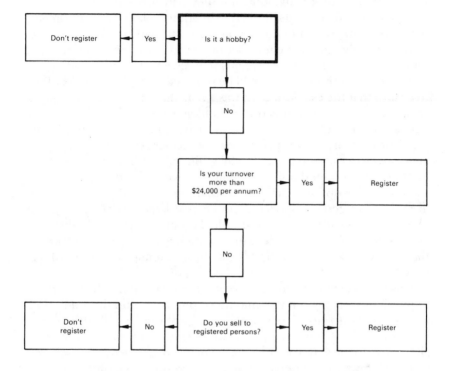

Source: New Zealand, GST Coordinating Office, *Self-Employed and GST* (Wellington, 1986).

taxable period would be a prescribed percentage of the aggregate amounts of tax shown on invoices of goods purchased for resale during that period. If it is assumed, for example, that the value added at the retail stage amounts to 25 percent of the value of inputs, the prescribed markup would be 25 percent. In this case, taxpayers subject to this scheme would pay a tax equivalent to one fourth of the VAT on their purchases (similar to the scheme operated in Portugal).

The tax would be payable quarterly even if most businesses pay monthly (again, this is a controversial matter and some authorities argue for only an annual liability—see the discussion above). The markup rates would be set to take account of losses from stock (due to theft or breakage) and bad debts. Those who felt the fixed markups were too high for their business would need to prove it by keeping detailed records, but they would have to pay the amount due according to the markup calculation until they had proved their case. The VAT paid on capital goods (limited to buildings, plant, and equipment) would be allowed as a deduction against VAT liability. Such a system should sharply reduce the number of returns that have to be rejected and the appeals against assessments that have to be considered.

Approval for this option would be required from the local tax office to ensure that the establishment was a bona fide trader and not, say, a retail outlet for a manufacturer supplying goods at artificially low prices, which would be recovered by charging a higher than normal retail profit margin. This could be checked by comparing the purchase invoices with the normal retail selling prices. The director of the local tax office should also have power to withdraw the approval for the use of this option, where more than, say, 50 percent of the sales are related to goods acquired from an associated trader. To prevent abuses, the local tax offices should be empowered to make VAT assessments in instances where information available or inspection of the taxpayer's premises indicates that invoice totals have been understated.

This scheme merely requires taxpayers to list and file their invoices of purchases, setting out the amount of purchases and the amount of VAT. During the transitional period, the authorities could evaluate the results of this option and decide whether to continue to offer this alternative to the taxpayer. One of the main advantages of this scheme is that it allows the tax department to concentrate on larger taxpayers during the initial periods of VAT by removing a considerable number of small taxpayers from the ordinary requirements of VAT.[11]

It must be stressed that this option is an *alternative* offered to small traders. They can, if they choose, use the simplified account books, which would be provided free by the tax authorities.

A taxpayer wishing to supply VAT invoices to his customers would have to come into the full VAT system irrespective of the volume of his sales. In addition, small businesses, who want to, may opt for paying according to normal VAT procedures.

It should also be stressed that this type of scheme works better for

---

[11]Turkey treated this intermediate group in a special way, but within the full VAT system, by requiring them to file every three months rather than every month required of the regular VAT taxpayer. In Belgium, taxpayers with a turnover under BF 4.5 million can opt to file a return only once a year and those with a turnover of less than BF 20 million can opt to file every three months (instead of monthly); however, the payment of (estimated) VAT is due monthly under all circumstances.

traders who sell goods than for those who provide services. There are two reasons. Typically, the purchased VAT-liable inputs of suppliers of services are few, infrequent, and at low cost. Second, generally, services have a much higher value-added content. Consider repair shops, hairdressers, painters, gardeners—all examples of small tradesmen whose taxable inputs are relatively trivial and where a scheme to base VAT liability on a presumed markup would founder. The input purchases could be too infrequent and erratic as a base; the high and maybe variable value added could create inequities in VAT treatment between traders and over time. Even where services can have expensive inputs (for example, computers, restaurant kitchens), these still tend to be infrequent and value added is still characteristically high.

It may be better to have a separate lower threshold for services. Those selling mainly to nonregistered persons would probably decide not to register. Those registering would use the simplified scheme but the authorities might wish to ensure that the assumed value-added markups were not sufficiently high to encourage traders to opt to fulfill the full requirements of the usual VAT.

Records for Small Traders

Present Policies

Based on EC guidelines, the VAT codes of all European countries require: (1) the strict enforcement of correct invoicing in taxable transactions between chargeable persons, and (2) the maintenance of a minimal standard of bookkeeping by all taxable persons sufficient for a trader to complete his VAT returns properly and for the tax authorities to audit them.

Small traders must keep records to satisfy the authorities. All purchases of goods and services received, whether taxed under VAT or zero rated, should have invoices from the supplier, and such invoices must be kept. All records of credits allowed or received must be kept. At the same time, the authorities should require businesses, including small businesses, to keep their normal business records, including orders and delivery notes, purchase and sales books, cash books, till rolls and any other records of daily receipts, documents relating to imports and exports, and the usual annual accounts.

In Latin America, the VAT law usually requires the businesses to issue a simplified invoice for retail sales except where it is clearly impractical (for example, in food markets and supermarkets). In most European countries, there are no requirements for the issue of documentation by retailers to final consumers for three good reasons. First, it is altogether unreasonable to harass traders with such an enormous burden in circumstances in which it is not already their commercial practice to give receipts or dockets to final consumers. Second, it creates invoices showing VAT that could be used, falsely, to claim credit against VAT liabilities. Third, it should be much more profitable to concentrate the revenue audit staff on controlling invoices relating to transactions between registered persons, working downward from importers and mining and manufacturing activities through wholesalers to purchases by retailers.

This does not mean that figures of retail sales are not checked; they are. But the primary concern is to ensure that all taxable transactions between registered persons are covered by invoices that correctly show the full consideration for every taxable sale, and that a more or less common bookkeeping system is installed, into which the relevant figures are channeled so that they can be readily checked by the revenue auditor. In this way through the production chain reliable particulars of purchases are established for retailers, and, as a computer operation, any trader, whose rate of gross profit as returned for VAT falls short of the norm over a period of time for his particular trade classification, is earmarked for investigation.

Korea, despite having an almost ideal VAT in many ways, provides a good example of the problems associated with a rigorous application of VAT to the small trader and why it should not be attempted in many countries. Compared with his European or Latin American counterpart, the position of the Korean retailer is more demanding. The law requires separate records to be kept for taxable and exempt sales, and no simplified schemes are available for apportioning total receipts between taxable and exempt elements. The law requires a standard form of bookkeeping for retailers as well as other traders. A separate entry is supposed to be made for sales transactions, giving particulars of the goods, quantity, and unit price. For each taxable sale, a retailer is expected to issue a "simplified tax invoice" and for each exempt sale, a "simplified income invoice." For mixed sales involving taxable and exempt items, a single simplified tax invoice may be used, the amount for exempt items being entered on the "remarks" columns. If an error is discovered after the issue of a simplified tax invoice, the latter should be recovered and canceled and a corrected simplified tax invoice issued in its place. If it cannot be recovered, another simplified invoice should not be issued instead. No matter how small a retailer's total sales may be, or how trivial an individual sale may be, he is required to issue a simplified tax invoice (or a simplified income invoice) for each sale.

A cash register docket fulfills the function of a simplified tax invoice or a simplified income invoice and, in the early stages of the Korean VAT, traders were encouraged to buy the appropriate cash registers by being allowed to levy a reduced rate of VAT if they did so. Purchasers of retail goods were encouraged to ask for receipts (or invoices) through lotteries related to numbers printed on the cash register sales invoices. The whole scheme was elaborate and small traders, not unnaturally, complained, despite actually being favored by a low tax liability. Ironically, as small traders were the most numerous tax-payers, their complaints appeared out of proportion to their actual contributions to VAT (in the early years of the Korean VAT they filed about 76 percent of all VAT returns but accounted for only about 5 percent of revenue). Nevertheless, they caused considerable embar-rassment to the authorities and gave the VAT an undeserved bad name for a time.

Preferred Solutions

All VAT systems operating at present are invoice based. However, many small businesses claim it would be helpful if they had the option to account for VAT on the basis of cash received and cash paid out. Some businesses operate in commercial circumstances that require them to provide lengthy credit facilities to customers. "Cash account-ing" improves the liquidity of many small businessmen who have to account for VAT due on invoices for which they have not received payment. It would also remove the problem of VAT on bad debts.

The main features of a scheme following the EC proposal, whereby VAT would be accounted for on a basis of cash paid and received, would be as follows: (1) it would be an optional alternative to the normal method of VAT accounting, that is, cash accounting would not be compulsory; (2) it would cover both input and output tax; and (3) it would be available to small businesses up to some fairly generous threshold; the threshold turnover suggested for the EC is ECU 150,000 (US$187,500).

Newly formed businesses would be allowed to adopt the scheme, on application, as part of the routine VAT registration procedures. Exist-ing registered traders would need to make a written application to the authorities, and a precondition would be that they were up to date with returns and payments. Businesses would need to agree to a number of conditions (about adequacy of records and accounts) and would normally have to remain in the scheme for two years.

To prevent steadily growing small businesses having to adopt nor-mal VAT accounting at a premature stage of their development, a tolerance of, say, 25 percent could be applied to the turnover limit. This would also reduce excessive movement between the normal VAT scheme and cash accounting. Businesses with turnovers already over the limit, but within the tolerance, would remain ineligible to adopt cash accounting.

These cash accounting scheme businesses, where turnovers exceeded periodic limits, would be obliged to adopt normal accounting at the start of the next accounting year, unless they could show that turnover was unlikely to exceed the tolerance during the year as a whole.

It can be argued that cash accounting schemes should not be allowed on the basis of some turnover figure but rather on the "nature" of the business. If cash sales are prevalent in a branch, cash accounting should be allowed; if they are not, accrual accounting should be the rule, even if turnover is low.

In any case, adequate records would have to be maintained. In particular, there would have to be comprehensive cash records, either by adapting existing summary records of sales and purchases by including settlement details or by setting up a cash book, which fulfilled the dual role of summarizing both transactions and individual cash movements. A clear audit trail would have to be maintained from the summary record back to the normal commercial evidence of the transactions (that is, copies of purchase and sales invoices and evidence of receipts and payments). Businesses would still have to issue tax invoices for sales to registered customers. Cash purchases would need to be supported by receipted tax invoices before input tax credit could be claimed.

Hand in hand with the receipt of payment (and not the supply) being taken as the taxable event is the regular payment of advance amounts (say, every month or each quarter), calculated on the basis of tax paid in the preceding year with reconciliation at the end of the year, that is, the business either pays a balance due or receives a repayment if its installments have exceeded the annual tax due. With newly registered businesses with no history of tax payments, a system of estimated payments against expected turnover might be adopted.

Suggestions also are made frequently to simplify the accounting problems of small businesses by allowing them to file returns less often than the regular VAT taxpayer. The attractions of an annual or perhaps twice yearly return appear obvious and the EC has made suggestions for quarterly returns; however, experience shows that it is precisely the smallest businesses that have the greatest difficulty in meeting their deferred payments, including tax liabilities.

In fact, small business associations have sometimes argued for the exact opposite treatment where small traders could make more frequent contributions to their eventual annual VAT liability so that they would not fall behind in their payments, find themselves unable to meet these obligations and then become liable for automatic financial penalties. The preference is not clear-cut, and it may be best to leave the smaller taxpayers on the same filing roster as other firms or allow less frequent filings, but encourage installment payments on VAT owed throughout the year.

Other Measures

It has to be accepted that in many countries, both developed and developing, the standard of bookkeeping and, occasionally, the standard of tax morality, leave much to be desired. Supplemental measures of control are used in such circumstances, entailing the physical checking of inventories against invoices of purchases and the inspection of merchandise in warehouses, storerooms, and business premises. Vehicles transporting goods are, in some countries, required to carry a manifest, corresponding to an invoice and giving particulars of what is being carried, and the names and addresses of the buyers and the sellers, with the VAT registered numbers. In fact, in countries where bookkeeping standards are suspect, much reliance is placed on this form of control though this moves VAT administration away from being an accounts-based tax back toward excises relying on police, customs, and excise controls.

In a few countries, the tax authorities provide assistance by initially providing model account books for VAT, free of charge. Given the importance of simple records in the VAT, the cost to the government of such free account books is a modest investment to improve taxpayer compliance. Guidance on keeping the necessary records is considered to be a fundamental feature of the VAT educational program for traders. Failure to keep minimal books correctly entails a penalty, sometimes a continuing penalty for each day of failure, which is strictly enforced by prosecution in the courts. This is in fact the main enforcement measure for VAT, and, on due evidence of noncompliance being produced, the courts award a penalty against a defaulting trader.

On the other hand, most tax administrators will prefer to rely on regulations and not court proceedings. In the Chilean and some other Latin American VATs, persistent noncompliance by a trader can lead to the authorities withdrawing his license to trade and closing his premises for a week or two (or eventually, permanently). The advantage of this procedure is that it relies on administrative order and not on a laborious legal proceeding. It is a swift decision that strikes at the heart of the business, and traders will react quickly to get back into business.

In general, the special schemes for retailers work reasonably well in most European countries. They are not regarded as departures from the principles of VAT made merely to suit commercial convenience, but as being so obviously necessary as to be intrinsic to any VAT system because without them the system would become totally unmanageable.

CHAPTER 7

Treatment of Agriculture

"And I shouldn't wonder," I said, for I was in a thoughtful mood, "if even herrings haven't troubles of their own."

"Quite possibly, sir."

"I mean, apart from getting kippered."

"Yes, sir."

"And so it goes on, Jeeves, so it goes on."

—P.G. WODEHOUSE, "Jeeves and the Song of Songs," in *Very Good, Jeeves!* (Penguin Books, 1979), p. 74

Agriculture poses special problems for VAT. In most countries, farmers are not easy to handle as taxpayers. For the most part they tend not to keep accounting books or, if kept at all, do not maintain them adequately.[1] In developing countries, they may not be well organized and may be located in places where the tax administration cannot reach them easily or even enforce the tax law with certainty. Their methods of farming are frequently rudimentary and even their culture can frustrate attempts to apply a VAT (or indeed, any tax), and make it rather impractical. There are a few striking exceptions from this general statement and, in a few countries, farmers are assumed to be like any other trader and are dealt with wholly inside the usual VAT legislation (for instance, in Chile, Denmark, New Zealand, Sweden, and the United Kingdom). However, VAT legislation usually tries to ensure that most farmers and fishermen do not have to make any VAT return and do not have to deal with the tax administration.

---

[1]A 1973 survey in the Netherlands estimated that under 3 percent of farmers kept accounting books in France, Italy, Ireland, and Austria, whereas over 80 percent kept books in the Netherlands and the United Kingdom.

141

The treatment of agricultural activities under a VAT has been the object of protracted discussions within the EC. Basically, the EC has recognized the difficulties that most farmers face in handling the normal system of VAT or even the simplified system available to small enterprises. Moreover, it has been accepted that agriculture is, in most countries, clearly difficult to deal with and politically sensitive.

The problems that agriculture faces are similar to those of small businesses. However, in farming, not only are many sales for cash and records of sales not kept; frequently, all records are poorly kept, which not only frustrates the authorities but also can work to penalize the farmer in compliance costs and in wrongly calculated VAT liabilities. In addition, farmers frequently produce and sell many products, and their products can be liable to different VAT rates (cereals, wine, cattle, and Christmas trees, for instance); their inputs are bought sporadically (for example, fertilizers and seeds or new equipment) and can also be liable to different rates of VAT. Sometimes farms are mixed with other taxable activities, for example, rooms rented for bed and breakfast, rental of caravan sites, provision of farm services, processing farm output, and transport of animals. Are thoroughbred stud farms or market gardens regular businesses or farming?

Possibly the best way to review these issues is to look at the EC's treatment of farming, and follow this with a discussion of other countries' treatment, and the preferred, or "last," solution.

The EC Common Flat Rate for Agriculture

The basic intent of the EC treatment is to try to make sure that the farmer is left alone in peace and that he is not disturbed by government paperwork or visits from VAT inspectors. It tries to anticipate the difficulties of dealing with farmers and does so by pushing the burden back onto farm suppliers and forward onto purchasers of farm output.

The EC's Sixth Directive provides a common flat rate scheme for farmers[2] to use, where the normal rate or the simplified scheme for small undertakings gives rise to difficulties. The farmer does not need

[2]See European Community, Sixth Council Directive, which defines a "farmer" as being a taxable person who carries on an agricultural, forestry, or fishing undertaking considered to be such by the member state within the framework of a list (in Annex A to that Directive). The list of agricultural production activities is as follows:

    I. *Crop Production*
      1. General agriculture, including viticulture.
      2. Growing of fruit (including olives) and of vegetables, flowers, and orna-

to register for VAT nor does he need to issue an invoice (see below). He is compensated for the VAT he pays on his inputs by a flat rate increase in the price he charges his customers. This percentage is a flat rate relief for all farmers and none are put at a competitive disadvantage in passing forward the increase; it can be claimed by the purchaser of the farm output as a credit against his (the purchaser's) VAT liability. In this way, only the seller of farm inputs (fertilizers, seeds, and equipment) and the purchaser of farm output are registered for VAT. The farmer has, normally, no VAT responsibility.

The Commission of the EC is responsible for monitoring the appropriateness of the flat rate compensation (for the VAT charge on farm inputs) determined by each member state. The flat rate compensation is fixed using a common method of calculation set out in the Sixth Directive. The computation is based on the national accounts figures for the preceding three years. Basically, this involves taking the figure for the total output directly derived from agricultural production; inputs consist of the total value of current inputs needed to achieve this production and the value of the gross fixed asset formation in all the specified agricultural activities. The ratio of VAT on inputs to farm output represents the flat rate compensation percentage (the last column of Table 7-1 shows some of the compensation rates).

Any changes in the flat rate applied in a member country must be agreed with the Commission to ensure that there is no significant

---

      mental plants, both in the open and under glass.
    3. Production of mushrooms, spices, seeds, and propagating materials, nurseries.
  II. *Stock Farming Together with Cultivation*
    1. General stock farming
    2. Poultry farming
    3. Rabbit farming
    4. Beekeeping
    5. Silkworm farming
    6. Snail farming
  III. *Forestry*
  IV. *Fisheries*
    1. Fresh water fishing
    2. Fish farming
    3. Breeding of mussels, oysters, and other mollusks and crustaceans
    4. Frog farming
  V. Where a farmer processes, using means normally employed in an agricultural, forestry, or fisheries undertaking, products deriving essentially from his agricultural production, such processing shall also be regarded as agricultural production.

subsidy to the agricultural sector by overcompensating farmers for VAT on inputs.

Problems with the Flat Rate Compensation

The Commission has identified certain minor problems in relation to the flat rate compensation scheme:

(1) Obviously the flat rate cannot compensate all farmers accurately. Spanish studies show that, depending on the particular type of farming, the VAT paid on final production could vary from 1.1 percent (for olives) to 5.7 percent (for intensive market gardening); VAT paid also varies by region from 2.9 percent (in Andalucía) to 4.7 percent or more (in Navarra, Aragón, Castilla-Léon, and Murcia).[3] A flat rate VAT allowance of 4 percent clearly only achieves rough justice.

(2) Some member states extend the rate to any farmer no matter how large or small his enterprise. If the flat rate is realistic, large farmers will probably opt for the normal system since their VAT inputs on purchases of capital equipment will make the flat rate unattractive. If the flat rate is generous, they may stay in the flat rate system. The Commission is of the opinion that the flat rate scheme should be confined to small traders—the ceiling being established by reference to criteria relating to turnover or quantities produced per hectare.

(3) Member states differ in their treatment of the disposal of capital goods. Some states exempt such sales by flat rate farmers, others include the disposal of such goods as part of the basis for calculating the flat rate compensation. In the latter case, the Commission suggests that the ratio for calculating the flat rate should be

$$\frac{\text{total input tax for the sector}}{\text{final production + resale price of used capital goods}}.$$

(4) Problems are raised by the inclusion or noninclusion of direct exports by flat rate farmers when compensation is calculated. Some countries authorize the farmer to collect flat rate compensation for his VAT on inputs on a basis that includes exports. Others exclude this possibility. Both arrangements present difficulties. States that authorize farmers to obtain compensation for direct exports both encourage farmers to export and relieve them of input tax—but the cost of the export to the foreign customer is increased by the flat rate percentage.

---

[3]García Azcárate (1986, pp. 139–40).

States that do not authorize compensation for exports keep the export price down, but at the same time farmers are not encouraged to export, and if they do they may not be compensated for input tax previously paid. This is a dilemma. The Commission suggests that direct exports by farmers should qualify for compensation and that the foreign customers, provided they are in the EC, or have reciprocal arrangements for VAT (for example, Austria), should be able to claim refunds under the VAT Eighth Directive[4] for the flat rate amounts they have paid.

(5) The status of the flat rate is ambivalent. It is not a VAT rate, but it is treated as such for deduction of input tax purposes by those who buy from farmers. It provides "rough justice"; if properly calculated, it provides adequate compensation for input tax to the "average farmer." So clearly, some gain and others lose, although year in and year out, a balance is probably achieved.

Article 25 of the Sixth Directive states that flat rates may not be used to obtain refunds for farmers greater than the VAT charges on inputs. This provision has two objectives: (a) to prevent distortion between member states and (b) to protect the payment of "own resources" to the Commission. In practice, it is the latter objective that is honored. This is explained below.

The EC is financed by payments by member states of all customs duties and a percentage (maximum 1.4 percent in 1986) of the VAT theoretical base. These amounts are legally due to the Community (its own resources) and are merely collected on its behalf by member states. Since balancing the Community budget is usually difficult and always contentious, the Commission is strict in obtaining compensation from states where the VAT system does not, in certain sectors, yield the full amount. This has been the case, for instance, with the flat rate scheme for farmers in the Federal Republic of Germany. In 1984, following a revaluation of the green rate of the deutsche mark, the German authorities decided to use the flat rate VAT mechanism to compensate farmers for the losses they suffered. This special aid was an addition of 3 percent to the flat rate. This move was attacked by the Commission because (a) it reduced the Community's "own resources" yield since more input tax was created, leading to a reduction in net VAT yield, and (b) it created a distortion in the treatment of farmers as between member states. In the event, Germany pleaded that the flat rate mechanism was the simplest method of compensating farmers

[4]See European Community, Eighth Council Directive.

both for input tax and losses due to the revaluation of the green deutsche mark; the authorities claimed that it was possible to calculate the loss in own resources to the Commission and to make a compensatory payment. This argument was accepted, and Germany was allowed to derogate from Article 25 of the Sixth Directive, provided the own resources account was corrected.[5] This incident demonstrates that the flat rate mechanism can be an administratively simple mechanism for compensating farmers for more than input tax, for instance, as a subsidy. It does mean, of course, a reduction in the net yield of VAT.

Although there is no evidence of flat rate compensation schemes for farmers leading to fraud, there is always the temptation for the farmer and his customers to conspire to increase the invoice price (hence the input tax deduction), but to settle in cash for a lower price. Of course, there should be legal penalties for such behavior.

Agricultural Invoices

Any claims for flat rate compensation by a registered purchaser must be supported by a proper invoice. As is usual in VAT control, the invoice is retained by the trader for inspection by revenue officials if required.

The unregistered farmer is not normally required to issue the invoice. This invoice is generally a matter for the registered purchaser, who must prepare and retain the invoice himself and give the farmer a copy, which the farmer retains.[6] The invoice must specify the net purchase price and the flat rate addition as well as the total price. An unregistered farmer, who accepts an invoice made out this way, recognizes the sale and validity of the flat rate addition to the price.

If there is a subsequent adjustment in the price or the sale is canceled, the appropriate VAT adjustment must be made and documented by the unregistered farmer (not by the registered purchaser) obtaining another invoice or destroying the old one. Failure to do so may leave the farmer liable for the tax involved and for penalties.

Sales by registered farmers to other registered persons are subject to the same requirements as sales by any other registered person.

There are no provisions in the VAT law for sales made directly by one unregistered farmer to another. If, however, the sales are of live

---

[5]See European Community, Twentieth Council Directive.

[6]In Luxembourg, Ireland, and in some states in Germany, the farmer himself issues the invoices.

cattle, sheep, or pigs and are made through a livestock mart or by auction, the seller can be entitled to the flat rate addition, since the mart or auctioneer will normally be a registered trader. Livestock marts, livestock dealers, and livestock auctioneers are deemed for VAT purposes to be simultaneously buying and selling live cattle, sheep, pigs, horses, and greyhounds. Sales of live cattle, sheep, and pigs are liable to VAT at the effective flat rate.

VAT Rates in Agriculture

By the time the Sixth Draft Directive was submitted to the Council, all the nine member states had determined their own provisions for dealing with agricultural activities (see Table 7-1). Only two of the EC member countries (Denmark and the United Kingdom) do not have a special regime for farmers. In both, farmers are treated the same as all other taxable persons, except that in Denmark they are allowed a longer time than other traders for paying the tax. In both countries this treatment of agriculture seems to work efficiently.

In the other member states, there are flat rate compensation systems which, in effect, mean that while the ordinary farmers may be technically within the VAT scheme, they do not have to keep books, issue invoices, or normally furnish VAT returns to the authorities. Of course, a flat rate farmer can, if he wishes, opt into the full VAT system, but if he does, he must remain in it for a minimum number of years.

Exceptionally in France, the flat rate relief is not given to the farmer by the purchaser of his produce, but by the Government, a procedure that enables the tax authorities to check the accounts submitted by the purchasers of output from farmers. The French farmer submits an annual return; this means he may have the disadvantage that he does not receive any compensation until later than farmers in other EC member countries.

In all countries, specialist farmers, whose activities are primarily of an industrial or commercial nature (for example, growers of flowers in Belgium), are required to register and are treated in the usual way. Apart from Denmark and the United Kingdom, where registration is compulsory for all farmers if sales exceed a fixed limit, only a relatively small proportion of farmers eligible to use the flat rate opted to register in the early years of VAT. Indeed, in some countries (for example, Belgium), all farmers must register regardless of turnover, but such registration does not oblige them to make tax returns unless they opt for the full VAT system.

Table 7-1. Summary of Agriculture Under VAT for Selected Countries, 1982–86

	Registered	VAT Rate (In percent)	Opt Out	Input VAT	Purchaser Credit Compensation (In percent)
Europe					
Austria	X	10.0	—	X	—
Belgium	X	2.0 (wood); 6.0 (food)	—	—	2.0 6.0
Denmark[1]	X	Standard	—	X	—
France	X	7.0 (food); 10.0 (wine)	X Turnover F 300,000 (US$53,809)	X Claimed from Government even if opt out	3.5 (eggs, poultry, pigs); 2.9 (wine, fruit, vegetables); 2.4 (other food)
Germany, Fed. Rep. of	X	6.5 (food); 13.0 (wine, beverages)	—	X	7.5 13.0
Iceland[2]	X	11.0 (wholesale); 25.0 (retail)	—	—	
Ireland	—	0.0 (vegetables); 1.0 (cattle, pigs); 10.0 (poultry, fish)	—	Principal inputs exempt from VAT and refunds on capital goods	2.2

Italy	X	2.0 (cereals); 8.0 (poultry, wine); 15.0 (milk, cattle); 8.0 (other)	As small business	—	2.0
Luxembourg	—	5.0	—	—	5.0
Netherlands	—	4.0	—	—	4.5
Norway	X	Standard	As small traders	X	—
Portugal	—	—	—	Zero rated	—
Spain	—	—	—	—	4.0
Sweden	X	Standard	As small traders	X	—
Turkey	—	Zero	—	—	—
United Kingdom	X	Standard but most food is zero rated	—	X	—
Western Hemisphere					
Argentina	—	Exempt (unprocessed); 18.0 (processed)	—	Principal inputs exempt from tax	
Brazil	—	—	—	Principal inputs exempt from tax	
Chile	X	Standard	—	X	
Colombia	—	Zero	—	Fertilizers and seeds zero rated	

Table 7-1 (continued). Summary of Agriculture Under VAT for Selected Countries, 1982–86

	Regis-tered	VAT Rate (In percent)	Opt Out	Input VAT	Purchaser Credit Compensation (In percent)
Ecuador	X	—	—	—	
Uruguay	X	Exempt (some unprocessed); 12.0 (bread, meat, beverages); 20.0 (processed)	—	Principal inputs exempt from VAT	
Asia and Pacific					
New Zealand[1]	X	Standard	—	X	
Philippines	—	Exempt	—	Fertilizers and seeds exempt	

Source: Various country reports.
[1]Approximately one third of all firms registered are farmers.
[2]Proposed.

Treatment of Agriculture in Other Countries

In general, most VATs in Latin America specifically exclude sales by farmers or exempt the first sale of unprocessed agricultural products. Chile is unique as it includes farmers as full registered traders and does not exempt any food from VAT.

In addition to the administrative reasons just mentioned, there are other arguments for eliminating farmers from the tax net. In the first place, the products they sell, especially food, are likely to be exempted anyway because they tend to be a large part of the consumption expenditures of the lowest income groups. Equity considerations frequently dictate, therefore, that to mitigate the regressivity of a general sales tax these products should not be taxed (but see discussions in Chapters 3 and 11 showing that this argument is not necessarily correct). If, on the other hand, the products become taxable through processing, or upon resale by merchants, no additional revenue would be gained by bringing even large commercial farmers within the scope of the tax, since full collection through "catch up" will take place at later stages of production or distribution. However, VAT collected earlier on farm inputs would not be credited. This is bound to create some cascade element and erode the neutrality of the system. In many countries, much of the farm output is exported and any VAT collected at later stages would ultimately be refunded. However, the VAT liability on inputs would remain and would put the export at some disadvantage.

So the problem remains, in Latin America as in the EC, of how to prevent multiple taxation of farm products when the farmers buy taxable items and, not being zero rated, are not allowed to claim a refund for the tax paid on purchases.

If the goods the farmer sells are processed further and become taxable, the subsequent processors and distributors receive no credit against their tax liability for the tax element contained in their purchase prices, and this causes cascading. The resulting cumulative effects, by comparison with the high value added by the primary sector, tend to be less significant. In simple peasant agriculture, the purchased inputs may be so small that the VAT content can be ignored. Nonetheless, some countries have attempted to meet this problem by allowing subsequent handlers of farm products an arbitrary credit for tax presumed to have been borne by the farmer; this procedure has been followed, inter alia, by Argentina. Admittedly, unless this credit is shifted backward to the farmer through higher payments for his produce, the system does not compensate the farmer for VAT paid on his taxable inputs.

Another approach, probably more suited to encourage increases in agricultural production, has been the outright zero rating of agricultural inputs that have no important alternative uses, such as animal feed, seeds, insecticides, and fertilizer. This still leaves an uncompensated VAT paid by farmers on purchases of tractors, trucks, fuel, fork lifts, and, indeed, all capital inputs, including buildings. As an alternative, larger farmers could be allowed to register and be zero rated, thereby obtaining a refund of the tax paid on their purchases if the tax element is considered significant enough to warrant adjustments. This could be an important possibility where farming was on a large scale with significant capital inputs. Indeed, in some countries, "agriculture," which has many of the characteristics of industry (for example, chicken farming, intensive pig farming, market gardening), can be required to be registered as a normal business.

Some countries such as Uruguay distinguish between farmers taxed on their actual income (and these are taxed under VAT) and others taxed on their presumptive income. Those paying income tax on a presumptive income are allowed to offset their VAT liability on purchase invoices against their income tax liability. Such tax payments can be made annually or, if preferred, on account monthly.

Moreover, in some countries, agriculture is organized along state or cooperative lines that frequently involve the agricultural organization in extensive manufacturing activity (such as, slaughtering livestock, manufacturing meat and dairy products, plant maintenance, machinery repair and manufacturing, transport, and retailing). Such multiple activities can lead to some complicated demarcation decisions on goods and services liable to different rates of VAT. It is clear that the nonagricultural activities have to be separated from the farming activities for the purposes of VAT and this may involve many difficult decisions on internal transfer pricing.

Preferred Solutions

As farming becomes more complex and capital intensive, so the value of capital inputs and bought-in services rises. Modern farmers may purchase the services of specialists (sometimes other larger farmers) to plough, sow, spray, harvest, and transport their crops.[7]

[7]A partial list of such services from the Sixth Directive is as follows:
—field work, reaping and mowing, threshing, baling, collecting, harvesting, sowing, and planting
—packing and preparation for market, for example, drying, cleaning, grinding, disinfecting, and ensilage of agricultural products
—storage of agricultural products.

These are basically business services and should be required to register as such.

In general, in more developed economies, as far as possible, the preferred solution is to treat farmers as a business. If their sales are small, they will be exempt under the small business exemption. If they are above the exemption limit, but below the limit that allows special treatment, then either (1) the flat rate compensation can be used or (2) agricultural inputs can be zero rated. Each system has its drawbacks but both relieve farmers of compliance costs. Farms with large turnovers or with the characteristics of commercial undertakings should have to register as full VAT traders. Naturally, all farmers should be given the option of registering fully for the normal VAT if they wish.

In developing countries, the government policy of encouraging farm production might be served best by a combination of exemption of farm inputs (or perhaps better, zero rating of farm inputs) and optional normal rating for large farmers.

Infrequent sales of agricultural products at the farm gate, or of fish at the house of a fisherman, through direct sales to the consumer at markets or through house-to-house sales, would not be considered to be taxable deliveries and would, therefore, not be subject to VAT. Of course, even if a flat rate compensation scheme operated, the farmer would not be able to claim any compensation and neither would his purchaser (who is an unregistered final purchaser anyway). Prices charged at such direct retail sales are presumed to recompense the farmer fully for all costs including VAT on inputs; otherwise, why would the farmer voluntarily make such a retail sale? However, if farmers are an integral part of the VAT system, they should not be allowed to claim VAT on all their inputs but suppress part of their sales; in this case, even their farm gate sales should be accounted for—as is the case in New Zealand. Again, in New Zealand, home consumption by the farmer of his own produce is supposed to be included as an output for VAT—clearly impractical in most countries.

Notwithstanding the zero rating of inputs specific to agriculture, the authorities may come under pressure to compensate smaller farmers for the VAT on inputs that remains, such as VAT on fuel, vehicles, and machinery. Some concessions may be needed. A scheme could be adopted under which a farmer, whose sales exceeded some very small figure, but who was still too small to be obliged to opt into the full scheme, could apply for repayment of the VAT on his inputs. He would have to keep and submit his invoices and make a formal claim. The invoices submitted by claimants would serve as a useful basis for audit when the supplier is visited by an audit team. Provided the qualification levels were fixed sensibly, the administrative burden should not be too heavy as the number of claims would not be large. There could however be a psychological benefit in that small farmers would know that exceptional purchases for their farms would be freed from the input tax burden. It would have to be made clear that farmers must expect to bear the input tax up to some minimum amount as the price of escaping the burden of bookkeeping for VAT.

CHAPTER 8

Federal VAT and Sales Tax Harmonization

> Differences in tax systems did not come about at random, but rather reflect social and political preferences that should not be ignored. . . . efficiency losses . . . may be an acceptable price to pay for retaining national diversity and autonomy.
>
> —SIJBREN CNOSSEN, *Tax Coordination in the European Community* (Deventer, Netherlands: Kluwer Law and Taxation Publishers, 1987), p. 49

The VAT is levied as a national government tax (except in Brazil). Sometimes, in a federal system, it can clash with existing state taxes. Even without a federal system, the central government VAT may not be easy to reconcile with existing local, municipal, and other sales taxes. However, some federal systems—such as in the Federal Republic of Germany, Brazil, Mexico, and Argentina—levy a VAT and short discussions of those systems follow. (India has introduced the "MODVAT," which is not a VAT but a federal excise to get around the powerful interests of the states and their state sales taxes, see Chapter 1, section on "Tax Evolution and Efficiency.") Next, there is a brief discussion of the VAT harmonization issues of customs unions, especially the EC. Finally, general federal-state issues are dealt with in the context of the United States and Canada.

VAT Used in Federal Systems

Federal Republic of Germany

In the Federal Republic of Germany, the states (Länder) actually collect the federally legislated VAT at common rates on a common base. The actual operation of the VAT is in the hands of each state, and uniformity of application is achieved throughout the country by court rulings on VAT. The total VAT revenue is split between the Federal Government and the states (roughly 70/30 percent), with some redistribution to help the economically weaker states.

As a model for other federal countries, the German VAT illustrates the need for agreed federal and state legislation on base, structure, and rates. Once established, the formula for splitting the proceeds may be the most clear and least contentious method of revenue distribution. However, it should be pointed out that even the limited flexibility in recent years of the federal/state split from 68/32 to about 70/30 was not achieved without considerable disagreement. In a federal system where the states tried to retain more discretion over their own exemptions, rates, and revenues, the system could not work.

Brazil

In 1988, a number of changes were proposed for the Brazilian VAT system (see below). Before that it was somewhat similar to the German system in that the Federal Government determined the base and rates. However, in all other respects it differed from the German VAT. The VAT base was much smaller as fresh food, agricultural inputs, fuels, minerals, and many services were excluded (and from time to time the federal authorities have granted other exemptions to try to stimulate economic expansion). In Brazil, the tax rates are different for interstate sales (11 percent) and for intrastate sales (17 percent). Moreover, the Federal Government levies the VAT on manufacturers' interstate trade (*impôsto valor agregado*—IVA), whereas the states themselves levy the intrastate VATs through to and including the retail sale. This creates a much more complicated structure than the German system and introduces some peculiar twists. For instance, a final consumer will be tempted to buy out of state because of tax at 11 percent instead of in state where the tax is 17 percent. (This is much the same as the present U.S. failure to collect from certain mail order firms the out-of-state retail sales tax—see discussion below.) Again, a firm buying any of the many tax-exempt inputs will have less credit to offset against its VAT liability on sales than it ought, and the VAT on its value added will be higher. Of course, this simply represents "catch up" on the VAT paid by the final consumer, and the tax collected by the government will be appropriate. However, there is continuous wrangling over "producer" versus "consumer" states. To try to pacify the consumer states, the agreement is to tax out-of-state sales at a lower rate; in turn, this leads to administrative complications and, possibly, to tax evasion.

Proposals for a new constitution (1988) transfer more tax authority and revenues to the states and the municipalities. The state VATs (*impôsto sôbre circulação de mercadorias*—ICMs) will have a wider base including services such as communications, consumer credit charges, electricity, and transport; it will also include fuels and minerals. Most important of all, however, the states are to have the right to set the state VAT rates themselves and to graduate them according to their individual assessment of "essentiality" of the goods and services. Thus, while in other countries there seems to be a general movement toward reducing divergences in tax rates between sectors and between countries to reduce distortions, Brazil seems to be moving in the opposite direction. The states are to get 75 percent of the new ICMs revenue and the municipalities are to get 25 percent. With multiple rates different in each state and a federal VAT on trade between states, the challenges to tax administration are obvious (see also Chapters 12, 13, and 14).

Mexico

Mexico has 31 states and a federal district. The collection and most administration of VAT is in the hands of the states. They remit the entire revenue to the Federal Government and get back only 19 percent. Although the situation is similar to that in the Federal Republic of Germany, the even lower payment ratio to the states seems to affect the efficiency of collection. The Mexican revenue-sharing formula is complicated and based on economic conditions in the different states. It does include a weight for the "effort" made by the state to collect the VAT; effort is defined as the ratio of change in the particular state to the total change in collection. Unfortunately, the reward for effort is small, probably less than a cent for a dollar's worth of effort. Second, the comparison with the revenue-sharing system under the 4 percent cascade tax the VAT replaced shows that previously the states kept 50 percent of the revenue they collected. The introduction of the VAT left the states feeling less enthusiastic about sales tax collection for the benefit of the Federal Government. Third, the federal district, despite having 50 percent of the taxpayers, collects only 20 percent of the revenue. Finally, the collection efficiency of the different states varies substantially; some states have much more sophisticated revenue departments than others and some more cohesive, perhaps federal, effort might be more efficient. These problems are recognized by the authorities, but clearly have deep institutional and political roots that are not connected to the VAT per se, but are an integral part of any federal structure of government.

Argentina

Argentina has opted for a federal VAT administered by the Federal Government. Revenue is shared with the states, using a revenue-sharing formula. Again, fiscal federalism creates problems; the Argentine states have the power to grant exemptions from VAT, which erodes the federal tax base, distorts economic policy and management, and creates administrative complexities.

Review of Issues

These examples illustrate that VAT can work in a federal system, but the states have to have an interest in making the collection system work and perceive that the formula for revenue distribution is fair. The VAT and fiscal federalism constitute an uneasy compromise. The worst alternative is probably that which gives the state administrative power for a federal tax; the best is that which relies on an agreed revenue-sharing formula, changed infrequently, and then only in response to agreed, objectively measured criteria. It should also be noted that in these examples there are no state level sales taxes independent of the VAT (as would be the case, at present, in the United States); this clearly complicates the issue and is discussed later.

Customs Unions

The usual country VAT is levied on a destination principle in that the tax is levied according to the rate levied on the final consumption of the good or service. The VAT is deducted from exports so exports are tax free. Imports are taxed at the full rate of VAT, equivalent to that levied on similar domestic goods.

This structure, in a customs union, still requires all the border VAT adjustments to be made despite the abolition of customs duties. The whole paraphernalia of border posts, customs officials, examinations, documentation, and so on are still needed. In recognition of these problems, the original designers of the EC looked toward a time when the EC VAT could be levied according to the origin principle.[1]

The origin principle implies that VAT is levied where the value added originates and not according to where final consumption

---

[1]See European Community, Commission of the European Economic Community, *The EEC Reports on Tax Harmonization: The Report of the Fiscal and Financial Committee* (1963).

occurs. Of course, for this to happen, the tax bases in the different jurisdictions should be the same and the rates should be identical, otherwise the "catching up" mechanisms of VAT would transfer VAT liabilities across borders. Recent proposals[2] have tried to limit countries to a standard rate, a low and a high rate of VAT, and to encourage a narrowing of the differentials between rates (no more than a 2.5 percent range of each other). Even more recently, the Commission has proposed only two rates, a standard rate between 14 and 20 percent and a reduced rate between 4 and 9 percent. The reduced rate would apply to foodstuffs, energy, water, pharmaceuticals, books and newspapers, and passenger transport.[3] It is recommended that member states fix their rates in the lower half of the band for the reduced rates.

It must also be recognized that it makes little sense to remove border controls for VAT if they remain for excises. Therefore, trade adjustment for such taxes might be shifted to "factory gates and retail outlets following agreement on uniform bases of assessment."[4] Of course, such agreements continue to be elusive and must suggest even further delays in EC tax harmonization.

As far as VAT is concerned, any customs union proposal should ensure that (1) traders are inconvenienced as little as possible; (2) the clearing system places as little additional burden as possible on the national fiscal administrations; and (3) the clearing system is self-financing.[5]

Traders are inconvenienced as little as possible by not having to distinguish between domestic and foreign sales. If traders simply apply the same rate of VAT to sales regardless of their destination, their task is made as simple as possible. Moreover, consider a trader who might consign goods to be trucked from the Netherlands to Italy; then, when the truck is in Paris, he changes his mind and diverts the goods to Germany. Imagine the complications if invoices must be changed (and checked at borders) for the change from zero rating at the Netherlands border to Italy and now altered to Germany. It is easier for the domestic Netherlands exporter to consider all his pro-

---

[2]See European Community, *Report on Behalf of the Committee on Economic and Monetary Affairs and Industrial Policy on the Removal of Tax Barriers Within the European Community* (1987, pp. 5–17).

[3]European Community, *Completion of the Internal Market: Approximation of Indirect Tax Rates and Harmonization of Indirect Tax Structure* (1987, pp. 8–12).

[4]Cnossen and Shoup (1987, p. 82).

[5]European Community, *Completing the Internal Market—The Introduction of a VAT Clearing Mechanism for Intra-Community Sales* (1987, pp. 4–5).

duction as one, regardless of destination. Where it goes after dispatch, as far as VAT is concerned, is no concern of his.

What happens under the Commission's present (1988) proposal is that each member state calculates its total VAT sales and purchases for intra-Community trade for the month by aggregating all VAT charged and claimed by registered traders on sales and purchases to EC members. The net position is calculated vis-à-vis the EC as a whole and not against separate states. So each country creates a monthly statement showing its total VAT input and output figures for intra-Community trade. The statement establishes a claim or payment. Under this system, there will never be "a final balancing of the VAT accounts, but must be seen as part of a perpetually on-going process."[6] Countries have different accounting dates, different rolling programs, different payments on account, and different seasonal trades.

A customs union clearing house will net out the national claims. "Large flows of revenue are at stake and Member States must have reasonable assurances that these revenues, important for their national budgets, are safeguarded."[7] Table 8-1 gives an idea of the size of these flows.

While it is relatively easy to recognize the benefits of such a simple system, it is also easy to anticipate the doubts that may rise about the accuracy of the claims involved in such large flows of money between countries with very different judgments about each other's accounting practices and efficiency. The Commission proposes four elements as means of control. First, the abolition of zero rating, which will extend the self-policing nature of VAT, and changes in the net surplus, which can help identify error trends. (There should be a surplus because VAT on exempt traders will be collected in exporting countries, but not credited in the importing country.) Second, the creation of standardized audit trails. Third, improved control and cooperation at the national administration level. Finally, better coordination at the Community level. All of these are desirable, but whether they are of sufficient substance in practice to persuade member countries to put at risk such large sums may be in doubt. "It would not be surprising if the national revenue authorities were more concerned to check that VAT had been paid on exports (for which they would have to pay money into the clearing system), rather than to scrutinise claims for

---

[6]European Community, *Completing the Internal Market—The Introduction of a* VAT *Clearing Mechanism for Intra-Community Sales* (1987, p. 7).

[7]European Community, *Completing the Internal Market—The Introduction of a* VAT *Clearing Mechanism for Intra-Community Sales* (1987, p. 9).

Table 8-1. EC Countries: Estimated Revenue Flows Resulting from Operation of the Clearing Mechanism[1]

	Net Amount to Be Paid or Received (*In millions of ECU*)[2]	Percent of GDP
Belgium/Luxembourg[3]	−747	−0.62
Denmark	680	0.82
France	2,421	0.34
Germany, Fed. Rep. of	−3,534	−0.38
Greece	437	1.08
Ireland	52	0.21
Italy	147	0.03
Netherlands	−1,509	−0.86
Portugal	77	0.26
Spain	132	0.06
United Kingdom	1,845	0.33

Source: Commission of the European Communities, *Completing the Internal Market—The Introduction of a VAT Clearing Mechanism for Intra-Community Sales*, Annex A (COM(87)323 final, Brussels, August 25, 1987); reproduced in *Intertax* (Deventer, Netherlands), January 1988, p. 26.

[1]Based on 1986 figures and assuming VAT rates of 16.5 percent (standard) and 6.5 percent (reduced).

[2]Positive figures indicate amounts to be received by member states from the clearing account and negative figures indicate amounts to be paid by member states into the clearing account (in both cases for the year as a whole).

[3]For technical reasons it has not been possible to distinguish between the constituent components of the Belgian-Luxembourg Economic Union.

input VAT (which they can, in turn, pass on to the Clearing-House)."[8]

The scheme leaves member states free to set their own VAT rates within the proposed limits. It is persuasively argued that this flexibility is especially needed in a full monetary union where national monetary policies are phased out and discretionary economic policy devolves to fiscal policy.[9] Whether such a clearinghouse scheme could work in federal systems may be debatable. Clearly, Canada with 11 provinces might well be dealt with in a similar manner to the proposed EC clearinghouse system. It is much less certain that such a system could be applied to the 50 states of the United States.

United States

Discussions on the possibility of introducing a VAT in the United States have recognized the crucial problem of the relationship of any

[8]Lee, Pearson, and Smith (1988, p. 23).
[9]Cnossen and Shoup (1987, pp. 74–82).

federal sales tax to the state sales taxes.[10] As shown below, there are four basic options.

United States: Possible Combinations
of Federal and State Sales Taxes

	Retail Sales Tax	VAT
State	a	c
Federal	b	d

Source: See text.

State and Federal Retail Sales Taxes (a + b)

The first possibility would be to run the existing state retail sales taxes in tandem with a federal retail sales tax (options a and b, above). This is a perfectly feasible alternative subject to one overriding criticism: most present state sales taxes use rates of about 5–7 percent; therefore, it would not be worth instituting the mechanism to collect a federal retail sales tax unless the rate was at least 5 percent. So the combined federal and state retail sales tax would be above 10 percent and, as already discussed in Chapter 1, that rate is one that has already proved too high for the retail sales tax, which has weaker collection and enforcement capabilities compared with the VAT. Quite apart from this fundamental problem, there are some additional problems about the precise method by which the piggybacking would be organized and the cost of administration borne between the two recipients of the revenue. Traders might well face increased compliance costs unless exemptions, tax periods, returns, audits, and penalties were identical in both the state and federal VATs. If they are to be identical, why bother to have separate taxes?

Federal VAT and State Retail Sales Tax (a + d)

The next possibility is to accept the existing state retail sales taxes and combine them with a federal VAT (options a and d, above). The principal problem is that compliance costs could rise sharply. Traders would be faced with two quite separate tax systems, probably taxing different goods and services with differing exemptions. There would be different, but frequently duplicated, systems for registration. The

[10]See, for instance, United States, Congress (1972, pp. 1–48), and McLure (1987b, Chap. 9).

calculation of tax liability would be different under each system and would involve quite separate forms and returns. Traders might have to tax some goods only under the state retail sales tax, some only under the federal VAT, and presumably most under both. If there were differential rates of VAT, the problems for traders would be multiplied. Presumably, audits and penalty structures would be different too. The treatment of retail state sales to out-of-state purchases might be complicated; a particular difficulty in the United States is the *National Bellas Hess (v. Illinois Department of Revenue, Case 386 U.S. 753)* decision that frees mail order traders from any obligation to collect taxes from a customer in a state and remit the revenue to that state unless the trader has a business presence in that state. This gives the mail order houses a competitive advantage over other traders.

The combination of options *a* and *d*, although possible, would likely be opposed by commercial interests and would certainly be a complex set of taxes, quite probably involving some cascading (insofar as the present state sales taxes create some cascading).

However, if the states could agree to zero rate and exempt exactly the same goods and services as the federal VAT and simply piggyback their retail sales taxes on the federal VAT, this could be a simpler option. Traders with no retail sales would pay only the federal VAT. Traders with in-state retail sales would have to calculate their state retail sales tax liability from the same figures, and probably a duplicate of the federal VAT form; payment would be made directly to the state. Traders making retail out-of-state sales (the mail order problem again) would have to tax at the rate appropriate to the destination state and remit the revenue to that state. Common sense (which does not always triumph in federal-state relations) suggests there should be joint agreement on audit and enforcement.

Both traders' compliance costs and potential evasion increase if multiple rates are used and increase even further if the rates are different for different regions. The desirable solution is to use a VAT as the way to collect revenue and then use a revenue-sharing formula to divide the resources between the different authorities. This can be arranged to allow each region to have its own rate (including zero if they wish); however, the differences between rates should not be too large otherwise interjurisdictional smuggling becomes a problem.[11]

[11]The problem occurs with VAT within the EC. The most recent example is that of the Republic of Ireland and Northern Ireland. It is estimated that 25–30 percent of color television sets in the Republic have been imported illegally from the north, because VAT and excises make them so dear in the south. See Ireland, Commission on Taxation, *Third Report* (1984, pp. 153–55).

Federal Retail Sales Tax and State VAT (b + c)

The other cross-combination of state VATs with a federal retail sales tax is improbable. It is certainly highly implausible that the states in the United States would shift from their present retail sales taxes to a VAT. Different state VATs with different bases and different rates would involve some peculiar "catching up"; the paperwork to ensure that interstate "exports and imports" were made fully VAT free would be considerable and would constitute a sizable impediment to trade, equivalent to breaking down the United States to the present different VATs of the EC with the added complication of a federal retail sales tax on top.

Actually, this parallel suggests a way in which federal revenue equivalent to a VAT could be collected. After all, the countries of the EC run their independent country VATs alongside a federal EC "VAT" to finance the Commission's expenses and programs. Currently, this "federal VAT" is levied at a maximum of 1.4 percent. It is, however, not really a VAT at all and is assessed only on a theoretical base. To ensure that all the EC members are treated equally, the Commission defines precisely how the theoretical tax base should be calculated from national income figures (see Chapter 7, section on "Problems with the Flat Rate Compensation"). The base is equivalent to that defined in the various EC VAT directives; all the various exemptions and deviations that can be used are ignored. It is on this broadest base that the "federal" EC Commission VAT is levied. Countries that prefer to exempt and zero rate many goods and apply their domestic VAT to a much smaller base (for example, Ireland, Portugal, and the United Kingdom), end up having to pay the federal VAT at 1.4 percent on a base they do not use and equivalent to a much higher effective VAT rate on their smaller base.

The practical problem with this method as a way to collect federal revenue is that each subnational unit (the states in the United States or the provinces in Canada) would have to compute, in an acceptably accurate manner, the household consumption for the state, broken down by various broad headings of goods and services consumed. The advantage is that as the traders are not involved at all in this tax collection, there are no compliance costs; the states can keep their own tax bases and rates but simply have to meet this federal charge, calculated on the basis of estimated value added, from their state revenues, however collected.

Naturally, this federal revenue collection on a theoretical VAT base could be used either in the example above (a federal retail sales tax and a state VAT), or with the final alternative, VAT used by both the federal and state authorities (options *c* and *d*, above).

Federal and State VATs (c + d)

If the federal VAT is levied on the principle of origin, it seems sensible to review the possibility of running the state schemes on the same principle. The mechanics appear straightforward. The VAT liability is assessed in the usual way. Then, either the revenue is collected by a federal agency and the states' share reapportioned from the federal government to the states on the basis of trader location and the state VAT rate, or the traders themselves could make separate returns to federal and state governments.

In practice, it is unlikely to be so simple. If states decided to levy different rates of VAT, then when commodities crossed state boundaries the VAT content of the good would be different, depending on which state the good came from[12]; this means that the tax credit on each invoice could be different for identical goods if they had originated in different states. It would be impossible for traders simply to apply the joint federal and state VAT rate to inputs to obtain their credit against VAT liability on sales, as their state VAT rate could differ from the VAT rate of the exporting state. There is no way out of this dilemma unless full harmonization of rates and coverage is obtained. It is recognition of this dilemma that has finally persuaded the EC to change its intention and not pursue the origin principle.

Even if complete rate and exemption harmonization was agreed, a further problem arises where group returns are allowed. To circumvent this problem, as described elsewhere, the usual practice in the EC is to allow companies with many subsidiaries to consolidate their return to eliminate all intracompany sales and purchases and to make only one return to the authorities. Such an arrangement is convenient and also ensures the allocation of federally collected revenues to the state where the group headquarters is located, unless the group returns specify the retail sales of companies in the group state by state.

Preferred Option

The simplest practical way to run a federal-state sales tax system (including VAT) is to adopt a form of revenue sharing (similar to that in the Federal Republic of Germany). This means the states hand over the sales tax to the federal authorities and, in return, get a portion of the revenue. There might be some slight advantage in the states' transferring the odium of levying sales taxes to the federal government, yet retaining the political kudos of spending, say, 50 percent of

[12]See McLure (1972, pp. 28–29).

the revenue. However, the arguments weigh heavily against this suggestion. The first problem is to agree to the appropriate revenue-sharing system. If the proportions of revenue in force before the new scheme is introduced are accepted, this fossilizes the allocation despite likely changing tax bases. Experience shows that the most contentious and difficult points in a revenue-sharing scheme involve any change in the formula, since what one participant gains can only be at the expense of another.

Second, states would have no latitude to use different rates or different bases. All in all, "this does not seem to be an appropriate or politically viable solution to the issues of intergovernmental relations."[13]

If this solution is unacceptable on grounds of state sovereignty, then the second-best solution is to use federal and state VATs on the same base, with the same definition and treatment of goods and services. Traders would register only once, complete the same forms, and make a single return. Presumably, audit and enforcement procedures could be the same for both federal and state VATs. In practice, this means that the states would give up most of their sovereignty over sales taxation and the solution may, therefore, be impractical. If differential rates were allowed, the invoice method breaks down. States with low tax rates would find their traders importing inputs from high-tax states offsetting their input liability and effectively reducing their VAT liability and the state revenue. Collections by states would become arbitrary.

A possible solution to this problem is to switch to a direct-subtractive method of calculating VAT. That is, each trader in each state would calculate his actual value added from his accounts, and the federal and state VATs could be levied at whatever rates were wanted. The VAT would probably be best calculated by the income tax authorities from the same accounts as the corporate income tax. If a flow of revenue were needed, interim payments related to the last year's figures could be made on account, subject to an annual reconciliation. This is a most attractive option and leaves the states with independence in their rate structures (and, possibly, in their bases) but, of course, it transforms the tax from a sales tax to a direct tax on business.[14]

As the tax content of invoices no longer matters, the intrastate and interstate trade could take place without invoices having to show any tax content. On the other hand, insuperable difficulties appear in

---

[13]McLure (1987b, p. 157).
[14]A variant of this approach is given in Poddar (1986).

compensating traders for the VAT content on international exports if states maintain differential rates of VAT on the origin principle, even using the direct-subtractive method. As McLure commented, "Imports would be diverted through the states with the lowest TVA rates and exports through the states with the highest rates."[15] Attempts to calculate average VAT compensation for exports would certainly contravene GATT rules. However, if a single rate VAT, common to federal and state jurisdictions, is used, then appropriate accurate rebates on exports and taxes on imports can be made. Whether these would be allowed under GATT, as indirect sales taxes, is another question.

Hybrid Options

Apart from these "pure" options, there are possible hybrids. For instance, the federal government could levy a VAT on manufacturing and wholesale sales and leave the states to tax the retail sales separately. This would be the innovation least invasive of state rights. The states could continue to tax retail sales as they do now. Only manufacturers and wholesalers would deal with the federal VAT.

While this sounds an easy way out of the problems discussed above, it has its own drawbacks. As discussed in Chapter 1, all wholesale taxes suffer from the problem of defining a wholesale price. Many manufacturers are also wholesalers; this should not cause a problem unless they come to an agreement with the retailer to allot most of the value added to the retail sale (if the retail VAT rate were lower than the federal VAT rate) or, alternatively, to put the value added into the earlier stages if their federal VAT rate were lower. However, frequently retailers are also wholesalers and their internal transfer price becomes crucial in allocating value added between the federal and state VATs. Even if the rates were the same for both federal and state VATs, the different value of the tax base (depending on the internal transfer price) could distort the apportionment of revenue between the federal and state authorities.

Trying to levy any sales tax at the wholesale level has always led to complex regulations to determine standardized discounts on retail prices to get back to the wholesale price. Alternatively, markups can be specified on factory gate prices to get at the wholesale value from the production end. In either case, the problems are difficult and any standard solution creates its own inequities as clearly not all producers

[15]McLure (1972, pp. 29–30).

Table 8-2. Advantages and Disadvantages of Alternative Tax Coordination Schemes

Tax Options	Advantages	Disadvantages	Assessment
1. **RST/RST** (uncoordinated)	Familiarity of RST;[1] state control of tax base and rate	Cascading of RST; difficulty of BTAs, vulnerability to evasion at high rates;[2] severe compliance problems;[3] no gain in *National Bellas Hess* area[4]	Not practicable
2. **RST/RST** (coordinated)	Familiarity of RST;[1] unification of bases; facilitates solving *National Bellas Hess* problem;[4] retains state control of tax rate	Cascading of RST; difficulty of BTAs; vulnerability to evasion at high rates;[2] loss of state control of tax base	May be feasible
3. **RST/credit VAT**	Familiarity of state RST; federal tax avoids cascading; accurate BTA for federal tax; administrative advantages of credit-method VAT; state control of tax base and rate	Severe compliance problems;[3] no gain in *National Bellas Hess* area;[4] cascading of state RST; inaccurate BTAs for state RST	Not practicable
4. **RST/subtraction VAT**	Simplified compliance on sales; familiarity of state RST; state control of tax base and rate	Defects of subtraction-method VAT;[3] standard problems of RST (cascading, BTAs); no gain in *National Bellas Hess* area[4]	Not practicable
5. **VAT surcharge/ VAT**	VAT avoids cascading; accurate BTAs; state control of tax rate	Not administratively feasible;[3] loss of state control of tax base	Not feasible
6. **VAT/VAT** (federal collection)	Simplified compliance;[1] saving in administrative cost; general advantages of VAT (no cascading, BTAs); state control of tax rate; implies solution to *National Bellas Hess*[4]	Loss of state control of tax base; appearance of complexity	May be feasible
7. **Tax sharing**	Simple compliance; saving in administrative cost	Loss of fiscal autonomy[3]	Probably not acceptable to states

Table 8-2 *(continued)*. **Advantages and Disadvantages of Alternative Tax Coordination Schemes**

Tax Options	Advantages	Disadvantages	Assessment
8. Revenue sharing	Simple compliance; saving in administrative cost	Loss of fiscal autonomy[3]	Probably not acceptable to states

Note: RST = retail sales tax and BTA = border tax adjustment.
Source: Charles E. McLure, Jr., *State and Local Implications of a Federal Value-Added Tax* (Washington: Academy for State and Local Government, 1987), p. 18.
[1]Indicates important advantages.
[2]Indicates potentially deciding disadvantages.
[3]Indicates overwhelming disadvantages.
[4]*National Bellas Hess* decision frees mail-order houses from obligation to collect sales tax on out-of-state sales—see text.

conform to the average. This option should not be ruled out but it does introduce its own undesirable elements.

Without using the federal manufacturer or wholesale VAT or the innovative direct-accounts method of calculating VAT (with a single common rate), the only really viable option seems to be a federal-state agreement on a common VAT base, with either a revenue-sharing agreement or, much less desirable, differential rates and cross-state border transactions subject to zero rating and import taxes as practiced in some customs unions; the administrative implications of this make it a poor option. Table 8-2 summarizes a series of options similar to those just discussed. McLure favors options (2) and (6), and if the retail sales tax is ruled out because of possible widespread evasion at rates over 10 percent, then this leaves only option (6), "an approach that entails considerable loss of state fiscal sovereignty."[16]

Whatever form of federal VAT is chosen, it should be pointed out that substantial administrative problems are likely. Present state retail sales taxes are made easier to administer by the exclusion of many services. The U.S. Internal Revenue Service (IRS) is used to administering withholding taxes (about 70 percent of receipts) but "in a VAT there is no such thing as withholding. The entire amounts that are due to the government must be paid by the registered taxpayers voluntarily at the end of each taxable period."[17] The suggestion is that compared with the taxes the IRS is used to dealing with, the VAT would require higher staffing ratios and more audit (see Chapter 13).

[16]McLure (1987a, p. 23).
[17]Casanegra de Jantscher (1987, pp. 303–304).

Canada

In 1987, the Canadian authorities published a proposal for sales tax reform.[18] Three possible sales taxes were suggested. First (and apparently preferred), a national sales tax. Although never exactly specified in the text, this represents a direct-subtractive-accounts-based VAT (see Chapter 1). The tax would have to be at a single federal rate on a uniform base for all provinces. However, provinces would be able to levy their own local variants on the rate. Thus, for example, the federal rate might be 10 percent, but Ontario might supplement this with a provincial rate of 3 percent, while Quebec might opt for 5 percent. Businesses engaged in interprovincial trade would apply the rate to goods at the combined rate (13 percent or 15 percent) in the province to which the goods were shipped (the destination principle). Provinces that decided to have no truck with the sales tax would be taxed at a zero rate. The tax would be federally administered on an accounts basis probably by the Income Tax Commissioners. The authorities maintained, "even though different businesses at different trade levels may have collected taxes at different rates, the national system ensures that the final tax collected on a product is the same as it would be under a combined retail sales tax of [X] percent in the province in which the goods are consumed."[19]

All this is possible. Taxpayers would be faced with a tax return that would have to show 11 columns (10 for other provinces and 1 for exports) for both inputs and outputs. This certainly sounds complicated. However, statistics on interprovincial trade indicate that the vast majority of businesses would only have to fill three or four columns, and interprovincial trade is not all-encompassing for all trades. (However, consider the problem applied to the 50 states in the United States.) Special rules would be needed for the cross-border flow of services, such as transportation and telecommunications. A computerized central clearinghouse would ensure that provinces were credited with the revenue appropriate to the value added originating in their province.

If the provinces cannot be co-opted to agree to the joint tax, then the federal authorities are prepared to go it alone with either a federally administered direct-subtractive VAT (called, as in New Zealand, a "goods and services" tax) or a straightforward VAT. The main difference between the two is that the direct-accounts-based tax neces-

[18]Canada, Department of Finance, *Tax Reform 1987: Sales Tax Reform* (1987).
[19]Canada, Department of Finance, *Tax Reform 1987: Sales Tax Reform* (1987, p. 50).

sarily implies a uniform base and a single rate VAT, whereas the second option could involve exemptions and multiple rates. It would require retailers to "keep track of their sales in four categories: sales subject to both federal and provincial taxes; sales subject to federal tax only; sales subject to provincial tax only; and sales exempt from both taxes."[20]

The national sales tax involves both federal and provincial agreement on the base but allows different rates. The federal only goods and services VAT is simple to operate but cannot accommodate exemptions and multiple rates. The federal VAT would be more flexible but also more costly to administer. However, "Each option is far better than the current federal sales tax and would be a major improvement in Canada's tax system."[21]

Municipal Sales Taxes

Not only do central governments and states levy sales taxes, so do cities and metropolitan areas. It is certainly undesirable to have yet another tier of VAT or retail sales tax imposed on traders. Many of these local taxes are undesirable in themselves. They can use numerous, extremely low rates (such as, 0.25 percent or 1 percent). They frequently list particular commodities or trades to be taxed; discriminations and distortions abound.

The obvious solution is to abolish such minor taxes at the time the VAT is introduced and settle with the local authorities to share in the VAT revenue by a formula or straight percentage. Other tax bases might be transferred to the localities (for example, property and vehicle licenses) to give an independent revenue source. However, the reality is that it may be easier, although still very difficult, to get states to agree on a common VAT with some revenue-sharing formula than it would be to get municipalities to do the same.

[20]Canada, Department of Finance, *Tax Reform 1987: Sales Tax Reform* (1987, p. 58).
[21]Canada, Department of Finance, *Tax Reform 1987: Sales Tax Reform* (1987, p. 58).

CHAPTER 9

Transitional Problems

I've always said we're only one President away from a VAT.
—CHARLES E. MCLURE, JR., reported in *Tax Notes*, Tax
Analysts (Arlington, Va.) January 12, 1987, p. 93

Academic discussions compare an economy where the VAT is operating with the economy and tax system which existed before. Not much attention is paid to the actual problems of getting from the state before VAT to the position after VAT. That is, the *process* of change from one state to another is assumed to be instantaneous.

In practice, the introduction of VAT should involve some sensitive initiatives on the part of the authorities to educate traders and the public about the new tax and to react with understanding to the concern of taxpayers about taxes already paid before the changeover. In the same way, there are problems about contract prices and continuous supplies that also complicate the changeover. However, the first problem concerns the public's perception of the VAT. Then there are problems about registration, educating traders about VAT, and the precise transitional treatment of inventories, capital goods, contract prices, installment prices, and various other small but worrying transitional matters. These topics are dealt with in the next sections.

Publicity

Countries that do not use the VAT can build up quite unreasonable fears about its introduction. Politicians argue that it will encourage the growth of the public sector (for instance, as anticipated in the United States), traders expect high compliance costs, and the public resigns itself to inevitable price increases. Publicity is important to explain the new tax and to combat such fears. Without a spirited publicity campaign, there is the danger of hostility in many quarters undermining the VAT before it even gets started. However, this point is now well taken, and in some cases the publicity has been so well produced and traders have been so overwhelmed by advice that the actual "VAT date" has been something of an anticlimax.

The authorities must assign a senior officer to be responsible for publicity. He should be involved in the early discussions on the form and structure of the VAT and gradually devote more of his time to explaining the application of the VAT as its introduction approaches. His activities should include the following:

(1) He should prepare a short explanatory booklet on VAT. There are numerous examples of these around the world.[1] The format is well established—about 30–50 pages explaining how a VAT works, and then an explanation of the broad heads of the legislation in simple language but sufficiently detailed to be useful to different traders.

(2) He should prepare, in collaboration with the technical staff, the staff guide and manual. These publications should be ready for the staff training sessions well in advance (a year) of the date of VAT introduction. (See also Chapter 12 on transitional staffing problems.)

(3) He should arrange for talks on radio and television and for press conferences. For instance, the Korean Ministry of Finance prepared and distributed 80 films on VAT; in New Zealand, amusing videos were made illustrating how (mythical) manufacturers of possum bikinis might deal with the VAT. Perhaps a little more sedate, the Dutch prepared a series of 13 ten-minute television programs that were screened early on one evening a week, with a second showing later to allow viewers to check up on the information given in the first showing.

(4) He should organize lectures and talks to public and professional groups. The success of VAT depends on the cooperation of the traders and for this reason it is important that they should feel their views have been taken into account. Therefore, meetings should be arranged for the authorities to explain the tax to businessmen and trade associations and, most important, for the authorities to listen to what traders have to say. At these meetings, neither the basic principles of the tax nor the rates of VAT would be a matter for discussion. Above

---

[1]See, for example, Ireland, Revenue Commissioners, *Guide to the Value Added Tax* (1972); or New Zealand, Inland Revenue, *GST Guide* (1986); or, for a very simple guide, New Zealand, GST Coordinating Office, *Working with GST* (1985).

all, "academic" discussions on such occasions about whether the tax falls on businesses or households are not profitable. What is useful is an exchange of views on the circumstances in which simplified invoices might be used and the particulars to be given on them—price tags and lists, the tax adjustments to be made in connection with discounts, returned goods, bad debts, simplified schemes to enable small and medium-sized retailers to calculate their monthly sales under each of the different rates of VAT without having to separate individual transactions, the period for which sales documents would have to be retained, and the procedures relating to the import and export of goods.

The VAT representatives might also wish to cover more fundamental matters such as the length of time to be allowed for payment of tax, the possibility of deferring payment of VAT on imports until the lodgment of the next monthly return, and even the question of having less frequent tax returns. It is of immense assistance in launching the new VAT if it is demonstrated to the trade representatives that their views are not only listened to, but are, where acceptable, acted upon.

The various organizations, interested professional associations, and chambers of commerce should be invited to submit their observations in writing within a certain time limit. These should be critically analyzed by the members of the central VAT coordinating unit and concise memoranda prepared for the consideration of the VAT commission or the ministry of finance on the revenue cost and administrative feasibility of the various suggestions.

In at least one case (New Zealand), the authorities employed a private sector businessman to organize the public relations for VAT (the GST Coordinating Office), including publicity, television, and videotape commercials. This appears to have been a most successful experiment.[2]

The Coordinating Office has at least three functions: "to explain the tax reform; to raise the level of public understanding; and to co-ordinate the efforts of the various organisations involved in the [VAT] education programme."[3] A nonpolitical organization, the Coordinating Office prepared and supplied leaflets and specialized booklets to households and various trade groups such as taxi proprietors, clubs, associations, charities, and farmers.

Finally, in at least one case (Korea), the authorities organized three

---

[2]See the description of the introduction of VAT in New Zealand in Douglas (1987, pp. 217–21).

[3]Douglas (1987, p. 218).

nationwide test runs to try out the new tax. In March, May, and July 1977, over 90 percent of the traders in the sample group concerned completed trial run filing exercises.

Registration

The VAT taxpayers must register, usually at their local office, before the tax starts. Regulations try to encourage registration some three months before the actual firm date for goods and services becoming liable to VAT; this allows the officials to get the computer and files readied, and avoids a log jam in a last minute hectic rush to register. One country (Indonesia) was remarkably generous in setting the date for the initial registration some three months after the start of the tax and this led to a slow initial rate of registration; a week before the VAT was due to start, only some 23,000 out of a potential 100,000 traders had registered. To have a smooth introduction of VAT, it is important that as many taxpayers as possible should be registered well in advance, and certainly before the introduction date. Then publicity material can be sent to registered traders and educational visits made. Registration involves recording the taxpayer's name, the firm's name and address, telephone number, date of registration, date of commencement of business, and the allocation of a VAT registration number. For statistical purposes, it is also useful to record the trade or industrial classification of the business.

Once the tax is in place, it is sometimes overlooked by commentators that the registration "churns" as new taxpayers enter the list and firms disappear. This churning creates a considerable administrative burden. It can be lessened by some concessions: for instance, by allowing small clubs or associations to register in the name of the club, rather than having to reregister each time the annually elected secretary changes, or by not requiring reregistration when one person of a partnership changes—see Chapter 17. Nevertheless, in general, there is a continuous onerous burden in keeping the VAT register up to date.

It is interesting that experience in some countries suggests that small taxpayers seem to see benefits in registration that outweigh the costs of compliance. Apart from the obvious benefits of receiving net refunds when large capital purchases are made and getting credit for inputs, there is the "avoidance of the appearance of commercial insignificance which accompanies nonregistration."[4] Having a VAT

---

[4]Turnier (1984, p. 459).

registration number on your invoices looks more organized and important. This is true particularly for the professions where the absence of a registration number betrays the fact of low turnover and when the client frequently is registered and wishes to claim a deduction for VAT paid.

Educational Visits

No matter how efficient the publicity about the VAT is, the most effective way to ensure that traders fully appreciate their obligations and rights under the VAT is the educational visit by officials from the local or district VAT office. Naturally, these visits should be made before the VAT is introduced. In practice, this is not always possible, but an educational visit should be paid to every trader not later than six months after VAT starts.

For many small and medium-size firms, the educational visit from the district tax office may well be the first opportunity they have of relating the legal requirements of VAT to their own particular situation. The impression of helpfulness and understanding of the taxpayers' problems by the local officials can contribute greatly to the successful launching of VAT and its future smooth administration. While the visiting officers should not be naive, the approach must be on the assumption that whatever may have been the position in the past, the great majority of taxable firms will be anxious to fulfill their obligations conscientiously. In most countries now using VAT, it was found that however extensive the overall publicity may have been, the general run of traders were puzzled by the implications of VAT and were in need of direct guidance on how to comply correctly, rather than having any intention to be dishonest.

The time available for each visit will be limited (in the Netherlands, for instance, the preliminary visit lasted only one and a half hours, but even so involved some 600 tax administrators to get all the visits done in time); but it serves no purpose unless it affords a taxable firm every opportunity to have its questions amply explained.

The following are an indication of the points that should be covered by the officials.

General

(1) Interview the owner or other responsible representative of the business.

(2) Confirm that the particulars on the application form for registration are correct.

(3) Check that the name agrees precisely with the official record.

(4) Confirm that the trader is chargeable to VAT by reference to the nature of his activities.

(5) If a trade classification coding is provided, confirm that the business is classified correctly.

(6) Give the taxpayer a copy of the VAT guide if he has not already received one. Check whether he appreciates the implication of VAT in relation to both purchases and sales. Clear up any points of difficulty.

(7) Draw particular attention to the chapter in the guide dealing with the completion of the returns and payment of tax and emphasize the importance and obligation to file returns and pay tax promptly.

(8) Ensure that the point when VAT becomes due is clear and unambiguous.

Invoices, Records, and Accounts

(1) Confirm that the firm has established a proper system of recording particulars of all invoices of purchases and sales.

(2) Unless the firm already has a satisfactory bookkeeping system in operation, provide a copy of the official accounts book for VAT if one is issued.

(3) Ensure that whatever system is adopted in relation to VAT it will provide for:

(a) Accounting for tax on all taxable supplies, including taxable self-deliveries.

(b) Proper recording of tax paid on taxable purchases and services and that only inputs that are properly deductible are claimed.

(c) Correct calculation of apportionment between taxable and exempt elements in the case of partly exempt activities.

(d) A system under which claims for repayment can be effectively checked by the local tax office.

(e) A VAT account being properly set up and maintained.

(f) Any distinction between current VAT obligations and year-end obligations (reconciliations).

Premises

Inspect factory premises—workrooms, stores, warehouses, show-rooms, and so on and consider whether all activities are correctly reflected in the return made for VAT.

Transitional Problems: Stocks and Inventories

The VAT frequently replaces sales taxes that have been incorporated in stocks and capital. If the tax replaced is, say, a single-stage tax, calculation of the tax content of inventories is relatively easy. If the tax replaced is a cascade turnover tax, then broad estimates must be made. For instance, in the Netherlands, refunds were made on the basis of a special list prepared by the Ministry of Finance, giving the turnover tax content of various goods that it would have been legitimate to refund had the goods been exported on December 31, 1968.[5] However, the basic question is whether such relief should be given at all. Some countries give it fully (Korea), others over time (the Netherlands and the United Kingdom), some partially (New Zealand), and some not at all (Chile and Indonesia).

Why Relief Is Justified

Most countries do grant some relief for taxes previously paid and included in the value of stock in trade (and stationery). Three main reasons can justify such treatment. First, from the point of view of equity, if no relief is allowed for the previous tax when goods taxed under the earlier regime are sold, there will be double taxation because some of the old tax would be included in the base on which the new tax is levied. Second, and more important from the point of view of getting VAT launched successfully, would be the danger of manufacturers increasing their prices unduly and permanently at the time of the changeover to compensate themselves for that temporary element of double taxation. Third, manufacturers might cut down their holdings of taxable raw materials and some processed goods during the period running up to the VAT introduction, planning to replenish them after VAT comes into force. This could disrupt trade, cause bottlenecks, and distort the opening months of the VAT.

[5]Cnossen (1981, p. 228).

How Relief Is Calculated

There are two basic ways to refund the sales tax previous to VAT on stocks. First, there can be a physical inventory of merchandise. The risk of this is that the inventory may be botched or done too casually, erring in favor of the company. Monitoring such physical inventories is extremely difficult. In practice, the traders' estimates have to be accepted unless their claims are wildly out of line with their previous pattern of trading. This leads to the second method; if a check has to be made in any case to assess how their physical inventory claim compares with the usual pattern of trading stocks, why not simply base the allowance on an average of their previous year's stocks? Or the previous year's quarter matching that before the VAT is to be introduced? This is basically what the Portuguese authorities allowed. Unfortunately, the law authorizing this treatment was published in August 1984, the year before the VAT was introduced on January 1, 1986. This, of course, allowed traders to anticipate their claims and perhaps artificially inflate their inventories for the last quarter of 1984, knowing this would validate their inventory for the last quarter of 1985, before the VAT was introduced. Another danger of using this method is that some firms, say, those with rapidly increasing needs for stocks, might be treated unfairly. This was also recognized in Portugal and a later law allowed a refund based on actual inventories as an option, provided that stock rotated in less than six months.

Generally, as the "average holding method" is likely to create many inequities, it may be better to require, at least on paper, a physical inventory.

Persons Who May Claim Relief and Methods of Making Claims

Only persons registered for VAT are entitled to relief for tax paid on stock in trade held at the date of the changeover. Moreover, it is not necessarily true for all registered persons in all tax systems; for example, manufacturers do not pay a wholesale tax, therefore, no question of double taxation arises in relation to their inventories and there is no case for relief. Traders wishing to claim relief must make a detailed valuation of stock on hand, or relate their stocks to some average holding at the changeover date, or within a period of, say, ten days before or after that date, showing appropriate adjustments for purchases and sales in the interim. They have to submit their claims on a prescribed form. To anticipate that some might try to inflate their inventories spuriously to claim a rebate for tax they never paid, reference on the form can be made, as mentioned above, to an average monthly amount of inventory. Forms for this purpose should be issued to all persons registered for VAT.

Stock Qualifying for Relief

Relief is confined to stock in trade (inventory) held in the country, provided that the stocks have borne the previous tax now being replaced.

For the purposes of relief, stock-in-trade comprises:

(1) Goods the taxpayer had bought for resale.

(2) Goods that the taxpayer had manufactured for sale (including partly manufactured goods and by-products.

(3) Raw materials and semiprocessed goods.

(4) Repair materials.

(5) Materials that are used in the manufacturing process, such as fuel, lubricating oil, detergents, and chemicals.

(6) Stationery, which is often allowed as a stock on which sales tax has been paid, although it is not strictly a stock in trade (see below).

No relief is granted for:

(1) Goods held outside the country or in a bonded warehouse or a duty-free shop.

(2) Goods awaiting clearance inward through the customs.

(3) Goods that have been cleared outward through the customs.

(4) Investment goods such as buildings, plant, machinery, and office furniture.

(5) Expense stock, such as loose tools and office stationery.

In general, as mentioned above, an actual physical stocktaking is probably required as near as possible to the changeover date. Where feasible, the stock should be listed at cost price, but for goods in the process of manufacture a different method of valuation has to be adopted. The situation in relation to different categories of taxpayers is examined in more detail below.

Treatment of Manufacturers, Wholesalers, and Retailers

No difficulty arises as regards raw materials for which proof of the sales tax borne on the stock is readily available. The same applies to goods in various stages of manufacture when the purchasers of the raw materials can produce invoices. The position is more complicated, however, if the tax has been suffered at one or more stages back from the manufacture of the final product or has cascaded through the distribution chain. A claim for such prior-stage tax should not be admitted without documentary proof of the tax base, or on the basis of typical examples furnished by the traders, although a generous interpretation should be applied in determining the amount of the relief where precise calculation would not be practicable and where the claim appears well founded.

Construction Industry

The stock qualifying for relief consists of building materials on hand and work in progress. For work in progress, the value on which relief is given is that relating to the proportion of the contract completed on the date of introduction of VAT, less any progress payments made up to then. The phrase used in New Zealand was "to the extent that materials and other work have been permanently incorporated in or affixed on the work on site."[6] The value of the work in progress includes the value of any work done by any subcontractor engaged by the main contractor. The subcontractors are entitled to relief for work in progress. To preclude double relief being granted, the value of the work in progress by the main contractor would have to be reduced by the value of the work of the subcontractors in progress. The figures would be determined by reference to recognized valuation practices carried out by an independent valuer.

Treatment of Importers

The VAT is imposed on the value of imports including customs duty, and this applies whether the importer is or is not a registered person. At the start of VAT, the importer will have on his hands goods imported by him which may have borne an existing sales tax at the time of importation and will be chargeable to VAT when they are subsequently sold. To avoid double taxation, the importer must be given relief for the amount of the previous sales tax paid on importation. This should be determined with precision from the import entry documents.

[6]New Zealand, GST Coordinating Office, *Understanding GST: A Guide to the Legislation* (1986, p. 26).

How Relief Is Given and Checked

A claim for stock relief should be submitted to the district tax office during the first taxable period after the introduction of VAT. Separate types of claim forms might be provided for (1) manufacturers, (2) building contractors, and (3) importers. The forms are issued automatically to all persons registered for VAT. The claim form incorporates stock sheets for completion by the claimant, and full details would have to be given of the different types of stock involved with valuations and the amount of sales tax borne on them.

In the local offices, the small claims would merely be checked for arithmetical accuracy, and the inventory compared with past returns made by the taxpayers. A field check should be made in perhaps 5 percent of the cases, or where VAT educational or explanatory calls are made on the factory, warehouse, or business premises. The larger claims might be examined more critically, especially with regard to the nature of the business, the kind of stock declared to be on hand, and the value of such stock in relation to the known sales or other information available in the tax office. Some traders should be selected for full examination at the taxpayer's premises. Large claims for relief should be authorized only after personal verification by the district chief. If, for any claim, it is evident that an excessive amount is erroneously included, an appropriate reduction should be made. Such adjustments can be contentious. In the words of one official, they were "energetically disputed." However, if definite evidence of fraud is established, such as a claim for nonexistent stock, there should be a prosecution for penalties and full publicity given to the court proceedings.[7]

Transitional Problems: Capital Goods

In a number of European countries, the cost of relief for inventory stock and capital goods held at the introduction of VAT was so high the relief had to be spread over one or two years.

There is a connection between the relief for stock in trade and the

---

[7]An interesting twist to the problems of stocks at the changeover to VAT occurred in Morocco, when some traders in Casablanca complained that the VAT would mean they would find it more difficult to "launder" illegal stocks of contraband and goods stolen from factories and from the port; they proposed a solution whereby the Ministry of Finance would "shut its eyes" to the existence and disposal of illegal stocks. Habibi (1986, p. 58).

often parallel problem of previously traded capital goods relieved of tax under the VAT. If nothing is done to anticipate this sudden reversal, it is likely that in the period before VAT traders will delay buying taxable capital goods until they can claim the full credit under VAT. To give the credit immediately on the changeover invites bottlenecks in capital goods orders. If the existing taxes are computed and are significant, some prorating of the full relief under VAT may be desirable.

In the Netherlands, the total cost of the relief was f. 1.6 billion, equivalent to 32 percent of the turnover tax receipts in 1968.

> The refunds on inventories were financed from the proceeds of a temporary investment levy, that is, the full deduction for tax paid on capital goods was not granted immediately, but was phased in gradually. The aggregate burden of turnover tax on capital goods in 1968 was estimated at 9 per cent of value. An immediate full credit would have involved a budgetary loss estimated at f. 5.0 billion, a sacrifice the Government was not prepared to make. Moreover, the credit would have encouraged businessmen to defer their purchases of capital equipment. The credit, therefore, was phased in, initially over a 3-year period, according to a scheme of 30-60-90 per cent of the tax. For budgetary reasons, the scheme was later extended by one year and changed twice. Ships, airplanes, and machinery used in the textile and shoe industries were exempted from the investment levy since these goods had not borne turnover tax or were utilized in depressed sectors. Actual receipts of the levy were estimated at f. 3.8 billion, or 13 per cent of total value-added tax revenues from 1969–72. Since the tax on capital goods would be completely eliminated under the new tax, it was decided that the investment allowance under the income tax would be phased out simultaneously.[8]

Table 9-1 gives some examples of the different treatments. Budgetary as well as economic considerations are involved because granting full VAT credit immediately on capital equipment means a substantial loss of revenue, and encourages the deferral of purchases of such goods until after the start of VAT. In the Federal Republic of Germany, for example, the cumulative burden of the old tax on plant and machinery was estimated to be 8 percent. The solution adopted was to allow full credit for capital goods bought after the changeover, but at the same time a special investment tax on capital expenditure was imposed from the changeover to VAT. It was set at 8 percent for the first year to correspond with the approximate burden of the former cumulative tax. It was reduced by stages over the succeeding five years

---

[8]Cnossen (1981, p. 228).

Table 9-1. VAT: Special Transitional Measures in Selected Countries

	Year VAT Introduced	Fixed Business Assets	Inventories
Austria	1973	A tax was levied at 12 percent in 1973 declining to 2 percent by 1977 and abolished in 1979; thus assets that had been taxed before VAT were only gradually freed from taxation	—
Belgium	1971	Only a partial credit (increasing during 1971–77) was allowed	Refunds spread over 1971–75, one third of which paid in treasury certificates with specific redemption dates
Chile	1975	—	No credit given
France	1968	Investment goods acquired in 1966 by enterprises liable to VAT were allowed full credit; those not subject to VAT received no credit; those subject to VAT for the first time in 1968 received only 50 percent credit	Full credit allowed spread over six years
Germany, Fed. Rep. of	1968	A tax of 11 percent levied from 1973 to 1975	—
Hungary	1988	No relief allowed	Full relief given by a price index
Indonesia	1985	—	No credit given
Ireland	1972	Investment goods were not taxed before VAT	Full allowance for wholesale tax
Italy	1973	The turnover tax paid on assets acquired before the VAT introduction but after June 1972 could be credited against VAT provided that the deduction did not exceed one half of the VAT due	25 percent of the turnover tax paid on raw materials and semifinished goods bought after August 1971 could be credited against VAT
Korea	1977	—	Full relief for replaced taxes in inventories
Luxembourg	1970	During 1970–72 a partial credit allowed: 50 percent in 1970 and up to 85 percent in 1972	Full refund of the cascade turnover tax
Mexico	1980	—	Credits allowed of 6 percent in the commercial sector and 4 percent for industrial firms for the 4 percent cascade tax
Netherlands	1969	Credit phased in over a period of a few years at 30-30-60-67 percent of tax	Refunds spread over two years

Table 9-1 *(continued).* **VAT: Special Transitional Measures in
Selected Countries**

	Year VAT Introduced	Fixed Business Assets	Inventories
Norway	1970	Tax of 13 percent levied on all business assets	—
Sweden	1968	A temporary 10 percent investment allowance granted in 1968 to encourage businesses not to delay their investment decisions	The old single-stage retail tax meant inventories were not taxed
United Kingdom	1973	Assets were already free of tax	Any wholesale tax paid was refunded in full when the food was sold from stock

Source: Various country reports.

after which it no longer applied. Provisions along rather similar lines
were adopted in Belgium and, as mentioned above, in the Netherlands. Presumably some such transitional provision for capital goods
might be made when South Africa substitutes a VAT for the present
sales tax that taxes capital goods.

Other Transitional Problems

Continuous Supplies

It is not practicable to start charging VAT on continuous supplies,
such as electricity and gas, on the day VAT is introduced. In most
countries such a charge is levied from the date of the first meter
reading after the start of VAT. If supplies are not metered or the
continuous supply is at a fixed periodic rate, VAT can be charged
proportionally based on the period covered by VAT over the total
period covered.

Effects on Contract Prices

Contracts entered into at a fixed price before VAT should have their
prices adjusted by the amount of the VAT applicable from the date of
introduction. This would include contracts for continuous hiring or

leasing (to which the proposals given in the section on "Construction Industry," above should also be applied where appropriate). Interestingly enough, this even applied to membership subscriptions in New Zealand and it was suggested that clubs might increase subscriptions at the beginning of the year to anticipate the introduction of VAT and their tax liability.[9]

Supplies: Treatment of Installment Payments

The treatment of installment payments made after the changeover to VAT for supplies made before the start of VAT gave rise to difficulties in some countries. The normal practice is that where the charge to VAT for goods purchased under an installment arrangement is the delivery of the goods, no charge is made on installments after the introduction of VAT. In such cases the title of ownership has legally passed before the changeover to VAT. On the other hand, if the title does not pass until payment of the final installment, the change to VAT normally applies only to the payments made after the introduction of VAT.

Exports Already Taxed

Some goods may have borne a sales tax, now replaced by the VAT, but are to be exported after the introduction of the VAT. Obviously, if at all possible, refunds should be granted in such cases. If this proves impossible, the difficulty is likely to be very temporary and advance notices, drawing attention to the problem, can help exporters anticipate such a tax liability arising, so that they can time their exports to ensure that as much as possible occurs under the new, and more advantageous, VAT.

Problems from Different Definitions of Taxable Transactions

The VAT legislation usually defines a taxable transaction and tax due date as the invoicing of goods (the essential element of the invoice VAT) or the performance of services. If the delivery of goods happens earlier, the VAT liability may be defined at that moment. Other sales taxes may use different definitions; for example, on a turnover tax it

[9]New Zealand, GST Coordinating Office, *Clubs, Charities and Associations & GST* (1986, pp. 15–16).

could be the sale of goods and not their delivery that determines when the tax is due.

Depending on the relative rates of VAT and the sales taxes it replaces, taxpayers may have incentives to predate their invoices or deliveries or both to reduce their tax liabilities. Special transitional provisions may be needed to cope with this sort of falsification; the first and last sequence numbers of invoices over the transitional period must be reported on the tax return. A taxpayer may be required to calculate and record periodic running totals in his account books.

Changes in VAT Rates and Liability to VAT

Finally, it should be noted that many of the problems discussed above are repeated, albeit in less serious ways, when the rates at which VAT is levied change, when the tax base is changed, and sometimes when traders register for the first time or when they deregister. Examples abound:

> Alterations and other home improvements, previously zero-rated, become liable to VAT at the standard rate of 15 percent on June 1, 1984. The government has refused to include any transitional provisions in the Finance Bill to deal with the problems, despite strong representations, so leaving the ordinary rules of law to apply. The sharp change of rate combined with the long lead-time on contracts in this industry make the problems more serious than those that have occurred on previous rate changes. . . . Consumer advice agencies have, predictably, been inundated with enquiries as to liability to pay, VAT in these circumstances. The position taken by VAT Offices is that 'the application of [the rules] in any particular case depends on the terms of the contract between the parties concerned; Customs and Excise cannot advise on individual cases.'[10]

Generally, VAT authorities are reluctant to create special provisions for such transitory costs consequent on rate changes or changes in definition; besides, VAT is exceptionally well suited to avoid the usual problems associated with the inventory costs of excises and single-stage pre-retail taxes where rates change, since full credit is claimed automatically under the VAT.

[10]Bragg and Williams (1984, p. 214).

PART II

Effects of VAT

CHAPTER 10

Effects of VAT on Prices

O chestnut tree, great-rooted blossomer,
Are you the leaf, the blossom, or the bole?
O body swayed to music, O brightening glance,
How can we know the dancer from the dance?
—W.B. YEATS, "Among School Children"

The effects of VAT, like those of most other taxes, are difficult to assess empirically. It is almost impossible to link, unequivocally, the change in VAT to the change in prices, efficiency, investment, employment, or whatever. There are usually too many variables to relate one change uniquely to another. Indeed, in some countries the introduction of the VAT coincided with the massive upheavals following the sharp increases in oil prices in 1972/73 and 1976 (Ireland, 1972; Austria, Bolivia, Italy, and the United Kingdom, 1973; and Honduras, Israel, and Peru, 1976), and the effects of the VAT pall besides those of the oil price changes. In some instances, we can outline what economic analysis might suggest and in a few examine the evidence of the actual outturn.

In all countries politicians and the public anticipate the impact of VAT on retail prices with trepidation. Studies are conducted to estimate the possible outcomes, and governments, with varying degrees of commitment, try to protect the public from price increases. A characteristic of all introductions of the VAT is uncertainty. Traders, particularly small businessmen, are uncertain what effect the VAT will have on their liquidity and on the costs of compliance; the public hear bits and pieces of information, and newspapers sometimes enhance the air of crisis by "scare" stories. In these circumstances, traders might well attempt to widen margins as a contingency against uncertainty, and the public may be persuaded to accept higher prices because speculation has suggested they should expect them.[1] Let us examine first, what common sense suggests should happen to prices when a VAT is introduced and when VAT rates change, then, how governments actually coped with the problems in real life, and finally review such empirical evidence as there is.

Price Change Forecasts

The first point is whether or not the VAT is intended to increase revenue or simply replace revenue lost from other taxes reduced or replaced. Table 10-1 shows that, in the majority of cases, the VAT introduction was designed to be an equal yield replacement for other taxes. In this case, the analysis must consider the effects of reducing the other tax or taxes. In an extreme example, replacing eight taxes in Korea by VAT could imply a complex mixture of changes in factor prices and producer prices at manufacturing and wholesale levels. Similarly, in Colombia, the changeover to a full VAT was combined with changes in income, property, capital gains taxes, and the abolition of many tax incentives. The problem in most countries is to find the data in sufficient detail to allow any ex ante estimates. Korea was unusual in taking great care to prepare a sample of several hundred businesses to assess the extent to which each of the taxes to be replaced by VAT were reflected in prices and, by implication, the price reduction or increase that might be expected when the taxes were removed and VAT imposed. This was a major exercise but it paid off in the detailed substantiated position the Government was able to take when the VAT was introduced (see below).

Even if reasonable data are available, some major theoretical issues must be faced. What is to be the assumption on shifting? The VAT is expected to be passed forward fully both because the legislation usually clearly assumes that this will happen and because, as a general sales tax, there is likely to be a general awareness on the part of traders that all will be affected similarly. Sometimes traders will take advantage of the confusion to raise prices "exorbitantly" and even to levy VAT when they are not liable (for example, taxi drivers in Portugal).[2] Naturally, differential rates will cause changes in relative prices. All traders will bear tax and compliance costs and wish to recoup them.

---

[1]For an examination of these issues and a different presentation of evidence, see Tait (1986).

[2]"Portugal: Effects of VAT," *World Tax Report* (1986, p. 9).

Moreover, the public is likely to be aware of a major tax change and gloomily expect the worst. But every business could pass along to its customers the full amount of its VAT liability only if the "enactment of the VAT were accompanied by repeal of the law of supply and demand."[3] Of course, the VAT need not be passed forward. It is quite possible to put forward the alternative that the money supply should not be increased to accommodate the increase in prices, that aggregate demand should fall because of other exogenous factors, and that traders might be forced to absorb the VAT, passing back its burden in lower factor rewards. As P.J.N. Sinclair, in his review of *Value-Added Tax: Lessons from Europe,* commented: "For example, suppose VAT is replacing other, less efficient, indirect taxes, with an unchanged total yield. The reduction in the distortionary waste generated by the tax system behaves like a rise in aggregate output. The demand for money should therefore rise. So long as this is the only effect upon the demand for money, and the supply of money is unchanged, the overall price level should fall."[4]

Whether or not forward shifting would be inflationary, as opposed to a once and for all change in the level of prices, depends not only on the possible offsetting changes in other taxes and an accommodating money supply but also on the reaction of wages, transfer payments, liquidity, and psychological effects.[5]

As Musgrave suggests,[6] consider five policy settings:

1. Wages flexible, monetary policy permissive
2. Wages downward rigid, monetary policy permissive
3. Wages flexible, monetary policy stabilises product price level
4. Wages downward rigid, monetary policy stabilises product price level
5. Wages flexible, monetary policy stabilises factor price level.

He remarks that case (2) might be the most realistic and that, therefore, "an absolute price increase is the most likely result."

For an increase in VAT to be inflationary would not only require forward shifting and an accommodating credit policy but also a determination on the part of labor to maintain its real consumption, increasing wages sufficiently to offset the increase in prices due to VAT. The ability of labor to do this, of course, depends on numerous considerations outside the compass of a discussion of VAT. One study shows that an increase in VAT, even if fully offset by a reduction in

[3]Ture (1972, p. 100).
[4]Sinclair (1983, p. 382).
[5]See the discussion in Tanzi (1983).
[6]Musgrave (1986, p. 215).

Table 10-1. Examples of Effects on Prices of Introduction of VAT

	Date VAT Introduced	Taxes Mainly Replaced[1]	Designed Effect on Revenue	Immediate Price Change General[2] (In percent)	Immediate Price Change Attributed to VAT[3] (In percent)	Other Concurrent Tax Changes	Any Other Concurrent Changes	Price Controls
Argentina	Jan. 1975	Wholesale sales tax	Equal yield	37.2	Minor	Provincial tax changes	Utility rates increased; devaluation	Yes, but relaxed
Austria	Jan. 1973	Cascade wholesale tax	Equal yield	2.4	Nil	Lower income taxes	Strict credit control	Yes
Belgium	Jan. 1971	Cascade wholesale tax	Equal yield	2.6	Nil		Increased wages	Yes
Bolivia	Oct. 1973	Multistage ring system	Equal yield or increase	9.5	Nil	New luxury tax rates; increased excises		No
Brazil	Jan. 1967	State sales and municipal industrial taxes	Equal yield	15.8	Nil			No
Chile	Mar. 1975	Cascade turnover tax	Increase	146.7	Minor	Taxes on gasoline, income, and property raised	Utility rates increased and rent controls relaxed	No
Colombia	Jan. 1975	Simpler VAT	Increase	12.9	Nil	Income, property, and capital gains taxes changed	Many incentives abolished	No
Costa Rica	Jan. 1975	Multistage ring system	Increase	...[4]	Nil	Increased excises		No
Côte d'Ivoire	Jan. 1960	Manufacturers VAT	Equal yield	—	—			No

Country	Date							
Denmark	July 1967	Wholesale tax	Increase	8.0	5.0	Lower income tax	Increased transfers and increased wages	No
Ecuador	July 1970	VAT was a new tax; some turnover taxes on mining and manufacturing replaced	Increase	8.7	(7.1)	Mining taxes reduced	Devaluation	No
France	Jan. 1968	Simpler VAT	Equal yield	2.1	1.0	Tax exemptions abolished and income tax adjustments	Increased wages	Yes, after VAT introduced
Germany, Fed. Rep. of	Jan. 1968	Cascade retail tax	Equal yield	1.5	0.6			Monitored
Honduras	Jan. 1976	Multistage ring system	Increase	1.0	Nil		Rapidly expanded credit	No
Indonesia	Apr. 1985	Production tax	Equal yield	3.5	Nil			No
Ireland	Nov. 1972	Wholesale and retail sales tax	Equal yield	5.5	Nil	Some tariff reductions		Monitored
Israel	July 1976	Various sales taxes	Increase	17.9	(9.0)		Increased wages and tax allowances	No
Italy	Jan. 1973	Central and local government sales tax	Equal yield	6.3	Nil		Increased wages	No
Korea	July 1977	Eight sales taxes representing 40 percent of revenue	Equal yield	4.1	Minor	Changed excises	Proposed VAT rate of 13 percent reduced to 10 percent	Yes
Luxembourg	Jan. 1970	Cascade wholesale tax	Equal yield	3.5	Nil			No
Madagascar	Jan. 1969	Cascade production tax	Increase	3.2	Nil			No

Table 10-1 (continued). Examples of Effects on Prices of Introduction of VAT

	Date VAT Introduced	Taxes Mainly Replaced[1]	Designed Effect on Revenue	Immediate Price Change General[2] (In percent)	Immediate Price Change Attributed to VAT[3] (In percent)	Other Concurrent Tax Changes	Any Other Concurrent Changes	Price Controls
Mexico	Jan. 1980	Cascade production taxes	Equal yield or increase	—	—	Lower border VAT of 6 percent		No
Morocco	Jan. 1962	Cascade production tax	Equal yield	2.4	Nil	Change in corporate and production taxes		No
Netherlands	Jan. 1969	Cascade wholesale tax	Equal yield	5.2	1.5	Lower income tax	Increased wages	Yes
New Zealand	Oct. 1986	Wholesale tax	Increase	8.9	6.5	Reduced income tax		No
Nicaragua	Jan. 1975	Multistage ring system	Equal yield	.. [4]	Nil	Reduced customs duties		No
Norway	Jan. 1970	Sales taxes on 65 percent of consumption	Loss	7.8	5.8	Reduced income and property taxes	Increased transfers and wages	Yes
Panama	Mar. 1977	Wholesale tax	Increase	5.0	(3.1)	Stamp taxes reduced and increased excises	Increased utility rates	No
Peru	July 1976	Cascade production tax	Increase	27.1	(13.5)			No
Portugal	Jan. 1986	Cascade sales tax and minor duties	Equal yield	10.0	(3.0)			No

Senegal	Mar. 1961	Manufacturers VAT	Equal yield	—	—		No
Spain	Jan. 1986	Cascade sales tax	Equal yield	2.8	2.0	Major administrative changes	Monitoring
Sweden	Jan. 1969	Retail sales tax	Equal yield	1.6	Nil	1 percent payroll tax to offset lost revenue	No
Turkey	Jan. 1985	Nine production taxes and duties	Equal yield	40.0	(10.0)	Wage earners rebate and vouchers	No
United Kingdom	Apr. 1973	Multirate wholesale tax	Loss	4.9	0.7	Selective employment tax removed	Monitoring
Uruguay	Jan. 1968	Manufacturers, wholesale, and retail taxes	Equal yield	66.3	(53.0)		No

Sources: IMF data and various country reports.

[1]This column is as accurate as a brief summary can be: "cascade production tax" refers to a cascade tax on business turnover, restricted to the production stage; "cascade wholesale tax" extends the turnover tax to include the wholesale stage; "cascade retail tax" extends the turnover tax to include the retail stage; "manufacturers," "wholesale," or "retail" taxes are single-stage taxes—some operated on a ring system, others on a credit system.

[2]The consumer price index for the quarter before VAT is deducted from that for the quarter after VAT and the difference expressed as a percentage increase.

[3]Figures in parentheses represent broad estimates based on examination of the data; other figures are based on external and contemporary commentaries.

[4]Monthly data unavailable for part of the period covered.

income tax, so that a worker on the average wage has an unchanged real net income, can still produce a rise in all unionized wage rates.[7] This increase in business costs could trigger the truly inflationary path of prices.

In addition to wages, there is the disturbing thesis put forward that recipients of transfer payments do not bear the burden of indirect tax increases, except perhaps in the short run, as governments will ensure that their real living standards are maintained.[8] Thus, a significant burden may be transferred to income taxes, raising again, in an intensified form, the possible reaction of organized labor.

Though, as Alan Walters points out, referring to the 1979 U.K. increase in VAT (from rates of 10 percent or 12 percent to a uniform 15 percent) fully offset by reductions in income tax, "it is difficult to see why such an obvious *step*—increase in certain prices, combined with *downward* pressure on the prices of excluded commodities, should lead to expectations of *higher* inflation (if, by inflation, we mean the *persistent* increase of prices year after year). Rationality would suggest expectations of lower price increases in future years."[9]

The actual ways in which the authorities have tried to estimate the effect on prices range from almost back of the envelope guesses to sophisticated general equilibrium analyses. However, most have used partial equilibrium studies and some, depending on the taxes to be replaced and the data available, an input-output model for a static general equilibrium price determination. The first difficulty is to allocate the taxes replaced, and the VAT (possibly at different rates), to the available input-output sectors. This inevitably means some substantial judgments, as there are likely to be fewer input-output sectors than taxed products. Having calculated the industrial-sectoral price changes these have to be reassigned to the constituent products that make up the household budget in the usual surveys and in the consumer price index; this demands another set of heroic assumptions. However, the anticipated price changes have matched the actual fairly closely and the apparent impact on inflation has been much as expected (see below).

Numerous countries, including Korea, Mexico, Morocco, New Zealand, Portugal, and the United Kingdom, have used partial equilibrium analysis to anticipate the effects of introducing VAT and the

[7]Sampson (1986, pp. 87–91).
[8]Browning (1978) and Browning and Johnson (1979); also see United States, Department of the Treasury (1984, Vol. 3, pp. 91–92).
[9]Walters (1986, p. 77).

results have, on the whole, turned out fairly well. Naturally, it is a bit difficult to know what influences what. Because the authorities have estimated the price changes that might occur, to some extent, those are the price changes that will be permitted to happen. As is shown below, governments undertake extensive actions to influence prices, from moral suasion to price controls, and these themselves reflect the judgments already made about expected price changes. Another difficulty, especially in complex substitutions, is that in some sectors, prices are calculated to fall (for example, the U.K. purchase tax and some Korean tax rates), and it is always easier for government to limit price *increases* than to require a price reduction. Usually in the estimates of the effect of the VAT substitution on the consumer price index, it is better to err on the side of caution when the *net* effects of price increases are offset by price reductions. Experience shows price reductions rarely reflect the full tax reduction and some allowance should be made for this. In the Philippines, many traders did not roll back their prices by the full amount of the sales taxes replaced by VAT. The VAT base thus included the previous sales taxes. However, in some complicated cases, the outcome appeared close to the forecast. In Korea, processed food, beverages, furniture, and some medical goods were expected to increase in price, whereas confectionery, electricity and fuel, and clothing were forecast to fall. The net effect was designed to be approximately neutral. In the event, the authorities assigned little or no net price effect to the introduction of the VAT. Indonesia expected a small (possibly 0.5 percent increase in the price level), and though there was a year on year consumer price increase of about 3.5 percent, only a trivial amount might be attributed to VAT.

Most countries have not had the data to permit the use of general equilibrium analysis and, to date, none of the VATs introduced have been tested against a general equilibrium prediction. The differences between this and partial analysis, for the VAT, can seem large. Conventional incidence analysis involves the attribution of taxes replaced and the VAT to commodities, but consumers will substitute out of taxed commodities, and general equilibrium could catch this adjustment.

The review that follows of the experiences of ten countries and their attempts to cope with the sensitive problems of price changes at the introduction of VAT may strike U.S. readers as describing extraordinarily interventionist policies. It is difficult to imagine the United States introducing a VAT in 1988 using a price freeze (Belgium, Korea, the Netherlands); price and wage controls (the United Kingdom); a national prices commission (Ireland); or profit margin control (Ireland, the Netherlands). The climate now is much more in favor of letting market forces operate and perhaps if these countries were to introduce VATs now, such elaborate checks would no longer be used. Nevertheless, the more recent examples (for instance, Hungary, Portugal, and New Zealand) show that governments remain extremely concerned about the reaction of consumers as well as of voters to the effect on prices of introducing a VAT or changing VAT rates. Perhaps these brief case studies continue to have something to teach authorities about VAT and prices. However, the basic message is that there is no reason to expect VAT itself to be inflationary; its effects on prices, if any, will be once and for all.

Actual Policies[10]

Belgium

Belgium changed over to VAT on January 1, 1971. Previously it used a complicated form of cascade tax with a rate of 7 percent extending to all stages except the retail level. This was modified for certain industries by the adoption of a single rate, purporting to be equivalent to the aggregate of the amount payable at the various chargeable stages. Certain basic foodstuffs were exempt, and some other foodstuffs bore a single-stage tax at 7 percent. In addition, there was an invoice tax of 0.7 percent on turnover. Capital equipment was taxable.

Since the changeover to VAT entailed a measure of credit for tax on capital equipment, and since a high proportion of Belgian industrial production was exported, it meant that for the same yield there would be a heavier tax burden on the domestic market. Moreover, basic foodstuffs, which were exempt before, became taxable under VAT.

Four rates of VAT were proposed, designed to correspond very broadly with the composite tax burden under the previous system. Basic foodstuffs were taxed at the bottom rate of 6 percent. A tax rate of 25 percent applied to goods chargeable at the former luxury tax rate, which had varied between 18 percent and 23 percent.

Price controls had operated in Belgium since 1945. A price freeze was in force for the first three months after the introduction of VAT on January 1, 1971. Applications to change prices had to meet a three-month advance notice. This measure, and a firm policy on price rises afterward, limited increases to 2.3 percent in the first three months of 1971 and to 5 percent for the whole of that year, which was not much higher than for the preceding years.

---

[10]This section has benefited greatly from help given by Seamus Duignan.

An interesting aspect of the Belgian situation is that the standard rate originally proposed for VAT was 20 percent with an intermediate rate of 15 percent. These rates were considered necessary if the degree of tax avoidance which allegedly existed under the earlier tax were to continue under VAT. Business organizations strongly resisted those rates, and they were ultimately fixed at 18 percent and 14 percent, respectively. It was generally believed that during the period of uncertainty about the rates, many businesses widened their profit margins to protect themselves against any adverse effects that the higher rates proposed might have had on sales later on.

Denmark

A comprehensive VAT at 10 percent on goods and services was introduced in Denmark on July 3, 1967, to replace a wholesale tax at 12.5 percent, which contained several exemptions, including food, medicines, fuel, and services. Because of the extended scope of VAT, its yield was estimated at double that of the earlier tax. It was accepted that the change was going to have a significant effect on prices. A reduction of income tax, especially for those at the lower levels of income, was promised and subsidy payments were applied to dairy products such as butter, cheese, milk, and cream. While the purpose of the subsidy payment was partly to relieve the consumer, the main object was to protect the producer in case home consumption of these items would fall if prices were to go up.

The effect of the VAT on prices in Denmark can be calculated fairly accurately, because there were two price indices, one, the consumer price index, which took account of tax changes, and the other, the wage regulation index, which, since 1963, excluded taxes. Between April and October 1967, the consumer price index rose by 8 percent and the wage regulation index rose by 3.1 percent, so that the VAT can be regarded as responsible for a rise of 4.9 percent in the consumer price index during the period. An increase of this order was expected because food and services were being taxed for the first time. No special price control measures were instigated. However, fairly large wage increases partially compensated for the erosion of real consumption.

France

From January 1, 1968, VAT, which had existed in France for many years, was extended to the retail stage, and services were also brought within the system. Previously, VAT was levied only to the wholesale stage, and there were separate taxes on retail sales and on services. These separate taxes were, of course, abolished. Bread, milk and other dairy products, and preserved meats were exempt under the earlier VAT, and bread, milk, and certain foodstuffs in general consumption were exempt from the retail sales tax. All these items became chargeable under the new VAT, so that a small increase in the consumer price index was expected.

In fact, during the first three months of 1968, the rise in the consumer price index was 1.15 percent, not all of which was attributable to VAT—probably less than 1 percent. Analyses of the prices of 78 products were prepared, and these showed that the differences in prices before and after the changeover correctly reflected the tax changes.

Federal Republic of Germany

On January 1, 1968, Germany replaced its multistage sales tax on goods and services, which extended down to the retail stage, by a VAT with a normal rate of 10 percent and a reduced rate of 5 percent on foodstuffs and agricultural products such as raw wool, raw hides, and timber. The change was to be revenue neutral and was not expected to have any significant effect on prices in general.

The rate of the replaced cascading tax was 4 percent (except at the wholesale stage where it was 1 percent, with an exemption for agricultural foodstuffs). The effective rate on a given item depended on the number of stages through which it passed before reaching the final consumer, but the broad implications of the change were that clothing and most foodstuffs would cost a little less, while services and building construction would cost more. Clothing would be taxed at 10 percent, compared with the earlier tax of 11 or 12 percent, and margarine, bread, potatoes, apples, beer, canned vegetables, sugar, eggs, coffee, and so on at 5 percent, compared with the earlier tax of about 6 or 7 percent. On the other hand, certain agricultural produce previously exempt, and meat formerly taxable at 4 percent, would bear VAT at 5 percent. The largest tax increases were for services, of which gas and electricity were the most controversial.

Price changes directly attributable to VAT worked out very much as expected, and accounted for a once and for all rise of 0.4 percent in the consumer price index. The largest increases were in the services sector, namely, hotels (4 percent), electricity (6.3 percent), gas (9.9 percent), public transport (5.2 percent), and cinemas (6.4 percent).

The VAT was introduced at a time of mild recession in the German economy, and this was thought to contain undue price rises. The states (Länder) operated a price monitoring system and no further control on prices was deemed necessary. All the larger traders were well versed in the mechanics of VAT, but there were problems with some small firms, which came under a special scheme where they were taxable at 4 percent without any credit for prior-stage tax. Some of these erroneously provided for tax at 10 percent in repricing on the changeover to VAT. Consumer magazines and consumer organizations, however, kept a close watch on prices, and because of their vigilance unjustified increases were quickly corrected.

More recently, it has been held that the price level has risen by more than the tax increase in the wake of increases of the VAT rate, which "suggests that enterprises use value-added tax increases as an opportunity to raise their own prices."[11]

Ireland

The changeover to VAT in Ireland on November 1, 1972 was in itself price neutral because, except for a few minor items of little commercial significance, the rates chargeable under VAT were calculated to produce precisely the same revenue as those under the replaced wholesale and retail sales tax on the estimated bases (even to the point of using some extraordinary rates to do so—such as 16.37 percent). Nevertheless, considerable public attention focused on the possible impact of the changeover on prices, and there was anxiety in case traders might try to widen margins.

The National Prices Commission, operating a system of price restraint, in its monthly report of March 1972 examined the likely outcome for prices of the changeover to VAT; it concluded that any effect should not be significant. The Commission added that in all cases that would come before them after the introduction of VAT, they would not recommend any price adjustment based on an increase in the absolute margin of profit or the application of that margin to a price that included any element of the tax paid at previous stages of production. If, following the changeover, prices were to rise appreciably it would be due to an unjustified reaction to VAT by manufacturers and distributors or to cost increases other than VAT. They announced that they would monitor the prices of a wide range of

[11]Dengel (1987, p. 279).

products during the period before and after the introduction of VAT and would publish the results.

The autumn review of the Commission, published in January 1973, bore out the forecast that VAT would have no significant impact on retail prices. While some price increases were reported, they were due either to seasonal factors or to passing on, with the approval of the Commission, higher costs of raw materials to the manufacturers. These were reflected in the rise in the consumer price index of 1.5 percent between August and November 1972.

Apart from the National Prices Commission, another organization, the Advisory Council on the Transition to VAT, which was appointed by the Minister of Finance to consider any transitional problems arising from the implementation of VAT, also directed its attention to prices. It carried out a publicity campaign through advertisements in newspapers, radio, and television, stressing that there would be no increase in the effective rate of tax on almost all goods and services, and recommending shoppers to report any cases of overcharging ascribed to VAT to the Department of Industry and Commerce, which had increased its inspectorate to investigate any such complaints.

In addition, the daily newspapers opened "Prices Desks," where consumers could report complaints or make inquiries about prices either in person or by telephoning. Where an instance of overcharging was brought to light, the name and address of the trader was published by the newspaper, as well as any observations he might offer to explain his case.

All in all, the Irish example might be considered a good example of a combination of government guidance on prices, official monitoring, and public awareness, successfully ensuring a smooth changeover to VAT with little net effect on prices.

Korea

The Korean VAT, introduced in July 1977, was the first VAT in Asia and as such was a major innovation; after all, the Japanese had toyed with the idea of a VAT since the 1953 Shoup mission, but had nervously postponed such a dramatic change in taxation. The Korean experiment was a brave initiative.

It was particularly courageous in that it involved the abolition of eight taxes, putting at risk a large proportion of revenue and, though the entire tax transformation was designed to be revenue neutral, there had to be numerous changes in relative prices. Naturally, there was the possibility, as mentioned above, that the changes might be asymmetrical so that prices would go up but other prices would not go down or would fall less than they ought. For instance, fuel, electricity, and clothing were expected to fall in price, while processed food, beverages, and furniture were expected to increase: the forecast change in the wholesale price index was 0.155 percent and the actual outturn was 0.061 percent; the retail price change was expected to be about nil and turned out to be an increase of about 1 percent. Overall, the limitation of the effect on prices, given the complex tax substitution and the great uncertainty, was an unqualified success.

The authorities consulted trade organizations before and during the design of the VAT and looked for cooperation from trading organizations. Government control over factory and wholesale prices for some 250 products produced under monopoly and oligopoly circumstances meant that such prices could be held constant. Just before the introduction, a widespread campaign informed the public of recommended prices for many consumer goods. Finally, the VAT was designed to be revenue neutral at a rate of 10 percent, but the authorities, nervous about the large amount of revenue at risk and the potentially disastrous consequences should there be a significant revenue shortfall, increased the statutory introduction rate to 13 percent. However, in what appears in retrospect to have been an inspired psychological move, just before July 1, 1977, the Government used a clause in the VAT legislation allowing it to adjust the rate plus or minus 3 percent (supposed to be for purposes of macroeconomic stabilization) to reduce the initial rate to 10 percent. As it turned out, this 10 percent rate was noninflationary and produced somewhat more revenue than expected. Oddly enough, the statutory rate of VAT remained 13 percent for many years, although the effective rate has continued to be 10 percent.

Netherlands

The VAT was introduced in the Netherlands on January 1, 1969. Before that there was a cascade-type turnover tax which stopped at the wholesale stage. Under it, certain unprocessed foodstuffs and fuel for domestic consumption were exempt.

The VAT was initially chargeable at a rate of 12 percent with a reduced rate of 4 percent applied, broadly speaking, to the areas that were formerly exempt. The changeover, therefore, entailed taxing basic foodstuffs and services for the first time. Although VAT was expected to yield the same revenue as the system it replaced, an increase in the consumer price index was inevitable. The Netherlands

Central Planning Office put the estimated rise at 1.3 percent. Agricultural products were expected to increase by 3.2 percent and other foodstuffs by 0.8 percent; textiles, clothes, and footwear by 5.1 percent; and furniture by 4.8 percent. On the other hand, decreases were anticipated in certain sectors, including a fall of 1.7 percent in transport and public utilities.

In the first three months following the changeover, prices rose by 5.2 percent, but the authorities considered that VAT accounted for only 1.5 percent of this. The main factor in the rise appears to have been wage increases that were not matched by increased productivity. An important and trend-setting wage increase in the heavy metal industry provided for a rise of 6.5 percent; in addition, the higher social insurance contributions by employers brought the total increase in wage costs to 9.5 percent. There was an impression, too, that some manufacturers and traders were using the occasion of the changeover to VAT to compensate themselves unduly for wage and other costs.

There had always been a system of voluntary price restraint in the Netherlands and no special measures were taken on the changeover to VAT. However, to meet a later incipient inflationary situation, the Government brought in a price freeze on March 14, 1969. It compelled certain industries, whose price increases were considered excessive, to roll them back. This helped to stabilize the position. Moreover, no increased labor costs due to further pay awards could be passed on in prices and no increases in profit margins were permitted; but increases attributable to the earlier rises in wages were built into the new price structure. The extent of this increase, however, was not very considerable. In the first nine months of 1969, the consumer price index rose by 6.2 percent, and this was in part accounted for by foodstuffs, which became taxable for the first time under the new system (the average increase in price in the four preceding years was about 5 percent a year). Prices fell significantly after March 1969, and the freeze was relaxed gradually in June and September 1969.

New Zealand

The VAT (known in New Zealand as the goods and services tax—GST[12] was introduced on October 1, 1986. The authorities made many estimates of the likely impact of replacing the wholesale tax by a VAT

---

[12]Suspected named after the Assistant Secretary to the Treasury, Graham Scott, as the "Graham Scott Tax"—see Douglas (1987, p. 209).

but, broadly, the once and for all expected increase in prices was about 5 percent.[13]

The authorities went to great lengths, using an extensive advertising campaign to reduce the public's fear about price increases and to contain any possible attempt by traders to take advantage of the uncertainty to widen margins. It was estimated that about half of the 10 percent VAT yield would be needed to replace the previous sales tax; this left about a further 5 percent net increase to be reflected in higher prices. As it turned out, some traders did increase their margins and the actual outturn for the first quarter, after the introduction of VAT, was a price increase attributable to VAT of 6.5 percent. The Government confidently expected the rate of inflation to return to the previous trend in successive quarters, as it did, so that the introduction of VAT can be seen, not as inflationary, but as a once and for all blip.

Sweden

Sweden brought in VAT on January 1, 1969, at a rate of 10 percent on tax-inclusive prices. It replaced a retail sales tax with the same rate. As, however, capital equipment was taxed under the retail tax, but tax free under VAT, the yield from VAT was expected to be less than from the former tax. The loss was made good by a 1 percent payroll tax.

The changeover was effected smoothly, and was looked on as being little more than a change in the method of collecting sales tax. The information for traders was entrusted to a large degree to the trade organizations, which trained their members on the operation of the new system.

The impact on prices was almost neutral, because the rate of VAT was identical with that of the previous retail sales tax. During the first eight months of 1969 the consumer price index rose by 2.3 percent, compared with an average annual increase of 5 percent in each of the preceding four years.

No special price restraint was instigated at the time of the changeover, but when the rate of VAT was raised to 15 percent (again on tax-inclusive prices) in January 1971, control measures were introduced, limiting price rises to the amounts justified by the change in rate.

A later econometric study suggests that the VAT is reflected in higher prices within a quarter of a year. It is held that the 1971 tax

[13]See, for instance, Douglas, *Statement on Taxation and Benefit Reform 1985* (1985, p. 10); see also Stephens (1987, p. 336).

increase (from 15 percent to 20 percent) increased the consumption deflator by 2.5 percent, compared to no tax increase; "however, the model does not include the institutional frame of labor market negotiations which is very important for Sweden."[14]

United Kingdom

The VAT was introduced in the United Kingdom on April 1, 1973 to replace two taxes: (1) the purchase tax, a single-stage selective sales tax then chargeable at three different rates (25 percent, 18 percent, and 11.25 percent, and these rates represented substantial reductions from previous levels in preparation for the introduction of VAT) on the wholesale values of many goods; and (2) the selective employment tax, which was assessed not on the price of goods but on the number of employees and the nature of the business.

Charges that VAT would be inflationary and regressive were made from the time the new tax was announced. Fear was expressed, in particular, that unless full relief were given for inventory stock held at the changeover, retailers would have to raise their prices unduly to recoup themselves for the double taxation burden. Anxiety on this score was removed when the Government eventually agreed to give full relief.

In May 1972, the National Institute of Economic and Social Research forecast that a VAT, which was to raise exactly the same amount of revenue as the taxes it would replace, would lead to an increase of 0.5 percent in the consumer price index, and that a 10 percent VAT with the coverage then envisaged might increase consumer prices by more than 1 percent.

A price and wage standstill instituted in November 1972 was to be succeeded by the "stage 2" relaxation at the time of the introduction of VAT in April 1973. Toward the end of 1972, consultations on price control began between the government departments directly concerned with price restraint. The outcome was the Counter-Inflation Bill, introduced in Parliament early in 1973. It contained a clause about retail prices in the period of transition to VAT, drafted after consultation with the Confederation of British Industry and the Retail Consortium, on the basis that a special temporary price control could be set in motion by an individual consumer's complaint about a particular price. The complaint would lead to an investigation of the

---

[14]Andersson (1987, p. 49).

facts; if it were found that the price change did not correctly reflect the tax changes, a notice would be served on the shopkeeper requiring him to correct the price. Disregarding the notice would be an offense. This approach was adopted because public anxiety about the impact of VAT on prices had to be allayed. It was recognized that, initially, many retailers might be genuinely perplexed and that not all instances of apparent overcharging could be regarded as profiteering. Some discretion and flexibility was considered necessary.

The U.K. changeover to VAT is unusual in that few countries have made the transition from taxing goods at high rates to taxing them at a uniform rate. (In some cases, the taxes were extremely high; jewelry, a few years before VAT, could have borne tax at 60 percent of its wholesale value.) The changes in relative prices were substantial, even though the size of the rate differentials had been narrowed in anticipation of VAT. The January before VAT was introduced provided a good illustration of the shoppers' dilemma. Should they buy goods at winter "sale" prices or wait till April when prices ought to be reduced under VAT?

The basic scheme to provide the public with facts on which to make judgments was to provide lists of goods and services with the price changes that could reasonably be expected for each, quoted first in ranges of pence per pound; then a typical price before VAT, and the typical change (or range of typical changes) in that price. The first government advertisements, full newspaper page length, appeared in mid-March with the lists divided between three panels headed "about the same," "up," and "down." Calculating the price changes, item by item, and checking whether the typical prices really were typical entailed inspection of shop shelves, catalogs, and advertisements, a task undertaken by the tax authorities. The lists were shown in advance to the Confederation of Industry and the Retail Consortium to give them an opportunity of commenting on the typical prices, the assumptions made about retail markups, and the detailed effects of abolishing the selective employment tax.

Apart from the press, radio, and television publicity, a leaflet giving the same information about prices was prepared with the title "Your Guide to VAT Prices," and 5.5 million copies were distributed free through post offices.

The press reports of the time show that, thanks to the effectiveness of the government publicity campaign, the changeover went smoothly, with, as anticipated, a large number of consumer durables becoming cheaper, and many services rising by up to 10 percent. There were complaints that some firms were not passing on the benefit of the abolition of the selective employment tax, but immediate attention was given to this, and the authorities said that over the country as a whole, the movement of prices and changes were very close to the estimates made when the publicity campaign was launched a month previously.

The Retail Consortium, representing about 90 percent of large retailers, had few reports of difficulties, and this is again ascribed to the thoroughness of the government advertising campaign.

The Central Statistics Office with the Treasury and Customs and Excise undertook a study of the increase in the retail price index over the four-week period from March 20. The April retail price index showed an increase of 1.9 percent on the previous month. Of this, it was estimated that higher food costs accounted for about 0.75 percent and raw materials another 0.5 percent. Since neither of these were affected by VAT, the result of the transition to VAT was less than 0.7 percent. Ministerial statements at the time said that the effect of the tax changes on prices had not been significant.

A survey carried out by the Consumers Association, whose representatives visited 800 retail shops three weeks before the introduction of VAT and again in the second week of April, said that of 2,188 prices checked, 40 percent went up less than expected, while 20 percent rose more than expected or were reduced by less than the amount set out in the shoppers' guide. They found there was more evidence of "fiddling" in the services, such as restaurants and cinemas, than in the shops.

Reports to the responsible ministries showed that during April the government inspections of complaints about prices proved that about 70 percent of them were unjustified and, in another 25 percent, voluntary reductions were secured as a result of the inspectors' inquiries. In only 12 cases, where the complaints were considered justified, was the trader unwilling to alter his price. In these cases, the inspectors issued statutory notices restricting the prices in accordance with the provisions of the Counter-Inflation Act, 1973.

The success of the U.K. introduction of VAT, despite a most difficult set of relative price changes, is principally due to the care the authorities took in cooperating with industry and the public to anticipate and meet their major concerns about VAT. The Government published periodic VAT bulletins for traders and tried to pay an educational visit to each before VAT was introduced. The monitoring of price changes by official agencies, consumer watchdogs, and newspapers undoubtedly provided a coverage that convinced everyone that the Government was serious about controlling unjustified price increases and ensuring price reductions when traders had been relieved of tax. Table 10-1 summarizes the main effects on prices of the introduction of VAT.

Table 10-2. Countries Allocated to Categories for Effect on Consumer Price Index

	Introduction of VAT		Changes in VAT Rates	
Cases	On data alone	Considering all circumstances	On data alone	Considering all circumstances
Shift	Bolivia Denmark Ecuador Haiti Netherlands Panama Turkey Uruguay	Denmark Ecuador Haiti Netherlands Panama Turkey Uruguay	Denmark, 1977	Denmark, 1977
Acceleration	Argentina Chile France Guatemala Ireland Israel Italy Mexico Morocco Peru Sweden United Kingdom	Guatemala Israel Italy Mexico Peru	Netherlands, 1971	
Shift plus acceleration	Honduras Norway	Norway	Ireland, 1980	Ireland, 1980
Little or no effect	Austria Belgium Brazil Colombia Costa Rica Côte d'Ivoire Germany Indonesia Korea Luxembourg Madagascar Nicaragua Senegal	Argentina Austria Belgium Bolivia Brazil Chile Colombia Costa Rica Côte d'Ivoire France Germany Honduras Indonesia Ireland Korea Luxembourg Madagascar Morocco Nicaragua Senegal Sweden United Kingdom	Belgium, 1983 Netherlands, 1973 Netherlands, 1976	Belgium, 1983 Netherlands, 1971 Netherlands, 1973 Netherlands, 1976

Source: Alan A. Tait, "The Value-Added Tax: Revenue, Inflation, and the Foreign Trade Balance," paper presented at World Bank Conference on Value-Added Taxation in Developing Countries, Washington, April 21–23, 1986.

Other Empirical Evidence

Changes in the consumer price indices, credit, and wages have been examined in 35 countries for two years on each side of the date VAT was introduced; another 6 examples of rate changes in existing VAT systems were investigated.[15] The actual outturns were compared to four hypotheses, first, that the VAT could lead to a once and for all shift in the trend of the consumer price index; second, it might generate an accelerated increase in the rate of growth of the consumer price index (that is, inflation); third, there could be a shift and acceleration in the consumer price index; and finally, there might be little or no effect. Table 10-2 summarizes the results.

An interesting outcome was the extremely clear indication of a pronounced shift in eight of the countries examined. However, only in one case (Norway) was the shift unambiguously combined with an acceleration in the rate of change of the consumer price index. In another (Bolivia), after looking at other evidence, it was concluded that the shift was not due to the VAT. So in all, there were 7 cases where the VAT created a shift in the trend of the consumer price index. In 5 countries, there was an acceleration; in 1, a shift and an acceleration; and in the rest, 22, or 63 percent of the countries, there was little or no effect of the introduction of VAT on the consumer price index.

Apart from the introduction of VAT, evidence of the effect of the tax on prices might be judged from changes in the rates of existing VATs. Examination of six rate changes (see Table 10-2) does not suggest any automatic link between VAT rate changes and inflation. Only one country (Ireland) suffered accelerated price changes, one country (Denmark) exhibited a shift, and the other four showed little or no effect.[16]

While some commentators have associated VAT rate changes with inflation,[17] the weight of evidence seems to be against it. Indeed, practical common sense suggests the opposite: "Price increases *remove* inflationary pressure; they do not add to it. Some light may be shed on the issue by pursuing the symmetrical argument for lower indirect taxes. If it were possible to excite inflationary expectations by a switch

[15]Tait (1981, pp. 38–42) and a more extensive and up-to-date discussion in Tait (1986).
[16]This is borne out by Sijbren Cnossen's reference; see Cnossen (1981, Table 5 and pp. 244–46).
[17]Hemming and Kay (1981, p. 82).

to indirect taxes, would it not follow that one could subdue such expectations by switches from indirect taxes to income tax? Or perhaps to more borrowing to finance some subsidies?"[18] In any case, further assumptions have to be made on an accommodating monetary policy and on the adjustments in wages and transfers.

[18]Walters (1986, p. 77).

CHAPTER 11

Effects of VAT on the Economy

Life can be one of two ways. Either it can be all about VAT or it can be all about God. It's perfectly clear that he has a lower percentage of VAT and a higher percentage of God than almost anyone else one knows.
—WILLIAM REES MOGG (about Cardinal Basil Hume, Archbishop of Westminster), February 1981

This chapter examines the effects of VAT on distribution, efficiency, savings and investment, foreign trade, public sector size, and management of the economy.

Distribution

General

The common case against the VAT is that it is regressive, reducing the real consumption of low-income households by a greater percentage than for high-income households. This general accusation depends on many particular assumptions about the taxes replaced, the exemptions and zero ratings, and any special compensatory features. However, the general view is that VAT is a broad-based tax levied on essentials, and as such must be regressive.

The first point is that for many countries, especially those outside the EC, it is important not to consider the distributional effects of the VAT in isolation but to determine whether the VAT's effects will be better or worse than any alternative measures used to raise revenue. Frequently, where income taxes are poorly administered and their revenue base limited, the alternative taxes to VAT for revenue are potentially equally or more regressive, such as excises on alcohol or tobacco and customs duties.

Second, in any country, it is not particularly useful to consider the impact of one tax in isolation; it is the overall distributional effect that is important and, indeed, not only the distributional effect of taxes on households but also the impact of government expenditures. That is, it is the net budgetary incidence that matters.

Furthermore, regressivity is usually measured against current annual household income. Some claim this is inappropriate because if all income were consumed over a lifetime, a general single rate tax on consumption would be proportional to lifetime income. Families save and accumulate capital; therefore, the sales tax would represent a higher proportion of a young family's income than of older families. However, offsetting this is the fact that the cross-section information is only a "snapshot" at a particular time. Households will be temporarily in a particular income category and, for instance, in the lowest category may well spend more than they earn for a year or two until they move upward; in this case, the conventional cross-section data would overstate the regressiveness of the sales tax.

Another problem, common to all users of household budget surveys, is that the sample always understates income toward the bottom of the scale, resulting in apparent persistent dissaving by low-income households. Once again, this probably leads to the regressivity of VAT being overstated. However, all in all, for most people and certainly for political presentation, the most understandable and most practical measure is annual household income. The professional economist can keep in mind that such a measure probably overstates the regressivity.

Let us look first at the evidence of regressivity, then at the effect of exemptions and zero rating, and finally at possible compensation schemes.

Evidence of Regressivity

The Dutch designed their introduction of VAT to be distributionally neutral.[1] The original rates of 4 percent and 12 percent approximated to the previous sales tax rates. The Central Planning Bureau computed that the change might have improved progressivity because services, which typically form an increasing proportion of household expenditure as income rises, were taxed under VAT. Later surveys

[1]Cnossen (1981, p. 240).

suggested that the Dutch VAT is roughly proportional, and that some adjustments to the tax base have actually worsened the distributional impact, for example, transferring hotel and restaurant services to be taxed at the lower rate and household fuels at the higher general rate.[2]

In some contrast, a single rate VAT at 10 percent in Korea proves to be regressive.[3] The VAT payments represented 5.6 percent of the lowest decile's income and only 3.9 percent of the highest. Farm households paid less VAT absolutely, but the regressivity appeared larger. These conclusions have been broadly confirmed in later studies.

Studies for France all found VAT proportional or mildly progressive, measured in relation to the levels of consumption.[4] In relation to income levels it was regressive, and certainly regressive compared with the exceptionally progressive income tax.

A calculation for the United States suggested that a 10 percent VAT could constitute as much as "17.97 percent of the pretax income of the average family in the lowest quintile, but would amount to only 5.57 percent"[5] in the highest quintile. The U.S. Treasury Report[6] estimated that a 10 percent VAT would lead to an 8 percent increase in consumer prices (assuming 80 percent of consumption expenditures liable and an accommodating money supply leads to a once and for all shift in prices); with no adjustments, this would require households in the lowest income class (up to $10,000 a year) to pay 14.2 percent of their income in VAT, whereas those with incomes of $100,000–200,000 a year would pay about 3 percent.

In the United Kingdom, the VAT is progressive mainly because of zero rating for food, housing, and children's clothing.[7] However, while the zero rating achieves progressivity, it does so at the cost of a great erosion of the tax base, large amounts of revenue forgone, and extraordinarily poor targeting of those groups supposed to be helped.

The Irish Tax Commission's Third Report gives an excellent account of the problem.[8] As Table 11-1 shows, because the zero rating of food benefits everyone who buys food, the richer households get an absolutely larger benefit (the top 10 percent of households gain the

[2]Cnossen (1981, p. 241).
[3]Heller (1981).
[4]Lienard, Messere, and Owens (1987, pp. 180–81).
[5]Greene and Fishbein (1986, p. 90).
[6]United States, Department of the Treasury (1984, Vol. 3, pp. 89–93).
[7]Hemming and Kay (1981, pp. 83–85).
[8]Ireland, Commission on Taxation (1984, p. 67).

Table 11-1. Ireland: Proportion of Total Weekly Expenditure on Food and the Share of Every £Ir 100 Spent on Food in 1980 by Decile Adjusted by Equivalence Scales[1]

Decile Groups (1)	Total Weekly Expenditure (In Irish pounds) (2)	Expenditure on Zero-Rated Food (In Irish pounds) (3)	Percent of Total Expenditure on Zero-Rated Food Items (3) as Percent of (2) (4)	Of Every £Ir 100 Spent on Zero-Rated Food Items, Each Decile Spends (In Irish pounds) (5)
Decile 1 (highest)	274.7	27.3	9.9	10.0
Decile 2	201.2	31.3	15.5	11.5
Decile 3	165.1	30.7	18.6	11.2
Decile 4	151.0	30.9	20.5	11.3
Decile 5	124.1	29.0	23.4	10.6
Decile 6	116.4	30.6	26.3	11.2
Decile 7	97.1	28.8	29.6	10.5
Decile 8	76.9	25.7	33.4	9.4
Decile 9	58.3	22.9	39.4	8.6
Decile 10 (lowest)	32.7	15.8	48.4	5.8

Source: Ireland, *Third Report of the Commission of Taxation: Indirect Taxation* (Dublin: Stationery Office, June 1984), p. 223.
[1] Equivalence scales provide a means of converting total household expenditure to a common basis to allow for differences in household composition.

benefit of tax relief on £Ir 27.3 worth of food a week contrasted to only £Ir 15.8 spent by the bottom 10 percent, although, of course, these represent 9.9 percent and 48.4 percent of total household expenditures). This is a most inefficient way to help poorer households. As the Commission points out, "Expenditure on zero-rated food, clothing, and footwear amounted to almost £1,700 million in 1983. Taxation on this expenditure would raise a sum *far in excess* of what would be necessary to compensate the poor for the regressive impact of a general value-added tax" (p. 67; italics added).[9]

Compensation Schemes for VAT

It is clear that exemptions, zero rating, and multiple rates are inefficient ways to tackle the potential regressivity of the VAT. It is also clear that if the tax were actually levied on the exempt commodities, the yield could certainly be used to compensate low-income households; but the question remains how to make sure that low-income households will be compensated. This has been recognized as a problem for many general sales taxes; some U.S. states (Hawaii, Idaho, Kansas, New Mexico, South Carolina, Vermont, and Wyoming) have experimented with credits to offset the cost of the state sales tax for particularly disadvantaged groups. Usually the credit is available against income tax for taxpayers with incomes under some specified amount (the highest limit is $2,751 in South Dakota). Massachusetts and Nebraska used to have similar credit schemes, but canceled them in the early 1980s. The evidence is that under half of the eligible households took advantage of the New Mexico scheme, and about only one eighth claimed the property tax credit in Michigan.[10] Obviously, it is possible to use tax credits to offset the regressivity of sales taxation, but the credits that have been used have been of debatable efficiency and they have not been used with the VAT, although their possible use has been debated.[11] What has been used is a form of negative income tax for poor people. New Zealand decided to compensate the poor for the price increase due to the VAT by ensuring a form of minimum wage paid by the employer (as agent for the Commissioner of Inland Revenue). "The employer recoups himself out of tax withheld from the remuneration of other employees," if he

[9]The same conclusion is drawn in McLure (1987a, pp. 12–14).
[10]Murray (1979).
[11]United States, Department of the Treasury (1984, Vol. 1, pp. 223–25, and Vol. 3, pp. 100–107); see also Canada, *Tax Reform 1987: The White Paper* (1987, p. 61).

has "so many low paid employees that he is out of pocket as a result of paying out tax credits he recovers the balance from the Commissioner."[12] This wage supplement was adopted deliberately to avoid introducing VAT exemptions for food and clothing; it was recognized that exemptions would be less efficient, more expensive to administer, and introduce problems of compliance.

There are three problems with credits for VAT. Credits against income tax will only help those who have income tax liabilities. In fact, for these persons it would be more efficient to adjust the income tax structure than to work through the cumbersome method of tax credits. For such persons, a better alternative may be to organize a cash refund (see below). Second, other persons, who might not be taxpayers, could be compensated through the social security system—the old, those on supplemental assistance, and so on. Indeed, it is argued that those receiving transfers from the government are automatically protected against inflation if the transfers are indexed.[13] However, this leaves a group who are still outside either category and who are likely to be many, especially in developing countries. Those with small rural incomes, the urban poor, and the old when there is no or only a rudimentary social security system, young workers, part-time workers, and all poor persons outside any social security system.

If credits can be organized to get to whom they are intended, they can be designed to leave households with exactly the same real purchasing power as before.[14] Moreover, the cost of the credit system can be limited, by designing the scheme so that credits are paid only to households below some "poverty" limit. The criteria must be kept simple: for example, households with incomes less than $7,000 could be allowed a credit of $100 for an adult and $50 for a child. The administrative costs of such a scheme could be kept low. Simple credit schemes also create sudden jumps into higher marginal income tax rates above the threshold income where they are phased out. More important, practically, there is no realistic way in which such schemes could be operated in many of the countries using a VAT. The idea of creating a vast transfer or credit system in countries such as Brazil or Mexico would not auger well for budgetary control—quite apart from the problems of monitoring even the most simple criterion, for example, the number of children in a household. It is striking that only New

[12]Prebble (1987, p. 14).

[13]United States, Department of the Treasury (1984, Vol. 3, pp. 91–92).

[14]Ingenious schemes can be concocted to replace both corporate and individual income taxes with a low, flat rate tax of the VAT type, but using personal exemptions—see Hall and Rabushka (1985) and McLure (1987b, pp. 89–91).

Zealand has tried a credit system directly tied to the cost of the VAT to compensate lower-income households. Where some offsetting action has been deemed desirable (Denmark, Norway, and Israel), adjustments have been made to tax allowances and transfers when the VAT is introduced.

In the final analysis, as pointed out earlier, it is not whether the VAT itself is regressive or not (and in some cases, it seems it is not, for example, the United Kingdom and Italy[15]), but whether the entire tax and expenditure system is achieving the pattern of household income net of taxes and gross of transfers and government expenditures that society desires. The case for VAT does not stand or fall on its regressiveness. The case for VAT is that it is an efficient way of collecting a large and buoyant revenue for government; other parts of the budget should take care of progressiveness, and the VAT should be kept as simple and efficient as it is intended to be—for that is its justification. The worst of all worlds is to end up with an eroded VAT base, complicated rates and exemptions, and a tax that is expensive to administer, all in the name of equity; instead of simplicity and efficiency, you end up with complexity, expense, and evasion—and all for the wrong reasons.[16]

Efficiency and Neutrality

In fact, it may be more worthwhile to emphasize the effects the VAT should *not* have. As first mentioned, the ideal VAT is an efficient tax precisely because it does not distort consumer choice. A VAT that taxes all goods and services (and the New Zealand VAT is an example that is as near general as it is possible to be) leaves consumers only with the choices of unbought and, therefore, untaxed services (for example, leisure and do-it-yourself work) and all goods and services taxed equally. Unlike the income tax, the VAT does not tax income from savings. In most countries, the income tax is riddled with distortions (in favor of owner-occupied house purchases, investment in government bonds, ownership of shares, development of certain industries or development areas, and so on), and in many cases the distortions arise because of an administration that is partial to certain persons and

---

[15]See discussions in Aaron (1981).

[16]"There is presently more concern for the administrative problems of IVA . . . The administrative mess and the huge evasion, which go hand in hand, are the truly outstanding and serious problems of the Italian IVA today," Castellucci (1987, pp. 234–35).

institutions. The VAT is likely to involve fewer distortions than the income tax.[17]

It has been stated that the introduction of a flat rate VAT in the United States, with an equal yield reduction in the personal income tax, estimated by using a general equilibrium model, would improve the efficiency of the economy; there would be "modest welfare gains."[18]

Such estimates can yield results indicating the marginal social costs of raising additional revenue by different alternative taxes. The evidence shows that the VAT has the lowest marginal social cost (only one third of a cascading wholesale manufacturer tax, for instance). In a U.S. study, the excess burden of raising extra revenue from a sales tax (on commodities other than alcohol, tobacco, or gasoline) was only a third to a quarter of raising the same amount by labor taxes on industry or by traditional income taxes.[19]

Of course, we must not compare a perfect VAT to a known imperfect income tax. Many VATs are far from general and, as soon as exemptions and exceptions are allowed, the neutrality is lost.[20] However, many VATs show that is possible to tax food and nearly all goods, including new housing. Few tax medical and financial services and clearly this distorts the tax, but not in an unacceptable way. More serious distortions occur with the zero rating of food and housing and lower tax rates on, say, clothing. The same general equilibrium model for the United States indicated that adopting the sort of differentiated rates common in the European VATs reduced the welfare gains from adopting VAT by 25–40 percent. Nevertheless, the same study concludes that a flat rate VAT, a differentiated VAT, and a progressive expenditure tax are more efficient, at the margin, than the U.S. pre-1986 personal income tax and, further, that the flat rate VAT appears to be far more efficient at the margin than an income tax surcharge.[21]

Savings and Investment

The usual case is a VAT replacing a previous sales tax. The old European cascade taxes frequently taxed capital goods (for instance in

---

[17]See McLure (1981, p. 149).
[18]Ballard, Scholz, and Shoven (1987).
[19]Ballard, Shoven, and Whalley (1985).
[20]Hemming and Kay (1981).
[21]Ballard, Scholz, and Shoven (1987).

Belgium, France, the Federal Republic of Germany, Italy, and the Netherlands), and as the VAT is designed to give full credit for capital goods, and to be neutral as regards the choice between capital and labor or investment and consumption, the substitutions should favor capital over labor and investment over consumption. The indirect taxes replaced by the VAT in Korea also taxed capital goods and it is considered that manufacturing, electricity, and gas sectors gained substantial benefits.

A broad-based VAT taxes present and future consumption the same and is, therefore, neutral between consumption and saving. The net effect of a VAT on saving and investment depends on the exact form of tax replacement discussed. A VAT that simply increased revenue would be potentially deflationary, would reduce consumption, and probably would reduce the profitability of future investment. At the same time, such an increase in revenue could be used to reduce the fiscal deficit, reduce the public sector borrowing requirement, allow interest rates to fall, and thus stimulate investment. The VAT could also lessen the danger of inflation from monetized deficits.[22] This might reduce interest rates and the real cost of capital. The net outturn depends on numerous behavioral relationships, but it is by no means clear that VAT harms investment and savings; there are several plausible arguments for the opposite.

The estimate for the substitution of a general consumption tax for an equal amount of the personal income tax in the United States is that it would increase saving by 6 percent of the yield.[23] This is a relatively modest contribution to saving. Given the decline in U.S. personal saving, currently about 3.8 percent against a postwar average of 6.8 percent, some encouragement might be welcome.

In general, VAT does not distort saving and investment behavior; if it replaces taxes that are distorting, economic efficiency should be improved.

Foreign Trade[24]

Though one of the main advantages of VAT is to ensure that international trade takes place on a transparent basis (and that is why GATT accepts the border adjustments for VAT), no one should claim that the net effects on foreign trade, as such, are likely to be large.

---

[22]Sinclair (1983, pp. 383–84).
[23]Goode (1976, p. 67).
[24]For a similar discussion, see Tait (1986).

Those that have thought foreign trade could be improved by, for example, substituting a VAT for a corporate profits tax, may have based their judgment, as discussed below, on a too narrow and partial a view of the tax change.

All present VAT systems are based on the destination principle, where fiscal frontiers must be maintained to ensure that exports are fully rebated for the VAT paid in the exporter's domestic market and where the VAT rates appropriate to the importer's home market can be applied. This is a major compliance cost, but the same cost would be involved by any sovereign nation trading across international boundaries.

There is the possibility of a minor distortion in foreign trade under VAT. To the extent that countries exempt goods and services, the suppliers are unable to recoup their VAT content. If these goods and services are used to produce taxable goods and services, then even though those activities can reclaim the VAT at the point of export, that amount cannot include the earlier VAT paid by the exempted activity. In this case, there could be differential amounts of hidden and unreclaimable VAT on different traded goods and services, depending on the exempted sectors in each country. The same holds true for any small firms that are exempted and export goods or services. In general, VAT removes distortions that existed in previous systems and the advantages to foreign trade of adopting VAT are those of getting rid of the previous distortions.

Replacing a Sales Tax with VAT

Retail sales taxes and most wholesale taxes are not levied on exports and, therefore, VAT offers an advantage only insofar as there is any cascading. Cascaded taxes are included in export prices and the tax content is different for different products or, indeed, for the same product, depending on the number of steps of production, the degree of specialization, and the amount of industry vertical integration. No matter how large the cascade content is in the export price, it cannot be rebated precisely for all products or for any one product without the danger of being unfair to other products. It was this arbitrariness of cascaded sales taxes that persuaded the EC to opt for the VAT, whose use ensures that the tax content is clear at any time.

When the VAT is substituted for a cascaded sales tax and the old export rebates are abolished, had the rebates involved an element of subsidy, the net position of the exporter might be worse. What happens then depends on the movement of exchange rates (they might depreciate), on the response of purchasers of the exports to the price change (which could well be small as the absolute price alteration is likely to be small), on the response of the exporters to the shift in producer prices and, finally, on the response of the domestic consumers to relative price shifts in favor of imported goods. Evidence from the Federal Republic of Germany[25] and Korea[26] suggests that perhaps the Government had inadequately compensated exporters under the old cascade taxes and that, therefore, the VAT, by giving the correct (and larger) rebates for domestic taxes, favored exports. Every country is likely to have a different outcome, and forecasting it depends on elasticities that are most uncertain, especially when disaggregated for particular products or sectors. In any event, the final net change does not seem likely to be large. In general, if factor prices are fully flexible, or if the exchange rate is floating freely, the usual domestic consumption type VAT will be neutral with respect to the allocation of resources.[27]

Replacing a Direct Tax by a VAT

The "VAT is also advocated as a means of stimulating exports. Under . . . GATT, a country may adjust the price of an exported item by indirect taxes but not for direct taxes, such as income taxes and social security taxes. As a result, goods exported from countries using VAT enjoy a comparative advantage; by contrast, goods exported from the United States bear the cost of high income and payroll taxes. By replacing such taxes, in part, with a VAT, some argue, the United States would no longer be at a competitive disadvantage since it would rebate the VAT on exports."[28] Some might argue this but it is based on a partial view of adjustment. To take the extreme view, if all direct taxes were rebated on exports, would that not give the greatest incentive? But the rebates on exports leave the government budget with a revenue shortfall. With a given government expenditure, the government must get its revenue from somewhere and what it gives with one hand it must recoup elsewhere. That is, the rate of VAT would have to be raised to maintain domestic revenue; this raises domestic prices and lowers real wages. If that position were sustained, exports might

---

[25]It seems the Germans undercompensated their exporters by approximately 3 percent; see Cnossen (1986a).

[26]See Han (1986).

[27]See Schenone (1981).

[28]Price Waterhouse (1980, p. 8).

indeed increase. However, if labor responds by demands for higher wages, domestic industrial costs rise and the competitive advantage is eroded. This argument that a VAT would increase exports only works if a real cut in domestic factor returns can be engineered, and that is based on social and economic considerations probably little connected with the VAT.

Even in the more limited case of substitution of VAT for some corporate direct taxes, the same argument holds. In addition, the argument must consider whether corporate prices fully reflect the reduction in corporate taxation; second, there could be cross-subsidization of exports from domestic pricing structures; third, a sustained expansion of exports and containment of imports might be countered by exchange rate appreciation. Finally, it has to be proved that the elasticities of supply of exportables and demand for imports are such as to yield significant advantages.

A provocative analysis by Gary Hufbauer suggests using a 4 percent VAT to eliminate the U.S. corporate income tax.[29] He argues that corporate profitability would be improved and the cost of capital would be reduced. However, the improved profitability would probably be short lived and, as Henry Aaron argues, the "effect of the tax swap on saving is many fold too high."[30] The VAT for corporate income tax swap would tend to increase domestic saving (because after-tax rates of return rise) and increase investment by U.S. businesses (because the cost of capital to the firm is reduced). At the same time, U.S. assets become much more attractive, and capital would tend to flow to the United States causing the dollar to appreciate and create an increased deficit on current account. In the longer run, the United States would have to run a larger current account surplus to finance the returns on the increased net holdings of U.S. assets by foreigners.[31] Whether or not this complicated and subtle series of changes on current and capital account would be to the ultimate advantage of the United States is difficult to assess. It is certainly dangerous to be dogmatic about cause and effect when so many uncertainties are involved.

It is not thought that the introduction of VAT had any significant effect on exports in Italy, Sweden, or the United Kingdom.[32] In the Federal Republic of Germany, the increases in exports at the start of VAT were associated more with constrained domestic demand and

[29]Hufbauer (1987).
[30]Aaron (1987, p. 211).
[31]Aaron (1987, pp. 212–13).
[32]Brecher and others (1982, p. 41).

higher productivity (lowering labor costs per unit) than with the tax change. The evidence is that "fluctuations in exchange rates and world demand" make the effects of VAT swaps (for personal income taxes—the United Kingdom and Sweden, or for social security contributions—Italy) "pall into insignificance."[33]

Overall, the argument and the evidence is that it is the customs union that drives up international trade and not the VAT; the VAT makes the customs union possible, but is not the agent that stimulates trade. Indeed, the VAT is designed to be neutral and not to give an edge to any one country. Any effect discussed above would be unlikely to be large and probably would be temporary.

There is, perhaps, a minor effect on international trade from using the VAT. It has been argued that importers must pay VAT as the goods physically enter the country, and that tax payment is deposited in the national treasury "for a fairly long period of time"[34] and, of course, no interest is paid on it. The trader, it is claimed, is at some disadvantage. This is exaggerated. Generally, importers do not pay VAT upon the entry of the goods, but are often allowed a month to pay. The "postponed accounting system"[35] allows the recipient of the goods, not the importer, to pay the VAT. Generally, this means an additional 15 days for which the tax payment can be postponed, and this synchronizes the import VAT with the domestic VAT. Unfortunately, the trend may be in the opposite direction, as countries such as the United Kingdom and Ireland, which used the postponed accounting system, have recently reverted to levying the VAT on the physical movement of the goods at import (despite a predominant wish on the part of industry that the postponed accounting system continues[36]) thereby gaining for their treasuries a once and for all gain at the expense of the importer.

Size of the Public Sector

Some commentators argue that the VAT allows the government to grow larger, including the President of the United States who, in his February 21, 1985 news conference said the VAT "gives a government a chance to blindfold the people and grow in stature and size."[37] The

[33]Brecher and others (1982, p. 42).
[34]Dekker (1985, p. 121).
[35]See European Community, Proposal for a Fourteenth Council Directive.
[36]Miles (1987, p. 2).
[37]"Reagan Sees Tightening of Business Tax," *Washington Post* (Washington), February 22, 1985, p. D3; see also Bannock (1986).

tax may offer policymakers a tempting way to expand their influence. Any revenue shortfall can be met by an increase in the VAT rates (and it is true that only in three countries, Chile, Costa Rica, and Peru, has the VAT rate been reduced from that at which it was initially introduced). In this way, there will be a temptation to increase public expenditures, knowing the buoyant VAT is waiting in the wings to help out. It is true that VAT, particularly in developing countries, often creates a more varied and broader tax base, which allows countries to tap resources that previously were unavailable. Also, because the VAT is levied on a wide range of goods and services, it automatically appropriates its "share" of consumption as the GNP grows and as prices rise.

In addition, it can be argued that since an ideal VAT taxes all goods and services, the taxpayer cannot shift his consumption pattern to alternative untaxed goods and services; if the VAT replaces a tax that has allowed taxpayers such a choice, then "tax distortion" is reduced. With no choice but to pay the tax, total tax revenues are likely to rise. At the same time, the VAT may have replaced taxes with high marginal rates and such a switch may encourage taxpayers to work harder. It may also reduce evasion. In both cases the tax ratio may be raised and the size of the public sector may increase.

An interesting "event analysis" of the introduction of VAT in 11 European countries suggests that the introduction of a VAT "immediately increases the tax ratio, which then persists at [a] higher level."[38] However, this particular test assumed that government expenditure is determined independently of government revenue, an assumption directly at odds with some of the arguments just made.

Other evidence does not support the thesis that VAT enables countries to have a larger public sector. Countries now using VAT tended to have a larger public sector before they used VAT than the countries that at present do not use VAT. As Table 11-2 shows, it is correct that 6 of the 11 countries reviewed did increase their average annual growth of public expenditure as a percent of GDP after the VAT, and that the group average reflects this.[39] However, Table 11-2 also shows that in most cases, receipts did not grow as rapidly as outlays and that, naturally, the difference showed up as increases in the rate of growth of the deficit. It is not so much that VAT triggers an increase in the rate of growth of the public sector, but rather that countries already with a large government expenditure look for efficient ways to finance that

[38]Nellor (1987, p. 1).
[39]See Alverson (1986); see also Stockfisch (1985).

government outlay and gravitate to VAT. They do so because they know that VAT is able to support general rates above 10 percent, indeed, typically at 15 percent, whereas the evidence is that a retail sales tax runs into difficulties at rates over 10 percent (see Chapter 1).

Table 11-2. The Government Sector Before and After the Imposition of VAT

	Years	Average Annual Growth in Outlays as a Percentage of GDP	Average Annual Growth in Receipts as a Percentage of GDP	Average Deficit or Surplus as a Percentage of GDP
Austria	1965–72	0.29	0.40	−0.01
	1973–82	1.01	0.53	−2.50
Belgium	1965–70	0.84	0.90	−3.56
	1971–82	1.65	0.89	−5.63
Denmark	1965–66	1.80	2.30	1.56
	1967–82	1.70	1.11	−0.81
France	1965–67	0.30	−0.10	−0.30
	1968–82	0.75	0.59	−1.36
Germany,	1965–67	1.00	0.60	−1.20
Fed. Rep of	1968–82	0.74	0.54	−2.39
Ireland	1965–71	1.23	1.40	−4.53
	1972–81	1.76	0.62	−9.10
Italy	1965–72	0.61	0.11	−4.34
	1973–82	1.90	1.28	−9.78
Netherlands	1965–68	1.73	1.70	−1.58
	1969–82	1.48	0.96	−2.83
Norway	1965–69	1.42	1.63	3.36
	1970–82	0.64	0.77	3.03
Sweden	1965–68	2.23	2.00	2.95
	1969–82	1.80	0.95	−0.10
United Kingdom	1965–72	0.53	0.51	−1.35
	1973–82	0.73	0.81	−5.22
Group average	Pre-VAT	1.09	1.04	—
	Post-VAT	1.29	0.82	—

Source: Terree Alverson, "Does the Value-Added Tax Contribute to Increased Government Spending and Taxation?" *Economic Outlook,* Chamber of Commerce of the United States (Washington), April/May 1986, Table 3, p.14.

Management of the Economy

The VAT has been seen as a possible tool for economic management, but with "fine-tuning" going out of fashion, not much has been heard recently about using VAT as a regulator. Some countries such as Korea have included a clause in the VAT legislation to allow the Minister of Finance to vary the VAT rate within 3 percent without immediate recourse to legislation. Some countries (for example, Italy) have used VAT deliberately to try to contain domestic demand.

The Italian example demonstrates a danger in using VAT in a too discriminatory way as a temporary surcharge; when a 4 percent VAT surcharge was applied to automobiles and "white goods" such as washing machines and refrigerators and a 2 percent surcharge was applied to electronic and photographic goods, it appeared that firms would have to reprogram their computerized accounting systems to accommodate these special separate rates.[40] The authorities allowed the surcharge to be merged with the existing VAT rates (increasing the 18 percent rate to 20 percent or 22 percent). However, such sudden and temporary switches in rates are administratively disruptive and the VAT is better left out of such short-run fiscal management.

It can also be argued that shifting to VAT from income taxes is a desirable part of long-run economic management. The disincentive effects of income taxes on work effort, savings, and risk taking are emphasized; VAT revenues replacing part of income tax could boost economic activity. According to one commentator, "It is a pity that the bad press accorded to the VAT increase of 1979 had tended to inhibit any further shift from income and capital taxes toward VAT."[41] On the other hand, it has been held that the composition of taxes for a given budget deficit critically affects the trade balance. "Under a value-added tax system, a budget deficit worsens the trade balance and raises the world interest rate; under an income-tax system, the same deficit improves the trade balance and lowers the world interest rate."[42]

Brazil has used the state VAT (ICM) to stimulate exports and promote certain projects of "national interest." Since 1975, such projects, including telecommunications, power, and steel, have not had to pay VAT on their inputs. During 1971–77, the usual VAT exemption for exports was supplemented by a subsidy (*crédito prêmio*); this was an

---

[40]"Italy: Tightening the Fiscal Belt," *World Tax Report* (1987, p. 8).
[41]Walters (1986, p. 78).
[42]Frenkel and Razin (1988, p. 297).

extra VAT credit expressed as a percentage of the firm's export value. Other countries have toyed with the possibility of using VAT as a tool of regional policy (basically impossible as the effects would rapidly spill over from the region—see Chapter 2). It might be feasible to create regional investment credits using the VAT refund mechanism. Traders, identified by the codes in the registration number identifying their region, could be allowed to claim refunds for investment expenditures in excess of the amounts actually paid. Of course, this would be open to all the criticisms of such regional incentives and, in fact, the VAT would only be used as a mechanism for distributing the capital subsidy.

Another suggestion has been to recognize that complying with VAT represents a significant cost for many small employers. If such small traders were exempted from VAT, this could remove an impediment to their survival and growth. As it is recognized that a substantial part of new employment takes place in small firms, it is argued that this concession could increase employment.[43] There is the added temptation that the exemption for small retailers would cost a relatively small proportion of the revenue and would release many VAT inspectors and other staff to monitor the tax on firms where the potential revenue loss (or revenue saved) is much greater (see Chapter 6).

It is always possible to devise ways to adjust the VAT and especially the VAT credits to affect investment, exports, and particular forms of consumption, but all this goes against the grain of the basic rationale of the VAT. The VAT is designed to be neutral. To use it for economic management, other than for broad-based demand adjustment, involves creating nonneutrality and is unadvisable.

---

[43]See Samuel Brittan, "Don't Let VAT Kill Off Jobs," *Financial Times* (London), February 18, 1985, p. 11.

PART III

VAT Administration and Compliance

CHAPTER 12

Administration and Staffing

The cost of administering such a simple tax has proved to be less than 1 per cent of the tax revenue. We estimated there would be 180,000 [VAT] registrations; at present there have been 282,000 and the number is still rising. Over 90,000 businesses previously unknown under the old tax system have registered. Even more amazing was the fact that public approval rating of the tax went up after it came into force. . . .

—ROGER DOUGLAS, Minister of Finance of New Zealand, in *Toward Prosperity* (Auckland: David Bateman), p. 221

Experience with VAT shows, once more, that in developing countries tax administration is tax policy.

—MILKA CASANEGRA DE JANTSCHER, "Problems of Administering a Value-Added Tax in Developing Countries,"IMF Working Paper 86/15, December 18, 1986, p. 18

The VAT may be complicated to administer but it is not as complex as personal or corporate income taxes. Compared with the administration of a sales tax at the manufacturer or wholesale stage, the VAT authorities must deal frequently with many more traders. Compared with a multistage turnover tax or a retail sales tax, although the number of taxpayers might be almost the same,[1] the information needed to levy the tax is more complex to provide and more difficult

[1]This may look surprising, but under a retail sales tax, particularly in developing countries, many manufacturers and wholesalers make occasional sales to final consumers and therefore have to be registered. The U.S. authorities estimated that there would be only 10 percent fewer taxpayers under a retail sales tax than under a VAT.

to check. However, three of the supposed advantages of the VAT are administrative: First, as each trader's sale is someone else's purchase, the invoices required for a credit-invoice VAT theoretically allow the authorities to cross-check the accuracy of a trader's purchases by adding up the supplier's sales. Second, the data on purchases and sales in the VAT returns should provide a valuable input to the calculation of profits for the purpose of income taxation, thus improving the administration of direct taxes. Furthermore, none of the complicated rules about uplifts, discounts, industry agreements, and special regulations under wholesale and manufacturers taxes are needed.

Usually, the introduction of VAT has been a major upheaval in a country's tax system[2] and the opportunity has been taken to reform a large part of the tax administration. This chapter is concerned with the details of VAT administration and staffing. Administration and staffing may appear to be a mundane preoccupation, but without it all the theory and broad generalities are vitiated. This chapter addresses four questions. First, who should run a VAT? Second, how should functions be specified and allocated? Third, how many staff are needed? And, finally, what are the likely costs of administration?

Who Should Run a VAT?

One of the earliest, and most important, decisions that has to be made is to determine which branch of tax administration shall be responsible for the VAT. In Latin America, most taxes are organized by functions such as collection, audit, and appeals, and automatically the department administering the internal taxes administers the VAT. In other countries, there are four options: the existing sales tax authority can run the new tax, the income tax, or the customs and excise, can take over, or a completely new authority can be established. Since the existing sales taxes being replaced by the VAT are likely to be simpler, they are also likely to rely on a less sophisticated administration and on a not so highly trained staff. Moving to a VAT is bound to involve extensive retraining and, probably, recruitment and upgrading of staff.

In most cases, where the income tax is efficiently collected, there are

---

[2]Not always; some Central American countries have adopted a form of manufacturing VAT almost by accident, through extending a credit mechanism for tax on inputs, as was the case in Costa Rica.

advantages in associating the administration of VAT with the income tax. As mentioned already, the potential for cross-checking between VAT and income tax liabilities is one of the advantages claimed for VAT. Such coordination should be much easier if the new tax is under the wing of the income tax organization. Nevertheless, there are sometimes doubts about expanding the scope of the income tax by adding such a large and important tax as VAT to what is already the biggest branch of taxation.

The U.K. VAT might be thought of as a good example for other countries to emulate. However, the U.K. case was unusual; the Customs and Excise had been responsible for the former purchase tax (a tax charged at the manufacturing and wholesale stages on wholesale values) introduced in wartime, when the income tax organization was understaffed and overburdened and when Customs and Excise was less busy than usual. Because of this accident of timing, the Customs and Excise gained experience in dealing with the wholesale trade in goods, and when the time came to introduce VAT, its experience in warehouse control, inventories, verification of customs import values, and factory visits for excise purposes was taken as a deciding factor in allocating responsibility for VAT administration. It was recognized that Customs had no experience in taxing services. The elimination of the purchase tax also freed 2,000 customs officers for other work. Perhaps there was also a feeling that the income tax authorities should not be made even more dominant than they were already. In general, few countries have followed this example, and it is not a road many tax advisors would follow.

Sometimes, the tug of war between the customs and excise and the income tax authorities can be such that to avoid antagonizing either, it is deemed more appropriate to allot the VAT to an entirely new organization, as has been done in Portugal, where the collection, audit, and legal interpretation under the Serviço de Administração do IVA, the VAT branch of the Tax Department, is a separate operational agency. However, there are dangers in this solution: staff may be reluctant to be transferred from income tax or customs and excise to a new sales tax; the personnel of the existing agencies may unreasonably resent the new organization; and there may be problems of cooperation among staff. It should also be borne in mind that, in any case, customs will collect usually a fourth (and sometimes much more) of the VAT revenue (on imports). Whatever is decided will require strong and sustained management interest and direction to get the new tax up and running.

Possibly the most complicated relationship between the income tax and VAT authorities is in Israel. In that country, the low rate (6.25

percent) is levied on municipalities and nonprofit organizations by the income tax authorities (as the VAT in this case is levied on organizations that make no profit, it can be viewed basically as a tax on *wages* and hence is collected monthly). The standard rate VAT (15 percent) is administered by the Customs and Excise except for financial services. The VAT on financial services is levied as a direct additive base on wages and profits (profits are defined as they are for the purposes of the income tax) and hence, in this case, the income tax authorities again collect the VAT on a monthly basis.

Even if the VAT is fully integrated with the income tax there is still the question of whether it is preferable to have a separate organization for VAT at headquarters or at regional or district levels, or whether to integrate the VAT into the activities at all, or none, of the administrative levels.

There are several basic arguments for having a separate VAT organization:

- It allows officers to identify closely with a particular function.

- There is better specialization; indeed, in developing countries especially, few officers are truly able to be good auditors for VAT and good auditors for income taxes at the same time.

- It allows for the integration of officers into the VAT (for example, customs or excise officers) who might not be readily accepted by the income tax personnel (who frequently consider themselves a more technically and financially sophisticated branch).

- The methods of operation of the VAT and the income tax are too different to make a combined effort efficient. For instance, audit for VAT is simpler and requires a less comprehensive accounting knowledge than an audit for income tax (basically because less analysis and less complex legislation have to be applied to the treatment of capital). This suggests a different and more frequent kind of audit than that for income taxation.

- Different interests may be difficult to reconcile. For instance, VAT inspectors are typically interested in the current fiscal year, whereas income tax inspectors tend to concentrate on earlier years.

Against this, or in favor of a more complete integration with income tax, are arguments such as:

- A more flexible use of manpower (provided the whole staff is highly trained).

- A less divided staff.
- Better appreciation of mutual problems in VAT and income tax, both within the offices and on the part of the traders.
- Better internal communications of ideas and solutions.
- Joint controls and audits check fraud and help identify undeclared activities.
- Probably less duplication of resources.
- No separate career paths to create jealousies and elite groups.
- Reduced compliance costs to taxpayers, fewer inspections, fewer communications with traders, and more consistent treatment that reduces conflicts.

However, whether or not the functions of the officer running the VAT can be combined with the existing income tax system sometimes turns on prosaic but unyielding structural considerations such as the civil service job-grading system. If income tax officials have been given a high job grading, they are, first, unwilling to accept functions for VAT that might dilute that grading and, second, those responsible for VAT will not work "under" an income tax officer. Such structural rigidities can stymie attempts to combine functions.

Two options (with suggested functions) for the district level are shown in Charts 12-1 and 12-2. In purely logical terms, the combined option (Chart 12-2) looks better. The structure is more cohesive and the duties can be combined more flexibly. The other two options of either shifting the customs and excise function from being primarily concerned with goods crossing international borders to taking on widespread domestic tax functions, or setting up a wholly separate agency, appear less happy.

The circumstances of each country are different and sometimes the decision to whom to give the VAT can depend on the personalities of the senior people involved. A young dynamic executive may seem more prepared to try new ideas with a new tax. Perhaps a well-tried experienced hand at the helm is needed to drive through a controversial new tax. The case has to be evaluated for each country, and Table 12-1 shows how diverse the decisions can be. Although the preference for a single department is clear, it is less so for a combined inspectorate. Whatever the decision, it has to be taken early and not left hanging while the planning for the new tax starts off in an administrative limbo. Senior appointees to the VAT administration should be participants in the initial planning and committee work and should be seen to have the authoritative backing of the senior revenue and treasury officials (as happened, for example, in New Zealand).

Chart 12-1. Possible Administrative Structure with VAT Operations as a Separate Organization at District Level

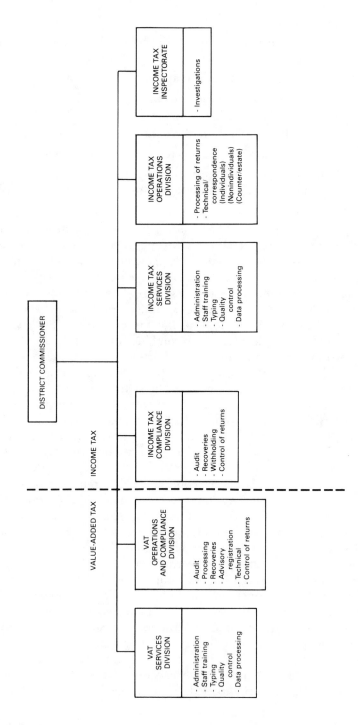

Source: Adapted from the Irish organization chart.

Table 12-1. Examples of Combined or Split Administration with Income Tax

	VAT and Income Tax Administrations	
	One department	One inspectorate
Austria	Yes	Yes
Belgium	No	No
Denmark	Yes	No
France	Yes	Yes
Germany, Fed. Rep. of	Yes	Yes
Greece	Yes	Yes
Ireland	Yes	No
Italy	Yes	No
Luxembourg	No	No
Netherlands	Yes	No
New Zealand	Yes	No
Norway	Yes	Yes
Portugal	Yes	Yes
Spain	Yes	Yes
Sweden	Yes	Yes
Turkey	Yes	Yes
United Kingdom	No	No

Source: Various country reports.

Central Versus Local Administration: Organization and Functions

There are several arguments in favor of decentralizing many of the administrative functions of VAT:

- Current management philosophy in many countries favors further decision-making power at the managerial and functional levels that have the information most immediately at hand for prompt action. Traders like to have ready access to local offices to register and to discuss VAT problems. The local staff get to know the traders, visit the trading premises, and carry out field audits. Traders should not feel they are dealing with an impersonal centralized machine.

- Since the VAT is a self-assessment system, voluntary compliance is important, and local personal contact between administrator and trader enhances the likelihood of good compliance.

- Decision making is quicker, although it may be uneven—see below.

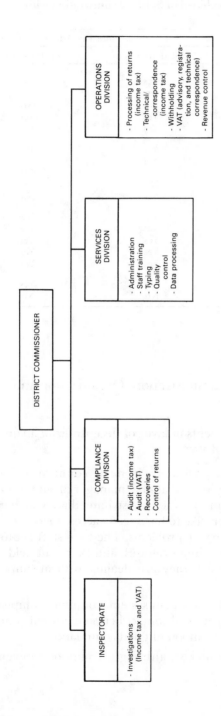

Chart 12-2. Possible Administrative Structure with VAT Integrated with Income Tax at District Level

DISTRICT COMMISSIONER

INSPECTORATE
- Investigations (Income tax and VAT)

COMPLIANCE DIVISION
- Audit (income tax)
- Audit (VAT)
- Recoveries
- Control of returns

SERVICES DIVISION
- Administration
- Staff training
- Typing
- Quality control
- Data processing

OPERATIONS DIVISION
- Processing of returns (income tax)
- Technical/ correspondence (income tax)
- Withholding
- VAT (advisory, registration, and technical correspondence)
- Revenue control

- Coordination between headquarters and traders is probably improved.
- Auditing, with local knowledge of trading conditions, is likely to be better.
- Regional offices are smaller and staff should be more versatile; if income tax and VAT are run together it should make for a more flexible use of staff, a most important consideration in many countries.

Against decentralization we have at least six arguments:

- Central control ensures uniformity of decision making and of equal treatment for all traders (but this can be countered by good training and up-to-date manuals).
- Officers from a central office are less likely to be swayed and influenced by local conditions and powerful local interests; they will not identify with local power structures.
- Corruption is less likely. This may be a crucial consideration in some countries.
- Decentralized offices may not have an even work load and, unless planning and execution are good, there can be underused staff; a central staff can be moved to even out local disparities.
- A large central operation may allow greater specialization.
- There are administrative advantages in having centralized records, accounting, and financial control.

As the points above illustrate, the balance of argument can go either way and each country's decision reflects its own political, administrative, and social priorities. It does seem desirable, for "customer relations" at the least, to have a substantial local presence, and, for staff morale, a reasonable degree of autonomy should be given to local offices. However, local staff must be capable of handling the responsibility; in some developing countries it has proved better to move gradually in this respect.

Sometimes external technical considerations can dictate the solution. In some cases, communications between the headquarters and districts are so poor that, despite any opposing arguments on technical grounds, the primary discretion on VAT decisions has to be left to the district. In another example, although a large central computing capacity existed, telecommunications links were so poor and inadequate that for at least ten years the authorities could only envisage main reliance on local administration. Indeed, the great advances in personal computer capacity and programming have meant that local offices can be given more duties to be carried out using local computing facilities with common software. Data can be transferred to the central authorities on tape or disk by the regular post or courier routes on a daily or weekly basis.

The way in which countries have decided to allocate responsibility for VAT illustrates the range and diversity of options. As mentioned above, the United Kingdom is an example of a country that decided to use the Customs and Excise for the VAT. Chart 12-3 shows the U.K. organization. Although the computer is centrally housed, some ninety local offices are located in principal towns (and some of these offices have suboffices in other towns).

> These offices are generally responsible, under collectors of Customs and Excise, for the local administration of the [VAT]. Staff are available . . . to advise traders about the tax and to deal with their enquiries. In addition, some 35,000 registered traders are visited at their premises each month to ensure that they understand the tax and their responsibilities within the system and that their tax returns are correct and their tax accounts adequate. These routine control visits are an essential part of the system, given its self-assessed basis; but local control is supplemented through use of the central computer system to check the credibility of traders' returns to draw attention to apparent inconsistencies in patterns of trade.[3]

By contrast,

> Enforcement of VAT is a local issue in Belgium. There is one Local Control Office [LCO] for every 2,000 traders and, as a trader, your local office is never very far away. The LCO consists of about 12–15 staff depending on the work load and it carries out all the functions of registration, enquiries, variations, typing, and most of the preliminary work connected with enforcement. . . .
>
> . . . when the LCO is satisfied that the return contains valid information they code the essential details on to a special magnetic roll and send these rolls each day to the Computer Centre (CTI). The CTI never gets any information direct from traders nor does it correspond with them. In this way access to the CTI and its sophisticated equipment is restricted to those who know how it works.
>
> The CTI holds a current account for every registered trader and every week it runs the LCO magnetic rolls against it. Payments are all made via one control "Office de Cheque Postale" in Brussels on a prescribed form.

[3]United Kingdom, Commissioners of H.M. Customs and Excise (1978, p. 7).

Payment information too is coded on a roll, sent to the CTI and this too is run against the current account. Thus the current account shows every movement in the traders position and to assist everyone the CTI sends a quarterly extract of the current account to the trader and to the LCO.[4]

The LCO has on line direct access to the CTI computer at all times. Regional CTIs deal with the collection of VAT and fines resulting from assessments by LCO officers.

Korea and Ireland are examples of fully integrated revenue services under common umbrellas, the Office of National Tax Administration (ONTA) in Korea and the office of the Revenue Commission in Ireland. However, the structure in each differs. In Korea, in the regional tax office, there are both direct and indirect tax bureaus, and the indirect tax bureau has separate sections for excise and VAT. At the district level, the VAT division is in charge of assessment and collection. The central computer prints lists of traders whose data are "nonmatching" (see below), and these are sent to the local officers who visit each trader to inquire the reasons for the discrepancies (which often prove to be figures transcribed wrongly rather than deliberate evasion).

The Irish organization is an interesting example of a homogeneous revenue agency working in a small country. As Chart 12-4 shows, the collection and inspectorate functions are general to all taxes, as are the head office functions of legislation and statistics, general administration, refunds, control audits, investigation, and fraud. At the local level, there are 14 districts (of which one, Dublin, covers about 50 percent of the registered persons).

In another small country, the Dominican Republic, VAT is administered from headquarters with all audit and enforcement centralized. Registration, VAT returns, and collection are made in 29 regional offices (one for each province).[5] In the larger Latin American countries, VAT is integrated within the tax department, electronic data processing is centralized, and auditing is decentralized.

New Zealand opted to integrate the VAT with the income tax at the district level (although in this case there was a peculiar problem in that the split of records for income tax between the two largest district offices did not necessarily form the ideal base for the VAT). On the other hand, Morocco, despite using the income tax to administer the VAT, decided that administration should be carried out from different offices.

[4]Barnard (1976).
[5]Meyer and Due (1988, p. 14).

Chart 12-3. United Kingdom: Organization Chart Showing Customs and Excise Headquarters Offices and Local Offices, and the Main Communication Links Between These and Traders and the VAT Tribunals, 1977[1]

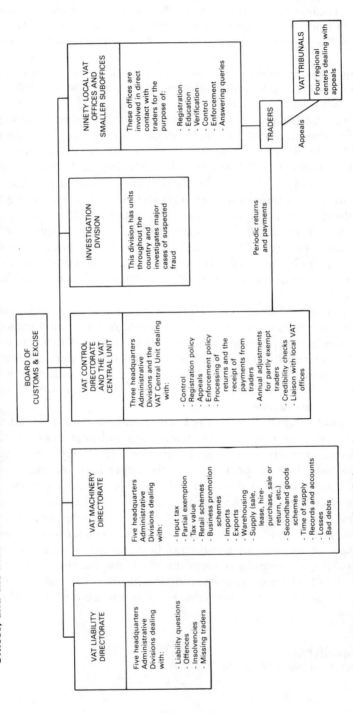

Source: Adapted from U.K. Revenue Commissioners.

[1] In 1977 there were 1.25 million VAT taxpayers in the United Kingdom. Total staff employed on VAT at headquarters was 2,000; local VAT offices and suboffices employed more than 7,500 staff.

In Brazil, the tax is run at both federal and state levels (federal at the manufacturing stage only, and state at all stages down to retail) and the states enjoy considerable autonomy in the administration of their VAT (and may, under the new Constitution currently being debated, have even more, including differential VAT rates). Alternatively, in Mexico, although also a federal system, the administrative discretion left to the states on the VAT is much less than that in Brazil. Nevertheless, collection and auditing are primarily the responsibility of the states and, as the same states do not have an immediate direct share in the revenue collected, this can give rise to strains between the central control and the states.

In the Federal Republic of Germany, the states collect and administer the VAT, and a formula is used to allocate the proportion to be remitted to the Central Government. In this case, the states have a clear interest in collecting all the tax due as this increases their own revenue as well as that of Bonn.

The desirable balance seems to be one where local offices are given administrative decision-making responsibilities that will be improved through local knowledge of local traders. These would include registration and deregistration, delinquencies, field and desk audits, complaints, and physical checks. Collection and financial control, including penalties, however, are probably better organized from a more remote center. Some control audits should also be made from headquarters. If state governments are to share in the revenue, better local administration will be obtained if that revenue share is seen to fluctuate directly with the VAT collections.

Staffing

Once broad agreements have been reached on the general structure and responsibilities of the administration of VAT, then the crucial question of staffing must be tackled. Of course, changes in the structure can induce changes in staffing levels, but basically the structure comes first. Thereafter, the variables affecting staffing must be considered, staffing levels in general outlined, and staffing by function allocated; finally, the staffing problems peculiar to the transitional period should be delineated.

Variables Affecting Staffing

The most important factor affecting staffing levels is the number of taxpayers. As the VAT usually covers more taxpayers than the taxes

Chart 12-4. Ireland: VAT Staff, January 1982[1,2]

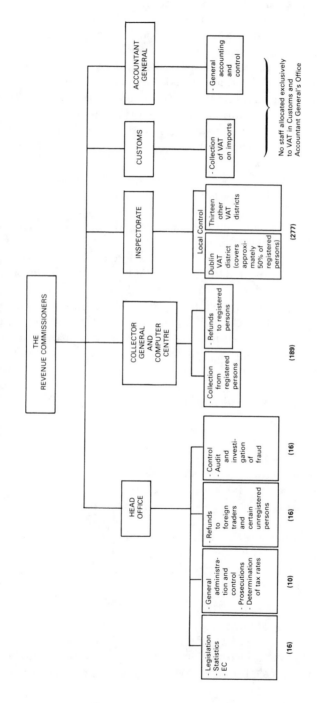

Source: Adapted from a chart of the Irish Revenue Commissioners.

[1]Not all staff are assigned full-time to VAT; for instance, at the Assistant Secretary level, approximately a quarter of their time would be allocated to VAT, and at the Principal Officer level, perhaps less than a third of their time.

[2]Numbers in parentheses refer to the full-time equivalent staff in each functional category; total revenue staff on VAT = 524.

replaced, the case is immediately made for an increase in staff. However, it should be noted that it is the number of registered taxpayers that is at issue here. Thus, staffing requirement is a function of the following:

(1) The exemption turnover limit.

(2) The exempted goods and services.

(3) The treatment of agriculture.

(4) The treatment of affiliated companies and group trading.

(5) The collection by other agencies.

(6) The staff transferred from taxes replaced.

(7) The frequency of returns.

(8) The complexity of tax rates;

(9) The standard of administration.

(10) The existing computer systems.

Each of these variables is discussed below.

(1) A high exemption limit can transform the scale of administrative problems. If many smaller traders need not register, the staff can concentrate on the more important and remunerative revenue sources. For instance, in Latin America, small traders typically make an annual return and quarterly or biannual presumptive payments. Of course, other problems increase, including evasion, company splitting, and a reduced tax base, but the saving in staff can be substantial.

(2) Similarly, if important lines of goods and services are omitted from the VAT, staffing needs are reduced. If, for example, all professional services are not included in the VAT base, an irritating and difficult to tax group is avoided, admittedly at the expense of revenue, neutrality, and equity, but fewer staff are needed.

(3) In many countries, farmers are the largest group to be left out of the VAT. In New Zealand, for instance, the difference between including all farmers as registered taxpayers (estimated 180,000 registered traders) and excluding them (120,000 registered traders) was 33 percent of the potential registration base. Ways to avoid requiring farmers to register, for example, the EC flat rate offset (see Chapter 7), not only avoid taxing a difficult sector, they greatly reduce the need for staff. However, in countries with advanced, literate, and numerate farmers, who frequently employ accountants to keep their books, registration and control for VAT need not involve a disproportionate number of administrative staff.

(4) Returns can be simplified by allowing subsidiary companies to register as a group, through a central parent company as the registered trader.

(5) The amount of VAT collected by other agencies affects staffing requirements. An island economy typically imports a large part of national consumption, whether as final or intermediate goods. The VAT is collected by customs officers at the point of entry. In some countries, this can represent over 60 percent of the VAT revenue and, even in Europe, can be as high as 35 percent and is probably the most secure portion of the VAT revenue. Moreover, in the control of VAT, the document established at the port of entry is the single most important control element. Manufacturers and wholesalers can be efficiently audited only if an audit trail is started by the import document. By contrast, if the United States were to introduce a VAT, the potential handle of collection at the import stage would be a much smaller proportion of consumption than in most countries now using VAT, so the likely demands on noncustoms staff would be higher. Similarly, state tax personnel can take over federal VAT administration, as has been the case in the Federal Republic of Germany.

(6) Staffing requirements are also affected by using staff released from the taxes abolished. Frequently this requires retraining and the strains between old and new staff in the VAT can persist and disrupt staffing for many years. Staff can be transferred only gradually since the taxes to be replaced still have to be administered for several months following the start of the VAT (see Chart 12-5, below).

(7) The volume of paperwork and hence the staff needed to handle it can be significantly altered by the required frequency of VAT returns. A balance must be struck between the evenness of cash flow to the government and the volume of administration. An annual VAT is conceivable but would create a large interest-free loan to the traders and leave the government with an uneven lumpy revenue, a potentially more difficult administration, and probably increase evasion. A monthly VAT is used (especially in Latin America where inflation is high), but the flow of documentation is larger. Indeed, in Chile in the mid-1970s, the authorities tried to collect VAT *in advance* every 15 days, to cope with high inflation. Many countries collect on a two-monthly or quarterly basis (with a provision for monthly returns for established cases where large refunds are due) with returns staggered through the period to ensure an even flow of work and revenue.[6] A

---

[6]Some advisors do not favor staggered returns; they argue that returns should be filed to ensure the best possible compliance and maintain that to concentrate on, say,

quarterly return should economize a trifle on staff, leaving more staff for audit by requiring fewer for processing returns.

In some developing countries, such as Argentina, Mexico, and Peru, VAT taxpayers have been required to file yearly returns but make provisional monthly payments. However, as one commentator noted, "Experience shows that the yearly return does not seem to add to the effectiveness of VAT administration because most administrations lack the resources to match the provisional monthly payments with it."[7]

(8) The more complex the VAT, the more staff is needed to run it. A single rate VAT requires less staff than a multirate tax. Legislators, anxious to exhibit their consciousness of equity, introduce multiple rates and complex exemptions; they ignore the cost to the taxpaying public of the extra staff required to administer the more complicated VAT. Even worse, legislators will introduce VAT complexities and not create the staff positions to administer the tax properly, thus actually creating more inequities than they "solved" by the new legislation. It is interesting that, broadly speaking, the trends in the newer VATs (Indonesia, Korea, Mexico, New Zealand, Spain, Taiwan Province of China, and Turkey) have been toward fewer rates, and those countries already using many rates (Belgium and Italy) have been trying to reduce the number.

(9) The standard of administration is a variable that can profoundly influence staffing. A quality system, sparing no expenses, might allow for visits to traders each year; in a less efficient system, the visits could take place, say, once every 6 years (one system acknowledges its audit frequency as once every 30 years, but this inevitably leads to greater evasion and is indefensible). Thus, it is clear that the level of compliance is an important factor in assessing staffing needs. There is always a trade-off between using staff to ensure that the really large VAT taxpayers are audited regularly and properly (and knowing that this would mean less staff is allocated to audit small traders who will, therefore, be evading tax) and needing staff to audit smaller traders (knowing that this could put some major revenues at risk). A typical frequency might entail visits to very large traders twice a year and visits to small traders once every four to five years. Much depends on

---

only four submission dates a year improves compliance. This may be true, but there are offsetting inefficiencies involved in bunching returns. The flow of work for accountants, advisors, and tax officials is better if returns are staggered—and the effect on compliance is not likely to be great.

[7]Casanegra de Jantscher (1986, p. 14).

the standard of accounting and auditing and the actual underpayments found at each type of trader.

(10) Whether to use the existing computer system or to upgrade it is the final variable. Of course, the VAT software must be unique to VAT but if there is hardware available, then staffing and other administrative costs may be reduced. Ireland, for instance, uses one computer for all taxes, as does Korea (see Chapter 15).

The range of variation shown in Table 12-2 is quite surprising: Italy employs one staff member for every 726 taxpayers, whereas the U.K. figure drops to 149. In one Asian country, the initial staffing ratio was 1:45 and in an African country, 1:31. What does seem clear is that the suggested staffing ratio for a U.S. VAT is way out of line. The U.S.

Table 12-2. VAT: Ratio of Staff to Taxpayers in Selected Countries

	Year	Ratio of Staff to Taxpayers
France	1982	1:173
Ireland	1984	1:130
Italy	1978	1:726
Netherlands	1979	1:280
Portugal	1986	1:215
Sweden	1982	1:250
United Kingdom	1983	1:149
United States[1]	1984	1:1,000

Source: Various country reports.
[1] Estimated.

Internal Revenue Service (IRS) audits about 2 percent of its income, estate, and gift tax returns and relies on withholding to collect. By contrast, countries using VAT audit 10 percent to 15 percent of traders annually, cannot use withholding for VAT and, typically, collect a higher proportion of the VAT through the (secure) customs import stage than would be true for the United States.[8] The various country examples indicate that the IRS may have to budget for a substantially lower ratio of staff to taxpayers than estimated hitherto. Looking at Table 12-2, a more traditional ratio would suggest 1:250 and a conse-

[8]Casanegra de Jantscher (1987, pp. 302–305).

quent fourfold increase in the number of staff needed (from 20,000 to 80,000) and in the expense (from $410 million to, presumably, something well over $1 billion). In turn, this emphasizes that to justify such an administrative expense, the U.S. invoice-credit VAT rate would not need to be 5 percent but more like 10 percent to 15 percent. Whatever the final outcome, the actual figure should emerge from the careful assessment of staffing at each level.

Staffing in General

BACKGROUND

The functions of the staff at different levels must be clearly specified, then the number of staff should be allocated provisionally, followed by a check on the overall ratio to see how the "bottom-up" approach matches the aggregative approach and estimates outlined above.

Naturally, staff ratios, at different functional levels and overall, would be country-specific, but to illustrate some not implausible figures as we go along, let us presume we have a country with 300,000 registered traders where three levels of administration have been chosen—district, regional, and head office. Broadly, the district offices would be responsible for registration, advice, troubleshooting, and compliance; the regional offices would deal with inspection control and some legal and personnel matters; and the head office would collect and process all the VAT revenues and be responsible for general administration, policy, and research. Naturally, these functions can be reshuffled in many ways; for instance, where postal, telecommunications, and banking communications are subject to delays, collection may be pushed down to the district level.

In the following sections, the functions and staffing of each level will be reviewed briefly to give an idea of the options and some acceptable staffing ratios (which, of course, will vary widely for different societies and economies).

THE DISTRICT OFFICE

Control.—The usual control functions of the district office would include the following:

- Dealing with applications for registration.
- Interviewing traders.

- Educational visits to new traders.
- Responding to inquiries.
- Identifying new registrations and making changes in existing registrations.
- Cancellation of registrations for traders who go out of business.
- Dealing with credit and refund problems.
- Low-level "audits" and inspections and follow-up action on the basis of inspection reports from regional and headquarters offices.

The ratios for these functions may be a general figure of about 750–1,000 traders to each staff member, which seems appropriate for a relatively simple VAT (a standard rate, a zero rate for exports, a fairly high turnover exemption limit, and, say, a two-month return period).

Filing.—The district office would need, in addition, staff for routing and filing duties, to

- Establish and maintain the filing system.
- Check out and retrieve returns for audits.

Experience shows that each sorter can be expected to control some 30,000 returns a year,[9] or some 4,000–5,000 taxpayers or cases.

Inspectorate.—Probably the most important function of the district office will be the inspectorate. The VAT functions better with a high-visibility inspectorate and the trader knowing there is a reasonable risk of an inspector's visit fairly frequently. The inspectors would be responsible for both routine visits and fraud investigations. Their duty would be to be seen in the field rather than at the desk. They would not be performing full audits—see Chapter 13. The inspectors should have the following functions:

- Make educational visits to potential or newly registered traders.
- Make routine visits, selected principally by computer, and conduct selective checks.
- Help traders to comply with VAT regulations.
- Ensure that traders' records are kept in a way that fulfills VAT regulations.

---

[9]"Returns" does not necessarily mean one piece of correspondence; in the U.K. context each "return" might involve three actual letters to the trader.

- Detect and follow up suggested cases of evasion or fraud.

The number of inspectors is crucially dependent on the frequency of their visits and on the number of visits an inspector can accomplish each year. Information is difficult to compare internationally, as administrations differ so much in what they expect officers to do in the field and in the office and, indeed, in the provisions they make for their staff to travel about easily and the time allowed to do so. Some visits may take only an hour, for example, for cross-checking some invoices or for explaining a new ruling, while a fraud investigation might take a week, and some time has to be allowed for office work, updating of records, and so on. However, with these allowances, inspectors should on average manage to make at least one visit every two days. Obviously inspectors will give priority to high-risk or high-yield traders (say, the building trade or retailers) and spend less time on low-yield or low-risk traders, but with approximately 226[10] working days in a year, an inspector should conduct at least 113 visits.

So, with 113 visits by inspector each year and a registered trader population of 300,000, the implied inspectorate is shown in Table 12-3. With a four-year cycle and 300,000 traders in our illustrative economy, 664 inspectors would be needed, a ratio of 1:452.

Arrears.—The final function of the district office in our example would be to ensure that VAT is paid, including VAT debts. Staff must visit traders, sympathetically assess the trader's ability to pay (it may be

Table 12-3. Implied Inspectorate for Different Frequencies of Visits[1]

Average Frequency of Visits by Each Inspector	Number of Inspectors Needed	Ratio of Inspectors to Registered Traders
One year (300,000 × 1/113)	2,655	113
Two years (300,000/2 × 1/113)	1,327	226
Three years (300,000/3 × 1/113)	885	339
Four years (300,000/4 × 1/113)	664	452
Five years (300,000/5 × 1/113)	531	565

[1] Assuming an inspector conducts 113 visits a year.

[10] Assumes a 5-day week, four weeks of holiday, and 14 public days or long-service days; but note, a European country assumed 240 working days a year.

a genuine temporary liquidity problem), arrange a payment schedule, monitor any arrangement, and be firm in following up delinquencies. In some countries (including European examples), staff do not visit traders to collect arrears as it is considered too dangerous! Instead, the taxpayer is requested to come to the tax office. To some extent, the staff needed depends on the automaticity of the penalties and the commitment of the courts to back up the tax prosecutions (see Chapter 14). However, arrears are also a function of the general perception of the government's relationship to the private sector. In some countries, traders have frequent experience of government agencies delaying payment of their bills and, in response, traders sometimes withhold taxes due. This can affect the relationship between the government and the entire commercial sector, undermining tax compliance and the authority of the staff. However, this is not a problem peculiar to VAT.

If we assume a ratio of staff to registered traders of 1:2,000 for the recovery of arrears, the overall implied staff for our example would be 150. Or, with a district office responsible for 10,000 traders, about 5 staff in that office.

Administration.—Support staff duties include secretarial, training, and management services. Every country has a very different idea about the desirable ratio of support staff to "professionals." The training function will be at its most demanding at the initial stages of VAT, but will continue even after the tax is up and running. Some countries prefer to have training a function of the regional office with training at the district level being more on the job. If district offices become large, then a separate training office can be allocated to that area. Similarly, depending on the size of the district, one or two managers can be added to the administrative staff.

Overall, in a district office with 10,000 registered traders, and with 300,000 registered traders altogether, the staffing needs might be as follows:

	District Office	Overall
Control	10	300
Filing	2	60
Inspectors	22	660
Arrears	5	150
Administration	3	90
Total	42	1,260

THE REGIONAL OFFICE

In our example, we consider there should be about one regional office for every 7 to 10 district offices; we will assume four regional offices to service the 30 district offices. The regional office, in this example, would deal with the following:

- Inspection control.
- Monitoring district office performance.
- Legal interpretation of VAT legislation and cases for revenue recovery.
- Personnel recruitment, training, and coordination.
- Support services to districts for emergencies.

The day-to-day responsibility for inspection would lie with the district; the regional office would have one or two inspectors to carry out spot checks on the regional offices and to take over extensive and difficult investigations of evasion and fraud.

Each regional office might need a regional attorney or advisor. Alternatively, if communications are good and/or the country is compact, the administration might prefer to keep all the legal services at head office. The regional legal offices would be available for opinions on request from traders, district inspectors, and the regional comptroller. If there are local VAT tribunals where appeals are heard, the regional legal advisor would present the government's cases.

The personnel officer would be responsible for recruitment in accordance with head office guidelines. He might develop and maintain training programs, monitor careers, ensure that annual performance reviews are conducted, and maintain regional records.

Finally, the regional staff might be expected to help district offices if there were special problem cases in the district or to arrange interdistrict coordination should one district be shorthanded or have particular difficulties.

As noted earlier, such regional VAT offices would probably be expected to work closely with existing income tax officers and would probably share their accommodations. In our example, we are looking at numbers approximately as follows:

	Regional Office	Overall
Inspection control	5	20
Legal advisors	3	12
Personnel/Administration	3	12
Total	11	44

THE HEAD OFFICE

In our example, the head office is responsible for revenue collection and running the main electronic data processing (EDP) unit. Other functions would include VAT policy and research, inspection, legal services, and management.

Data Processing.—An important duty of data processing staff in VAT is to scan returns to ensure that the required data are available for entry and that they are entered correctly. A typical, uncomplicated VAT return would need checking for the following:

- Trader registration number.
- Taxable period.
- Goods and services sold liable to VAT correctly specified.
- Goods and services sold correctly exempted.
- Goods and services sold correctly zero rated.
- Goods and services purchased liable to VAT.
- Goods and services purchased exempt from VAT.
- Goods and services purchased zero rated.
- Net VAT due or net credit and evidence of payment.

A way to approach the problem of estimating the number of staff needed would be to take the total number of registered traders (300,000 in our example), and assume the two monthly return periods, crediting 150,000 returns a month, on a staggered basis. Evidence from some pay-as-you-earn (PAYE) and VAT data suggests that a staff member deals with some 3,000 to 4,000 payments a month, which means that some 38 to 50 staff would be needed. However, even the simple VAT entries discussed here suggest that, depending on the precise form of VAT chosen, more time will be needed than for PAYE. So the staff needed might be 50 percent to 80 percent more, say, 57 to 90; for our example, let us assume 75 staff for EDP screening (depending on expertise and duties this figure may be toward the high end of the options).

Similarly, data entry, updating the data base, and keeping the master file and the tax deduction ledger base requires about double the number of fields to be keyed, compared with PAYE. Therefore, using the same ratio as before, the staff needed for EDP entry might be about 85 (again, a possibly generous figure).

Policy and Research.—Although policy and research are most important for the launch of the VAT, they must be kept running after the initial decisions and problems have been dealt with. Obviously, many of the staff who have considered the issues and have thought and written about them more carefully would be valuable in advising regional and district offices. Nevertheless, governments keep changing the VAT structure and the head office must advise ministers on the practicality and cost of changes proposed; it should keep in touch with developments overseas, help prepare legislation and regulations, analyze data, and think ahead about potential improvements in the VAT. These functions are often underrated in the staffing of VAT, but in fact are crucial to the continued effectiveness and development of the tax.

Inspections, Legal Services, and Management.—The inspection and compliance staff at headquarters are, in a sense, the "keeper of the crown jewels" for the VAT. They should be the most highly qualified officers with field and desk experience to provide specialist investigation services, highly trained accounting support to the regions and districts, and have the ability to scrutinize computer selections for possible fraud cases and tax intelligence. Such a staff should certainly include statisticians, accountants, and inspectors.

Legal services would have to be employed to meet the casework load generated by VAT. This would depend greatly on the complexity of the tax, the attitude of traders to tax administration in general, and the general litigiousness of the society. The better the staff at the district inspectorate are in explaining and tactfully defining issues at the trader's level, the less the need would be for the expensive services of legal staff at the head office.

Finally, the head office should provide management and office services. These responsibilities would include the following:

- Publicity, including radio and television.
- Manuals, both initial and updated.
- Design of forms.
- Checking on the flow of reports and job sheets.
- Checking that recognized office procedures are followed in districts and regions.
- Overseeing personnel, training, and staff development.

Of course, the number of staff allocated to these functions would vary greatly, but for our example could be summarized as follows:

Head Office

EDP screening	75
EDP data entry	85
Policy and research	4
Inspection and compliance	10
Legal services	4
Management and office workers	25
Total	203

Another way to look at the head office figures, if the head office is responsible for raising returns and monitoring and running the VAT collections, is to estimate, as the British did with quarterly returns from over a million traders, that the average number of communications received by the central unit each working day would be about 50,000 (an average of three communications per trader per return—some are monthly—and 240 working days a year). Say an average of five minutes per communication and each effective seven-hour working day yielded a staff of 600 to add to the 300 needed for computer operations. In this way, an estimate of the staff needed for the central office alone amounted to about 1,000. However, "it may seem even more astonishing, and it certainly depressed us"[11] that the complementary staff for a head office—initial establishment, training, solicitor's office, the accountant, comptroller general's office, investigation, clerks, typists, registries, messengers, and cleaners accounted for another 1,000. Another general rule of thumb is that such staff is about a 1:1 ratio to the professional staff. So the U.K. Control Office was estimated to need a staff of about 2,000, which indicated a local staff of about 6,000 and 8,000 overall. With about a million traders, the implied staff/trader ratio was 1:125.

In our example, using the U.K. rule of thumb, with 226 working days, two monthly returns, and three communications per return, the implied staff needed for scanning would be 284. With about 84 staff needed for computer operations, the basic staff for the head office would be 368, and if the 1:1 ratio of head office complementary staff is needed, the head office ends up with 736—which appears a high figure for the example of our relatively small country. Clearly, such calculations are country-specific, but it pays to be aware of the underlying perceptions of the given advice—particularly if you are paying for the consultant.

The total staff in our example is 1,260 at the district level, 44 at regional offices, and 203 at the head office, making 1,507 in all. As the

[11]Johnstone (1975, p. 47).

assumed number of traders is 300,000, the overall staff ratio is 1:200, which is above the French and the U.K. figures, about the same as that for Portugal, but well below the figures for Italy or that suggested for the United States (see Table 12-2). However, it should be noted that no figure has been added for the proportion of time spent by customs officials collecting VAT. Whatever figures would be added for this in terms of full-time staff equivalents would reduce the staff/taxpayer ratio.

Table 12-4 shows the proposed percentage distribution of staff calculated for the U.S. VAT (with a staff to taxpayer ratio of 1:1,000). Compared with the example just considered above, both allocate exactly 35.8 percent to processing returns, computers, and statistical services; however, within this figure, the United States seems to assign an extremely small number to actually run the computers (this may simply reflect a different description of functions). For the rest, the U.S. Internal Revenue Service appears to assign more staff to taxpayer services and appeals, at the expense of the examination services.

It must be emphasized that the example discussed above does not represent any country and is not intended as a recommendation; it does, however, highlight the issues to be discussed and gives at least an idea of possible relative levels of staffing and allocation of functions.

Table 12-4. A Comparison of the Percentage Distribution of Staff in the Example in the Text and in the Proposed U.S. VAT

| | Example | | United States | |
	Number	Percent	Number	Percent
Total staff required	1,507	100.0	20,694	100.0
Of which:				
Returns processing	380	25.2	7,389	35.7
Computer and				
statistical services	160	10.6	22	0.1
Subtotal	540	35.8	7,411	35.8
Examination	670	44.5	7,032	34.0
Taxpayer services				
and other costs	131	8.7	2,407	11.7
Appeals and counsel	16	1.1	940	4.5

Sources: See text and United States, Department of the Treasury, *Tax Reform for Fairness, Simplicity, and Economic Growth: The Treasury Department Report to the President,* Vol. 3: Value-Added Tax (Washington: Office of the Secretary, Department of the Treasury, November 1984), Appendix 9-B, p. 128.

Chart 12-5. An Example of Recruitment and Placing of VAT Staff

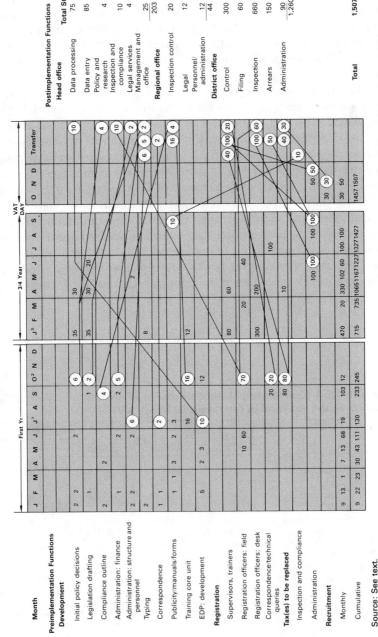

Source: See text.

Note: Recruitment numbers are shown in preimplementation functions *before* the circular boxes: *after* the circular boxes recruitment is shown with reference to the postimplementation function.

1 Date when skeleton head office starts.
2 Date when regional offices are set up.
3 Date when district offices open.

Transitional Staff Problems

Recruitment and Transfer

Whether the VAT replaces existing taxes or is introduced as a new tax, there are important transitional issues for staffing. The VAT staff cannot be created with a complete hierarchy overnight. Senior staff for all levels must be brought in from elsewhere in the service.

Unfortunately, real life does not allow such a simple smooth changeover. The taxes to be replaced must be monitored up to and past the day on which the new tax is introduced. No matter how desirable it may be to detach staff from the old tax for training and thinking about the new tax, the machinery of government has to be maintained so that only a limited number of trainees can be released at any one time. Moreover, personnel have to continue working on the old tax, overlapping the staff of the VAT; collections must be made, delinquents chased, audits conducted, and penalties collected. For a time the two systems will operate side by side and this requires a "hump" of staff during the changeover. This is no easy matter to arrange and is certain to cause strain. The responsibilities and timing of job changes need to be worked out in detail well ahead, so that everyone is fully aware of what is to happen and unpleasant surprises are minimized.

It is wasteful to recruit permanent staff solely for the temporary "hump," when careful anticipation of retirements or re-employment of recently retired staff for the temporary overlap can cut the long-run costs of staffing the VAT. Chart 12-5 gives one example of a possible schema for the recruitment and placing of staff. Duties are divided into preimplementation and postimplementation functions and the transfers are shown so that the cumulative recruitment problem is presented, literally, as the bottom line. Again, this is only an example, and each country will create its own method of analyzing the problem, but the types of problems are similar and can be represented in similar ways.

The assumptions behind Chart 12-5 are that 21 months are allowed to plan and introduce VAT. Legislation for VAT will be introduced during this period; the exact timing depends on political and legislative situations unique to each country (Hungary put the legislation through only three months before the VAT was introduced). Obviously, administrators cannot train and organize for the VAT until they have a clear mandate from parliament. In our example, legislation might be introduced at the end of the first year. The first six months involve an initial design team of about two dozen persons and the first major recruitments are the 70 trainee supervisors, 10 for the head office eventually and 60 to form the core groups of six at the ten district offices. Another early and important recruitment is that of the 10 EDP staff to develop the computerization of the VAT at head office. Indeed, half of this group is recruited in the second month of planning and is involved in all the early discussions. Further main EDP and data processing recruitment is left to later in the program.

In the example shown in Chart 12-5, only 280 (250 for inspection and compliance and 30 for administration) persons are transferred from the taxes being replaced; naturally, this figure could be much larger, depending on the number employed in the taxes replaced. However, experience shows that sometimes it is difficult to get people to leave the existing tax administrations and, even when they do move, frequently their skills and motivation are not necessarily suited to the VAT.

In this example, the monthly recruitment reaches a peak nine months before the VAT is introduced, with the addition of EDP personnel and a large batch of trainee supervisors and field and data registration officers, all bound for regional offices for control and inspection functions. The total cumulative number recruited for VAT, 1,507, is the same as that used in the earlier discussion on relative functional responsibilities; the totals under each function at headquarters and at regional and district offices is, similarly, the same as that described earlier.

Finally, three dates are assumed to be important. A skeleton headquarters is set up after 6 months (that is, 15 months before the VAT is started). The small regional offices are opened 2 months later and, a year before the "VAT date," the district offices are started with 6 inspection control "core" trained officers each, and 10 more officers to be trained by the core officers. After another 3 months, a further 380 officers are added to the districts (30 for inspection and 8 for control in each office) to be trained by those already trained. There is another influx 3 months later, and the final additions occur just before and after the VAT starts, as staff is transferred from the taxes replaced.

Plans for Staffing

The planning for VAT can take many forms, depending on the political, administrative, and legal relationships and responsibilities. The first thinking about VAT might best be conducted in a small cohesive committee with an outside (academic?) chairman, government lawyers, and administration economists (such as the format in Portugal). Such a committee would consider the feasibility and broad implications of VAT for revenue, prices, savings, equity, and so on and as such is not shown in Chart 12-5. The committee's report would be a precursor to the decisions to adopt VAT after which the timetable outlined in Chart 12-5 could start.

If it is desirable to push ahead more quickly and involve from the outset those who will conduct the VAT, then the outline organization for planning the VAT could take the form shown in Chart 12-6. This embodies some of the structure used in the United Kingdom where the planning (and the present VAT administration) is split into two broad categories—"VAT liabilities" and "VAT machinery" (not the

Chart 12-6. A Possible Outline Organization for Planning VAT (I)

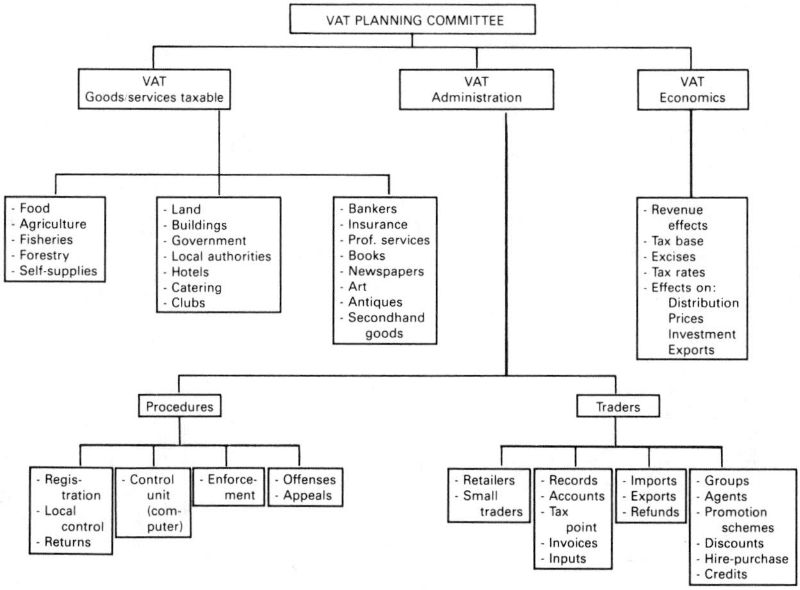

Source: See text.

Chart 12-7. A Possible Outline Organization for Planning VAT (II)

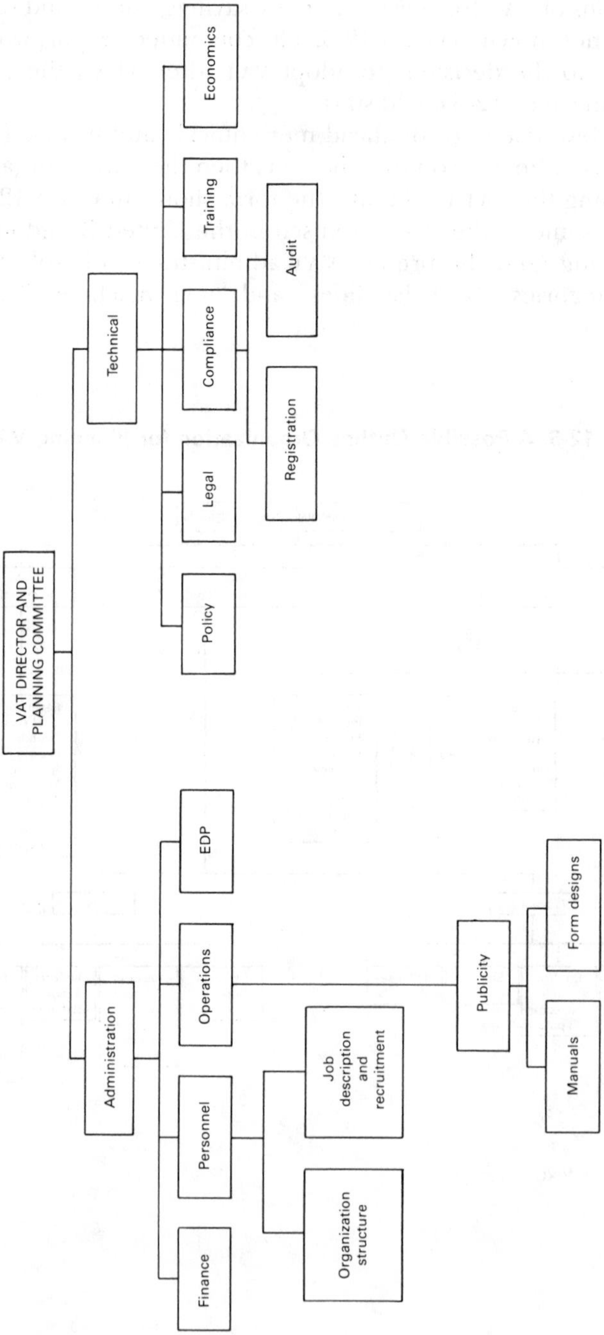

Source: See text.

most elegant usage). In Chart 12-6, it is suggested that "VAT: Goods and services" would deal with the liabilities of different goods and services to tax and another principal branch "VAT: Administration" would be subdivided into problems connected with "Procedures" and others connected with "Traders." Of course, few distinctions are watertight, and those dealing with, say, "retailers" would also have to know about, for instance, the decisions being made in "food, agriculture, hotels, and secondhand goods." Indeed, this whole division might be too complex for a country where the number of traders was below, say, 300,000 and some consolidation might be needed. An alternative organizational structure is given in Chart 12-7, which draws on the experience of New Zealand.

In Chart 12-6, a third major responsibility is shown for the economic effects of VAT (this responsibility is subsumed under the main subheading "Technical" in the New Zealand example—Chart 12-7). Ministers are keenly aware of the potential political ammunition provided by the introduction of VAT and those responsible will be asked for initial assessments (and continuous updates) of the likely effects on prices, household expenditures, investments, and exports. As some of the earliest work on VAT will involve the calculation of alternative tax bases and possible combinations of tax rates, this unit should be created at the beginning of the planning stage (and, indeed, may include the continuation of the original appraisal committee referred to above), but would be run down and abolished, or phased into research, once VAT was introduced and working efficiently.

It may be desirable to create a small legal team to advise the VAT planners on the numerous issues involving the law in nearly all aspects of early decisions on VAT (this is shown in Chart 12-5, with two persons recruited in the early stages of thinking about VAT and eventually assigned to VAT headquarters).

Training for VAT depends on the tax it is replacing and the officers to be trained. If the income tax department is responsible for VAT and uses its own officers, the training may be an extension of its existing courses, simplified to the extent that VAT audits do not need the full galaxy of accounting tools used in income taxation. If, however, the VAT employs many officers previously used to administer taxes based on physical controls, such as customs and excise, then they will have to be retrained to administer a tax based principally on financial returns and controls.

Whatever the scale of retraining, the broad methods are similar. A small group of officers is selected to be trained, say, 12 to 18 months before the VAT is to be introduced. This "core" group may have to be taught for 4 to 5 months, perhaps helping draft manuals, often with

Table 12-5. United Kingdom: VAT Statistics, 1978/79–1982/83

	1978/79	1979/80[1]	1980/81	1981/82	1982/83	Percentage Change, 1978/79 to 1982/83
A. MANPOWER, CONTROL, COSTS, AND REVENUE						
(Numbers in thousands)						
VAT manpower						
Directly employed on activity	10	...	10	...	10	1.9
Directly employed on activity and domestic administration	13	12	12	11	11	−7.3
Registered traders at March 31	1,286	1,327	1,338	1,380	1,398	5.4
Control visits	400	368	357	358	335	−16.3
(In millions of pounds sterling)						
Underdeclarations of tax discovered on visits	61	84	146	169	290	375.4
Overdeclarations of tax discovered on visits	4	4	10	5	24	585.7
Cost of administration (including domestic administration)	99	105	130	145	155	48.0
Revenue outturn	5,218	8,706	11,450	12,363	14,413	65.6
(In pounds sterling)						
Average underdeclarations discovered per visit	152	228	409	472	866	469.7

B. COST OF ADMINISTRATION AS PERCENTAGE OF REVENUE

VAT	1.90	1.20	1.14	1.17	1.08	−40.0
Excise duties	0.44	0.41	0.44	0.39	0.37	−5.0
VAT and customs and excise	1.59	1.35	1.36	1.32	1.26	−21.0
Inland Revenue duties	2.00	1.89	1.98	1.72	1.73	−13.5
Inland Revenue and National Insurance	1.41	1.31	1.40	1.23	1.24	−12.1
Ratio of registered traders to manpower directly employed (VAT only)	128	139	141	147	149	16.4

Sources: United Kingdom, Commissioners of H.M. Customs and Excise, *76th Report*, Cmnd. 9655 (London: H. M. Stationery Office, 1985), and Board of Inland Revenue, *Report for the Year Ended 31st December 1985*, Cmnd. 9831 (London: H. M. Stationery Office, 1986).

[1] Revenues increased in 1979/80 because of the increase in the VAT rate to 15 percent (from 8 percent and 12.5 percent).

the aid of counterparts from other countries. After their training, each of them becomes a teacher to train similar groups on, say, three- to six-week courses. In one developing country, a typical course designed for training local (district) junior officers engaged on the straightforward administration of VAT involved approximately three weeks: for tests (three days); theory and practice of VAT (two days); VAT law (one day); bookkeeping and accounting for VAT (four days); "control" visits (four days); reports on control visits (one day); and fraud, law of evidence, and psychological aspects (one day). Depend- ing on the size of recruitment and training, the "teachers" can con- tinue training successive groups of officers, and their newly trained personnel can themselves return to provincial centers to teach yet more staff. Whatever system is adopted, it has to be articulated well in advance, so that the cadre of trained personnel will be available at the locations on the dates needed to implement the VAT (see possible sequences outlined in Chart 12-5).

Costs of Administration

It is notoriously dangerous to relate costs of tax administration to the revenue collected. First, it is often difficult to designate precisely which officers administer which taxes; often the responsibility be- tween taxes is blurred for one tax helps another (after all, one point in favor of VAT is that it is supposed to help the income tax). Second, changes in rates of duty and tax may need more staff, yet greatly "improve" their efficiency ratios. Conversely, multiple rates of VAT might both raise revenue and require more staff, thus not improving the ratio at all. Nevertheless, as long as we are not wedded to the significance of these ratios to several places of decimals, their broad movement over time and their relation to other similar tax ratios may be informative.

Table 12-5 shows how the costs of administering the U.K. VAT have fallen over the period 1978/79–1982/83 and amounted to only about 1.08 percent of revenue in 1982/83. Of course, as the table also shows, excises were the cheapest taxes to administer (under 0.5 percent of revenue collected). Indirect taxes were less expensive, in toto, to administer than personal and corporate income tax (above 1.72 per- cent). It should be noted that if national insurance is included as part of direct taxation, the administration costs as a percentage of revenue fall to a figure much the same as that for indirect taxation.

A fair comment seems to be that in 1982/83 there were about 150 registered traders per person employed in administering the U.K.

VAT (up from 128 five years earlier). However, as noted earlier, this ratio can be as high as over 700 (as in Italy) or even 1,000 (as proposed in the United States), but at the expense of the number of control visits. As Table 12-5 shows, each control visit in the United Kingdom on average uncovered underdeclarations of £866 (US$1,561), so that the potential revenue costs of *not* employing sufficient staff can be high.

Thus, evidence indicates that a VAT introduced at low rates would need almost the same number of staff, yield less revenue, and be less revenue effective as a VAT at much higher rates. Given the complexity of the changeover, the recommendation has to be that the costs of the VAT can only be justified if it is a major revenue source which, in the best of circumstances, generates sufficient resources to allow the government leeway to make discretionary changes in other taxes (a point debated in the U.S. context). The buoyant revenue from a broad-based single rate VAT also can be used to compensate low-income households through transfer payments for equity costs incurred through the introduction of a VAT (see Chapters 1 and 11).

CHAPTER 13

Control

> It is the . . . fear induced in ordinary decent trading citizens that they might inadvertently have done something wrong . . . or done or omitted to do something which could land them up before the Magistrate like a serf before a Tsarist Court . . . which is at the root of the unpopularity of this tax.
>
> —UNITED KINGDOM, COMMITTEE ON ENFORCEMENT POWERS OF THE REVENUE DEPARTMENTS (Keith Committee), *Report*, p. 80

The provision of adequate controls is crucial to a VAT system. Controls are exercised through a number of means, including taxpayer registration, deregistration, invoices, refunds, and audit. These topics are dealt with in separate sections below.

Taxpayer Registration

Purpose of Registration

Registration brings a person within the control of the tax authorities. Usually this means he is required to make periodic returns of purchases and sales and, at the same time, pay the VAT. However, in some countries (for example, Belgium), all traders must register whether or not they will actually be liable for VAT. The compilation and maintenance of a comprehensive and accurate register are essential to the successful introduction and operation of a VAT. Steps toward its compilation must be taken well in advance of the start of the tax. Moreover, VAT information must be sent to all registered persons at various times to inform them of any changes in procedures and their responsibilities to register or not under the law.

The number of taxpayers is not a function of country size as Table 13-1 demonstrates. The highest percentage of taxpayers as a proportion of total population is in New Zealand, a relatively small country; two other smaller countries, Haiti and Niger, have the lowest percentage. The principal influences on the number of taxpayers (see Chapter 12) are the exemption threshold, the treatment of farmers, the treatment of groups, and the coverage of VAT. Low-exemption countries such as Denmark will tend to have more registered taxpayers as will those who tax farmers, as is the case in New Zealand and, again, in Denmark. However, the United Kingdom, even though it taxes farmers, has a lower percentage of VAT taxpayers partly because its exemption threshold is higher. Less sophisticated economies and those where the VAT does not cover the retail stage, for instance, Colombia and Peru, will have fewer taxpayers, as will those where substantial sectors such as services are untaxed. Finally, as described below, a generous willingness to allow groups of companies to register as one taxpayer reduces the number of registrations.

Exemption Limit for Registration

The operation of a sales tax is kept within manageable proportions, either by granting exemption to small enterprises by not requiring those with a low turnover to register, or by ignoring small tax liabilities the collection of which costs more in administrative expense than is worthwhile. A small retail taxpayer under VAT usually buys his goods for resale at tax-paid prices and all that is given up by the government through the exemption is the tax on his margin. As suggested in Chapter 6, small enterprises with annual sales under a fairly generous exemption limit should not be required to register or pay any VAT. The exemption limit should be designed to keep initial VAT registrations to manageable proportions. Through time, with unchanged exemption limits, inflation will increase the fraction of firms having to register.

Preparatory Work on Registration

The appropriate time between the date of registration and the start of the VAT depends on at least three factors. First, whether another form of sales tax already exists in the country; second, whether the coverage of the VAT is to be similar to existing sales taxes or whether it is to embrace a wider range of goods and services; and third, the likely number of VAT taxpayers. For example, for the successful introduc-

Table 13-1. VAT Taxpayers as a Percentage of Population Ranked by Size

	Number of VAT Taxpayers (*In thousands*)	Population	VAT Taxpayers as a Percentage of Population
New Zealand	282	3,246	8.7
Italy	4,601	56,945	8.1
Denmark	385	5,101	7.6
Norway	295	4,144	7.1
Korea	1,168	20,357	5.7
Belgium	561	9,853	5.7
France	3,027	55,133	5.5
Austria	400	7,545	5.3
Sweden	400	8,330	4.8
Chile	399	11,990	3.3
Netherlands	468	14,486	3.2
Panama	4	2,180	3.2
Ireland	110	3,560	3.1
Germany, Fed. Rep. of	1,857	61,065	3.0
United Kingdom	1,500	56,618	2.7
Argentina	514	30,531	1.7
Uruguay	50	3,004	1.7
Peru	13	18,653	0.7
Colombia	150	28,418	0.5
Ecuador	22	9,367	0.2
Niger	0.4	6,391	0.01
Haiti	0.5	5,451	0.01

Sources: World Bank, *The World Bank Atlas 1987* (Washington); "The Rise of VAT: U.S. Holds Out, Hungary to Join," *Financial Times* (London), June 12, 1987, p. 20; Milka Casanegra de Jantscher, "Problems of Administering a Value-Added Tax in Developing Countries," IMF Working Paper WP/86/15 (unpublished; Washington: International Monetary Fund, December 18, 1986); and various country reports.

tion of a VAT entailing a change from a ring-type sales tax at manufacturers' level to a VAT at the same level, a period of 6 to 12 months may be needed to train inspectors and to instruct businessmen on the operation of the tax and on their responsibilities to the government. However, the number of taxpayers is more or less unchanged and the tax register should be the same; therefore, the preparatory work on the register is only to ensure it is up to date.

If, however, no form of general sales tax exists, or if the number of taxpayers is likely to be substantially increased (in Spain 400,000 previously unrecorded taxpayers were discovered), a period of at least 18 months or more may be needed. Interestingly enough, in centrally planned economies (for example, in Eastern Europe or some Asian countries) the existing demands on state enterprises and cooperatives by the ministry of finance for detailed returns for both revenue and economic planning purposes mean that the administrative changes needed for a VAT may not be as great as in more market-oriented regimes. Indeed, the greater concentration ratios of centrally planned economies with larger and fewer enterprises, and state-owned activities that include retailing, mean that the registration and accounting for VAT is easier.

To allow for flexibility, the latest date for registration need not be fixed in the law, but provision can be made for its determination by Ministerial Order at whatever might be considered an appropriate time. The intended date should be announced, however, when the draft bill is circulated and, of course, should ensure that all taxpayers are registered before the start of VAT and not, as in one developing country, leave the final date for registration three months into the operation of the new tax. Information about VAT is sent before the final date for registration to all persons already registered for whatever tax is to be replaced and, of course, checked against the register for other taxes (for example, on corporate income). There should be extensive publicity in the press, radio, and television to ensure that all likely taxpayers are aware of the registration requirements.

Unit of Business for Registration

Where a trader operates through two or more places of business, he may find it convenient to register each unit separately or, alternatively, as one entity. However, safeguards must be provided to prevent the provision being used for tax evasion by splitting up a business into two or more separate units to bring each below the limit for registration. To check such avoidance, a provision can state that if the aggregate sales of the various branches exceed a certain amount, they will all be chargeable to VAT on their sales, either as a group or individually.

Another consideration is that a group of closely related taxable persons might wish to register as a single unit and to have the business carried on by the various members of the group treated for VAT purposes as if it was carried on by one of them. Such treatment is particularly advantageous under a VAT because invoices would have to be issued only for sales transactions outside the group and VAT liability arises only on such transactions. This procedure creates administrative savings both to the taxpayers concerned and to the authorities. Such arrangements need the approval of the tax authorities, and the members of the group have to undertake to be jointly and severally liable to comply with all the statutory provisions of VAT. In some countries, all group registrations are dealt with in a special control unit or tax district that handles group registration for the whole country; this seems a sensible treatment given the specialized law and accounting issues that can be involved.

Penalty for Nonregistration

Failure to register must be treated as a serious tax offense and a significant penalty for nonregistration must be specified and imposed. The advantages of such a provision are not always appreciated in developing countries. Liability to VAT should not depend on registration; VAT is liable whether or not the trader is registered, as long as his sales exceed whatever threshold has been fixed. A trader who "forgets" to register is still liable to pay VAT. Thus, any tax for a period before registration should be recoverable in full with penalties. The penalty for nonregistration can be a percentage of the VAT unpaid increasing the longer the amount is outstanding. As such calculations can be subject to protracted dispute, the authorities can be given the option to levy a lump sum, plus a continuing accumulating penalty for each day of nonregistration.

Keeping the Register Up to Date

To ensure that the register is up to date, taxable persons should be required to inform the tax authorities of changes in circumstances affecting registration, including death. The local tax offices should review periodically against other information in the office (even the humble telephone book—especially the yellow pages—can be most useful) the lists of registered persons to ensure that new traders are brought on to the tax rolls, and particularly that those whose sales have risen beyond the threshold for treatment as small enterprises are brought into the full VAT.

Table 13-2 shows the result of an interesting exercise in Argentina. The existence of firms was established by checking many sources, including the telephone yellow pages and lists of professions and farmers. These numbers (Column 1) were compared with the actual number of taxpayers (Column 2); that implied the possible percentage

(Column 3) of evaders. For example, 90 "restaurants" emerged in the sample, of which only 49 percent appeared as taxpayers (that is, approximately 50 percent evasion) or, of "ladies apparel" businesses, in which only 39 percent showed up as evaders, contrasted with "bookstores," all of which were registered.

Persons Who May Elect to Register

It is a good idea to allow a supplier of taxable goods and services, whose sales do not exceed the minimum annual exemption limit, to elect to register if he wishes to do so for trade reasons. Persons who volunteer to register are subject to the same obligations as other registered persons. The procedure for electing to become registered is identical with that for traders who are obliged to register.

A person who is not obliged to register might consider it advisable to become registered (1) if he supplies taxable goods or taxable services to registered persons—because he could then pass on a tax credit to his registered customers or clients; (2) if he exports goods—since as a registered trader, he would have no tax to pay on his export sales and could claim a credit or repayment of any tax invoiced to him on his purchases relating to the goods exported; or (3) if a VAT registration number can make his business presentation (letterhead, invoices) look more professional.

Usually a registered person is chargeable on all taxable sales even if his turnover does not exceed the exemption limit (but not in Belgium —see above).

VAT Registration Numbers

A taxpayer identification number is essential for VAT. Some countries adopt the existing tax identification system for the VAT and some use the introduction of this major new tax as the occasion for an overhaul of the identification system. Indeed, one of the principal contentious issues, that thwarted the 1987 attempt by Japan to introduce a VAT, was the obligation of traders to seek a code number designed to guard against fraudulent tax paid invoices and "other irregularities."[1] Tax identification numbers seem to be provocative; in

[1]"Japan: Sales Tax," *World Tax Report* (1987, p. 14).

Table 13-2. Argentina: Characteristics of a Sample of Hard-to-Tax Groups, July 1968

Type of Business or Profession	Total Number in the Sample	Of which: Number of Taxpayers	Of which: Nontaxpayers *(In percent)*
Jewelry stores	67	41	39
Furniture stores	75	57	24
Dentists	114	98	14
Physicians	143	114	20
Beauty parlors	83	46	45
Representations	74	60	19
Restaurants	90	44	51
Insurance agents and companies	58	44	24
Civil engineers	90	73	19
Exporters	21	15	29
Importers	32	27	16
Funeral homes	38	33	13
Real estate	78	75	4
Hardware	78	56	28
Clothing manufacturers	77	59	23
Shoe stores	88	59	33
Advisers	108	62	43
Ladies' apparel	64	39	39
Electric appliances	51	38	25
Architects	103	93	10
Lawyers	190	159	16
Tourism	45	33	37
Bakers	81	50	38
Bookstores	54	54	0
Dairy shops	23	14	39
Liquor stores	35	22	27
Night clubs	34	17	50
Cattle raising	145	112	23

Source: Adapted from Federico J. Herschel, "Tax Evasion and Its Measurement in Developing Countries," *Public Finance* (The Hague), Vol. 33, No. 3 (1978), p. 254.

1987 the Australian Government was obliged to drop a similar proposal. By contrast, every Swede is given a taxpayer identification number that "the law-abiding Swedes accept without noticeable complaints [so] that even personal checks are embossed with the ID number, regardless of the fact that the number starts out with six digits revealing the birthday of the holder."[2] If the income tax author-

[2]Mutén (1988, pp. 2–3).

ities are to administer the VAT scheme, the use of income tax code numbers for both the VAT and the income tax can be useful. Some countries use the old tax code with an additional suffix to denote the VAT. An identification numbering system common to both importers and traders is useful for cross-checking; frequently an audit trail can be established for a particular imported shipment and traced through to wholesalers and retailers. This can be particularly useful in smaller developing countries (particularly, island economies). If such codes do not exist, the VAT can be made the occasion for their introduction.

The most important key to an effective computer system is the unique identifier that can distinguish one record from another. In the case of a taxpayer master file, the identifier ensures that each taxpayer's account contains all the relevant tax and payment data for that taxpayer alone. The best identifier is one that is unique, and permanent. It must be capable of being easily checked for transposition of numbers and other errors. It should be easy to remember as it is used frequently by others. It should not be offensive (as can be the case with three or more letters).

The identification number system shown below meets most of these conditions. Only the first eight digits are permanent and susceptible to computer check. New codes of ten digits or more (Latin American countries typically use eleven-digit codes) can be produced (see Chapter 12 for another example):

1	2 to 7	8	9 to 10
Type of taxpayer code (corporation, individual government agency, etc.)	Sequential	Check digit	Branch office code

The first eight digits are designed to be permanent numbers, the eighth digit capable of detecting error in the first seven digits using a standard formula, but modified to designate the reciprocal of the remainder as the check digit. The last two digits, which are not subject to error detection, can be used to identify the home office or main office of a taxable firm and each of its branch offices separately. Such a number will be entered by the authorities on the registration form—see Appendix I.

The other extreme is to have no identification number, as at present in Japan. This, of course, makes computerization of returns much more difficult, introduces the possibilities of duplication and error, and greatly complicates audit. Basically, a taxpayer identification number is essential.

Application Forms for Registration for VAT

Application forms should be provided free of charge, and they should be widely available not only in tax offices but also in banks and other public institutions (or perhaps sample forms can be available in such public places). A copy of the trade classification list showing the definitions of special traders (for example, hotels, boarding houses, rental accommodation, and restaurants) and the VAT Guide should be supplied along with this form. See Appendix I for a sample of a VAT registration form.

Checking VAT Forms by Local Tax Offices

The details on the initial VAT application forms must be checked during the educational visits by local tax officers. The particulars given by businessmen on their application forms for registration under VAT are of vital importance, especially the trade classifications allotted to businesses, because these may be used at a later stage to select cases for audit. Where a claim is made for treatment under the small trader scheme, the local office should satisfy itself at registration that the annual turnover is likely to be no more than the limit for the first year.

Reregistration and Deregistration

It is often not appreciated that net changes in the number of registered traders from year to year do not reflect the whole picture of the work of keeping the register up to date. Thus, in the United Kingdom, with approximately 1.2 million VAT taxpayers, as the Commissioners of Customs and Excise pointed out:

> In the 12 months up to September 1977 there were 170,000 new registrations and 158,000 cancellations, and in the following 12 months there were 153,000 new registrations and 164,000 cancellations. In other words, the Department has been required each year to deal with over 300,000 movements in the VAT Register, while the total of registered

traders increased by 12,000 in the first year and fell by 11,000 in the second.

Each movement in the Register gives rise to a substantial amount of work. Accurate information must be recorded about every new registration; this is essential to facilitate the smooth operation of the computer system, to ensure that any repayments of tax are made to the person properly entitled to receive them and to safeguard the position should it be found in the future that the registered person has failed to comply with his legal obligations to render returns, etc. Many registrations are followed by advisory visits to the trader's premises. Before a registered person can be removed finally from the VAT Register care has to be taken to ensure that any outstanding liability to pay tax has been identified and discharged.[3]

There are really no short cuts to keeping the register up to date. However, it is recommended that where an existing legal entity wishes to reregister as a new legal entity it should be allowed to do so with the minimum of formality. Unincorporated associations should be registered in the name of the association (and act in the names of representative members, that is, treasurer, vice chairman, etc., where otherwise a change of member would require a reregistration). Further descriptions of work on registrations will be found later in this chapter.

Invoices

The invoice is the crucial control document of the usual VAT. It establishes the tax liability of the supplier and the entitlement of the purchaser to a deduction for the VAT charged. Invoices must be carefully completed and kept as records. The law and regulations of each country lay down the form of invoice, the time limit for its issue, changes in invoices, and the use of credit notes. In the EC, each member state may determine criteria for admissibility of invoices.

The invoice must normally show the following:

- Name and address of person issuing the invoice.
- VAT registration number.
- Serial number of the invoice.
- Date of issue of the invoice.

[3]United Kingdom, Commissioners of H.M. Customs and Excise (1978, p. 16).

- Date of supply of the goods or services (if different from the date of invoice).
- A description of the goods or services.
- Amount charged, excluding VAT.
- Rate (including zero rate) and amount of VAT at each rate.
- Name and address of customer.

To prevent a possible black market developing in the use of tax invoices (which are a claim on the government, tantamount to printing money and the classic way to evade VAT—see Chapter 14), the requirement to give the name and address and reference of both seller and buyer, as well as the other statutory details should be strictly enforced. In the EC, most countries do not require a VAT registration number on the invoice, on the ground that if the other particulars are tampered with it is unlikely that the number will be correct. Where the buyer is not a taxable person it may seem preferable to issue an invoice quoting the consideration inclusive of VAT. On the other hand, legislators think this procedure conceals the tax from the public and the requirement should be to show the VAT separately on all sales, including retail sales. The EC practice is to quote prices VAT inclusive for retail sales only. Of course, retail invoices can be of a more summary nature.

As long as the required particulars are included, the invoice can take any form the company wishes. Some authorities standardize the invoices for VAT, such as in Taiwan Province of China, but given the variety of business and accounting practices, it imposes a heavy burden on many traders to use only one "official" invoice, and this at a time (the introduction of the VAT) when the authorities are seeking the greatest cooperation from the business community.

As a minimum, one copy of the invoice is kept by the supplier and the other by the purchaser. Each trader retains his copy of the invoice at his office to be inspected, if required, by a VAT auditor. In Chile, three invoices are required, one each for seller and purchaser, and the third to be kept by the seller in a separate file for inspection by the VAT authorities. Korea adopted a more rigorous system whereby each general taxpayer (that is, those who are not small traders) has to complete four invoices for each sale at the time of the supply of goods and services. One copy is kept by the person or business making the sale, another copy is sent by that person to the district tax office, the third copy is kept by the purchaser, and the fourth copy is sent by the purchaser to his district tax office. The two copies of the invoice held by the appropriate tax offices are then sent to the computer data processing unit which carries out a cross-check of sales against purchases. Tax invoices issued or received were to be kept for five years. Tax invoices in which the value of a transaction exceeded W 300,000 (US$236) were computerized for audit. This was a most ambitious attempt to use the underlying theoretical structure of VAT to cross-check purchase and sale one against the other.

Korea is the only country to have adopted this system, and Table 13-3 shows the progress in the first two years of the VAT. At first, nonmatching data was 7.2 percent of all general returns. The "learning curve" was steep in the first year as the nonmatched data fell from 7.2 percent to 4.4 percent, 3.4 percent, and after two years to 3 percent. Similarly, the number of errors detected fell from 6.4 percent to 1.8 percent. Of course, as both percentages fell, it might become more debatable as to whether it was worthwhile committing the administrative resources to completing the matching process. Indeed, the open question is whether any tax administration other than the Korean could succeed in such an effort and, even if they could, whether the necessary staff and computer resources might be better employed on other controls.

The Retail Invoice: Cash Registers and Other Schemes

Korea is unusual for another aspect of control associated with invoices. Usually, in other countries, traders may issue invoices for all business transactions but are not obliged to do so for transactions with nontaxable companies and individuals (except for registered persons entitled to repayment—for example, farmers). In Korea the authorities recognized that the final retail sale was the weakest link in the chain and decided to try to oblige retailers to issue invoices. Article 32 of the VAT law required traders to install cash registers that would issue receipts. The Government would advance 80 percent of the cost of buying the cash register (repayable without interest over 18 months) and the trader was entitled to deduct from his VAT bill an amount equivalent to 0.5 percent of his taxable sales; he kept the tally roll in fulfillment of his obligations under VAT law. However, the most valuable benefit was conferred by Article 83 whereby the retail customers could obtain "compensation" from the Government of 1 percent of the amount of their purchases covered by the cash register dockets. To further encourage such customers to ask for and keep their "invoices," the Government ran lotteries based on consecutive

Table 13-3. Korea: VAT Nonmatching and Error Data, 1977–79

	1977 (Second Half)			1978 (First Half)			1978 (Second Half)			1979 (First Half)		
	Total	Output	Input	Total	Output	Input	Total	Output	Input	Total	Output	Input
	(In thousands of won)											
Total	52,245	34,128	18,117	55,490	35,713	19,777	56,649	35,304	21,345	51,523	32,338	19,185
Nonmatching	3,761	1,566	2,195	2,428	897	1,531	1,909	699	1,210	954	705	249
Error	3,363	2,201	1,164	2,223	1,508	715	1,430	1,002	429			
	(In percent)											
Ratio of nonmatching data to total	7.2	4.6	12.1	4.4	2.5	7.7	3.4	2.0	5.8	3.0	1.4	5.7
Ratio of error to total	6.4	6.5	6.4	4.0	4.2	3.6	2.5	2.8	2.0	1.8	2.2	1.3

Source: Korea, Office of National Tax Administration.

numbers on the tally rolls. This elaborate scheme sacrificed a significant element of the VAT revenue and required increased administration for, perhaps, a rather uncertain extra yield. However, it is an
interesting example of a developing country trying to ensure that the
weakest link in the VAT chain, the retailer, complied with the law.

The twin pillars on which any system of VAT must rest are, first, the
issue of tax invoices for all transactions between taxable persons and,
second, the maintenance of an adequate system of bookkeeping. In
some developing countries, the use of cash registers for retail sales
and their rolls as VAT checks has become a major preoccupation of the
authorities.[4] (For example, Mexico is about to embark—in 1988—on a
scheme to get traders to use one kind of cash register.) However,
requiring the use of cash registers for retail sales is no guarantee that
significant "back-door" unregistered sales are not also being carried
on from the same premises. Only by auditing a trader's books by the
tax officers and the occasional unannounced check on stock-in-trade
can such transactions be brought to light.

The use of a cash register is only one element in a proper system of
bookkeeping and to equate it to the fulfillment of the bookkeeping
obligations under VAT would be tantamount to giving a trader a
license to evade tax. In Korea there was a strong belief that the
extensive use of cash registers at the retail level could be of great value
in introducing retailers to obligations of running a modern tax system
like VAT and this may be true for other developing countries. But the
scheme as planned was costly in terms of money and administrative
overheads. If a government allows small retailers to write off the cost
of buying a new cash register in a year, that should be enough
compensation. No EC country gives a tax reduction to traders for
using cash registers or to customers for the submission of cash register
dockets. Governments get more revenue from using the VAT staff to
audit the larger cases where the discovery of fraud often results in
substantial payments of tax.

The Turkish authorities tried a different device to encourage
households to ask for receipts. Wage earners were allowed to offset a
proportion of the VAT paid on their retail purchases against their
income tax liability. This was meant to offset some of the regressivity
of VAT but, at the same time, households could only claim the credit
for VAT paid on production of invoices showing the purchase and this,
it is claimed, stimulates households into demanding invoices for their
purchases. Of course, it also opens the door to further evasion

---

[4]See the list of problems with cash registers in Panama in Porras (1979).

through false invoices, and it erodes the income tax base and creates uncertainty about the yield of both VAT and income tax.

The most prevalent type of evasion under any sales tax that includes the retail stage is the underdeclaration of sales to final consumers, and it is understandable that this should cause concern. There is, however, much less ground for worry under a VAT than under a retail sales tax, because under VAT reliable figures of purchases can be established, and, by applying computer tests, the cases where the figures of sales appear to be underreported can be picked out and investigated.

Payments and Refunds

The VAT is basically a self-assessed tax. As such, registered traders are expected to submit their payment with their completed assessment forms. Indeed, in some countries such as Indonesia no VAT return is accepted if it is not accompanied by payment, unless, of course, a refund is claimed. This eliminates the need to match returns and payments later. Returns and payments can be processed both centrally and regionally. In some countries, including Denmark, the government GIRO (post office banking system) system is used; in others (for example, Argentina, Bolivia, Brazil, Chile, Colombia, Peru, and the Philippines) the commercial banks collect taxes on behalf of the authorities, and are willing to do so, providing they get four to ten days' use of the money. Using banks to collect VAT can be particularly efficient where local collectors may not be fully reliable and where the postal system is suspect. Authorized agent banks can be required to sort out returns into three groups: those where the amount paid is the same as that shown in the return; a second group where the amount paid is different to that in the return; and a group where credit exceeds tax liability. Banks stamp all copies of the returns showing the date of receipt and validate receipt of the VAT. The tax return serves as evidence of the tax paid.

In Argentina, Spain, and Hungary, the authorities supply a booklet with slips containing data printed in magnetic characters relating to the registered taxpayer. This slip is used by the trader to identify his tax return. This procedure is claimed to prevent taxpayer errors in transcription and shortens the administrative time to record the taxpayer's information.

Returns are frequently filed monthly, as is the practice in Brazil, Chile, Costa Rica, Ecuador, Honduras, Mexico, Nicaragua, Panama, and Uruguay, but many countries use a two-month or quarterly system. Argentina and Mexico are among the few countries that have adopted annual filing (with provisional monthly payments), but, as mentioned in Chapter 12, this has not proved particularly useful.

One of the features of the VAT is the possibility of generating balances in favor of the taxpayer through the credit mechanism. Indeed, in one new European VAT, monitoring refunds absorbed almost 70 percent of the initial control effort. If the balances are clearly of a temporary nature, the problem is easy to solve; they will be offset by debit balances in a relatively short period of time. There are, however, situations in which the credit balances not only are created but once created keep growing. A VAT is intended to be a tax on consumption and not a tax on business; in principle, all excess of input tax over output tax should be refunded at once. Failure to do so alters the nature of VAT by making it, in part, a tax on business. The tax law must provide a solution for these cases. These fall into five main categories, which are described below.

Balances Resulting from Export Operations

Since exporters are normally allowed to recover the tax paid on their purchases and there is no tax on their export sales, it is easy to see that they will tend to accumulate credit balances. Application of the destination principle, therefore, requires that taxes paid by exporters be refunded. Ideally, any excess should be refunded promptly. Alternatively, it has been suggested that exporters could be allowed to use their balances against other tax liabilities, for example, income tax, as in the Dominican Republic. Of course, liabilities should always be enough to absorb the balances without undue delays. However, it is not a good principle to mix the liability and collection of two quite separate taxes. This can be especially true in small developing countries where the refunds claimed can be concentrated in very few companies (for example, in Panama, one third of the taxpayers claim credit and pay no tax and of these taxpayers just two account for most of the tax credit).[5]

Sometimes exporters are allowed to claim their VAT on imports in anticipation of the exports. For instance, under the Chilean "second method,"[6] the exporter makes a sworn return specifying by when the export will be made and estimating the amount. Once approved, the refund is made within five days. The exporter must provide a nota-

[5]Porras (1979).
[6]See "Chile," in International Bureau of Fiscal Documentation (1986, pp. 51–52).

rized guarantee represented by a bill of exchange or promissary note. If the exporter cannot demonstrate that the export has been carried out within the period promised, he must reimburse the amount, adjusted for inflation, plus 1 percent a month interest.

Balances Resulting from the Use of Multiple Rates

This situation can occur when the products sold are subject to a rate that is lower than that applicable to inputs used in the manufacturing process. In practice, this would be unusual as rate schedules are set up to avoid it happening. The solution should be the same as in the preceding case, that is, credit balances should be refunded. If a single rate is not feasible for political or other reasons, as the EC suggests, the lower rate should be set at a level that is high enough ordinarily to allow complete absorption of the credit originated by tax paid on inputs.

Balances Resulting from Zero-Rated Goods

This case is similar to the preceding one and it arises when taxable inputs are used to produce zero-rated goods. But, as discussed in Chapter 12, administrative considerations may make exemption preferable to zero rating; if so, the taxpayer will not be able to recover the tax paid on purchases and will have to treat it as an additional cost element.

Balances Due to Purchases of Equipment

Large purchases of fixed assets by taxpayers may also give rise to credit balances and their volume may be such that it would take a long time to accumulate the debit balances to allow complete offsetting. During all this time, the tax paid on the purchase of the asset becomes a financial burden for the taxpayer that, if severe, may strain his liquidity. This may be particularly important in the case of new firms that are confronted by substantial investment in equipment. It follows that, as for balances from exports, quick refunds are the best solution. It should be noted that this requires most careful administrative checking and inspection. Also in this case, another possibility would be to use the balances to pay other taxes. In Chile, if credit for fixed assets is accumulated for six consecutive tax periods, it can be offset against other tax liabilities, including import duties. Again, new firms frequently make little profit and hence incur no liability to corporate taxation and, in any case, two tax structures should not be mingled in this way. Such credits in Argentina must be spread over three years and can be claimed only annually.

Balances Resulting from Temporary Conditions

There are a number of situations that may give rise to temporary credit balances, for example, substantial increase of inventories or seasonally slumping sales. By their very nature, these credit balances will tend to disappear quite quickly. Any credit should be settled within the normal tax period. Some countries, however, allow the taxpayer to offset such credits only against future debit balances (that is, only export credits are paid at once). Others (for example, Belgium) allow credit to accumulate for three months before they are paid. Spain allows the credit to be claimed at the end of the year.

In discussing the treatment of credit balances, mention should be made of the so-called buffer rule. It originated in France (*règle de butoir*) and has been adopted, with changes, by some Latin American countries, such as Argentina and Uruguay (*regla del tope*). Basically, the French approach meant (it was abandoned in 1972) that the tax paid on purchases could be credited against the tax due on sales only up to the latter's amount and that any excess over the tax on sales was not creditable. The Argentine law went further and established that the creditable balance was limited to the amount that would result from applying to the taxpayer's purchases the rate that would be applicable to his sales.

This is an undesirable feature that should be avoided. It could distort business organization, leading firms, for instance, to merge to use credits. Ideally, the total tax burden on any particular product should be equal to the rate applicable at the point of final sale to the consumer, and the only way of achieving this result is to do away with these artificial ceilings on credit balances, whenever possible. These difficulties are another argument to minimize the use of exemptions and to avoid multiple rates.

The EC's Sixth Directive leaves the decision on the means of dealing with excess deductions to the discretion of the country: "Member States may either make a refund or carry the excess forward to the following period according to conditions which they shall determine."[7] In practice, the treatments vary but most countries repay any excess credit within a month.

[7]European Community, Sixth Council Directive, Article 18(4).

The Sixth Directive also permits member countries to ignore cases where the excess for a given taxable period is insignificant. With the increasing use of computers, most countries find it more satisfactory for the tax administration and for taxable persons to settle the account for each taxable period as it arises rather than to carry a balance forward from one taxable period to the next. In general, European countries provide for repayment of VAT within about three weeks from the end of the taxable period; if a firm is in a continuous refund position, returns are accepted more frequently than usual and re-funds made promptly. In all countries abnormal claims are subjected to prior verification.

However, in many developing countries, the refund is perceived as the major potential weakness of the VAT and the main avenue of evasion; therefore, the authorities are reluctant to be too prompt on refunds, preferring to have time to inspect, in detail, large refund claims. This is a prudent requirement in any VAT system.

Audit

Relationship to Income Tax Audit

Efforts should be made to coordinate VAT audit with the internal and field audits carried out for the income tax. The relationship and exchange of information between the VAT and the income tax is discussed in Chapter 12, but it is assumed that the legislation allows a close relationship. Audit for VAT is usually undertaken independently of income tax audits because the work is less comprehensive and can be done, in some instances, by less technically experienced staff. Some countries, including the Netherlands, consider VAT audit to be as comprehensive as the corporate income tax audit. In these cases, the size and nature of the firm determines the staff to be responsible for the audit. In any case, recent income tax audit reports should be available for examination by the VAT auditor beforehand. Equally, VAT audit reports should provide a useful input for income tax audits.

The universal method for the control of VAT and the prevention of tax evasion is the auditing and spot checking of records, coupled with a system of adequate penalties for detected cases of fraud. Only by an effective audit program can instances of tax evasion be brought to light. Therefore, the central tax administration must have one arm for the direction and control of the audit programs and another for the investigation of cases of suspected fraud. The central audit management division and the investigation division may well deal with income tax and VAT as a joint operation.

Often staff to administer VAT are transferred from other departments or tax offices (for example, staff with experience in manufacturers sales taxes, excise, and wholesale taxes) that have relied more on physical control than on financial appraisal. Before the VAT is introduced a substantial amount of time has to be allowed to train the new staff in VAT administration, including simple financial audit. The training for VAT audit can be used as a staging post on the way to fulfilling the revenue department's qualifications to be a full income tax auditor.

Physical Checks

There is still a place under VAT for physical checks on warehousing and movements of goods. In the opinion of many "hands on" VAT administrators, physical checks are crucial to effective VAT control. Physical checks establish undeniable facts; paper and records can conceal facts. A VAT fundamentally must tax a fact, the delivery or supply of a good or a service; it should not tax just an invoice. Others claim that physical checks are out of place in a financial accounts based tax. This debate can become quite fractious. There is merit in both views. Most VAT is collected and audited on documentary evidence, but the physical check and the threat of physical checks continue to be important. Truck drivers can be required to carry consecutively numbered manifests corresponding to an invoice giving particulars of what is carried and the names and addresses, with registered number, of the buyer and seller. In Europe, some of the more blatant (and successful) schemes for VAT evasion have involved illegal movement of goods across international boundaries, and physical checks are useful in this context. These physical checks on merchandise and of the movement of goods ought to be considered as additional tools of enforcement. They are usually carried out by staff operating under the immediate control of the district and regional offices and can be especially useful in developing countries in checking on suspected VAT fraud.

Definition of Audit

There must be a common understanding of the definition of an "audit." A VAT control visit does not necessarily constitute an audit (see Chapter 12). Control visits are meant to ensure, primarily, that the statutory provisions for VAT are being complied with; that, in cases picked at random, the records of purchases and sales are correctly completed from original documents; that monthly returns for selected months correspond with the totals in the records of purchases and sales; and that the totals under the different columns for the month are correct and the records accurately reflect the business operations. When the control officer detects what he thinks may be evidence of fraud, he merely notes the facts. He does not attempt an investigation but makes a report so that a full audit can be made.

An audit for VAT purposes differs from an audit by a chartered accountant. A VAT audit is a selective review of the taxpayer's books and records, including year-end statements, balance sheets, and profit and loss accounts, to ensure that the major areas of purchases, sales, and stocks are *substantially* correct, not that the taxpayer has filed a perfect return. An error can be found pertaining to almost every return, but frequently its significance is not really material, particularly when viewed in terms of auditing and processing costs. The usual audit is limited to the significant issues of the current year. If notable changes to the current returns are made, the audit should be linked also to those same issues in the two preceding years, plus any other issues in those years that are apparent on the face of the return. Only in unusual cases should the audit be extended beyond the two preceding years, even though there may be, for instance, a five-year statute.

The purpose of the VAT audit is to find out, according to the law and regulations, the actual VAT liability of the taxpayer. This generates both revenue and voluntary compliance. Voluntary compliance is generally enhanced more by increasing the number of taxpayers audited than by auditing fewer taxpayers with large tax potential. Perversely, revenue is enhanced by concentrating on those taxpayers where a large amount of revenue is at risk. These opposing concerns will always pull audit teams in opposite directions.

The audit report should also include a recommendation as to whether frequent audits should continue. The taxpayer's books and records should be evaluated, and if found deficient, the taxpayer should be advised that underreporting coupled with inadequate books and records are prima facie evidence of an intent to evade taxes and, therefore, subject to severe civil or criminal penalties or both. In such a case, returns should be earmarked for potential audit, and if inadequate records persist, recommendations may be made for severe penalties or prosecution or both.

Type of Audit

There are two main types of audits: field audit and office audit.[8] A field audit is conducted at the taxpayer's place of business. It frequently involves third party contacts with suppliers or other government entities to obtain information to validate the accuracy of the books and records, or to reconstruct net income. A field audit can require, in addition to a thorough knowledge of the tax law, the application of accounting principles, and auditing knowledge and techniques. A field audit can include an audit of associates such as parent and subsidiary corporations.

An office audit for VAT does not require an extensive knowledge of accounting or auditing principles. It is generally limited to the checking of returns for arithmetical correctness and general conformity with legal requirements. It can include the verification of exemptions, claims for credit, and checking for self consumption, etc. Audits can also be described according to the function. For instance, in Denmark an "accounts analytic audit" is an introductory survey of the facts; a "system analytic audit" is for large companies and identifies weak and strong areas; and a "transactions audit" is more time consuming and investigates in depth areas of weakness.

Audit Management Activities

Audit management activities, which management should design, organize, monitor, evaluate, adopt, correct, and approve, include the following:

- Search for unregistered taxpayers.
- Identifying the information needed by the taxpayers about VAT.
- Establishment of criteria to select audit cases.
- Selection of cases.
- Collection of information about trader practices.
- Preparation of VAT audits.
- Performance of office and field audits.
- Reporting on audits.
- Discussion and decisions about the outcome of audits.

---

[8]Some would classify audits as (1) examinations, that is, the administrative check of returns at the district office; (2) verifications, which basically are field audits; and (3) in-depth audits, usually where a suspicion of fraud exists.

- Processing of results for use in other audits and for management decision making.
- The quantity and quality of audit work.
- Training needs for audit.
- Staffing requirements.

The management responsibility for each of these activities can be explained by considering, for example, the first activity mentioned above of a "search for unregistered taxpayers" in terms of definition of problem, the criteria needed, the options, and the possible solutions.

The problem in this case is that there are persons and companies that according to the law are taxpayers but are not yet registered. The criteria involve testing the possible solutions for their cost effectiveness, that is, the cost of the extra audit against the possible revenue obtained.

Possible operations could include the following:

- Creating a publicity campaign using radio, television, the press, and videotapes.
- Mounting an information campaign through locally organized meetings to inform potential new taxpayers.
- Seeking the collaboration of organizations (trade, professional, journals) to inform members of their obligations to register and possible penalties for not doing so.
- Using readily available information sources (for example, telephone yellow pages, business guides, local newsletters, publications of professional organizations, newspaper advertisements, and local tax officials' observations).
- Making checks on unregulated retailers to ascertain the sources of their stocks.
- Cross-checking with other tax sources, especially customs clearances in economies that rely heavily on imported raw materials and finished goods; checking excise returns, property tax registrations, and even business truck registrations.

Probably the first three operations have already been tried, so that attention would be concentrated on the last three. Having selected the thrust of the activity, management must assess the resources to be used and then organize the activity. Although it sounds obvious, experience in many countries suggests any organization of work should be kept as simple and cheap as possible. Paperwork should be reduced to the minimum commensurate with what is needed to monitor the activities.

Monitoring should try to establish effectiveness without fuss. A big difficulty, experienced in many businesses (even in international organizations), is that people tend to report only positive things to their superior (or things they think their superior wants to hear). To anticipate this, the VAT manager needs to devise simple statistics on a weekly or monthly basis to keep himself informed of what is going on and, of course, to make it clear that fake reporting will not be tolerated. At the same time, the VAT manager should ensure that all VAT officials involved are kept informed of the overall situation so that the information flows both up and down. Some suggestions are as follows:

- Regional directors conduct a sample check in their regions.
- Headquarters conducts some direct regional sample checks..
- Results from different regions are compared and large differences must be explained.
- All regional results are reported to every other region.

Once the activity is under way and monitored, it needs to be evaluated and, if necessary, corrected and improved. However, the core of audit work is actual office and field audit, and reporting on audits, as mentioned above.

Outline Procedures for Audit of VAT at the District Level

In general, most tax administrations stress the uneasy relationship between the tax officer with obligations to secure revenue and traders with businesses to run. Traders cannot be expected to welcome VAT control visits; equally, the demands of most revenue services on traders are infrequent and reasonable: "Officers will often have to pit their wits against the keen business minds of traders who are, as it were, playing on their own ground. They should accept this as a challenge and strive to maintain the Department's reputation for courtesy, commonsense, shrewdness and fairness."[9]

PRELIMINARY INQUIRIES

Before visiting a taxpayer, the auditor should:

- Check that filing of periodic returns and payments are up to date.

---

[9]United Kingdom, Committee on Enforcement Powers of the Revenue Departments (1983, p. 686).

- Examine the annual summaries of monthly (or quarterly) sales and compare them with the returns for income tax.
- Check the most recent income tax audit report available before making the audit.
- Examine the file for any peculiarities or uncompleted matters from previous visits.

GENERAL APPROACH

At the beginning of the audit the auditor reviews the business activities in a general way with the proprietor or with a responsible officer of the company to gain an overall picture of operations—the main sources of supply, whether goods were paid for in cash or by check, the number of employees, amounts withdrawn for private use, how cash receipts were dealt with, and so on. This should help to pinpoint the areas that might require special attention.

THE FIRST VAT AUDIT

The duties of a VAT auditor (always remembering the overriding requirement to be fair and courteous) on the first audit to a taxpayer could be summarized as:

- Ensuring that the taxpayer is in no doubt about his legal obligations and the procedures he is expected to follow.
- Analyzing and recording in the file the bookkeeping procedures and records. He should be prepared to educate the taxpayer in the best way to carry out his obligations under VAT.
- Arranging for payment of tax where underpayments have been discovered and to ensure the correct operation of the system by the taxpayer in future.
- Considering any impact on income tax that comes to light.

The training of the junior auditors should be directed toward exercising sound judgment and discretion in handling any features which seem to point to irregularities. In particular, they should not seek to investigate fraud but should obtain enough information to enable their office to decide whether the case is one calling for full investigation.

While VAT provides certain built-in checks in that the output items of taxable sellers constitute the input items of their taxable customers, if the cross-checking of such items does not bring any discrepancy to light, it does not mean that everything is satisfactory, as items might be omitted by both the seller and the buyer.

The nature of the taxpayer's business can suggest possibilities for special scrutiny. Confidence in checking is acquired by junior auditors, as part of on-the-job training, by examining in the first instance 20 or 30 cases that are believed to be operating satisfactory bookkeeping systems. While examining the accounts in those cases, the junior auditors familiarize themselves with any features which might be new to them.

SUBSEQUENT AUDITS

At subsequent audits, the following additional procedures should receive attention:

- A particular month is selected and the figures of purchases and sales on the monthly returns are checked against the original documents.

- The totals for purchases and sales are compared with the bank statements.

- Whatever records that are kept for goods withdrawn for private use are examined, and inquiries made to verify their reliability. If there are no records, agreed estimates are made.

- A search is made among the invoices of purchases for any items that might be destined for private use. This search might be extended to invoices outside the particular month selected. The purpose of the search is to ensure that a deduction was not claimed for tax on such expenditure and that it has been excluded from the business "expenses" for income tax purposes. Any unusual items appearing in the record of purchases are investigated to see to what use they were put.

- The accounting system is examined generally, with particular reference to the calculation of the figures for taxable sales and any changes in the system as recorded in the file being noted.

- Special attention is paid to the treatment of payments and receipts in cash.

- Records of payments are checked against receipts issued as well as invoices received.

- The most recent inventory is examined, particularly items related to the records of purchases and sales.

- In a few selected cases the last two inventories can be examined and a reconciliation sought with the figures returned for purchase and sales in the intervening period.

- Checks are made for claims for tax credits based on invoices in the names of other firms (that is, multiple claims associated typically with groups of companies).

- Checks are made that sales to tourists are genuinely exported. See Chapter 16 for a further discussion of the items officials may look for from the trader's point of view.

In the beginning of the U.K. VAT, traders were to be visited, on average, once every three years. As trader experience with compliance grew (and there was some pressure to reduce staff), this frequency fell to one in four. (By comparison, income tax audits can be as infrequent as one every ten years.) Audits for the U.S. state retail sales taxes are strikingly infrequent, from below 1 percent of accounts audited annually, up to a maximum of 8.8 percent (in Mississippi).[10] In one Latin American country, the probability of audit is at most once every hundred years, but in Chile it is once every seven. Clearly, the greater the likelihood of a visit, the better compliance should be. It is also true that in all countries, commissioners of tax can show that the employment of an additional inspector will easily pay for his salary through the increased tax collected. Yet, no legislature will authorize increases in numbers of tax inspectors up to the level where the marginal inspector's salary just equals his additional collections. Any decision on the inspectorate is a compromise. An average of about once every four years would seem about as infrequent as is compatible with keeping a grip on the tax. Of course, some taxpayers might be visited very infrequently and others much more so.

Number of Audits

Auditing capacities of field offices are determined by calculating the number of returns that can be audited, using estimates of the number of returns each field and office auditor can reasonably be expected to complete during one year. There should be an overselection of 25 percent to 30 percent of audit capacity. With proper pre-audit planning, strong supervision, and effective use of the review staff as a training vehicle, it is not unreasonable to expect an office auditor to complete an average of 10 to 20 cases a month, and for a field auditor (exclusive of auditors dealing with controlled cases) to complete an average of 4 to 6 cases a month.

[10]Due (1983b, Table 9.5, p. 232).

Table 13-4 shows a typical presentation of data on central visits. Part of the assessment of the required number of visits is clearly the effectiveness based on the net receipts and the staff effort involved.

In a tax department operating in an environment where there is a widespread belief that most tax returns are underreported, careful planning is needed, otherwise there may be an overselection of returns for audit, with the result that the inventory of work in process will increase to unmanageable proportions and make an orderly approach to an annual audit work plan impossible. The first step in a monthly work plan is to devise a system to control the work load and to accumulate data to refine the audit plan. The results of the audit and the characteristics of the return before and after audit must also be checked. Computers can provide control for each return selected for audit, and for accumulating the data on audit results.

The frequency of audit is a contentious issue. The judgment is always a delicate balance between the threat of audit to check the temptation to evade and the cost. Some countries are prepared to envisage a high frequency of audit (for example, Indonesia) but usually, where the VAT system is fairly well established, audits of 15 percent to 20 percent of registered traders a year are sufficient. In the Federal Republic of Germany, small traders may be audited by the tax authorities only once in every 8 to 10 years.

However, it is not only the crude number of audits that is the most useful measure of need. The form of audit is important. Often too

Table 13-4. United Kingdom: VAT Control Visits, Year Ended March 31

	1980	1981	1982
Number of control visits (in thousands)	368	357	358
Number of underdeclarations (in thousands)	144	142	133
Value of underdeclarations (in millions of pounds)	84	146	160
Average value of each underdeclaration (in pounds)	583	1,028	1,203
Number of overdeclarations (in thousands)	13	11	8
Value of overdeclarations (in millions of pounds)	4	10	5
Average value of each overdeclaration (in pounds)	308	909	625
Approximate staff effort in control visits (in thousands of pounds)	4,200	4,100	4,100
Net receipts (in thousands of pounds)	8,189	10,967	11,856
Net receipts per visit (in pounds)	1,949	2,674	2,892

Source: Adapted from United Kingdom, Committee on Enforcement Powers of the Revenue Departments, *Report*, Vol. 1, Cmnd. 8822 (London: H. M. Stationery Office, 1983), p. 74, Table 2.

much time is spent on each audit visit; in some countries, five days on average has been noted, whereas this should be reduced to one to two days with an average of one and a quarter days. Again, for each trader, the checks appropriate to his business should be set out and applied selectively on each visit. Also the number of individual inquiries can be reduced by ensuring that the trader's file contains cross-references from audits of other firms as they are received, which are dealt with in bulk on the next inspection visit.

An allocation of about 200 cases a year should be reasonable for an experienced junior auditor, who should be eligible for advancement to senior auditor after fours years of satisfactory service in that grade. Usually, where serious irregularities are discovered, or where fraud is suspected, the case, in coordination with the income tax auditor, should be reported for attention by the regional office.

In Panama, a "preventive audit" has proved effective in detecting and preventing violations. This is a spot check control over inventories designed for the time of the year when sales activities increase, as during Easter, Carnival, and Christmas; sales by the month are taken and combined with a review of inventories of seller and purchaser companies.

Refunds of VAT on exports must be closely monitored. Auditing of the larger manufacturers is carried out by senior auditors under the control of the regional offices. Audit visits in such cases is undertaken yearly, if possible. Manufacturers not sufficiently large for audit of that nature are dealt with by the local tax office, where the more straightforward cases are handled by junior auditors and the more complex cases by senior auditors.

Audit Selection Criteria

There are several sources from which the audit work load is derived. Returns will be drawn for audit from these sources by either selecting returns through a special process, or selecting returns through a routine process, based on developed or established criteria.

SPECIAL PROCESS

This category could include the following:

• Controlled cases as defined.
• Sectoral audits made to establish guidelines to be used for reference purposes during audits.

- Cases that must be audited based on policy decisions. These should be kept to a minimum. A most common case of this type is one including a large refund. Others might be repeated claims for refunds or "nil" returns. Also included would be traders who repeatedly fail to file returns or those whose category of trade suggests a higher rate of VAT than that returned. Small builders and restaurants fall into this category.

- Cases on which information is received from external sources, often a dissatisfied competitor. These should not be automatically audited; they should be reviewed, and only those that appear to contain substantial error should be audited.

- Cases on which information was developed through the audit of another taxpayer. These should also be screened to select only those involving a substantial omission.

- Returns audited as a result of a project to determine compliance within a specific profession or industry, such as advertising and contractors.

The investigation to assess compliance can be more general. In Colombia in 1983, the Government organized a special audit of some 7,000 commercial traders. Those audited produced revenue more than 5 percent higher than the comparator group not audited. No penalties were levied, but advice on compliance, and a warning, was given. Subsequently, one fifth of those audited were visited again to see whether the recommendations were adopted. Four fifths of the sample had adopted at least some of the recommendations and the remaining 20 percent were subject to a "punitive audit" and the full application of penalties.[11]

An interesting special method was found useful in Argentina when government purchases were used as a starting point for audit. It was found that up to 50 percent of some traders' sales to the Government had not been reported and, of course, this resulted in substantial assessments for underpayments.

ROUTINE PROCESS

The balance of the work load should be selected through a regular classification procedure.

Regular classification consists of selecting returns in one of two ways, by audit ratios or by computer selection. The audit plan should

---

[11]Perry and Orozco de Triana (1986, p. 43).

calculate the number of returns to be audited from each audit class. From this, a ratio of returns to be audited to total returns filed by class can be determined. Generally, a higher ratio of returns should be selected from the higher income and higher turnover groups. The ratio should be used to determine the number of returns to be reviewed to select those for audit. All returns are, of course, not reviewed. A balanced plan might assume the following:

- For large returns, a selection is made of 30 percent to 40 percent of the returns reviewed.
- For medium returns, a selection is made of 10 percent to 20 percent of returns reviewed.
- For small returns, a selection is made of 1 percent to 5 percent of returns reviewed.
- A small percentage, say, 1 percent, to be selected purely at random.

A balance must be maintained between returns selected through the special classification and returns selected through regular classification. In some countries, the number of returns that can be selected through special classification—basically informants—exceed the entire annual work load. To actually select them would congest the audit plan and result in a deterioration of compliance. Theoretically, the ideal balance seems to be for some 40 percent to be selected through special classification and the rest through regular classification, although conditions vary greatly among countries. Based on the above, a projection of the number of returns that should be reviewed can be made.

Strict monitoring is required since it is difficult to refrain from reviewing an excessive number of returns, especially when there is a belief that most taxpayers are underreporting. Over a period of time serious underreporting will, however, be identified through the random qualities of the process.

The auditors assigned to the task of reviewing the returns should be experienced in auditing and well versed in the law. They should recognize the importance of the duty, be able to read, analyze, and interpret financial statements, and adapt to the confining task of sitting at a desk, reviewing return after return. A good classifier should be able to review some 75 to 100 of the larger returns a day. It should be noted that the classifier is not reviewing the return for the purpose of making an assessment; he is exercising judgment in determining returns offering the best potential for audit.

A checksheet should be developed that lists the reasons (by line item) why the return was selected for audit. The checksheet should accompany the return through the audit process, and, at the end of the audit, should be used to evaluate the effectiveness of the classification program and the effectiveness of the individual classifier. Checksheets can also be used to generate statistics on noncompliance. For a representative sample of a particular class of taxpayer, the ratio of unaudited tax liability to the correct tax after audit gives the level of compliance. Staff can concentrate on areas where compliance is low.

The classifiers should be given training on their special responsibilities. They should learn the process of developing an audit plan and the process of analysis required to determine whether a taxpayer should be selected for audit, as well as the criteria used in selecting a taxpayer for examination. These criteria can best be developed by conveying a group of experienced auditors to adapt criteria to the circumstances of each country.

COMPUTER SELECTION

Within each tax district a certain number of tax officers are available for field audit work. To direct those field auditors into the most productive inquiries a computer-based case selection system can be invaluable.

Computer selection for sales tax audit has been used for many years.[12] Interestingly enough, computer selection for the relatively simple retail sales taxes of the United States has not been an unqualified success. A major problem has been the growth of multiproduct stores so that the norms are more difficult to establish and, even if established, their validity does not hold for long. However, more sophisticated analysis has produced estimated dollar returns from audits or a ranking of firms on the basis of potential audit productivity.[13] Nevertheless, experienced auditors still express strong reservations about the usefulness of computer-generated selections, especially in developing countries.

To help select those taxpayers who appear to warrant auditing more than others, the information already stored within the computer on each trader's tax and trade performance over a period of 12 months should be compared with performance of his competitors in the same class of business. Those taxpayers who are showing much lower-than-average gross profit margins should be the subject of early audit.

---

[12]See an interesting account by Due (1985).
[13]Due (1985, p. 238).

The output and input tax and the sales purchases for a current year should be calculated and used to calculate for each taxpayer: (1) the markup (output minus input as a percent of inputs) and (2) annual sales growth (current sales less previous year sales as a percent of the previous year sales). It should be borne in mind, however, that opening and closing stocks may fluctuate and therefore affect the apparent markup.

Each taxpayer's figures should be calculated individually and should be used to calculate the average markup and sales growth for the business classification as a whole. The comparative performance data should be calculated separately for payment and refund taxpayers.

There should also be a separate performance ratio calculated to assess the comparative growth of sales of exempt goods and services over successive tax periods. The calculation should be total exempt sales as a percent of total sales.

Each general taxpayer should be assigned an indicator within the computer relating to performance over a two-year period. The indicator values should take into account the following:

- Markup over the period compared with other taxpayers in the same business classification.

- Returns performance—if any returns have been submitted late or have had to be corrected.

- Tax performance—whether or not the tax has been paid promptly.

The range of values might go from "good" (one) to "bad" (four) in four stages. It would be set by reference to statistics extracted from the computer record or by reference to the local tax officer or by both.

In any selection for audit, the potential revenue risk should be assessed. For taxpayers with a high tax base the risk is generally greater than one with a low tax base if other indicators are the same. Accordingly, selections for audit should be biased toward the larger taxpayers. Naturally, the computer selected returns for audit still need a senior auditor to scan them to make the final decision about which traders should be audited.

The more traditional tax administrators who view computer selection with a jaundiced eye maintain that plain random selection generates the same results with less effort and less administrative cost. A problem with the so-called random selection is that too often it can degenerate into personal selection and, in bad examples, into bias and personal vendetta. Some rules have to be made and kept whether or not they are computer generated.

Audit Manuals

The preparation of an audit manual is a complex job and is particular to each country although, of course, many of the procedures (as indicated above) are common. What needs to be emphasized is not only the importance of creating a detailed manual but of insisting that officers use it and continuously review and update it.

In many countries, it is sad to report, tax manuals are written and used when a tax is introduced or when it is radically overhauled. Within a few years, officers refer to them infrequently, often ignore the recommended procedures, and indeed, sometimes cannot even find a copy of the manual in their office or in the offices of the staff they are supervising. Manuals are meant to be used and their procedures followed. To the extent they are not, it usually indicates the erosion of the tax base.

It follows that one way to keep attention focused on manual procedures is to have statistical records on the procedures the manuals recommend and to issue regular updates to the manuals that, on inspection, are expected to be included in each officer's copy.

CHAPTER 14

Evasion, Enforcement, and Penalties

Some of them are running from lovers
Leaving no forward address
Some of them are running tons of ganja
Some are running from the IRS
— "Banana Republics," composed by Steve Goodman,
Steve Burgh, and Jim Rothermel

Frustration, including annoyance with the compliance costs, may tempt a trader to evade the VAT. Straightforward greed may also tempt him. All commentators describe the theoretical self-checking mechanism of VAT and all go on to elaborate how this does not work. Estimates of VAT evasion range from 2–4 percent of revenue forgone (the United Kingdom) to 40 percent (Italy).

Only Korea has tried formally to cross-match sales and purchase invoices (see Chapter 13). The Korean study shows that for the two years 1980 and 1981, the largest penalties were associated with invoices for VAT liability or credit and that delayed submissions of invoices were twice as costly as nonissuance and nonsubmission. These results suggest that better collection and enforcement to trace deliberate fake invoices were important. It is also interesting to note that nonregistration continued to be a major problem in Korea four years into the VAT.

Like other taxes VAT is evaded;[1] like other taxes that are basically

---

[1]Sales tax evasion is by no means restricted to shady middlemen and to the VAT; in spectacular charges, the City and State of New York charged fashionable retailers

self-assessment systems VAT requires a firm enforcement system with known and applied penalties culminating in (although rarely used) criminal prosecution. Deterrents should exist that increase the risk of underreporting commensurate with the degree of flagrancy and revenue involved. A taxable person who underreports is in effect stealing and misusing funds that have been paid by his customers and that belong to the government. For a penalty to improve tax compliance it must reflect the gravity of the offense and not merely increase the risk for underreporting by more than the cost of borrowing funds (such as interest).

All taxpayers must be seen to be treated equally if all taxpayers are expected to pay their fair share. If an enforcement program is consistently directed only at a particular group or class of taxpayer, usually one producing a high yield per audit, that group will eventually lose faith in the fairness of the system and its levels of compliance will be vitiated. Other classes or groups to which little investigation has been devoted will tend to comply less since the risk of detection will be seen to be small.

Some countries have tried to co-opt the taxpayer's own interests to declare his VAT liability. In Turkey and Bolivia, the trader's VAT liability is allowed as an offset against a gross income tax. In the Turkish case, the amount allowed to be offset diminishes as income increases so that the concession can be considered progressive but, nevertheless, is still expensive in revenue forgone.

Of course, public attitudes toward taxation in general, and VAT in particular, are important. A U.K. survey showed that 70 percent of the sample did not consider it "morally wrong" to pay a trader in cash who volunteered not to charge VAT and 65 percent appeared to consider it acceptable behavior to take cash for work performed to evade VAT or income tax.[2]

In another survey of those who tried to evade tax, on a scale of one (never) to ten (always), the Irish scored 3.35, compared with a European average of 2.64; moreover, the sample indicated that the younger the person the more likely he is to take a casual view of tax

---

(Cartier Inc., Ben Thylan Furs Corporation, Bulgari, and Christie Brothers Fur Corporation) with evading the retail sales tax (at 8 ¼ percent). One customer was said to have evaded tax on purchases worth a total of $250,000. See account in *New York Times*, August 8, 1985, p. B3. It is also estimated that as much as 75 percent of the "ring"-type sales tax in Paraguay is not collected. In Belgium, "tax evasion and avoidance is rife;" see "Belgium: Income Tax Changes Ahead," *World Tax Report* (1987, p. 9).

[2]"Cash, Sir? That'll Do Very Nicely . . . ," *The Times* (London), October 28, 1985, p. 10.

evasion (the index for the 18–24 age group was 4.05, compared with 2.11 for those over 75).[3]

Although prevention of tax evasion within the EC remains primarily the responsibility of the national authorities, the Community has issued two Council Directives, one for mutual assistance in the exchange of information and the other for mutual assistance in the recovery of VAT.[4] Increasing rates for VAT make the tax conspicuous and makes successful evasion all the more valuable to trader and public alike.

Forms of Evasion

There are numerous ways to categorize evasion. The following list gives a flavor of various forms of VAT evasion.

Traders Who Are Liable to VAT but Do Not Register

Traders have an obligation to assess their trading turnover (or whatever other criteria are used to establish the VAT threshold—see Chapter 6) and if they qualify, they must register for VAT. If traders initially are not within the VAT limits, most legislation requires traders to notify the authorities either ex post when sales exceed the limit, and even, in some cases, when there are reasonable grounds to believe that sales in the coming 12 months will exceed the annual threshold. The problem of evasion is created when traders who should register do not.

This means that although they pay VAT on their purchases, their sales are not liable. Their value added, therefore, escapes VAT and they are in a better competitive position than those who pay tax. The government loses revenue.

On the whole, this is a minor problem because, principally, only small traders will fail to register (although not only small, that is, "special" traders in Korea, as the penalties show in Table 14-1) and relatively little revenue is at risk. Another, perhaps larger problem, is those traders who are outside the approved legal structure, such as bookmakers, operators of sauna parlors, and call girls. As one govern-

[3]Ireland, Commission on Taxation (1985, p. 144).

[4]Council Directives 79/1070/EEC and 79/1071/EEC; see European Community, "First Report from the Commission to the Council on the Application of the Common System of Value Added Tax," reproduced in Intertax (March 1984, pp. 103–22).

Table 14-1. Korea: VAT Penalties Imposed, 1980–81
(In millions of won)

Type of Tax-payer[1]		Total	Non-regis-tration	Invoices		Tax Returns		
				Non-issuance or nonsub-mission	Delayed sub-mission	Errors	Proxy errors	Zero-rating errors
Jan.–	Total	407	112	25	125	85	46	14
June	General	318	30	25	125	78	46	14
1980	Special	89	82	—	—	7	—	—
July–	Total	601	124	40	191	152	36	58
Dec.	General	512	41	40	191	146	36	58
1980	Special	89	83	—	—	6	—	—
Jan.–	Total	542	122	67	165	129	37	22
June	General	496	80	67	165	125	37	22
1981	Special	46	42	—	—	4	—	—
July–	Total	682	107	103	229	194	18	31
Dec.	General	642	71	103	229	190	18	31
1981	Special	40	36	—	—	4	—	—

Source: Korea, Ministry of Finance (Seoul).
[1] "Special" broadly refers to "small" or special-scheme taxpayers.

ment's internal document put it, "These individuals also could be liable but probably will not register."

Exaggerated Refund Claims

One of the simplest ways to evade VAT is to inflate the claims to deduct VAT paid at earlier stages. In the Netherlands, it has been estimated that 44 percent of all VAT fraud involved fake claims for prior-stage tax. The simplest method is to fabricate fake invoices for purchases never made. Indeed, businesses have been established solely to invent and print false invoices for sale to those wishing to defraud the revenue. Clearly, there is a limit to the scope for this as too many fake invoices would squeeze the taxable values to the point where the authorities would become suspicious and, in any case, audit would identify the fraudulent invoice.

A more complicated, but more remunerative (and riskier), device to claim fake refunds is when a new business is started, because then the authorities could expect VAT deductions to exceed VAT liability since there would be large purchases of capital equipment and raw materials. Most authorities will pay refunds quickly to avoid squeezing business liquidity; this can mean that before the time comes around for an audit the firm goes out of business and disappears. For this reason, among others, some countries will not make large refunds—especially to newly established traders—without first checking the complete authenticity of the claims.

Unrecorded Cash Purchases

Small traders (and sometimes large ones) will buy goods from a primary (unregistered) supplier, such as a farmer, and because the transaction is not recorded, the purchaser will be able to sell the goods without charging VAT and no record will exist. In general, this is not a serious problem because most purchasers will want to record the sale to claim the VAT as credit. But if the production chain is short, which it frequently is in developing countries, then this can become a major form of evasion. In addition, if income taxes are high, then it will be a double incentive to avoid both VAT and income taxes, which will increase the value of the evasion.

Credit Claimed for Invoices from Unregistered Suppliers

Credit for VAT paid on inputs can only be claimed when the purchase is made from a registered supplier. An unregistered supplier could be an exempt or a small trader, perhaps already enjoying a special treatment for VAT, or it could simply be a private person. The input purchases may be perfectly valid and it may be that the purchase does actually involve paying a price inclusive of VAT that is impossible to claim because the supplier is unregistered. That is just too bad. If the trader who has purchased from the unregistered supplier pretends that the purchase invoice has a VAT number, or creates an imaginary VAT number, the authorities are defrauded.

The sums involved are unlikely to be great since large suppliers will be registered; nevertheless, the practice is illegal and as the authorities may have made special provision earlier in the production chain (for example, under special schemes for retailers or purchases from farmers) to compensate for such sales, the revenue could lose twice over.

Credit Notes on Purchases Including VAT Not Shown on Returns

This is a minor item, but if a credit note is issued on a purchase and the credit for VAT is claimed on the full invoice before credit, the authorities will allow more VAT credit than they ought. The trader's books may all be in order and all the purchase invoices may be properly kept and available for inspection. The cheating may show up only through a financial match on checks issued against (sometimes numerous aggregated) invoices from the same supplier. Sometimes the cross-check can be initiated from the credit invoices of the supplier.

Credit Claimed for Taxable Supplies Used in Exempt Activities

If a business is wholly exempt, no credit can be claimed. The problem arises when a trader is selling both taxable and exempt goods and services. It may prove quite easy to divert purchased inputs on which VAT credit is claimed against taxed sales to help produce and sell exempt items. The problem is that some such decisions can be, in all good faith, extremely uncertain. The VAT content on the capital purchase of a shop and its equipment should be split between the sales that are exempt (say, unprocessed food) and the rest that are taxable; in this case, the VAT authorities may simply allow the credit in direct proportion to the split between taxable and exempt sales. It is much more difficult when the same raw materials may be inputs to exempt and taxable outputs and some traders may deliberately offset more credit against VAT than was actually involved. Again, this is unlikely to be a major problem unless legislation has created numerous exemptions that require traders to make many such borderline decisions. It is, of course, another argument against creating exemptions.

Credit Claimed for Purchases That Are Not Creditable

The best-known example of this type of fraud is the credit claimed for an automobile for business purposes when, in fact, it is used for nonbusiness purposes and should be classified as nondeductible. Some countries employ a blanket prohibition against allowing credit for ordinary passenger automobiles used in businesses for precisely this reason. Once discretion is allowed as to whether the automobile is used fully, partially, or not at all, for business purposes, the door is opened to misassigned claims for credit. One potential solution is to allow credit for VAT in the same proportion as the income tax allows the claim for the capital cost as a business expense. Another is to disallow automobiles, but then borderline cases arise with jeeps, trucks, and pickups.

Again, the revenue loss may not be great but the potential inequity between traders and between the public is created.

Imported Goods and Taxed but Unreported Sales

Goods imported illegally, sold with the full VAT added, reward the trader not only by his illegal sale but by a tax revenue pocketed. It may seem especially greedy for traders who are already acting illegally by selling smuggled goods to want to charge VAT on the illicit wares. But it does happen and on a large scale. "We estimate that £120m has been lost in rackets involving the sale of gold alone."[5] Gold is the best example, but for any commodity to be used in this way there has to be a sizable legitimate trade in the good and fixed retail prices (wine, spirits, and cigarettes are other possible goods); the goods are sold through fake names and addresses and premises on short-term rentals so that the trade can be completed and the VAT received before the authorities can catch up with the bogus operation. The rate of VAT charged on the sale is, of course, an additional profit to the criminal at the expense of the revenue.

Underreported Sales

Understating sales is the most usual way to evade VAT. The lower the value of sales, the less the VAT owed. The only dangers are that if an invoice is issued, the purchaser will claim his VAT deduction and this would not be matched in an audit against the VAT paid—but this danger depends on the likelihood of audit.[6] Again, any trader who underreports on a scale even slightly out of line with the average for other traders in similar categories may be picked up by the computer as a case for audit.

Of course, the question of nonmatching invoices does not arise if the sale is retail. Again, taxpayers may be picked for audit if their reported sales as a ratio to purchased inputs is lower than average over a period of years; but where shops carry many different lines,

[5]Chief Investigation Officer, H.M. Customs and Excise, quoted in "Goldmine in VAT Frauds Exploited by Criminals," by Andrew Hogg, *Sunday Times* (London), February 3, 1985, p. 4.

[6]In one country, the probability of corporate audit for sales tax worked out at once in 30 years—hardly a major threat to the evader. In West Virginia, the chance of being audited for the state sales tax during 1978–80 was about once in every 300 years! See Due (1983b, p. 232).

when trading practices are changing and lines stocked alter, and when shops carry on business in different localities, such checks are imprecise, and more sophisticated methods of detection may be called for.

Traders may try to meet these ratio checks by underreporting both sales and purchases, thus preserving an acceptable trade value added. However, here the VAT mechanism does limit the revenue loss as the trader cannot claim tax credit on the purchase not reported.

The authorities can check inventories and warehouse stocks to catch these evasions. However, such searches are time consuming, expensive, and sometimes annoying to the honest trader who is attempting to comply with all the regulations.

It must be appreciated that the VAT at risk is only for the particular stage of production or distribution. Earlier processes will have declared their sales and purchases and paid the VAT appropriate to their value added. Indeed, if the invoice for the nonreported sales is suppressed (other than at the retail stage), the VAT liability will catch up at the next stage as the purchaser will be unable to claim his VAT deduction. Of course, VAT may be fully at risk if the seller does not report the sale, but the buyer takes the VAT credit on his purchase and this tax credit will cover all value added in previous stages of production.

Retail services are particularly prone to evasion through underreporting. European experience shows that in trades such as decorating, carpentry, plumbing, and gardening where taxable inputs are small and value added is high, evasion by small operators is common. The customer is offered a lower price and the sale is not reported. Frequently, cash sales evade both VAT and income tax. It may be impossible to check the sales compared to purchased inputs if the trader decides to pay the VAT on his inputs as a retail purchase, such as for paint, plumbing or electrical hardware supplies, or gardening tools. An antique trader, required to keep a record of the names and addresses of purchasers, maintained that she used to go through the telephone book with a pin and write down any old name and address.

This type of evasion has been tackled in various countries. In Belgium, for example, service retailers such as garages, restaurants, hotels, and builders are required to issue numbered receipts giving their name, address, and VAT registered number. Service businesses sometimes gave receipts for less than the amount charged. The consumer, "although paying the full price, paid the VAT only on the invoiced amount. In an effort to combat such fraud, the Belgium government now requires hotels, restaurants, and cafes to use pre-numbered invoices, and automobile shops to register the license numbers of all cars they repair. But this system has not prevented businesses from failing to fill out any invoice at all, or from filling out numbered invoices for reduced amounts."[7] Nevertheless, the threat of such checks has some deterrent effect.

In Italy, customers of restaurants and hotels can be stopped by the police on leaving the premises and asked for the receipts showing the VAT paid; this is supposed to encourage the customer to ask for the receipt and may discourage him from being a willing partner with the retailer to evade VAT. However, in a classic demonstration of mounting ingenuity to evade VAT, restauranteurs employed "escorts" who accompanied patrons to their car or for a few blocks and then pocketed the receipts.

Finally, another widespread unreported sale is the farm gate sale of agricultural products direct to the consumer. In Denmark, these sales are wholly forbidden (and, in any case, farm sales in Denmark are nearly always made through the cooperatives). However, farm gate sales are usually exempt from VAT but they can become a serious source of evasion if undertaken on a basically commercial scale as happens in some areas in France.[8]

VAT Collected but Not Remitted to the Authorities

This is a straightforward example of evasion that is particularly pernicious in the construction industry where small traders may collect VAT and then disappear. In Belgium, to meet this evasion, VAT was able to take advantage of an anti-income tax avoidance device; the client is made liable for the VAT if the building firm he employs is not registered (and the registration system is specifically designed to keep track of the small builders—not only for the VAT but also for social security).

Of course, in some countries, sloppy administration may allow traders to keep VAT proceeds longer than the prescribed periods and unless penalties are automatic (and automatically applied and collected), traders will take advantage of this liquidity. The most efficient way to shorten the period during which traders hold VAT receipts is to use a post office GIRO banking system, or the commercial banks, for VAT payment; this system can be used to require traders to pay within a week—and certainly within two weeks—of the end of the taxable period.

[7]Oldman and Woods (1983, p. 325).
[8]Oldman and Woods (1983, p. 327).

Multiple Rates and Incorrect Descriptions

Multiple rates of VAT are the bane of VAT administration. Tax forms become more complicated as VAT at the appropriate rate has to be applied to both inputs and outputs; the chances for genuine error are enhanced and the opportunity for deliberate misclassification is widened. Where traders are buying and selling goods and services that may be liable to three or more rates of VAT, clearly the compliance costs rise and the reduction in tax liability by shifting goods from "luxury" to standard rates can be tempting; equally, the refunds can be inflated by allocating an undue proportion of sales to exempt or low rate categories.

The classic opportunity to combine underreporting sales and misclassification of goods occurs in retailing. In a small shop, the owner can persistently misallocate goods for a lower VAT in ringing up the sale on the cash register. In larger stores, an assistant can favor friends, defrauding the revenue, in exactly the same way. An even more direct way to falsify till roll records is to start a new roll halfway through the day and submit the half roll as the record of the day's sales.

Checking such evasion is difficult without effective audits and even then a pattern of deliberate misclassification has to be established to identify evasion rather than error. This consideration emphasizes the need to limit the number of tax rates and exemptions to as few as possible.

Omission of Self-Deliveries

Small traders frequently use their own production for their household consumption. This is true particularly for small retailers but can be done by builders, garages, textile producers, wholesalers, and so on. All VAT legislation requires traders to record goods used privately as a sale liable for VAT. While it is unrealistic to expect all such consumption to be recorded for VAT, if it rises to a substantial amount (and especially when extended to family and friends), the amounts can be quite large.

Typically, the authorities can spot businesses that are "at risk" and audit them specifically for this sort of evasion.

False Export Claims

Companies that export much of their output are often in continuous credit to the government. Completely false export sales can be invoiced and the claim for VAT refund made—very like printing money. This fraud can be caught because export invoices are usually associated with customs and shipping documents and it is difficult to fabricate all the paperwork required. More difficult to check would be the export of computerized data (through a service agency); the use of telecommunications means no documentation need be used and, therefore no documents may be available for audit. The Dutch claim to have used a system of spot checks to improve detection of this form of evasion.

Bogus Traders

Also difficult to check is the creation of short-lived bogus companies. These can fabricate fake export invoices and claim VAT rebates on goods that have never been handled. Alternatively, they may actually sell the goods on the domestic market but claim a VAT rebate on a bogus export invoice. In one example, a trader set up 48 fake companies to "work the export racket"; the rebates claimed in each case were relatively modest but in total were substantial. "A customs officer said, 'If the chap is 'reasonable' and prepared to put in perhaps a year's work organising it, that number of claims, each for about £1,500, could net him nearly £75,000. To make that amount by stealing, you would have to present a fence with something like £500,000 in stolen property.'"[9]

Barter Arrangement

If there is collusion between seller and purchaser to exchange goods and services with no payment and no invoice record, then there is no documentary liability to VAT. There may be, of course, depending on the VAT law, an implicit liability to VAT that ought to be reported. Again, collusion can involve a sale for cash of, say, color television sets and issuing false invoices for an equivalent value for the sale of some other items that the same purchaser would be able to represent as an input to his business (for example, fishing nets in a Danish example involving the offsetting barter of television sets).[10]

Such collusion is difficult to check except through careful analysis

---

[9]Andrew Hogg, "Goldmine in VAT Frauds Exploited by Criminals," *Sunday Times* (London), February 3, 1985, p. 4.

[10]Oldman and Woods (1983, p. 328).

of the inventory of goods but, compared with any single-stage tax, the revenue at risk is limited to the VAT liability at the stage of production. Such collusion is difficult to arrange, awkward to sustain, and may be difficult to keep secret.

Accounting "Errors"

This can be the innocent type of error and generally the penalty will be the same as the late payment penalty (linked with the period during which the accounting error delayed the receipt of VAT revenue due). However, "creative accounting" can be extraordinarily ingenious and tantamount to fraud.

For example, if there are companies closely associated with one another and goods are sold to the "sister" company, the company purchasing the goods can claim the VAT involved in the purchase price as a credit. However, the seller may issue a credit note and can delay for many months any proof that VAT has been charged. The VAT credit received by the purchaser represents an interest-free loan until, eventually when the credit note reconciliation is sorted out and the transaction is canceled. Large sums can be "borrowed" in this way (especially, for instance, in the construction industry) and when done on a sustained basis can be a major form of evasion.

Enforcement

The frequency of evasion under each heading differs according to each country's enforcement and according to the particular quirks of VAT legislation. Numerous rates will invite evasion by misspecification; generous provisions for suspending VAT liability for imported raw materials may encourage the diversion of goods on to the domestic market. Field audits that are known to be infrequent will tempt the use of "manufactured" false invoices. The proportions in the United Kingdom for 1985/86 offense cases were 73 percent for failure to furnish returns, 6 percent for failure to pay tax, and 21 percent for other forms of fraudulent evasion.[11]

How much effort should be put into enforcement? Obviously all revenue departments show that far more dollars are collected for each dollar spent on investigation and enforcement. As mentioned earlier, this can hardly be used as a justification to go on spending on enforce-

[11]United Kingdom, Commissioners of H.M. Customs and Excise (1986, p. 23).

ment until a dollar spent gains only a dollar in extra revenue. Yet it is difficult to say how much should be spent. One view is that the acceptable minimum yield from tax enforcement is the real cost of raising the same revenue by general taxation; the cost is the loss of output and consumers welfare from the (small) increase in taxation to compensate for the revenue forgone through fraud. Estimates suggest that in the United Kingdom, this implies that for each pound spent on enforcement about five pounds should be raised in revenue.[12]

Assessments

Any self-assessed tax such as VAT needs a power of assessment by the authorities to be used when they suspect traders may have misreported their tax liability or when returns are not presented at all.

All VAT systems allow for such assessments; however, the scope varies. In France, the assessment relates to incomplete or inaccurate returns and not the failure to make a return. In the Netherlands, the authorities can also issue an assessment for incomplete returns or failure to file a return. In the Federal Republic of Germany, the United Kingdom, and New Zealand, the authorities can assess for inaccurate or incomplete returns and for failure to submit a return. In Italy, in addition, assessment can be made where traders destroy records or fail to keep satisfactory records.[13]

Record Requirements and Provision of Information

Traders must create and keep sufficient records to allow the authorities to check on the validity of tax liabilities and claims for credit. A balance has to be struck between the demands of the revenue authorities for a reasonable volume of records to be kept for a length of time sufficient to ensure that mistakes will be found out, and the commercial needs of the traders to select what documents (and in what forms) should be created. Also, the cost of storage and retrieval to the trader should be minimized. Some (for example, New Zealand) even specify that the records shall be kept in a specific language (English); this could be important in countries that have a significant

---

[12]See Topham (1984) and Smith (1986, pp. 27–28).

[13]United Kingdom, Committee on Enforcement Powers of the Revenue Departments (1983, Vol. 2, p. 678).

foreign trading community or a commercial language that is not required for tax (for example, Chinese).

Most VAT legislation specifies clearly the crucial role of invoices in the system and the need to create the chain of invoices. Most countries leave the precise form of the invoice to the trader concerned (although some will encourage small traders to use standardized invoices issued by the government). In the EC, Italy attempts to control records more than most. The records to be kept are specified. A trader must have his record book stamped and the pages numbered by a VAT official or a notary public, the substantial cost of which is borne by the trader. In addition to the usual records, the Italian trader must submit an annual return of customers with their transactions; this is supposed to form the basis for the cross-checking audit. However, the more onerous such requirements, the more the trader is tempted to conceal the transaction and hence save himself the trouble and cost of compliance.

All countries require traders to keep their records of sales and purchases for a number of years; the requirement is four years for France, five years for Italy, six years for Germany and the United Kingdom, and ten years for the Netherlands and New Zealand. The usual legislation allows the authorities, on visits to traders, to demand evidence that supports their VAT return, including invoices for the supply and purchase of goods and services, the right to take samples of goods, and power to inspect, use, and check the working of any computers and machines used to produce invoices or information related to invoices. Some legislation will allow officials to take copies or extracts of documents (Germany, the Netherlands) and some do not (France). In general, documents must be examined at the premises of the trader, but some legislation allows a trader to produce his records at a tax office (for example, Germany—but not usually enforced).

In general, it seems sensible that VAT, by the very nature of the tax, defines the records that must be kept, and common sense suggests that authorities will wish to accommodate taxpayers by not making unreasonable demands on the time and place when records are to be examined or on the length of time they should be kept.

Much more contentious are the powers to be granted to officials to search for documents and seize evidence where fraud is suspected.

Entry and Search

As the U.K. Keith Committee stated, "there seems to have been confusion in public discussion between the power of entry and *inspec-*

tion of business premises, and the power of entry and *search* under warrant for evidence of VAT evasion."[14] All countries give officials the right to search premises where VAT fraud is suspected, usually when a warrant has been obtained (in Germany and the United Kingdom from a judge, in Italy from a magistrate) after convincing the legal authorities that the suspicion is valid and sufficient circumstantial evidence exists to justify the search.

Much of the discussion about complaints against the authorities using these powers prove to be exaggerated when examined in detail.[15] It is never convenient, either in place or time to execute a search warrant; as an experienced lawyer has remarked, "when [you] want to pounce on these serious criminals time is very important and it is nearly always between about 4 am and 7 am in the morning, because that is about the only time the criminal fraternity seem to be at their addresses."[16] In general, the authorities must be given the power to enter and search premises and it is expected they will be suitably cautious in exercising such powers.

Penalties

Penalties, of course, reflect the particular circumstances, social priorities, and history of each country. Table 14-2 gives a representative list in Ireland of 16 VAT offenses liable to penalties. Broadly, there are four forms of penalty: automatic financial, automatic nonfinancial, criminal financial, and criminal nonfinancial. Some authorities lean heavily toward one form, for instance, automatic financial penalties in Belgium, while others appear to rely more on the threat of criminal proceedings even if they are not actually implemented.

Automatic Financial Penalties

The automatic financial penalty is probably the best known and the most favored sanction for VAT crimes. It is particularly useful where the offense could be construed as neglect or forgetfulness; it may not

[14]United Kingdom, Committee on Enforcement Powers of the Revenue Departments (1983, Vol. 1, p. 66).
[15]For a vivid example of public reaction to the power of entry and search, see Waugh (1986, p. 8), "what right [do] these VAT inspectors have to go snooping in the drawers and cupboards of a private citizen."
[16]United Kingdom, Committee on Enforcement Powers of the Revenue Departments (1983, Vol. 1, p. 255).

Table 14-2. Ireland: Examples of VAT Offenses Liable to Penalties

1. Failure to register.

2. Failure to issue an invoice by a "flat rate" farmer.

3. Failure to keep proper records and/or retain them for the minimum required period.

4. Noncompliance with obligations to issue invoices, credit notes, etc.

5. Noncompliance with obligations to produce records to an authorized officer.

6. Noncompliance with obligations to furnish tax returns and remit tax payable.

7. Nonregistered person issuing an invoice which states an amount of VAT liable.

8. Person improperly issuing an invoice which states an amount of flat rate addition.

9. Company/association/club secretary's liability where any of the above offenses are committed by a body of persons.

10. Obstruction of an authorized officer.

11. Fraudulent or negligent use of an incorrect invoice or return.

12. Fraudulent or negligent use of incorrect invoice or return by a body of persons.

13. Secretary's liability where a body of persons makes use of an incorrect invoice or return fraudulently or negligently.

14. Misrepresentation to procure improper tax-free importation of goods.

15. Fraudulent or negligent issue of invoice or credit note.

16. Assisting in or including the making or delivery of incorrect return, invoice, etc.

Source: Ireland, Commission on Taxation, *Fifth Report: Tax Administration* (Dublin: Stationery Office, October 1985), pp. 324–25.

carry any overtones of criminality and yet can represent unwelcome business costs. Such penalties are not always a cost; in France, penalties for late payment (3 percent for the first month and 1 percent for each succeeding month) are a deductible expense for the purpose of corporate income tax. Penalties for underdeclaration, bad faith, and fraud are not deductible.

Such penalties are triggered automatically by failure to do something—register, send in a return, or settle overdue accounts with the authorities and are commonly used in VAT systems (for example, France, Belgium, Chile, Ireland, and Argentina). Oddly enough, the U.K. legislation until 1985 did not allow automatic interest penalties on unpaid VAT; "interest had to be awarded by a VAT tribunal before it became due,"[17] thus, civil penalties did not exist and the only

[17]de Vries (1985, p. 204).

penalties of fines and imprisonment had to be substantiated by the burden of proof for action in law.

A good example of the automatic financial penalty is provided by the Belgian practice. If a return is missing three months after it is due, or if the state is owed money, the Computer Center closes the trader's account to "zero" and converts the disputed amount to a special account. For each return missing, a fine is levied, payable within a month. When returns are made eventually, three further penalties are incurred: (1) a fine for each month late; (2) a late payment fine of 5 percent of the tax due for the first month, 10 percent for the next month, and 200 percent (the legal maximum) for the months thereafter; and (3) an interest charge on the accumulating outstanding debt balance. The system seems to work as 95 percent of monthly returns are entered by the due date and 99 percent within three months.[18]

Following the recommendations of the most interesting 1983 Report on Enforcement Power (the Keith Committee), the U.K. authorities can now issue default surcharges on traders who are persistently late with VAT payments. Penalties for the first time range from a small amount (£30—equivalent to $54) up to 5 percent of the VAT due (similar to Belgium); for each new default the penalty rises by 5 percent to a maximum of 30 percent. There is also a category of "serious misdeclaration," defined as an amount of tax lost equal to or exceeding (1) 30 percent of the true tax for the period; (2) the greater of £10,000 ($18,032) and 1.5 percent of the true amount; or (3) 15 percent of the true amount (for persistent offenders, the penalty is 30 percent of that tax).

In Argentina, a VAT taxpayer who fails to issue an invoice for a taxable transaction is subject to a penalty ranging from 50 percent to 100 percent of the tax evaded. If he has acted fraudulently, the penalty ranges from twice to ten times the tax evaded. If the taxpayer is found to have omitted issuing an invoice on a second occasion, imprisonment for up to 30 days is applied in addition to the monetary penalty.

Countries usually also apply automatic noncriminal financial penalties for not keeping records and for breaking regulations about registration and deregistration.

It should be pointed out that such penalties do not necessarily imply simple outcomes. To take the example given above of "the true amount of tax" which is, of course, the net difference between VAT on output and credit for VAT on inputs; the variations between these can

[18]Barnard (1976).

affect whether a trader is viewed as making a "serious misdeclaration" or not, and also in its effect.

For example:[19]

	(a)	(b)	(c)
		(In pounds sterling)	
Output tax liability	33,830	33,830	33,830
Input tax recovered	− 500	− 8,000	− 30,500
True amount of tax	33,330	25,830	3,330
Whereof 30 percent	9,999	7,749	999

In (a), an error of £9,000 should not give rise (provided that the "two offenses" in four out of six previous years had not been violated) to a penalty, as it is within 30% of the true amount of tax and no serious misdeclaration arises—but it would exceed the 15% margin and so contribute to the "two offenses" rule.

In (b), an error of £9,000, which may be precisely the same error as in (a), would result in a serious misdeclaration and a penalty of £2,700; it also exceeds the 15% margin.

In (c), the permitted margin of error is only £999 and is clearly exceeded by the £9,000 error; however, the penalty would still be £2,700, although the error giving rise to it would be fundamentally the same one. . . .

The penalty is always 30% of the amount of the tax which would have been lost had the inaccuracy not been discovered.

Of course, there should be symmetry to these penalties. Should the authorities fail to refund net credit due to traders promptly (especially in cases of large capital purchases or exports), then the government should have to pay interest at the commercial borrowing rate (or some rate close to that and periodically reviewed) to the trader who is out of pocket.

Finally, in some countries, the purchaser of the good or service can be held responsible and fined if he knows that VAT has been evaded (Chile), or if he does not ensure that VAT is levied (on buildings in Belgium or, theoretically, on restaurant bills in Italy).

Automatic Nonfinancial Penalties

Automatic nonfinancial penalties have proved, in the opinion of some tax administrators, more effective than financial levies. For example, in Chile, failure to register for VAT makes a taxpayer liable

[19]"Value Added Tax: Finance Act 1985—Keith Committee Proposals," *Accountancy* (1985, p. 37).

to an automatic fine. Failure to issue an invoice for a taxable transaction draws a fine of five times the sales amount. More important, however, in addition, the premises (shop, factory, etc.) where the infraction was committed may be closed down by the tax authorities for a period of up to 20 days. If a taxpayer commits the same offense again, he may be subject to imprisonment for a period of three to five years.

It is the knowledge that his business may be closed down, even for a day or two, that is the greatest penalty to a trader. (This provision has been included in the Philippine VAT legislation.) It should be noted that this action requires no special warrant and no threat of criminal proceedings or ultimate sanction of imprisonment. It is wholly within the control of the revenue department.

Criminal Penalties

Criminal penalties are commonly legislated to be both financial and nonfinancial, that is, to back up the monetary penalty with the threat of imprisonment. In practice, countries do not make much use of actual imprisonment for tax offenses and indeed criminal proceedings are not pursued enthusiastically. For example, in a typical year 1980/81, in the United Kingdom the number of prosecutions was 98, of which 79 pleaded guilty and out of the 19 contested cases only 4 convictions were not achieved. The small number of failed cases suggests that the authorities were applying very high standards of evidence to ensure success. However, it is also noteworthy that the U.K. Inland Revenue with 20 million direct taxpayers in 1979/80 sought only 156 criminal prosecutions, whereas the Customs and Excise started proceedings against almost 2,800 of the 1.25 million VAT taxpayers (0.2 percent) and by 1985/86 this had risen to about 5,500 out of approximately 1.5 million taxpayers (0.4 percent).

In some countries, the authorities may even have the stiff penalties and power to prosecute in the legislation but find themselves frustrated by the courts. The legal officers may be slow to move on tax cases; they may find it difficult to put together the evidence needed, and when the case is proved the judiciary may tend to be more indulgent to the taxpayer than they would be for other crimes. In some countries, the legal delays can take up to five, or even ten, years.[20] It is true, of course, that criminal prosecution is the most feared penalty of all. It threatens to deprive an individual of his

[20]Perry and Orozco de Triana (1986, p. 47).

freedom and often (depending on constitutional law) conviction for a felony strips one of certain rights. Extreme caution should be exercised in prosecuting a taxpayer for tax evasion, since it has devastating effects on both his social and business endeavors. However, once the facts indicate that there is convincing evidence of fraud, there should be no hesitation in proceeding with prosecution.

Criminal prosecution without publicity limits the deterrent effect. Extensive publicity of convictions should, therefore, be given. Generally, any evidence used during the prosecution becomes public, and news releases should be issued highlighting the basis for the prosecution. As far as the administrators of VAT are concerned, information on prosecution cases should be distributed to all district offices, and the district officers should be encouraged to seek publicity in their districts.

Whether payment is required automatically or as a result of criminal prosecution, there will always be cases where payment is not forthcoming for reasons partly or wholly outside the taxpayer's control. For example, substantial additional tax may have become due because previous payments have been inadequate through an innocent misunderstanding of the law, or a taxpayer may have had his business disrupted through a disastrous fire. In such cases, what is at issue is not the taxpayer's willingness to pay, but his ability to pay, and the normal procedure in such circumstances would be to accept payment of outstanding tax installments over a reasonable period, on the understanding that all future liabilities would be met when due. So as not to impede the smooth working of the collection machinery, cases requiring this kind of special treatment should be separated from the mainstream of the collection office. This special office engages in the necessary correspondence with the taxpayer and arranges the installment payments. Such facilities should only be granted, however, in exceptional circumstances. For instance, of some 5,150 VAT offense cases in the United Kingdom, 528 (10 percent) were settled out of court.[21]

In general, the public views tax evasion in a different light to most other crimes and, rightly or wrongly, it makes administrative sense for the tax authorities to rely on sanctions other than criminal prosecution. As far as possible, financial penalties should be automatic and other sanctions, such as closing the business temporarily, should be at the discretion of the tax commissioner.

---

[21]United Kingdom, Committee on Enforcement Powers of the Revenue Departments (1983, Vol. 2, p. 338).

CHAPTER 15

Computers and VAT

You've never seen an IRS computer at work. It can add, subtract and counter-
mand, all at the same time, and also send your refund check to Nome, Alaska.
Once your return goes through our computer the game is over for you and
anyone you love.

—ART BUCHWALD "Form 1040: The 1 Percent Solution,"
Washington Post, January 15, 1987, p. C1

Everyone gets a promotion when I install a computer system.
—SOL DUBROOF

A well-designed computer system is a useful tool of tax administrators, and when used effectively can reduce the cost of operations,
improve the efficiency of controls, and assist taxpayers to comply with
tax legislation.[1] However, the benefits of computer processing are
offset by associated expenditures. These include not only the capital
costs of purchasing or leasing equipment, software, and telephone
lines, site preparation, and other supporting apparatus but also the
recruitment, training, and management of specialized personnel to
operate the equipment and to plan, design, test, implement, and
maintain the computer system. This chapter surveys some broad
issues of the choice of system, user requirements, some important
assumptions, security issues, and ends with an Annex that illustrates a
possible computer system for VAT.

---

[1]This chapter could not have been written without using the accumulated wisdom of
Sol Dubroof who, of course, carries no responsibility for the actual text.

324

General Considerations

Advantages and Problems of Computerization

In recent years, the efficiency, capabilities, and capacities of computer hardware have steadily increased, while hardware costs have declined. Maintenance has also become easier. All this has made the use of computers more straightforward, especially in developing economies. On the other hand, salaries and other costs of computer technicians have increased to a point where it is not unusual for the software, design, and other personnel costs to equal or exceed the hardware costs. In addition, experienced computer technicians are scarce in many developing countries and learning basic skills by education, special training, or on-the-job application usually requires several years, and must be updated frequently as techniques and computer systems' capabilities are constantly changing. Moreover, in a small administration the loss of a handful of the top computer center people can cause a major dislocation in keeping the system running.

Two recent developments have reduced this problem. The first is the development and mass marketing of personal computers, which are powerful, versatile, reliable, economical, have interchangeable components, and can operate on battery power. They are also less sensitive to climate and are easy to use, enabling them to be operated in almost any environment. They can be programmed with fairly simple common languages.

The second breakthrough is the enormous variety of preprogrammed, economical, and reliable software packages that have been tailored for the personal computer. They are convenient for both the VAT administration and the traders who must comply with VAT. For example, a highly rated accounting system package ("The Shoebox Accountant") costs only $395 and the highest-rated accounting software ("4-in-1 Basic Accounting") costs only $995.[2] A general software package, such as an accounts receivable program, can be modified to fit the specific tax administration requirements of a VAT system.

For a small VAT administration, the total computer system, including all hardware components and software packages, can be acquired for less than $50,000, depending on the complexity of the VAT system and the number of revenue offices that will issue, receive, or process VAT documents and therefore will require computer terminals, printers, and communications equipment.

[2]*Software Digest Ratings Newsletter* (1986).

Experience in VAT administration in Latin American countries and elsewhere, even with a relatively small number of VAT taxpayers, has confirmed the need to apply computer processing to VAT taxpayer registration, returns, and payments, and to assist in other compliance and enforcement areas such as collection and auditing.

Therefore, during the process of deciding to install a new VAT system or to replace an old simpler turnover, business, consumption, or other type of sales tax with a VAT, the resources implications should be fully identified. The estimated costs of the computer system, the personnel, the preparation and printing of forms for public use, the information and instruction materials for taxpayers and government employees, the supplies, and external technical advisors should all be included in setting the VAT rate and estimating net revenues from the VAT system.

In many countries, a computer system is already used to process other types of taxes, payroll data, statistical reports, and many other applications. For instance, in Mauritius the central computer not only processes tax data but also the examination results for the Ministry of Education. In such cases, the additional costs in hardware and software for VAT may be minimal, as the new basic investment costs can be avoided and experienced systems technicians would be available.

It may be appropriate to indicate how computerization can reduce handling costs (for example, automatic printing and dispatch of tax returns) and how it can save manpower. It should be possible to calculate this saving with some accuracy. It should also be possible to quantify all such savings, put a value on other improvements (for example, quicker banking of money), and arrive at a total benefit that can be set against the cost of purchasing hardware and the training and retention of computer specialists.

The point should be made that it is sometimes better to start with a manual system, or to stay with one, until it is cost-effective to change. Clearly, such factors as the number of registered persons and the complexity of the VAT itself are important elements in this decision. But if a manual system is decided upon initially, then it should be the intention of the planners to computerize in due course. Procedures and forms should be designed to make the switchover smooth (for example, the VAT return in the manual system should be designed so that it can easily be adapted as a data input document).

The manual system should be considered only as a temporary substitute for the computerized system. You do not have to go back to a horse and buggy, feed the horse, and shovel manure for a year before adopting an automobile. Even simple VAT systems need purchase accountability, sales, nonrefundable credits, refunds and payments, and quick identification of nonfilers, nonpayers, and under-payers for adequate tax administration.

The argument that manual systems are more desirable in economies that have plenty of educated but underemployed people—such as India, Pakistan, and Egypt—is mistaken. Computers do not eliminate jobs. They do supersede boring and repetitive tasks, but create more interesting work (for example, audit and investigation), using educated manpower that commands higher salaries. As an illustration, since computer technology was adopted in 1957, the number of U.S. Internal Revenue Service employees outside Washington, D.C. has more or less doubled (from 48,000 to 90,000) but the cost of collection has remained at 49 cents per $100.

Prevalent Concepts

There are two general approaches to computerizing a government's tax administration system, including the VAT, and either can produce satisfactory results. In the centralized concept, the design, development, and operation of the computer system is provided by an organization (usually independent of the tax department) that is responsible for satisfying the requirements of all or most government agencies.

Brazil's Serviço Federal de Processamento de Dadaf (SERPRO) is a typical case. A small staff of the Government's operational departments gathers information concerning the agency's requirements, presents and coordinates them with the computer service agency's technical staff, and participates in evaluating systems' outputs to ensure that the expected results are produced.

In Ireland, an example of a smaller system in a geographically compact country, all taxes are processed on a central mainframe. There is immediate access to data on the computer master file, through a widely based teleprocessing network that provides direct access to all significant collection files in the revenue data base, including the VAT master file. For this purpose, a subset of the data recorded for each case on the magnetic tape VAT file is placed on a magnetic disk file and is kept fully up to date with events on the main tape file. Terminals are installed in all VAT offices throughout the country; these are linked by leased telephone lines to the central computer. Each terminal typically comprises a visual display unit with an associated printer and, if authorized, may be used to access any disk file in the revenue data base. An official retrieves and examines a case from the VAT computer file on the screen and enters an appropriate message through the terminal. The official can request a printout of any information on the screen for a more permanent record. The terminal can also be used to enter and update a VAT master file account.

In other countries, each ministry may apply the centralized concepts to its operating departments. So, in the United Kingdom, for instance, the Customs and Excise computer at Southend deals only with VAT. The VAT administrators cannot have direct access to income tax data as they could in a more unified system.

A third possibility, opened up by the development of powerful desk top or personal computer systems, is to decentralize many record keeping functions to the regions or districts, with only periodic information processing and data storage being sent to the central organization. For a country with a limited number of potential VAT taxpayers, the modern personal computers can offer a cheap, efficient, and reliable way to run a VAT.

The Appropriate Choice

While the initial choice of which concept to use depends on several factors, such as capital expenditures and efficient use of computer hardware, the major deciding factor is often the existing official computing setup. Since VAT is usually a tax introduced as a complete innovation within the last 20 years, it generally enters into a tax registration and collection system that has already been created for existing direct and indirect taxes. Frequently, VAT has to make do with the existing data center. Sometimes VAT is used as a justification for a massive expansion of the data center, as in Korea, or for an overhaul of the entire ministry of finance computerization, as in Indonesia. In many cases, the existing computer system is likely to be a major molder of the VAT computer system's supporting administrative services.

Another deciding factor often is the availability of adequate numbers of skilled computer technicians. But, as computer costs fall, or when the number of available technicians increases, and/or the services provided by the central computer organization are inadequate or become unresponsive in terms of scheduled work or unplanned events (such as a last minute, significant tax legislation change), a mixed approach evolves. Tasks that must be done on time, such as issuing receipts for taxes, answering inquiries, and issuing refunds, may be performed by the operating department's newly acquired decentralized computer system; however, large master file operations and outputs, such as labels for tax returns, mathematical verifications, assessment notices, delinquency checks, audit selection, and other complicated master file operations still may be performed by a central government data processing agency or department.

Sometimes the results are not those intended, as in Portugal, where the intent was to link the 22 VAT districts with terminals and printers to the Central Collection Office. However, the telecommunications linkage was not achieved and, after a year into the VAT, the data (for instance, selecting taxpayers to be audited) had to be sent by courier or mail. Much the same is true for the difficult geographic links between the 69 Indonesian district tax offices and the computer center.

In another example mentioned earlier, physical circumstances forced the authorities to accept a decentralized system. Telecommunication links were so poor, and were not expected to be upgraded for at least ten years, that the officials decided that substantial computerization had to be placed in local hands on personal computers and data passed to headquarters on disk by biweekly courier.

Furthermore, of course, often a third to a half of VAT is collected by customs; as the customs department is often already computerized, VAT should complement the customs system, and data should be freely accessible between the VAT and customs systems.

A point that might be made about a decentralized system is that the computer in each region should be compatible with, and have identical software as, those in other regions. It is better if the purchasing and assessment of requirements are done centrally even though each region will have its own computer. This may seem self-evident, but in the Federal Republic of Germany, there was no harmonization of computer treatment of tax returns in the states, and this has caused problems (although it is being harmonized).

Finally, as already mentioned, the size of the modern sector of the economy can suggest whether a mainframe or some combination of personal computers should be used. Computer technology is changing so rapidly that what seemed necessary five years ago is likely to be outdated today.

Planning

Long before hardware is procured for a new computer system, the major objectives of the system should be confirmed, the basic assumptions and rules described, and the users' requirements defined. These activities, when combined with hardware, software, installation, training, and conversion considerations, can form the basis for a master computer system implementation plan (see Appendix II and the Annex to this chapter).

Objectives

General objectives could be described nontechnically as (1) making the administrative system and procedures simple and effective; (2) aiding the department's officers and the public to carry out their obligations; (3) improving the processing and filing system so that information can be quickly, accurately, and easily retrieved; (4) providing collection and statistical information required by the tax authorities; and (5) providing timely, exact, quick, and accurate management information for policymakers and executives.

User Requirements

Defining user requirements is usually a time-consuming task as it requires educating the users on what their needs are and what the computer system can do for them. Software requirements may be unique to each country, and while it may seem sensible to call on the expert help of the company selling the computer, often the vendor is not necessarily the best person to solve an individual country's problems (they may not appreciate the subtleties and may be too willing to sell their own programs even though they do not fit the user's needs). Moreover, new users need to be aware of the likely conflict between systems analysts and tax experts that can be time consuming to sort out. Therefore, an effective project manager is essential. In any case, there must be thorough quality assurance tests on the systems analysts' and programmers' translations of user requirements into practice. In at least one major country, serious problems have arisen because systems analysts failed to meet fully user requirements. The VAT staff did not detect this until late in the installation because quality assurance tests were delayed as there were too few staff.

The following lists give some idea of the typical potential computer output for VAT, typical inquiries and displays, file posting, and analysis.

Computer System's Paper Outputs:
- Labels or preaddressed VAT returns and payments vouchers.
- Letter assigning a registration number to taxpayers or printing the VAT registration certificate.
- Alphabetical and numerical directories of all registrations assigned for revenue offices' use.
- Errors lists (data on return or document invalid).
- Unpostable lists (wrong registration numbers or other errors that prevent posting to master file).

- Letters requesting missing data on tax returns.
- Refund offset notices.
- Credit notices or refund checks.
- Assessment notices—underpaid tax returns.
- Demand notices—arrears accounts.
- Stop filer or nonfiler notices.
- Lien or property seizure notices.
- Registration forms for new applicants or changed names.
- Stock or inventory reporting forms for pre-VAT credit.
- Audit selection control and summons.
- Audit case closing report.
- Audit deficiency assessment notices.
- Collections reports and accounts receivable.
- Statistical reports.
- Operational reports.
- Management reports.
- Transcript of accounts.

Input and Outputs via Terminal Inquiry:

- "Where's my refund" inquiries.
- Look up missing registration numbers on tax returns.
- Other taxpayer inquiries about credits or payments.
- Research and input for unpostable accounts.
- Input of data from taxpayer responses to inquiry.
- Entering payments vouchers data to delinquent accounts.
- Audit inquiries about assigned and related taxpayer's or income tax data.
- Audit posting of results of cases closed.
- Display of audit inventory and activity.
- Inquiries about status of accounts in arrears.
- Display of open account activities.
- Display of arrears account activities.
- Entering adjustments to accounts.
- Updating taxpayer accounts with name and address changes.
- Obtaining document location numbers of paper documents.

Master File Posting and Analysis:

- External and internal source data matching—identify nonfilers and new taxpayers as well as underreporting by comparing VAT data with income tax data.
- Identify unpostable records—duplicates and inconsistencies.
- Identify audit criteria cases.
- Set triggers for scheduled future events such as issuance of follow-up notices or reversal of a holding action.

Basic Assumptions and Rules

The following major assumptions and rules are put forward also as an example. The list is probably not complete and, of course, will be different for every country and its VAT system, but it can provide the basic outlines of a system's design.

(1) A most powerful assumption is that taxpayers will register and will be issued a unique tax identification number (TIN) for all ministry of finance tax-related activities (not just the VAT department, but for customs and excise and income tax as well). This identifier could be the income tax identification number with a prefix or suffix added to it and, assigned to each taxpayer, should be used as a VAT registration number for all tax-related purposes in all the departments of the ministry. The TIN number will be required to be entered on all departmental forms and other related documents, such as payment vouchers, tax returns, and import/export invoices. This unique number is a powerful tool in tax administration, naturally, but it is not enough merely to assign a number to taxpayers—experience in many countries indicates that taxpayers cannot be relied upon to provide accurate numbers on tax documents. The percentage of missing or bad numbers can be substantially decreased by computer preaddressing on turnaround forms. The time and expense needed to check that large quantities of identification numbers are correct far exceed the cost of issuing labels (as was realized in Spain and Hungary) or preprinting identification data on tax forms. In addition, the delays in processing and posting data to tax accounts become intolerable when error rates exceed 10 percent. Therefore, the VAT computer system should be able to print labels or preaddress payment vouchers and tax returns for new applicants, and indeed, for existing taxpayers.

(2) Tax returns (monthly, quarterly, or annually for VAT and probably for withholding and income tax as well) may be made in the local

offices or at a data processing center. Here, data preparation tasks such as an initial review for completeness of data, coding, editing, controlling, and batching are performed. Data entry, that is, key punching, and error correction tasks are also performed. Tax returns are available pending selection for audit and other taxpayer contacts.

In one of the older VAT systems, that of Belgium, labels are computer printed and sent to a local office when requested by a trader. The preaddressed slips and tax returns are sent to the trader who sticks the label to his declaration form. This decentralized taxpayer contact method shifts the responsibility to the taxpayer and the local offices.

In the newer VAT systems, such routine tasks as preaddressing returns, declarations, and payment vouchers are centrally controlled and automatically sent directly to taxpayers at prescribed intervals, and the tax returns are mailed directly to a computer processing center. When the local office receives the tax return and is satisfied that the return contains valid information, local officials code the essential details on to a special magnetic roll, and send them to the computer center daily. The computer center never gets any information directly from traders nor does it correspond with them.

In the Belgian system, the maintenance of the taxpayers accounts and receipt of payments is centralized in one place. For example, as described in Chapter 12, a current account for every registered trader is held in the computer center and run against local office accounts every week. Payments are all made via the Office de Cheque Postale in Brussels on a prescribed form. So, every movement in the trader's position is shown in the current account, and, to help everyone, the computer center sends a quarterly extract of the current account both to the trader and to the local office.[3] In other larger countries, payments are received in many places—the customs department, any authorized bank, or a finance collection office.

(3) The tax department computer center should print and provide each district office with a quarterly list of all taxpayers who have registered and an annual consolidation for backup and research purposes.

(4) Appropriate paper document data should be put on the computer, at the first place of receipt that has computer input equipment, to establish control quickly and reduce paper handling.

(5) Only a limited number of authorized persons in the tax department need receive, handle, or process cash, checks, or other remit-

[3]Barnard (1976).

tances from taxpayers. Post offices, authorized banks, customs offices, and treasurer's offices should receive, validate, control, and deposit most payments for VAT taxes. Paper payment vouchers need not be sent to the tax department's regional or district offices for data preparation or entry, when the treasurer's office can produce magnetic media (probably cassettes or diskettes) as a by-product of cash register entries, or when the regional computer service centers can enter payment vouchers. After the data are entered, the payment vouchers should be sent to the district offices for storage, for research for disputes, or for unpostable re-entry purposes.

(6) Paper documents should be reduced to an absolute minimum in number and size (another reason to prefer a single rate VAT). Preferably the tax department should receive only one copy of any document (in the case of a payment, the taxpayer retains his receipted or validated copy or stub, while the tax department keeps the other copy or part of the payment voucher). Each form should be designed to serve all necessary purposes. For example, the notice of a TIN will be a carrier for other forms, such as monthly vouchers returns and their related instructions. Also, all forms should be standardized and designed for quick and easy completion by taxpayers, and for accurate and quick data entry to minimize errors by taxpayers and processing personnel (see example in Chapter 13). This is easy to say but extremely difficult in practice. The cost of creating good forms should never be underestimated.

(7) All external use, turnaround forms, letters, notices, and cards should be designed as self-mailers or for easy standard window insertion. They should be preaddressed, including the TIN from the most current computer master file data to assure reliability of the taxpayer's identification number, to accelerate data entry, reduce key strokes, and to minimize errors and corrections work. Also, all notices should contain a telephone number or an office address or both where taxpayers can call or go to receive prompt and reliable explanations or advice.

(8) Each paper document should be given a unique number, the document locator number (DLN), by machine imprinting (cash register or hand numbering machine) or by computer. This number is needed to control, identify, and locate a paper document and to reduce data entry strokes and time.

System Design and Responsibilities: Assumptions

(1) A centralized taxpayer master file system of a ministry of fi-

nance, either for VAT or for all taxes, located in the tax department's computer center, should be the legal file to contain all permanent data on disk, diskettes, or magnetic tape for all tax-related material. These data could be speedily updated by authorized persons and could be accessed quickly and used for research and administration. For example, urgent data could be accessed and transmitted on line via terminals, while other outputs, such as labels, notices, and lengthy reports could be printed on the computer center's high-speed printers and sent to those requesting the information via terminals, messengers, or postal services.

(2) When the regional service centers and the tax department's local offices are fully computerized and operational, the main computer center should not receive any paper tax documents. The center would receive data via magnetic tapes, diskettes, disks, or cassettes.

(3) It is assumed that a data processing headquarters office has overall responsibility for the design, development, and operation of the taxpayer master file system. Other technical experts may provide assistance on specific projects under the general direction of the data processing division, but the responsibility for physical control of the central taxpayer master file and its physical magnetic disk or tape files remains centralized. The general structure of the master file should be organized and formulated on the concept that there is an account for each taxpayer based on his TIN, and each account would contain appropriate information sections. At a minimum, each taxpayer's account would have an entity section, an accounting section, a tax return section, a balance (arrears or refund) section, an audit section, and history sections. To illustrate the contents of one section, the entity summary section should contain permanent identification data such as the taxpayer's TIN, name, address, and telephone number, the type of tax the taxpayer is liable for, the date of registration, the month his tax year ends, accountant's registration number, type of business code, indicator of unpaid balance due (VAT refund freeze indicator), and audit in process or results of completed audit codes.

(4) It is assumed that the centralized taxpayer master file would not contain all the detailed tax return and other data received or entered by the tax department to verify tax computations, to select returns with high potential for audit, and to make statistical samples and other detailed processing and validation checks. Only significant permanent data, which may be required for cross-reference with other files, for legal accounting, management, reporting, and other ministry of finance purposes, would be extracted from other computer files that have detailed records and would be retained on the master file. When

detailed data are required, it can be retrieved from paper documents, microfilm, or disks and tapes, if it is received at the local or regional office.

(5) The system should be designed to be flexible, especially during the earlier periods when pilot offices, system's tests, and other interim processes are being phased in. Thus, the system should be capable of accepting input data in different media from various sources at different stages or times. For instance, in Spain, each registered business is required to submit a list of sales above a certain (high) value, together with details of the purchases, and the computer center is required to compare the input tax credit claimed by the purchaser with the list provided by the seller. This serves a double purpose, a preaudit control and a control over the input VAT credit claims, especially at the introduction of the VAT. All VAT systems are vulnerable to fraud in the form of overdeductions of input tax at the start of the tax, and cash flow is damaged (see Chapter 14). Therefore, this verification provides valuable flexibility at the outset.

(6) The system should be designed to handle the volume of data expected for the next five to ten years to ensure that the computer capacity and other resources are adequate in the medium and longer term.

Personnel and Training

(1) Sufficiently trained staff should be recruited to run the computer center, and they should be paid enough to retain them. This seems an obvious statement but experience shows, whether in developed or developing economies, that computer staff turnover is high, and experienced programmers and systems analysts can command substantially higher salaries in the private sector. Typically, especially in developing countries, they are internationally mobile.

(2) Training courses, lasting one or two weeks, should be set up for the operational, managerial, and executive staff. The courses should cover the subjects listed below, followed by on-the-job training as appropriate:

- Establishing a master file system.
- Structure and contents of a taxpayer account.
- Programming requirements preparation.
- Posting and analysis techniques.
- Data and accounting controls.

- Transaction and command codes.
- Validity checks concept.
- Application of document locator numbers.
- Error and unpostable resolution standards.
- Computer-generated transactions and notices.
- Returns processing procedures.
- Processing cycles.
- Password and other security features.
- Data base management concepts.

Quality and Security Assurance

(1) All computer programs should contain adequate controls and validity checks. As a minimum, the programs should verify the correctness of each TIN, using the check digit, the date, tax period, type of tax, and amounts (see Chapter 13). Controls of amounts accounted for and the numbers of forms processed should be effectively applied to all documents and batches of work processed. A log should be kept of all transactions, terminal input entries, and audit trails; tax department security officers should be responsible for controlling and assigning employee command codes, passwords, badges, and other physical security standards in all tax department offices that have computer equipment and software.

(2) Each terminal user should be in possession of an identification badge and, when using it to "sign on" to the computer, should also supply the password that is currently associated with his badge. The prerecorded data on the badge identify the user to the computer system and thereby establish the range of actions and data that will be available to that user. The initial issue of badges to users should be a strictly controlled procedure involving documentation requiring the signature of the security officer or other appropriate senior officer. The ongoing custody of badges and the assignment of passwords in the various user areas should be subject to careful controls and unannounced checks. All sign-on badges normally should be changed by the network controller at the computer center at irregular intervals not exceeding eight weeks.

(3) The range of commands or actions allowed to a particular badge should be strictly controlled. This control is applied by means of an authority code that is assigned to the badge and employee's

assignments at the time of issue and as required for the employee's work and tasks.

Subject to badge and password restrictions, access to the VAT system can be further controlled by:

- User identification code—identifying a VAT taxpayer, usually by a prefix or suffix to their TIN.

- User group code—identifying the tax official's office or location of the terminal.

- Tax office code—messages confined to the offices of the inspector of taxes are further controlled so that an official from one local office may not input a transaction to another local office other than that for which the sign-on code was issued.

- Authority code—which may permit the user to retrieve and inspect and to modify or enter new data, or restrict the user to inspection only.

- The computer transmission of an alert message, if attempts are made to input data with an ineligible badge, by an unauthorized office, an improper terminal, or by other types of intruders.

- Log tapes of which badges were used to access and enter data (journalizing).

(4) It is assumed that backup systems, including pairing with a compatible computer, retention of grandfather tapes or disks in another location, uninterceptable power supply, and other security standards will be provided.

Computerized Accounts

Finally, there is the growing general use of computerized accounts to be considered. Not only does the revenue department in many countries use computers, but frequently customs and excise departments have been in the forefront of computerization and, as already mentioned, the systems should be designed to complement each user, especially as customs can be expected to collect a large portion of the VAT in most countries.

In many countries, commercial businesses are far ahead of the government in the use of computer-kept accounts. The reasons are that business accounts are basically on a much smaller scale than government accounts and also that the software is usually available in standardized format, whereas government accounting systems must often be designed afresh or require program modifications. However, most administrations are under pressure to audit computerized business accounts and verify the correctness of related tax returns, declarations, and evidence of inventory changes based on this media, in lieu of paper records. This raises a number of issues and may become increasingly important as "the incidence of fraud perpetuated by companies using computer accounting systems has recently increased considerably."[4]

The VAT officials therefore should have the right both to operate and to have access to data in the business taxpayers' computers. This, of course, requires VAT operators who themselves are trained to use and appreciate the nuances of small- and large-scale systems. Some administrations have been training their own auditors in computer techniques for many years (in the United States there has been a post of "computer audit specialist" since 1971) and it is generally recognized that it is better to train auditors to use computers than try to turn computer specialists into auditors.

Regrettably, this is not the end of the story. Accounts can, and increasingly are, kept on foreign computers and only the end-product data needed for the tax returns is transmitted transnationally. What should the appropriate stance of the VAT authorities be—to accept, or not to accept, such evidence? This is a question that remains open-ended as the scope and reach of tax authorities is a contentious debate and no clear guidelines have yet emerged.

Computers have been used to misclassify and erroneously describe imports and exports and to evade duties and levies. Once misclassified, for whatever reason, to ensure consistency, the fraud must be continued for other records, including VAT returns. Clearly, there are numerous large international companies that keep scrupulous computer-run accounts and these often are those that are important in VAT (for example, producers of petroleum, tobacco, alcohol, and automobiles). Nevertheless, because the revenue involved is so large, the authorities must be able to monitor the computer records and this requires substantial initial costs and continuous training to keep abreast of developments. As accountants have recognized, the "level of audit assurance that the auditor can derive from the results of a [computer-assisted audit technique] is directly related to the degree of independence achieved in its use";[5] that is, the more the auditor has to

---

[4]United Kingdom, Committee on Enforcement Powers of the Revenue Departments (1983, Vol. 1, p. 102).

[5]"Auditing Guideline: Computer Assisted Audit Techniques," *Accountancy* (1982, para. 25, p. 117).

rely on the enterprises' own staff to run the computer programs, the more the credibility of the audit is eroded. That goes for the VAT audit as well.

Many computer systems of accounts can be checked by use of audit trail and interaudit software programs, but this cannot be relied on to the exclusion of all other checks. They should be used as one technique in an armory of internal and external audit checks to frustrate computerized fraud.

The use of computers for VAT is an enormous subject. This brief review indicates the potential and some problems. Although many VAT officers caution relying too much on computers (for example, to select companies for audit), it is clear that the tide is one way and computerization has a crucial role in helping administer the VAT.

ANNEX

A Possible Automated System

The flow diagram (Chart 15-1) tries to pull together the various strands of Chapters 12–15 to give an example of how they may be interlinked. The reference numbers used below can be found in Chart 15-1. They relate to each flow. The assumed system and the volume of flows are relatively small and approximate to a medium-sized developing country.

An estimate of the costs in time and money to install such a system is given in Table 15-1. It is assumed the design and installation will take 18–36 months. The assumed computer system has a capacity of at least eight megabytes, capable of handling on-line traffic from 200 terminals (about 120 in district offices and others at regional headquarters and customs offices).

Estimated Annual Volume	*Suggested Procedures*
	(1) Regional offices (and the excise department, if involved) send data via their terminals or lists to establish their potential VAT taxpayers on the taxpayer master file. Thereafter, all new TIN assignments and VAT-related transactions must be verified with the master file via computer terminal.
130,000 (Total potential VAT taxpayers)	(2) Potential nationwide VAT taxpayers are purged of duplicate names and TINs. All taxpayers in the revised list are sent a preaddressed letter and VAT registration application form from the entity section of the master file.

120,000 (VAT taxpayers)	(3) VAT taxpayers send back VAT application form; some do not qualify; some are no longer in business or do not respond. Those who do not respond are sent a second letter and application form.
2,400,000 (Monthly payments are assumed)	(4) Eighteen preprinted payment forms or labels, with a VAT category prefix to the TIN, are sent to each VAT taxpayer—one for each month plus extras—with instructions. Taxpayers may request more forms as payments can be made more frequently, but the forms must show only the one TIN.
480,000 (Quarterly returns are assumed)	(5) Approximately 20 days before the due date of the VAT return, a preaddressed blank form is sent to each taxpayer with instructions for completion of the tax return.
300,000 (Three mailings are assumed)	(6) Periodically, additional information is sent to the press, business associations, accountants, and taxpayers about the VAT system. One mailing would include stock relief claim forms, a one-time mailing to establish business tax credit for inventory at the beginning of the VAT system, but only for full VAT taxpayers.
2,200,000 (VAT payments, except to customs department)	(7) Fifty percent of the preprinted forms or labels are used to make payments to banks and to regional and district cashiers. Checks and cash are deposited in the bank, while reports of collections are sent to the comptroller general. Data from the payment forms are transmitted electronically wherever possible, to the VAT account section of each taxpayer's account in the master file.
2,200,000 (VAT payments received by customs)	(8) Fifty percent of the preprinted forms or labels are used by importers and exporters who must pay VAT to the customs department with each transaction. Each week, customs sends a magnetic tape of its VAT collections in TIN sequence to the revenue department. The revenue department consolidates transactions by TIN and posts one weekly total per account as a credit. (Up to 20 credits and 10 debits per quarter are provided in each account.)

Chart 15-1. A Proposed Automated VAT Administration

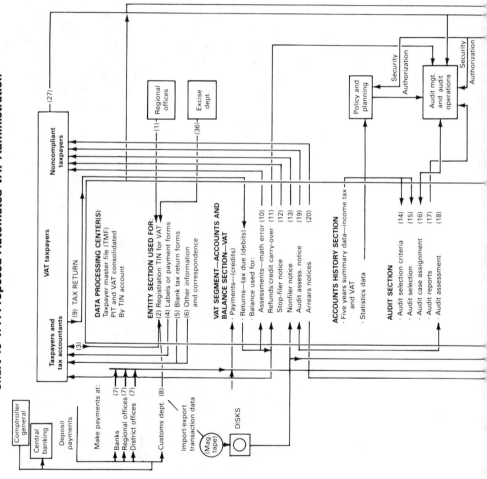

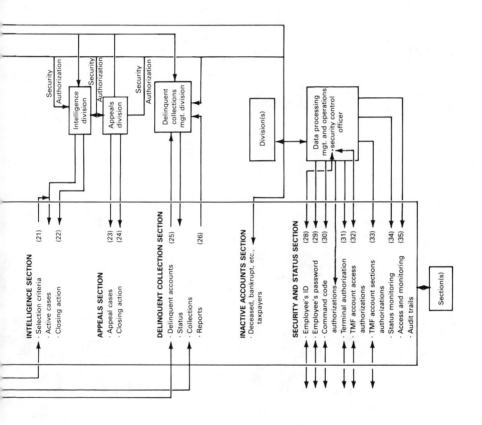

INTELLIGENCE SECTION
· Selection criteria (21)
· Active cases
· Closing action (22)

APPEALS SECTION
· Appeal cases (23)
· Closing action (24)

DELINQUENT COLLECTION SECTION
· Delinquent accounts (25)
· Status
· Collections
· Reports (26)

INACTIVE ACCOUNTS SECTION
· Deceased, bankrupt, etc., taxpayers

SECURITY AND STATUS SECTION
· Employee's ID (28)
· Employee's password (29)
· Command code authorizations (30)
· Terminal authorization (31)
· TMF account access authorizations (32)
· TMF account sections authorizations (33)
· Status monitoring (34)
· Access and monitoring (35)
· Audit trails

Table 15-1. An Example of Resource Costs and Timing of Implementation of an Automated System

	Automated VAT Administration System		
	U.S. dollars (In thousands)	Man-months	Other information
1. **Major decisions made and approved** by ministry of finance, including schedule and computer utilization; elapsed time in calendar months			3 months
2. **Funding commitments obtained**, including funds for external assistance; elapsed time in calendar months			4 months
3. **System development stage:** requirements: analysis and recommendations			
3.1. Elapsed time in calendar months, including obtaining officials' approval			4 months
3.2. External assistance—VAT software, accounting specialists	85.1[1]	26	
3.3. Additional revenue department computer technicians, including external technical training	42.6	12	
4. **Hardware acquisition**			
4.1. Elapsed time in calendar months to acquire computer hardware—normal/expedited			36/18 months
4.2. Mainframe computer system			
4.2.1. Annual leasing cost	1,548.0		
4.2.2. Purchase cost	3,483.0		
4.2.3. Annual maintenance charges	387.0		
4.3. Number of mainframe locations			1
4.4. Additional data-entry terminal systems—purchase, including maintenance	212.8		
4.5. Additional complete on-line intelligent terminal system(s)			
4.5.1. Purchase costs, including maintenance	1,160.9		
4.5.2. Number of additional systems			200

5. Software design, programming, testing, and technical training			
5.1. Elapsed time in calendar months			7 months
5.2. External assistance	135.5[1]	35	
5.3. Additional revenue department computer technicians, including external technical training	69.7	105	
6. Facilities preparation and electrical additions			
6.1. Elapsed time in calendar months			6 months
6.2. Number of locations			116
6.3. Total estimated cost for facilities and electrical additions	2,322.0		
7. System's implementation			
7.1. Elapsed time in calendar months			13 months
7.2. Preparation of manuals and training for all officials, managers, and supervisory personnel of revenue, customs, and excise departments			1,000 employees
7.3. Give training to all potential tax return preparers, VAT taxpayers' comptrollers, and bookkeepers on VAT records, invoices, and procedures			3,000 persons
7.4. Run system's acceptability test simulation in one revenue department office using the old business tax volume and data but new VAT forms			4 months
7.5. External assistance	282.5[1]	59	
7.6. Revenue department technicians			
7.7. Revenue department operational staff to be trained at processing division and other offices	100.6	195	2,000 employees

Source: Various country estimates.

[1] The estimates for external assistance are based on the following technical personnel requirements: a part-time computer specialist; two full-time senior systems analysts; a full-time systems analyst; two full-time program analysts; and, for the first two months of the preparation, a full-time VAT computer specialist and a full-time accounting software systems specialist.

4,000
(Invalid TINs or potential
nonfilers or stop-filers)

(13) If posting customs' tape of transactions to establish credits discloses no master file account, or an account without a debit (no VAT return) entry 30 days after the tax return was due, this triggers an inquiry or the issue of a delinquent filer's notice. There is a quick follow-up investigation for failure to respond to the notices. If appropriate, a temporary TIN ("T" prefix) could be issued for taxpayers who pay but have no master file account, and used to establish a new master file account; alternatively, a nonprefixed TIN could be used, and a status code would identify the account as a temporary one.

432,000
(VAT returns received)

(9) Ninety percent of taxpayers file quarterly returns that cover three months or 13 weeks each, four times a year, 20 days after end of the quarter.

43,000
(Arithmetic errors and
underpayers)

(10) Ten percent of the tax returns have arithmetic errors or computer analysis indicates they have substantially underpaid VAT either monthly or with the tax return. Assessment notices are sent to them, including the underpayment penalty, when appropriate. Sixty percent pay in full upon receipt of an assessment notice or the matter is otherwise settled.

17,200
(Arrears status)

(20) The status of the remaining 40 percent is changed to "arrears," and arrears demand notices are sent to them. If enforced collection becomes necessary, their status should change again to delinquent collections and control of the accounts should be transferred to the delinquent accounts section (see steps 25 and 26, below).

86,400
(Refunds and credit claims)

(11) Twenty percent of tax returns filed each quarter show refunds or credits. (This may be much higher in the first few quarters because of stock relief claims.) Approximately 20,000 are for exporters who will regularly overpay VAT and should not be referred to audit, except in special cases.

9,280
(Audit VAT assessment)

(19) Large, unusual, or unexplained refund or credit claims should be referred to audit promptly for verification of claims and

possible income tax audit. Additional audit assessments are made in 20 percent of these cases. Refunds are reduced for another 20 percent.

48,000
(Stop-filers)

(12) Matching quarterly VAT returns with VAT accounts registered on the master file discloses that 10 percent failed to file VAT returns and make VAT payments. Computer-generated stop-filer notices should produce responses, for example, one half with tax returns and the other half with valid reasons such as out-of-business, duplicate TIN, etc. The latter master file accounts should be moved to the inactive accounts section (see step 27).

10,200,000
(Immediately accessible
VAT/income tax
summary data fields
on the taxpayer
master file)

(14) Summaries of debits, credits, and balances from five years of VAT quarterly returns and five years of similar data from corporate or personal income tax returns are retained.

(15) Audit has access to the current VAT and income tax accounts data for selecting cases for audit.

44,000
(Nonrefund VAT/
income tax cases
assigned to
auditors)

(16) Ten percent of nonrefund VAT returns are selected for audit review and/or examination in conjunction with income tax audits.

30,800
(Audit nonrefund
assessments)

(18) Seventy percent of these joint VAT/income cases result in audit assessments.

60,000
(Audit examination
reports and
monthly inventory
and closing reports)

(17) Audit examination letters and reports to taxpayers are computer generated with preprogrammed paragraphs and formats. Monthly case reports of inventory aging and of closings are also compiled and computer printed for each officer and each office, as well as by region and entire country.

5,000
(Intelligence cases)

(21) One percent of the VAT returns and documents are referred to the intelligence division for

(22) further investigation, after correlation with other internal and external data.

5,300
(Appeals from revenue
assessments)

(23) Twenty percent of the taxpayers who receive underpayment or audit assessment
notices

(24) appeal and eventually are adjudicated.

8,600
(Delinquent accounts)

(25) Fifty percent of taxpayers in arrears do not
pay VAT in full and are referred to the
delinquent collections division for enforced action or part payment agreements.
Various collection actions, both office and
field, are taken and collections are enforced.

20,000
(Delinquent accounts
division reports)

(26) Monthly reports by collection officers are
prepared by computer, as well as inventory
reports by age of cases, status of pending
cases, closing actions, summaries of
monthly receipts, and closing for each office and summaries of all activities and
statuses, as well as collections data. Quarterly and annual reports are compiled by
computer and printed promptly.

120,000
(Inactive accounts)

(27) Deceased, out of business, duplicate VAT
number, etc., accounts are moved to the
inactive section of the master file and retained there for five years. This should be
done as soon as possible so that the active
section of the master file reflects valid data
about VAT accounts and activities.

20,000
(Employees, terminals,
offices, and other
security activities)

(28) A complete security and privacy protection system is required with employee
identification,

(34) passwords, command code authorizations,
and account access authorizations. Terminal usage authorizations, master file section authorization, and account status and
access monitoring are also required.

6,000,000
(Audit trail transactions)

(35) A complete audit trail of every terminal
access to a master file account and data
retrieved must be maintained and be
quickly retrievable for security, searching,
and other uses.

CHAPTER 16

The Trader's Point of View

Do not take for granted that because Customs and Excise is an official Govern-·
ment body it is right. This is not always the case.
—IAN HILLS, *VAT: A Working Guide for the Small Business*
(London: Telegraph Publications, 1987), p. 90

Most discussion of VAT is about whether or not a government should
introduce VAT or about the practical difficulties of administration. It
is often forgotten that the other half of a successful tax depends on the
trader's reaction and that reaction depends, in part, on the businessman's feelings about the costs to him of complying with the requirements of VAT.

This chapter looks at trader decisions in anticipation of VAT,
problems of compliance costs, invoices, pricing, profit margins, bookkeeping, and visits from VAT officials, and the need to review company decisions for their possible implications for VAT.

The Trader's Anticipation of VAT

Traders have an obligation to find out whether they should register
and to register if necessary. They should receive an educational visit
from an official of their local VAT office and this should form the basis
for reasonable working relationships at the district level.

Before the VAT has started, or in opening a new business under a
VAT regime, registered traders should anticipate the tax and consider
whether or not the following should be taken into account.[1]

---

[1]Many of these points on the New Zealand VAT were suggested in the article by Dodd
(1986).

- Appoint a senior staff member to ensure that things get done at the right time and in the right order to prepare for VAT; this staff member should be responsible for training staff at all levels to understand VAT and how it may change their work in-house, with suppliers, and with customers (for example, in a retail store, the paperwork needed to reimburse tourists for the VAT on their purchases).

- Review the accounting system to ensure that it creates the proper and convenient entries for VAT returns.

- Review and modify, if necessary, existing stationery, especially the design of "tax invoices" for the supply of goods and services. Arrange for printing new forms well in advance as many others may be making similar demands on printing.

- Modify cash registers.

- Modify computer programs.

- Identify the activities, transactions, and categories of revenue and expenditure for which VAT could have implications. For instance, separate records will have to be kept of sales at different rates of VAT.

- Identify the precise stage at which VAT applies to each type of supply.

- Determine whether or not some activities are eligible to use the "cash" option for VAT instead of the invoice (accounts) basis; if the option is available, evaluate which is the most advantageous.

- Determine whether a change in the accounting period is needed to satisfy the requirements of VAT.

- If an activity is conducted by a company that is part of a group for income tax purposes, determine whether (in the light of administration and cash flow) it should register separately or whether the group should register.

- Depending on the taxation of stocks and capital goods under the earlier sales tax and the transitional provisions for reimbursement, decide whether such purchases should be advanced or delayed.

- Assess whether VAT will have any effect on contract obligations.

- Ensure that marketing personnel understand the basis for price displays on price tags, price cards, and in advertisements (see below and the discussions of "Discounts" and "Credit" in Chapter 17).

- Review any possible advantages from in-house provision of "exempt" services.

- Carefully review the firm's cash flow position, remembering that though liquidity may be improved (because stocks bear no VAT), the VAT is due to the authorities whether or not the cash has been received from the customer. Failure to pay VAT promptly can have serious financial consequences in many countries as severe automatic penalties may be incurred.

Compliance Costs

What are the compliance costs for a business fulfilling its obligations under VAT? Most businessmen do not actually compute what it costs them to comply with government requirements; they just know it costs money and they resent it. Even before the VAT was introduced in New Zealand "by far the most widespread concern about the proposed form of GST [VAT] relate[d] to a perception that it will impose very heavy costs on those obliged to account for the tax."[2] In the United Kingdom in 1985, VAT was considered the most serious officially created burden on business; twice as serious as the next tax problem (PAYE).[3]

To estimate VAT compliance costs needs an evaluation of the size and costs of the resources committed to VAT work within the business. This includes the wages and salaries and fringe benefits of full- or part-time workers involved with the tax, including accounting, clerical, and sales staff. The overhead costs (office space, depreciation, utilities, and so on) of the employees should also be costed, as should computer hardware, software, time, other equipment and supplies, and any outside advice contracted. Of course, the real costs of all this is what these people and productive capacity could have earned the company had they not been dealing with VAT; but usually it is just their market cost that is computed.

Against these costs there may be offsetting benefits. Smaller firms may be obliged to keep better records than they would have kept without VAT. This may improve their management and decision making. Some businesses may gain a cash-flow benefit. Usually traders collect more VAT on sales than they pay on purchases. They

---

[2]New Zealand, *Report of the Advisory Panel on Goods and Services Tax to the Minister of Finance* (1985, p. 3).

[3]United Kingdom, Department of Trade and Industry (1985, p. 31).

will, therefore, enjoy a cash-flow benefit that will vary according to their relative sales and purchases, their commercial credit periods, and the proportion of annual VAT payments held on average throughout the year.[4] For example, a large retailer selling mainly for cash but enjoying, say, a three-month credit from suppliers, would do very well indeed. Others, selling on credit and getting little supplier credit (typical of smaller firms) would not gain this advantage. The scale of advantage depends on the interest rate and, of course, the gain is not to the economy, but only represents an interest-free loan from the authorities to the traders or perhaps another tax on consumers.

These advantages are undoubtedly real but, in most cases, are not included in survey assessments.[5] However, their scale is well exemplified in Table 16-1, which shows *net* (after offsetting cash flow benefits, but not management benefits) compliance costs for the United Kingdom halving the gross compliance costs in 1984/85.

While traders' compliance costs are undoubtedly real, they are also extremely difficult to assess. The only practical way to do so is to ask those involved to make an informed computation. Table 16-1 shows seven examples of such surveys of sales taxes. The results suggest that compliance costs can be between 3.7 percent and 30 percent of the sales taxes paid. The highest costs were associated with an extremely small sample of retailers paying VAT during the year the tax was introduced and it is hardly a general sample. Otherwise, the results suggest costs below 10 percent of taxes paid, lower costs for the retail sales tax, and small firms suffering higher (sometimes much higher) compliance costs than large firms.

Regrettably all such surveys suffer from the problem of self-selection of respondents producing a self-fulfilling prophecy. If you set out to ask a group by mail whether they are unhappy, it is likely that those who reply will be those that are sufficiently unhappy to take the trouble (and suffer the cost) of filling in the survey. The sample is automatically biased to weight heavily those who consider tax compliance to be a vexatious cost. To balance the results would require an implied weight to be assigned to those who did not reply; presumably these nonrespondents found the sales taxes to be insufficiently burdensome to make a fuss about. It is worth noting that in each case

---

[4]In the United Kingdom, this would average $5/24$ of the VAT they collect annually—made up from a three-month collection period with an average of one and a half month VAT, that is, $3/24$, and the "grace" period of one month before tax is remitted equivalent to one month's VAT, that is, $1/12$ or $2/24$.

[5]For a good appraisal of the problems, see Sandford (1981, pp. 10–12) and (1986).

(except for the tiny face-to-face sample of Matthews) about two thirds of the sample were not used, largely because they did not respond. If, for example, a cost of 2 percent was attributed to these members, it could halve the 9 percent compliance costs of the 1978/79 U.K. VAT survey.

Not only is the sample self-selecting in that only those who are concerned respond but, presumably, those responding have an interest in assigning as much cost as possible to tax compliance. If the respondents think the results will be published, and presumably they cooperate in the hope that their complaints will encourage changes in the tax, then it is possible they think that the more they complain and the higher are the apparent compliance costs, the greater will be their impact on policy. So not only is the sample selection likely to be biased, the replies themselves are likely to include a further bias.

It is difficult to know what to make of this debate. Perhaps it is best if it is recognized that these costs do exist and they can be important, especially to smaller businesses. The VAT administration should be aware of them and should do as much as possible to mitigate them.

The Invoice

General

Having anticipated VAT and registered, what other concerns about VAT does the trader have? He must usually keep a number of records, including normal accounting records; a VAT account; sequentially numbered sales invoices; purchase invoices; and import and export documents.

The authorities might also require other information to be kept, for example, stock control sheets. However, invoices are the most important documents, and examining agents place great store in the availability (or absence) of invoices.

The invoice is the crucial control document in all existing VATs. The requirement to issue invoices, showing the VAT liability, should impose little extra obligation on most businesses as the recording of sales and purchases is part of the normal accounting system of any business that has a proper system of bookkeeping. Accuracy in such records is essential for the financial control of the business. However, in some countries, such as in Indonesia before the introduction of VAT, enterprises did submit a sales tax return showing how their tax liability was computed, but there was no specific stipulation that an invoice had to

Table 16-1. Sales Tax Compliance Cost Studies

Study	Year	Country	Tax Surveyed	Sample Size	Replies Used	Compliance Costs as Percentage of Tax	
						Gross	Net
Sandford[1]	1984/85	United Kingdom	VAT	—	3,000[2]	5.1	2.3
Sandford[1]	1980/81	United Kingdom	VAT	—	3,000[2]	4.8	0.8
Sandford/Goodwin[3]	1977/78	United Kingdom	VAT	9,094	2,799	9.3	7.6
Goodwin[4]	1973/74	United Kingdom	VAT	68	29	21–28	—
Yocum[5]	1960	United States	Retail sales	—	—	7.6	—
Matthews[6]	1957	United States	Retail sales	7	7	5.4	—
Haig[7]	1934	United States	Retail sales	1,600	163	3.7	—

[1]Cedric Sandford, "The Costs of Paying Tax," *Accountancy* (London), June 1986, pp. 108–11.

[2]1984/85 estimates from an update of the 1977/78 survey.

[3]Cedric Sandford, Michael R. Goodwin, Peter J. W. Hardwick, and M. I. Butterworth, *Costs and Benefits of VAT* (London: Heinemann Educational Books, 1981).

[4]Michael Goodwin, "VAT Compliance Costs to the Independent Retailers," *Accountancy*, (London); September 1976, pp. 48–60.

[5]James C. Yocum, *Retailers' Costs of Sales Tax Collection in Ohio*, Bureau of Business Research Monograph No. 100 (Columbus, Ohio: Bureau of Business Research, College of Commerce and Administration, Ohio State University, 1961).

[6]Milton P. Matthews, *A Measurement of the Cost of Collecting Sales Tax Monies in Selected Retail Stores* (Salt Lake City, Utah: Bureau of Economic and Business Research, University of Utah, 1957).

[7]Robert M. Haig, "The Cost to Business Concerns of Compliance with Tax Laws," *Management Review* (New York), November 1935, pp. 323–33.

be issued for tax purposes. This could put the country at a disadvantage compared to others when introducing a VAT.

The directives of the EC specify that taxable persons must issue invoices for all supplies of goods and services to other taxable persons. The requirements in relation to invoices are emphatic: every invoice must show, among other particulars, the price of the goods or services exclusive of VAT and the corresponding amount of VAT. Under the laws of various countries, the purchaser is not entitled to any credit if the tax is not clearly and correctly shown on the invoice. In this lies the control nature of the invoice as an instrument of tax enforcement. The system does not envisage the compulsory issue of invoices showing tax at the retail level or indeed in any transaction other than one between two registered taxpayers.

Since the invoice is not relevant in relation to imports, the appropriate customs form for certifying payment of VAT constitutes the control document for the purposes of a claim to tax credit.

The laws of different countries lay down specific requirements, including a time limit for the issue of invoices, credit notes, and related documents, and these should be strictly applied. A taxpayer must be aware that if he issues an invoice stating a greater amount of tax than is correct for the transaction, he is liable for the whole amount of tax invoiced and may also be liable to penalties. Buyers should not be allowed to take credit for any VAT that proves to be overstated. The VAT law precludes an unregistered person from issuing an invoice and if he issues an invoice showing an amount of tax he is liable for the amount shown. He also leaves himself open to penalties.

None of the European countries requires the use of an official form of invoice. In fact, in all of them, the tax authorities have been ready to meet the convenience of businessmen by accepting as valid documents for tax credit purposes any piece of paper that is in use commercially and that contains the appropriate information required on a VAT invoice. In the case of small sales, simplified forms of invoices are accepted. However, in Taiwan Province of China, traders in goods and services are obliged to issue uniform invoices. These invoices are printed and sold by the authorities. Enterprises can be authorized to print their own invoices, provided they are approved by the Ministry of Finance. In some countries, small-scale traders are exempted from this requirement and just issue ordinary receipts.[6] However, in most countries the tax authorities are authorized to issue regulations for the issue of simplified invoices in certain circumstances, for example, in

[6]Jap (1986, pp. 318).

relation to passenger transport, agricultural markets, and cash-and-carry wholesalers. But note that because of potential VAT evasion through cash-and-carry sales, there are usually regulations to require such traders to ensure that their till rolls show a product code clearly identifying the different classes of goods. In addition, the till roll must be prepared to show all the details required on a VAT invoice and, of course, till rolls must be kept for the full statutory time.

Failure to issue a tax invoice, where the law requires it, or the issue of an invoice falsifying the amount of the consideration strikes at the foundation of any VAT system. It is treated as a highly serious offense, and the penalties applicable to it are likely to match its gravity.

Question of Issuing Receipts to Final Consumers

No European country requires invoices for sales by retailers, but a VAT invoice may be issued by a taxable retailer when asked to do so by a taxable customer.

In Belgium, suppliers of certain services are required to issue officially approved receipts numbered consecutively for all transactions with final consumers. Hotels, restaurants, garages, car wash businesses, and building construction come under this rule. A similar requirement in relation to certain services exists in a few other countries.

In a country in which the legal requirements to issue documentation to final consumers has been consistently ignored by many retailers and the bookkeeping standards are poor, the tax authorities are faced with two alternative courses of action. On one hand, they can commit themselves to raising bookkeeping standards and building up an effective and efficient audit force. On the other, they can try to enforce the requirement that simplified tax invoices be issued to final consumers (for example, in Latin America and Turkey), in the hope that consumers will ultimately be transformed into auxiliary tax officials. (In reality, this is a pious hope because consumers also see themselves as benefiting from the tax evasion.) If the choice is the second, valuable administrative resources will be diverted to profitless pursuits instead of carrying out effective audit programs that are the key to proper VAT control. Traders should try to influence the tax authorities to discourage such a course of action. Small and, indeed, many medium-sized retailers have sufficient difficulty in mastering the essentials of VAT, without the additional and unnecessary complication of documentation to final consumers. In an exercise of give and take, which will be of considerable expense to the government and must exert a serious upward push on costs, it is better to avoid multiplying the vexatious meetings between traders and VAT officials.

The position as regards services is, however, different. Suppliers of certain services with high added value, such as restaurants, garages, building contractors, and allied traders, are often required to issue receipts with printed consecutive numbers in books approved by the tax authorities. The totals for each day's receipts can be entered in the sales book from the trader's own copies of the receipts, which would be the only ones apart from those given to the customers. The tax auditor checks the receipts against the cash book entries and assesses their reliability from the general nature of the business, the stock carried, number of employees, and other criteria.

Pricing

Some countries require the VAT content of a price to be shown clearly and separately from the tax-free price so that the buyer is fully aware of his tax liability. Others claim that buyers want to know the full cost of a good including tax and do not wish to be faced with an additional impost at the till. "Members of the general public may not want to know the exact amount of tax included in each item purchased, they will usually want to know the all up price (including [VAT]) before taking the item to the counter or check out."[7] The New Zealand authorities specified that prices could be shown for a $99 item inclusive of VAT as:

- $99.00, or
- $99.00 (including VAT), or
- $90.00 + $9.00 = $99.00, or
- $90.00 + $9.00 (VAT) = $99.00;

but what would *not* be acceptable were the following:

- $90.00, or
- $90.00 (excluding VAT), or
- $90.00 + VAT.

Every country has its own priorities, but traders must be clear about what discretion they have and make the appropriate adjustments to their price tags and price lists. What happens when this is not anticipated is well exemplified by the case of Greece. "Last week Greece's

[7]New Zealand, GST Coordinating Office, *Pricing & GST*, pp. 2–3.

entire retail sector slowed down as merchants grappled with the new and confusing set of VAT rates. . . . So befuddled were many Greek shopkeepers that 1,500 government officials had to fan out through the country to help them compute prices."[8]

Profit Margins

Sometimes traders set their profit margins on an "into-store" cost. This may or may not include any tax element levied before VAT. With a single-stage tax (say, at the manufacturing level), retailers are quite likely to include the tax element in their base for markup. However, under VAT, the traders act as tax collectors and pass the tax forward fully to the final consumer and, unless traders adapt their practice when VAT is used, profit margins could be distorted.[9]

For example, Table 16-2 shows that if a trader originally (in Column 1) had a 50 percent markup on a purchase price, including a 10 percent sales tax, his selling price would have been $165.00 and his profits, if he considered himself as having paid the sales tax, $45.00. Under a VAT (Column 2), his purchase price will be liable to a VAT of $10.00, his markup remains the same, but his VAT liability is only $6.50 ($16.50 minus $10.00), and his profits after paying VAT rise to $48.50. However, if the trader under the old sales tax did not think of himself as paying the sales tax, his accounting gross profits would

Table 16-2. Profit Margins and VAT
(In U.S. dollars)

	Single-Stage Sales Tax (1)	VAT (2)	VAT (3)
Cost of goods	100	100	100
Plus sales tax at 10 percent	10	10	10
Into store cost	110	110	110
Markup	55	55	62[1]
VAT	—	7[1]	7[1]
Selling price	165	165	172[1]
Profit after sales tax (2)	45	49[1]	—
Profit after sales tax (3)	55	49[1]	55

Source: See text.
[1]Rounded.

[8]"A VAT Spat in Greece," *Newsweek* (1987, p. 37).
[9]New Zealand, GST Coordinating Office, *Pricing & GST*, p. 6.

show $55.00, and the equivalent under VAT would be $48.50. To regain his $55.00 margin under VAT, he would have to raise his margin to (approximately) $62.00 (Column 3).

In each country, the pretax and post-tax profits will be different and will require careful consideration by each trader, taking into account all changes in relative prices. Of course, the tax revenue to the authorities will be quite different under two of the schemes in Table 16-2, but that simply exemplifies that here we are looking at the VAT from the *trader's* point of view and not that of the revenue department.

Bookkeeping Requirements

Importance of Adequate Records for VAT

Under a VAT, the tax authorities are concerned not merely with the figures of sales by taxpayers and the relevant tax but also with the figures of purchases and their liability. To calculate a taxpayer's VAT liability for a given period, there must be adequate records of both purchases and sales. The bookkeeping requirements for the trader can, however, be quite simple (see below), but the existence of more than two rates introduces an element of complexity and even more so if the number of rates exceeds two or three.

Link Between Invoices and Bookkeeping

There is a close link between the proper use of invoices for VAT purposes and the maintenance of a satisfactory system of bookkeeping, because the most essential factor in an adequate system of bookkeeping for VAT is the recording in a systematic way of all invoices of purchases and also all invoices of sales to taxable persons.

Main Bookkeeping Requirements for VAT

Both the directives of the EC and the laws of the various countries establish that chargeable persons must maintain a sufficiently detailed system of bookkeeping to allow VAT to be levied and checked by the tax administration. These requirements, as set out below, should apply to any taxpayer under a VAT except for small traders allowed to keep simplified accounts.

Every taxable person must keep records of all taxable goods and services he receives or supplies in the course of business, distinguishing between taxable transactions liable at different rates of tax, as well as any taxable self-supplies and goods applied to personal use. Such entries should be cross-referenced to relevant sales documents. He must also keep a record of all exempt supplies that he makes or receives. It may be inappropriate to clutter books of account with self-supplies; many VAT authorities allow taxpayers to estimate their self-supplies at the end of the year and make an annual adjustment.

The records must be in sufficient detail to allow the taxpayer to calculate correctly the amount of VAT that he has to pay or can reclaim, and to complete the necessary returns. He must also keep them in a form that enables the tax authorities to check the completeness and accuracy of the VAT returns. Records and accounts do not have to be prepared in any special form, but if they are not regarded as satisfactory, the tax authorities may direct a businessman to make the necessary changes. Records and accounts have to be maintained up to date, and preserved with all relevant papers (such as orders, invoices, delivery notes, and correspondence) and other documents pertaining to the business (such as trading accounts, profit and loss accounts, and balance sheets) for a period that varies according to the law of the different countries.

In developing countries, and for small traders generally, the authorities would expect a sales book and a purchase book shown in Examples I and II.

Example I: Sales Book

			Sales		Sale	
Date (1)	Seller (2)	Items (3)	Invoice Number (4)	Transactions Contents[1] (5)	Amount (6)	VAT Amount (7)

[1]In Column 5, quantity, unit price, and other necessary matters should be recorded.

Usually, traders should keep separate purchase and sales books (or separate pages in a single book for a small trader). Usual bookkeeping requires an order day book (that is, a daily record of all invoices received and cash payments made).

For retailers, a simple form of a purchase book and a sales book would be adequate. Something on the lines of Example II would suit a mixed business with chargeable and exempt sales. It would also suit a business handling taxable goods only.

Example II: Purchase Book

			Purchase		
		Invoice	Taxable		
Date	Supplier	Number	Amount	VAT	Exempt
(1)	(2)	(3)	(4)	(5)	(6)

The invoices for taxable and exempt supplies should be numbered consecutively in separate series. If no invoice is received for exempt goods, a pro forma invoice should be prepared and numbered. All invoices should be filed safely for audit reference if needed.

A trader engaged solely in taxable activities would have no entries in Column 6 in Example II. Purchases of goods and services "not for resale" should be specially indicated, so that at the appropriate time any necessary adjustment of input tax may be made for exempt activities.

In the case of retailers, the essential requirement for VAT is to get the correct total for each day's sales (or receipts, if, as is usually permitted for retailers, a "receipts," rather than a sales basis, may be used for arriving at output VAT).

To ensure reliable figures of takings, a balanced cash book would also have to be maintained and entered up each day.

Auditing the accounts of a retailer who maintains a purchase and a sales book and a balanced cash book on the lines indicated is a simple operation and, with a little experience, the tax auditor can quickly conclude whether or not honest records are being kept. The inconvenience to the trader is minimal. Innocent errors, especially at the initial stage, are dealt with usually by payment of the tax, plus a small administrative penalty. Of course, deliberate, carefully conceived fraud would involve the usual VAT penalties, depending on the seriousness of the offense.

Trader Relations with VAT Officials

Usually, VAT officials at three grade levels visit traders.

- Officers, who are often young, newly recruited, personnel. They visit smaller establishments. They are not qualified accountants. However, they have been trained to audit for VAT and the more experienced will have a good knowledge of accounting practices.

- Senior officers, in charge of a number of offices will usually visit larger traders with more complex accounting systems. Some may have additional qualifications specializing in computer accounting techniques. Others may develop special knowledge about particular trades and industries (for example, brewing, building).

- Management officers, who manage local districts, check reports of their offices, and visit some of the traders.

Visits by officials can often trouble the trader whether or not he has anything to hide. Traders worry about whether VAT officers are experts in business affairs. "Few VAT officers have experience in actually running a business because they are career civil servants, although they are trained to be observers of business and draw reasonable conclusions. . . . There could be a communication problem because the VAT officer may not appreciate the way a business operates and its specialised terminology. Accordingly, VAT officers' questions should generally be answered in the clearest possible language on the assumption that the officer has little understanding of the business."[10]

Similarly, a trader may ask, "Why me?" when his premises are chosen for a visit from the VAT authorities. It is as well that a trader should know that an officer's suspicions may have been alerted by a customer invoice with an error that suggested mistakes in the selling business, or an invoice may have been selected at random from another audit to be cross-checked in this trader's business. Usually, of course, visits depend on the size and type of business and will be more frequent if officers have reason to believe something is wrong (persistent default, late returns, errors in returns, and so on).

To the question, "Should I have my tax advisor present during an inspection?" the answer sensibly is, "not usually"; however, if the authorities request a follow-up visit, then it probably pays to have a VAT specialist present because his presence ensures that the authorities "do not have complete freedom in placing their own interpreta-

---

[10]From a good series of responses to possible traders' questions in Somerville and Arnold (1985, p. 20).

tion on the law and on the way in which you do business. Once a VAT officer has made a decision, it is very difficult to get the ruling changed."[11]

The trader should understand that the VAT officer on a routine visit is carrying out basic checks to verify the VAT returns submitted and to review the business to check on possible mistakes in categorizing goods and services or any signs of VAT evasion or fraud. The trader should anticipate that the VAT official may carry out some or all of the following credibility checks:[12]

- Sampling batches of invoices to check that the correct rate of VAT has been charged.
- Checking that invoices have been correctly posted to the VAT records.
- Checking page totals.
- Checking calculations relating to any special schemes, for example, small traders, building traders, hotels, and secondhand goods.
- Spot checks on extra documents such as bank statements and sales correspondence.
- Testing purchases (especially for retailers) followed by checks to ensure that the sale was correctly recorded.
- Checking till rolls and observing cash sales to make sure transactions are correctly entered.
- "Comparing VAT returns with annual accounts, which may reveal that a cash difference has been added to sales in the profit and loss account to overcome a discrepancy between recorded cash expenditure and recorded cash income. [Officials] may infer from this that the outputs have been underdeclared on VAT returns and this may form the basis of a subsequent assessment."[13]
- Calculating the relationship between particular purchases and sales, for example, electricity consumed and sales, gasoline and taxi takings, gallons of water and average gallons per wash in a launderette.
- Checking markups on purchases against sales returns for VAT.

[11]Somerville and Arnold (1985, p. 28).
[12]See the interesting account in Buckett (1986, Chap. 3 and pp. 64–65).
[13]Buckett (1986, p. 64).

Such calculations can be contentious and traders can discuss with VAT officials the need to take account of different markups for different goods at different times of the year, stock losses, pilferage, inflation, and wastage.

It is also good advice for traders to make notes about the visit of VAT officials, so that the discussions and comments are recorded while they are fresh. It is also worth noting that a VAT officer's advice is often not given in writing and as such need not be binding; if the trader suspects an error (for example, if he knows his competitors are paying VAT on sales on which he has just been told he need not), he should take the matter up officially with the VAT office.

Continuous Review For Potential VAT Ramifications

Traders can, in the normal course of business, make decisions that, unknowingly, create VAT liabilities. The mistakes are made through genuine ignorance, but they can be expensive.[14] An example might be a multinational company that decides to fill suddenly created posts by seconding staff from its overseas affiliates; the VAT could be chargeable if the fees were paid to the affiliates, and an alternative way of contracting staff should have been used.

For example, "In many cases, it is possible, through careful planning, to ensure that management changes actually improve the VAT position of the corporate group. Where, for instance, a partly exempt member makes a taxable supply of management services to a company which can recover the input VAT, it may increase the proportion of its own input VAT that can be recovered, depending upon its agreed partial exemption method."[15]

The basic message is that the implications of business decisions for VAT liability should always be considered especially in the choice of new lines, asset sales, group treatment, overseas transactions, and intragroup transactions worldwide.

---

[14]Buckett (1986, pp. 11–16).
[15]"See VAT: Avoidance Methods on Management Charges," *International Tax Report* (1985, p. 10).

CHAPTER 17

Definitions

Dreich, *adj.*, dreary, long-lasting, persistent; tiresome, hard to bear; . . . *of sermons*, . . . long-winded; dry, uninteresting; . . . *of tasks*, . . . difficult, requiring close attention. . . .

—*The Concise Scots Dictionary*, Mairi Robinson, ed.
(Aberdeen University Press, 1985)

Academic discussions of VAT refer to "businesses" or "firms" paying VAT, but there is rarely any recognition of the problems of defining just who, exactly, is liable to pay VAT. In practice, all countries must begin by defining, under the law, who is liable to pay VAT. At bottom, the question in applying the law is, who can be prosecuted for non-payment of VAT? Practices differ but the problems are, broadly, common to all countries, and some comment is in order on what existing VAT codes have found to be the problems, with some speculation on "best" solutions. Some comment is also appropriate on the problems of defining place and time of supply, what is the value of a sale, and the definitions of "goods" and "services."

Who Should Pay VAT?

Taxable Persons

A clear way to think about liability to VAT is to recognize that though VAT is charged on the supply of goods and services, these are supplied by "taxable persons" who must register for VAT and be accountable to the authorities for the tax they have collected. Essentially, the taxpayer must be a legal entity that can be sued. Thus, the definition of "taxable person" is important.

Though it is a person who is liable for VAT, not all persons are liable; they are liable only if they carry on a business. If a private person sells something, say, furniture or clothing, generally he would not be liable to VAT. However, this apparently neat distinction leads to many borderline cases (how often do I have to sell furniture to turn it into a business?), and it is best to look first at the definition of a person and then at the definition of a business.

A person carrying on a business (which achieves a turnover, or employs a number of persons, or whatever criterion is used to place it above a minimum size—see Chapter 6) is liable to tax. If the person has two branches, each below the minimum size but together above, he must amalgamate his turnovers (supplies) and be liable to register (see below for further discussion). A person or company, acting as an agent and paying bills on behalf of another taxable person, is not usually treated as making a supply but as performing a service for which he will be charged separately. The VAT will be charged (if applied to services) on that agent's supply of his service.

Partnerships

Partnerships are a most difficult business relationship to tax. The partnership in Anglo-Saxon law is not a legal entity and cannot be sued; it is the individuals forming a partnership that can be (ultimately) taken to court. However, because a partnership is a flexible arrangement where persons can change partnerships and be members of many partnerships—or sometimes the same persons can be members of different (but identically composed) partnerships—much administrative time can be occupied chasing the registration, deregistration, and reregistration of changing partnerships. Moreover, the very nature of a partnership where profits, as well as liabilities, are borne individually means that when the composition of a partnership changes, the VAT liability has to be recalculated before and after the change.

In civil law countries (broadly derived from the French code), partnerships can be legal entities and as such can be registered for and be liable to VAT. Such a solution seems more straightforward and undoubtedly avoids the tangles into which the British VAT law gets itself over this issue. Even in the United Kingdom, it has been accepted for VAT that a partnership can be registered in the name of a firm. However, in most civil law countries, most partnerships are not legal entities; they are usually registered in the managing partner's name. Generally, all partnerships can be sued, but if there is a "sleeping partner" (who provides capital), he can only be sued up to the amount of capital he has provided.

If the same individuals carry on several different businesses, under separate partnership agreements, they should have to aggregate their supplies for VAT. If the partnerships were composed of different individuals, they could each be registered separately. This provision can allow a limited number of partners to combine in different groups, but never the same combination, to reduce their VAT liability. It also can involve the authorities in numerous reregistrations each time a partnership name changes. There is no simple solution to this problem and each country has its own devices.

Clubs

To reduce the administrative hassle of reregistration each time the "taxable person" of, say, a club changes (this could be annually if it were the elected treasurer), it might be acceptable to make the firm or club, as a legal entity, the taxable person, while retaining the usual requirement for most cases that an individual must be named the taxable person. Similarly, tax tribunals or courts must be able to look behind the firm as necessary to establish if the taxable persons are responsible for more than one firm or club.

Groups of Companies

It is usual to allow a group of companies to register as a group. This allows all intracompany supplies to be disregarded for VAT and a single return made for the entire group.

For this legislation to be operated, a "group of companies" has to be defined. For instance, in New Zealand, companies are in a group when they have two thirds common ownership or control. "Ownership" and "control" are further defined as proportions of the paid-up capital, the nominal value of allotted shares, the voting power held by persons, or the prescribed portions of profits to which persons would be entitled if profits were distributed as dividends.[1] Such groups can apply to the Commissioner to be treated as a group for VAT and one company must be nominated to be the representative member. The representative member has the responsibility for filing VAT returns and making tax payments on behalf of the group. All members of the

[1]See Price Waterhouse (1986, pp. 308–309).

group must adopt the same taxable period and use the same accounting basis, and all members are "jointly and severally" liable for any tax payable by the representative member.

The member designated as the person in the group is responsible for signing the VAT return. Experience has shown that sometimes staff members in remote subsidiaries are unaware that their figures are used in a VAT return and mistakes subsequently can embarrass the signing person.[2] It is important for groups to ensure that everyone is aware of his responsibilities in supplying information for VAT.

Other Persons

Provisions should be made to cover other possible taxpayers. These include personal representatives, liquidators and receivers, agents for absentees, and auctioneers. The liability of a new company for tax payable by former companies with substantially the same shareholders should also be covered. This last is needed to anticipate a possible evasion of VAT by a company going out of business owing VAT and reformulating itself anew for trading without the obligation to settle the old liabilities.

A taxable person is liable to VAT if he supplies goods or services in the course of carrying on a business. Therefore the next question usually is, what is a business for the purposes of VAT?

A "Business" or "Taxable Activity" for VAT

Some form of "business test" must be used. To avoid confusion with the "badges of trade" type tests in the income tax acts and to indicate that it is likely to be a wider concept, the term "taxable activity" might be used, as is the practice, again, in New Zealand. The sort of tests used include the following:[3]

- *Continuity*
  Supplies should be made regularly and fairly frequently as part of a continuing activity. Isolated or single transactions will not usually be liable to VAT.

- *Value*
  The supplies should be for a significant amount; trivial, even if repeated, transactions would not usually count.

---

[2]Buckett (1986, pp. 63–64).
[3]See, for instance, Bertram and Edwards (1984, p. 611).

- *Profit (in the Accounting Sense)*
  Not necessary; after all, large concerns can create substantial value added and pay large sums in wages, yet make no profit (many publicly owned firms do precisely this). Such firms should certainly pay VAT.

- *Active Control*
  Control should be in the hands of the supplier. He should be actively engaged in the "control or management of the assets concerned" (including operation through an agent).[4] The proprietor should be independent and, hence, should be excluded from coverage.

- *Intra Versus Intertrade*
  Supplies should be to members outside the organization and not just between members of the organization.

- *Appearance of Business*
  The activities should have the characteristics of a normal commercial undertaking with some acceptable method of record keeping in place.

Recognizing what is a business for the definition of a "taxable person engaged in business" does not end the matter. Taxable persons may decide to break up their large (and hence taxable) business into several smaller units each with a turnover below the VAT exemption limit, thus reducing tax liability. Such behavior is more likely the higher the exemption limit. Authorities are always torn between the temptation to reduce administrative costs by raising the exemption limit and the danger of increasing avoidance by making the breakup of business into nontaxable units more attractive.

There have to be supplementary criteria to the definition of business to help define what is a separate business. This is also important when defining the taxable person carrying on a business. It is quite possible for a single businessman to claim that his twenty shops are all separate businesses (or even partnerships with each individual manager as a partner with the central businessman). Examples of such rules follow:[5]

- *Premises*
  The person carrying on the business should own or rent the premises and equipment.

---

[4]Bertram and Edwards (1984, p. 611).
[5]See Wheatcroft and Avery Jones (Vol. 2, p. 5731, Sect. 5-786).

- *Records and Accounts*
  These should be maintained for the separate business.

- *Invoices (Both Purchase and Sale)*
  All invoices must be in the name of the person carrying on the business, and the arrangements for the supply must be directly between the taxable person and the customer.

- *Legal*
  Legal responsibility must be with the taxable person.

- *Bank Accounts*
  These should be in the taxable person's name.

- *Wages and Social Security Contributions*
  Such contributions should be paid by the taxable person.

- *Income Tax Benefits*
  These should be identified separately for the business.

If these criteria are met, the business might be considered separate for VAT purposes, but even so, in some countries, if it could be proved that the intent was to evade VAT, then tax might still be claimed. However, in most cases, objective and independently verifiable criteria have to be evaluated to establish either VAT liability or registration as a taxable person carrying on a separate business.

In general, the scope of the tests (depending on each country's decisions) should ensure that it encompasses not only companies but also self-employed individuals (including, ideally, members of professions), partnerships, cooperatives, trusts, charities, clubs, government departments (see below), state corporations, and local authorities.

There always will be marginal debatable cases. For instance, although a charity may be defined as a taxable person, exemptions can be made for certain welfare supplies by charities and public bodies. Such services would have to be supplied for nonprofit reasons (that is, no net consideration could be thought to be made) and would be associated with health care or spiritual care. Even this can cause danger; a place of spiritual retreat has to be distinguished from a health farm or from a fake church.[6]

Of course, this will still leave some debatable cases. If an individual is in the habit of selling secondhand goods, for example, in the United States if he held frequent "garage sales," that might be construed as a business liable to be registered for VAT, as, indeed, it can today for the state sales taxes.

---

[6]See "Exemption of Welfare Supplies by Charities and Public Bodies," *Accountancy* (1986, p. 35).

Generally, VAT administrations readily assume that a "business" is taxable, since a basic rule for the authorities is always to tax until you run into a final consumer or an exempt activity.

Traders Versus Descriptions of Business

Some VATs do not apply to all stages of production. It is possible to have a manufacturing-stage VAT (Indonesia) or a VAT through the wholesale stage but stopping short of the retail stage (see Chapter 1). On the purely technical side, it is easier to achieve simplicity with a broad-based tax using no distinctions between stages of production.

Taxpayers under VAT should be known as "traders" or "businesses" and not as "wholesalers" or "retailers." It is almost impossible to produce a watertight definition of a manufacturer or wholesaler; some manufacturers are also wholesalers and many wholesalers are retailers. This sort of distinction almost always leads to complex rules about minimum markups or maximum retail percentages that, in practice, create more distortions than they solve (see Chapter 1, section on "To the Retail Sale?"). Taxing all traders eliminates the need for price adjustments when the taxpayer skips the last taxable stage in the chain of production and distribution and sells the goods at a stage that is outside the tax coverage. Another advantage is that complex rules to deal with transactions that are not at arm's length are no longer required, since there is no incentive to split up companies to minimize the portion of value added subject to tax.

Place of Supply

To be liable to VAT, the supply of goods or services must be made within the country. That may seem simple, but first "country" has to be defined to include the continental shelf and territorial sea (important in these days of supplying oil rigs, or covering a complex archipelago), and to exclude free ports or free zones (see below).

Goods are considered supplied where they are physically located when they are allocated to a customer. If the goods are outside the country when allocated, the supply is outside the scope of VAT. Of course, if the same goods are subsequently imported, they become liable to VAT at importation. If goods are installed or assembled, then the place where that is done is the place of supply.

The usual place of supply for services is where the service is "rendered," or, as a secondary alternative, the usual place of residence of an individual supplying the service or the country where the supplying country is legally incorporated.

This concept of service "rendered" is not the same as that used in the U.K. and New Zealand VATs, where services are treated as made in the place where the supplier "belongs." The concept of "belonging" is peculiar to VAT legislation, but is now more usually replaced by the idea of the place where the service is rendered or performed. The two are not necessarily the same. If advice is given on advertising, say, by a person visiting a country, then the value of that advice can be deemed to be taxable in the country where the individual has his fixed office or establishment. Alternatively, the VAT liability can arise in the country where the service is rendered.

Generally, it seems more desirable to identify where the service is rendered, otherwise substantial amounts of value added supplied abroad could be tax free; in these days of computer data banks and swift international information, the movement of services might prove too difficult to pin down, except in respect of the person or agency who actually gains advantage from it (see section on "Imports and Exports," below, for further discussion).

Finally, there are three relatively minor points. First, the supply of services connected with land (for example, services of real estate agents and architects and for site supervision) should be deemed to be rendered at the place where the land is situated. Second, services relating to the international transfer of passengers should be deemed to be supplied outside the national territory. Third, services that can be deemed to be supplied where they are physically performed; these include cultural, artistic, sporting, and educational services, as well as activities connected with the transfer of goods (for example, loading, handling, and temporary storage), the valuation of goods, and cottage industries.

This leaves only self-supply as a relatively minor issue. If goods produced by a business are used internally, instead of being purchased from outside in the usual way, there is no purchase invoice and there can be a loss of tax credit to the business. Sometimes the authorities allow companies to claim self-supply. However, to avoid many trivial cases, such treatment is usually restricted to only a few significant items. For example, if an automobile manufacturer or a retailer supplied a vehicle, this could be sufficiently frequent and expensive to merit special treatment. An unusual example is that under U.K. legislation, the self-supply of stationery in an exempt or partially exempt business is allowed if the value exceeds the registration limit.

Time of Supply

The important point about time of supply is that the VAT is liable at the rate applicable at a particular time. If the rate changes (and VAT rates frequently have, usually upward—see Chapter 2), then determining the time the supply took place can make a substantial difference in tax liability and is especially important on major purchases (for example, new housing or plant and equipment). Countries employ different rules, some of which tend to confuse the issue of invoices, the requirements for invoices, the dates when goods were actually moved to a purchaser, and the dates when they were available to a purchaser. Special time of supply provisions usually cover transactions such as placing bets, lotteries, coin-operated machines, deferred-payment agreements, employee fringe benefits, and door-to-door sales.

In general, the clearest way to express the options on this issue is as follows. The time of supply is the *earlier* of:

- When the invoice is issued. This is the best, and clearest, dated documentary evidence.
- When the goods are made available to the customer or the services rendered.
- When payment is made.

These rules can cover most contingencies. However, for products with continuous supply (for example, electricity), the good is available and used by the purchaser but VAT can only be levied when the invoice is issued. In other cases, for example, if goods are supplied on a sale or return basis (where the customer has the option to return a good and not pay the full amount if he is dissatisfied or has no further use for the item), the time of supply is when the customer receives the goods; if there is an increase in the VAT rate after he gets an invoice, the appropriate rate to be applied would be that in operation when the customer physically received the goods. These seem to be sensible, straightforward, and generally applicable rules that, once more, can be open to interpretative ruling by the authorities.

Value of Goods and Services Supplied

All businesses under the VAT must make a return of their turnover. The concept of gross takings is crucial to any business, no matter how large or small. However, as simple as this may be to state in theory or in textbooks, in practice the flexibility of business creates numerous problems for actual VAT administration.

Businessmen will often come to formal or informal agreements with their customers on the means and promptness of payment. Relatively few traders get paid immediately in cash. Credit sales in developed countries are the most common form of sale with payment delayed for a month or two. Sales can be settled by check but, depending on the efficiency of the banking system, checks can take some time to clear (up to two months in one large and complex developing country) and span different VAT periods. Even more difficult are the numerous ways in which business can accommodate customers by making provisional sales, by partial down payments, and by sale or return agreements. A point to remember is that the crucial evidence of supplying a taxable good under VAT is the *invoice*. It is the invoice showing the tax content of the goods supplied that is the essential document of control. However, the following points need to be clarified and are exemplified in the examples shown in Table 17-1.

Discounts

There are three forms of discount: unconditional, prompt payment, and contingent. The most obvious example of an unconditional discount would be a shop having a sale; if the item is purchased, the discount is claimed and settlement is made at the time of purchase. When the customer pays the discounted amount, the VAT is levied on the discount price and shown on the invoice for that discounted amount.

The most common form of trade discount is conditional on prompt payment. Most traders will try to encourage payment within, say, 28 days, by offering some discount. Indeed, in some promotional schemes, even a retail sale discount can be supplemented by allowing credit to run for three months. The sale invoice issued at the time of purchase will show the VAT liability on the discounted price. If the customer does not take up the offer, the tax value is on the undiscounted amount. Modern billing procedures provide two amounts— the full price and the VAT, and the discounted price and the discounted VAT.

Finally, there are discounts that are contingent on the customer doing something else. For instance, a discount can be allowed with a provision that the customer will later earn the discount by buying a certain quantity of further goods. In this case, the VAT supply invoice will show the full amount to be paid without the discount; should the purchaser later act in a way that means he can obtain this discount, the amount of tax liability can be adjusted by issuing a credit note.

Credit

Credit, or a contingent discount, can permit a purchaser to reclaim all the tax on the supply as an input tax. The scheme can operate in two ways. Both seller and purchaser can agree that the credit need not affect the original VAT (usually because the credit is going to be used in the near future and is not permitted to be used for a good with a different rate; that is, the credit will be used for a similar good to that originally purchased). Alternatively, the credit can be held for some time and allowed to be used for the purchase of some other good liable to a completely different VAT rate. In the latter case, both purchaser and seller should adjust the original VAT charge and a credit note should be issued to the purchaser with, of course, the seller keeping a copy. The credit note shows the details of registration numbers and addresses, but also must show the total amount credited excluding the VAT and the rate and amount of VAT credited. When the purchaser receives a credit note which includes VAT, then he must reduce his input tax by the amount shown in the tax period when he receives the credit note.

Credit notes (like invoices) are valuable documents, not only in respect of their commercial value but also because they affect the input tax liabilities and output tax liabilities of traders. Therefore, the administrators of VAT have an interest in defining clearly conditions under which credit notes can be issued and the adjustments that must be made to the VAT returns in respect of credit notes.

If goods are returned (because they are damaged or in some other way unsatisfactory) and the original supplier replaces them, then the original VAT charge can be allowed to stand or it can be canceled and an entirely new transaction established. If the replacement goods are identical and at an identical price and are supplied free of charge, then no further VAT responsibility is involved. If the replacement goods are supplied at a lower price than the original goods, then a credit note can be issued; if the replacement goods are supplied at a price higher than the original goods, then a supplemental VAT liability can be established for the difference (see Table 17-1, examples 13–16).

Trading on Credit

Credit cards are commonly used for retail purchases in cash-and-carry outlets. Such sales are considered to be cash sales and must be

Table 17-1. New Zealand: 10 Percent VAT—Examples of Supply, Value,[1] and Consideration[2]

Type of Supply	Other Names	Example	Value,[1] Tax, and Consideration[2]	Time of Supply: Invoice or Payments Basis	Frequency
1. Supply for consideration in money only (or expressed as money)	Cash sale, "arm's length" transaction, counter sale, trade-in	Customer purchases a radio from a shop for $NZ 220	Amount paid less tax = $NZ 200; tax = $NZ 20; total paid = $NZ 220	Earlier of: invoice or date of payment	Vast majority of supplies
2. No consideration (other than to an associated person)	Gift, free samples, give-aways	Free sample to prospective customer	Nil	...	Frequent
3. Periodic payments and hire arrangements (*not* including hire-purchases; see No. 4, below)	Lease, rental, hire of tools	A businessman rents a computer for 12 months; payments of $NZ 550 are due monthly	Consideration less tax = $NZ 500 monthly; tax = $NZ 50 per payment; total paid = $NZ 550 per monthly payment	Earlier of: date payment due or payment received	Very common
4. Goods or services under a hire-purchase agreement	Hire purchase, "tick," "never, never," extended payment, installment plan	Customer purchases refrigerator on hire purchase over three years; cash price = $NZ 1,100 (including VAT); interest = $NZ 600; total = $NZ 1,700	Cash price less tax = $NZ 1,000; tax = $NZ 100; total = $NZ 1,100	Time when hire-purchase agreement signed	Common
5. Layby sales	Reserved goods	Store sells cricket bat in May for $NZ 55 to be picked up in September	Consideration less tax = $NZ 50; tax = $NZ 5; total amount = $NZ 55	When ownership passes, i.e., when full payment is made (September)	Fairly common

6. Canceled layby sales	Reserved goods canceled	Customer buys cricket bat on layby for $NZ 55; gives up game; retailer retains deposit of $NZ 11	Amount retained less tax = $NZ 10; tax = $NZ 1; total amount retained = $NZ 11	Date of cancellation	Occasional
7. Supply to an associate who may claim an input tax credit (i.e., a registered person)	Gifts to associates, any sales to associates	Registered person sells spouse goods for use in spouse's business for $NZ 22 (normally sells for $NZ 100)	Amount paid less tax = $NZ 20; tax = $NZ 2; total = $NZ 22	Earlier of: invoice or date of payment	Occasional
8. Supply to unregistered associate or to a registered associate for private use, for no consideration or for less than open market value of that supply	Gifts to associates, sales to associates	Registered person sells goods to uncle for private use for $NZ 300 (open market value $NZ 434.50 including tax)	Amount paid less tax = $NZ 395.00; tax = $NZ 39.50; open market value = $NZ 434.50	Date when supply physically occurs unless invoice issued or payment made promptly	Occasional
9. Consideration not known at time goods are removed	—	Farmer contracts to sell his produce to a cannery in return for an initial payment of $NZ 770,000, and:	Consideration less tax = $NZ 700,000; tax = $NZ 70,000; total = $NZ 770,000	Earlier of: invoice or payment due or payment made	Common
		A "wash-up" payment at the end of the season dependent on export prices received; it turns out that his payment is $NZ 110,000	Consideration less tax = $NZ 100,000; tax = $NZ 10,000; total = $NZ 110,000		
10. Tokens with no face value	Redeemable vouchers	Two milk tokens sold by a dairy for $NZ 1.10	Cost less tax = $NZ 1; tax = $NZ 0.10; total = $NZ 1.10	Earlier of: invoice or date of payment	Common
		Those two tokens are later used to get two bottles of milk from the milkman	Nil	…	

Table 17-1 (*continued*). New Zealand: 10 Percent VAT—Examples of Supply, Value,[1] and Consideration[2]

Type of Supply	Other Names	Example	Value,[1] Tax, and Consideration[2]	Time of Supply: Invoice or Payments Basis	Frequency
11. Tokens with face value	Vouchers, record tokens, etc.	Department store sells gift voucher for $NZ 11	Nil	Earlier of: invoice or date of payment (by way of voucher for goods) in return for goods for which voucher swapped	Fairly common
		Voucher later swapped for $NZ 1.10 worth of goods from store	Consideration less tax = $NZ 10; tax = $NZ 1; total = $NZ 11		
12. Purchase of secondhand goods	—	Registered person buys tools for business in garage sale for $NZ 110	Amount paid less tax = $NZ 100; tax = $NZ 10; total = $NZ 110	Earlier of: invoice or date of payment	Occasional
13. Debit notes issued	Undercharging penalties for late payment	A business issues a debit note for $NZ 60.50 in relation to a previous supply	Total debit less tax = $NZ 55; tax = $NZ 5.50; total = $NZ 60.50	Date when it is realized that charge for original supply is too low or date payment received	Common
14. Debit notes received	—	A business receives a debit note for $NZ 60.50 in relation to a supply previously received	Total debit less tax = $NZ 55; tax = $NZ 5.50; total = $NZ 60.50	Date on which debit note is issued or payment made	Common
15. Credit notes issued	Overcharging discounted	A business issues a credit note for $NZ 77 in relation to a previously invoiced supply	Total credit less tax = $NZ 70; tax = $NZ 7; total credit = $NZ 77	Date when it is realized that charge for original supply was too high or date payment made	Common

Item	Examples	Scenario	Consideration/tax	Time of supply	Frequency
16. Credit notes received	—	A business received a credit note for $NZ 77 in relation to a previously invoiced supply	Total credit less tax = $NZ 70; tax = $NZ 7; total credit = $NZ 77	Date on which credit note is issued or date payment received	Common
17. Late tax invoices	—	Goods received with invoice and paid for $NZ 550; no tax invoice received	$NZ 500; tax = $NZ 50; total = $NZ 550	Earlier of: invoice or date of payment	Common
		Tax invoice for above goods not received until six months later	$NZ 500; tax = $NZ 50; total = $NZ 550	Earlier of: invoice or date of payment, but not before tax invoice received	Occasional
18. Commercial accommodation up to 4 weeks	Hotel stays, motel stays, short stays in boarding houses	Person stays in a hotel for two days at cost of $NZ 165	Amount paid less tax = $NZ 150; tax = $NZ 15; full charge = $NZ 165	Earlier of: invoice or date of payment	Common
19a. Commercial accommodation over 4 weeks	Long-term stays in hotels, motels	Person on transfer stays in motel for 10 weeks	Consideration less tax; tax fraction of consideration in money; 60 percent of accommodation charge for the fifth to tenth weeks	Earlier of: invoice or date of payment	Frequent
19b. Commercial accommodation over 14 weeks in a residential establishment	Rest homes, hospitals	Elderly person residing in a rest home	Consideration less tax; tax fraction of consideration in money; 60 percent of accommodation charge from first day	Earlier of: invoice or date of payment	Frequent
20. Coin operated machines	Slot machines, vending machines, parking meters, video games	The owner of a video parlor removes the day's takings of $NZ 60.50 from a machine	Takings less tax = $NZ 55; tax = $NZ 5.50; takings from machine = $NZ 60.50	Date on which machine is emptied	Common

Table 17-1 (continued). New Zealand: 10 Percent VAT—Examples of Supply, Value,[1] and Consideration[2]

Type of Supply	Other Names	Example	Value,[1] Tax, and Consideration[2]	Time of Supply: Invoice or Payments Basis	Frequency
21. Door-to-door sales	—	Salesperson visits a home and sells $NZ 55 worth of cosmetics on January 16, 1987 (purchaser does not subsequently cancel the sale)	Consideration less tax = $NZ 50; tax = $NZ 5; total = $NZ 55	On eighth day after purchase date (January 24, 1987)	Common
22. Progress payments	—	A builder enters into an agreement to build a house for $NZ 231,000 (including tax); the agreement provides for payments to be made as follows:	Consideration less tax =	Earliest of: date progress payment is due, or date progress payment is received, or date invoice relating to progress payment is issued, or date of payment	Occasional
		10 percent on signing = $NZ 23,100	$NZ 21,000; tax = $NZ 2,100; total = $NZ 23,100		
		25 percent when foundation laid = $NZ 57,750	$NZ 52,500; tax = $NZ 5,250; total = $NZ 57,750		
		35 percent when roof on = $NZ 80,850	$NZ 73,500; tax = $NZ 7,350; total = $NZ 80,850		

	Examples	Transaction	Calculation	Time of supply	Frequency
23. Contract variations	—	Builder contracts to erect building for $NZ 770,000	Consideration less tax = $NZ 700,000; tax = $NZ 70,000; contract price = $NZ 770,000	Earlier of: invoice or date of payment	Common
		25 percent when internal work completed = $NZ 57,750	$NZ 52,500; tax = $NZ 5,250; total = $NZ 57,750		
		5 percent on completion = $NZ 11,550	$NZ 10,500; tax = $NZ 1,050; total = $NZ 11,500		
		Builder-owner requires extra room to be added at a cost of $NZ 55,000	Consideration for variation less tax = $NZ 50,000; tax = $NZ 5,000; total = $NZ 55,000	Date when payment for variation made	
24. Grants and subsidies	Government grants and subsidies, research grants	Government, through the Ministry of Agriculture, pays a grant of $NZ 22,000 to a laboratory for fishing research	Consideration less tax = $NZ 20,000; tax = $NZ 2,000; total payment = $NZ 22,000	Earlier of: invoice or date of payment	Fairly common
25. Raffles and other prize competitions	Lotteries, bingo, housie, coin poker	Sports club runs a raffle; total cash prizes = $NZ 2,200; sales of tickets bring in $NZ 6,600	Money received less cash prizes less tax on difference = $NZ 4,000; tax = $NZ 400; money received less cash prizes = $NZ 4,400	Date on which result is first determined (e.g., when drawing commences)	Common

Table 17-1 (concluded). New Zealand: 10 Percent VAT—Examples of Supply, Value,[1] and Consideration[2]

Type of Supply	Other Names	Example	Value,[1] Tax, and Consideration[2]	Time of Supply: Invoice or Payments Basis	Frequency
26. Rate payments to local authorities	Local property levy for services	Local authority assesses rates of $NZ 880 for a property	Consideration less tax = $NZ 800; tax = $NZ 80; total = $NZ 880	Earlier of: invoice or date of payment	Common
27. Racing bets	—	Total of $NZ 110,000 is placed as bets on a horse race; of this amount, 20 percent is required to be deducted before dividends are paid	Total deduction less tax = $NZ 20,000; tax = $NZ 2,000; total deductions made = $NZ 22,000	Date on which deductions are made	Common
28. Insurance indemnities paid	Cash claim payments made	An insurance company pays $NZ 1,650 cash on a claim made by a business	Amount paid less tax = $NZ 1,500; tax = $NZ 150; total = $NZ 1,650	Date of payment	Rare—only insurance companies affected

Sources: New Zealand, Inland Revenue, *GST Guide* (Wellington, June 1986), pp. 34–39, and *Goods and Services Tax: Supplement to the GST Guide* (Wellington), pp. 10–11.

[1]Value is the tax-exclusive amount paid (or consideration less tax).
[2]Consideration is the tax-inclusive amount paid (or value plus tax).

treated for VAT in the same way as would a cash sale. The value for VAT liability should be based on the full retail price and not on the assessment net of credit company charges.

Deposits

A cash deposit can be made for two purposes: the deposit can be a down payment to secure the eventual supply of a good or the deposit can act as a security to ensure the particular good is kept in stock for that particular customer until he can pay the rest of the price. In the first case, where the deposit is an initial payment, VAT should be charged within the taxable period in the normal way; the further VAT liability, when the eventual supply is made, is liable in that appropriate tax period.

The deposit, which is made as a security, can be excluded from gross takings and treated simply as a temporary expansion of business liquidity until the full payment is made and the good is actually supplied to the purchaser when the VAT will be liable.

Sale or Return

Many businesses allow goods to be removed from the premises "on approval." The goods are not actually sold and can be returned within some agreed time. Sometimes, a deposit of the full value is required from the recipient, for example, on sales of automobiles. For VAT, it is usual that this transaction is not considered as a supply until the time when the purchaser agrees to purchase or to pay. In the interim, the seller must continue to view these goods as part of his stock. Once the goods are agreed to be bought by the customer, then the sale is put through with a VAT invoice in the normal way. Similarly, of course, if the sale is not retail, the purchaser cannot claim the VAT shown on his purchase document as an offset to his VAT liability until he has confirmed the purchase and has been issued the appropriate invoice by the seller.

Finance Houses

Many businesses use finance houses to provide the liquidity for their sales. The credit is arranged for a purchaser through the finance house, which formally adopts the ownership of the goods sold. In this case, the sale is a cash sale to the finance house and should be shown as such with the tax charged on the cash sale value.

Promotion Schemes

Many businesses, both retail and other, indulge in promotional schemes to induce customers to trade with them. These are common in both developed and developing countries and, while understandable from a commercial point of view, they are an annoyance to the tax administrator. The basic point is clear; the VAT is liable on the price actually paid by the customer. However, some examples can show the potential hazards.

A frequent retail scheme is one in which a coupon is attached or claimed when an article is sold that can be redeemed when a further charge is made for another article. The public can collect the coupons attached to the existing articles or from magazines and newspapers or, indeed, sometimes obtain them through the post. The VAT treatment in this case is straightforward. The tax at the appropriate amount is charged on the second good at the normal retail price for which that second good usually sells, regardless of the coupons given in lieu of cash payment. If the seller is financing the scheme himself (say, through newspaper advertisements), this is the end of the transaction as far as VAT is concerned. If, on the other hand, the scheme is financed by a finance house or by the original manufacturer, then it is expected that the seller recoups the value of the coupon from that original supplier. The actual goods in the transaction have been invoiced through the usual trade channels at the full invoiced price.

There are other schemes (and no doubt many more will be invented), where coupons are supplied with goods, but the coupons can be redeemed for other goods without any further charge (see Table 17-1, examples 10 and 11). As far as VAT is concerned, the tax liability is on the goods with the coupons sold in the normal way, and the assumed result of this is that the VAT is charged (in advance on the redemption of goods at the same rate as that applied to the original goods sold). Should the redemption of goods actually be liable for rates quite different from those applicable to the original goods, obvious problems arise. For instance, this could happen even in a simple standard rate VAT system if a purchaser were allowed to "redeem" a package holiday abroad on some substantial purchase, such as an automobile. While the car purchaser might be paying VAT at the standard rate, the holiday abroad, if travel agents' services were not taxable, would be tax free.

Perhaps this is one of those cases where the possible abuse of the system is so slight that it does not deserve any special treatment as far as the tax authorities are concerned. However, should the authorities wish to tackle this issue, methods have been tried. For instance, the U.K. legislation requires the seller, if the original goods and redemption goods are taxable at different rates, to make adjustments so that the tax on redemption goods is levied at the rate appropriate to those goods at the time when the coupons were sold. And the value of the redemption goods is either the price paid on the original goods and coupons together or the actual cost of the redemption goods to the seller, whichever is higher. Alternatively, the whole transaction can be treated as one sale and the VAT calculated on apportioned values of the goods concerned.

In some countries, trading stamps involving elaborate redemption centers and cumulative books of trading stamps are used. These schemes can involve extremely large sums of money and substantial implied costs to the purchaser and, further, a complex differential liability to different rates of VAT. There are various ways of tackling this issue, but all keep to the basic principle that the usual sale on which the purchaser can claim the trading stamp is taxed under VAT in the normal way. The redemption centers themselves must pay VAT on the value of the implied sales from the centers. This can involve taking their purchase prices of items and using markups to achieve the implied selling price of the goods claimed by coupon redemption.

It should be noted that when a retailer, for instance, purchases trading stamps from a stamp promoter, there is no tax liability. However, any charge made by the company promoting the stamps to the retailer for his services is taxable. The charge will be shown on the promoter's sales invoice, and this can be recouped by including it in the retailer's input VAT deductions.

Small Retailers' Alternative Methods for Calculating Sales

The usual VAT liability is determined by the issuance of a tax invoice. However, in most developed countries, for small retailers and indeed for most retailers, invoices for sales are not issued or are only issued as a till slip. Moreover, the numerous discounts and promotional schemes can make the assessment of gross takings difficult. Some countries have offered small retailers two options. In the first, they can use a cash basis for calculating their sales. Under this, all payments are recorded as they are received. Credit sales are not recorded until payment is received. The advantage of this, as used in

New Zealand, for instance, is that no VAT is payable on bad debts. An alternative is to use the more normal VAT liability on the amount that is charged (but not necessarily received at the time of supply).

The second option is practiced throughout Latin America, where retail traders must complete a "simplified invoice"; this invoice includes the seller's name and registration number and specifies, in summary terms, the goods sold. Frequently, such invoices are provided by the government in books and are marked with special watermarks or stamps to prevent forgery. Sometimes the consecutive numbers on the invoices are used for public lotteries to encourage purchasers to ask for and keep the retail invoice. Indeed, it is these invoices that can be used as an administrative check on retailers; inspectors check on the issuance of invoices and, if they find they are not given, and if this happens three times in the same establishment, then the trader's shop is closed automatically, at once, for two or three weeks. The police check on restaurant invoices in Italy as described in Chapter 14 is similar. Technically, patrons themselves could be guilty of a VAT transgression, as the law required them to request a bill showing the VAT paid.

The choice of an appropriate system depends largely on the retailers' methods of trading and accounting.

Supply of Goods

It is generally agreed that neutrality and resource allocation are least jeopardized by a broad-based sales tax taxing most goods with few exemptions (see Chapters 1–5). It is better to start by including everything, and then define those items not taxed, than to try to itemize each commodity to be taxed—that way lies madness (though some countries have pursued this latter option).

In practice, the actual definition of "supply" needs some elaboration. Buying and selling goods clearly involve a transfer for a consideration. However, the development of leasing has meant that almost any good can be hired, so the supply of goods must include the letting of goods on hire, the loan of goods, and lease-sale contracts (where the final transfer of ownership is optional).

Most legislation holds that goods are "supplied" when:

- Exclusive ownership is passed to another person.
- The transfer takes place over time under an agreement such as a lease or hire purchase.
- Goods are produced from someone else's materials.

- A major interest in land is provided, that is, the use of land for a long period of time.
- Goods are taken from a company for private use.
- A business asset is transferred.

Such transfers should be a taxable supply undertaken in the course of a business and should be subject to VAT on the invoice price in the same manner as the usual supply of trading stock. If a business is sold as a going concern, VAT liability arises on the payment for the capital (and trading) assets of the business. A deduction of the VAT paid against VAT liability will then be allowed to the new owner.

There are two more activities usually mentioned. Many countries define the provision of electricity, heat, refrigeration, ventilation, power, or gas as a supply of goods. This is simply a linguistic problem. If these items are not included as goods, they will certainly be included under services, so the only question is where they should be mentioned. Some prefer to think of electricity and gas as services, but more usually they are defined as goods.

The second point, which needs to be mentioned, is that goods given free to employees (within some defined maximum amount) solely in the course of employment are not usually taxable.

Supply of Services

Services are intrinsically less easy to identify than goods. They are best defined as a residual rather than through individual itemization. In this way, any transfer or provision for a consideration that is not the supply of a good is automatically the supply of a service. This is a particularly useful method in countries (such as those in the Middle East or the Far East) that have, typically, expanded their taxes on goods and services by adding individual items to an ever lengthening list. This residual solution breaks that approach (which lends itself to exemption and special pleading).

So services include:

- Any supply for a consideration that is not a good.
- Lending goods.
- Hiring goods.
- Agreeing not to do something for a consideration.
- Surrendering a right for a consideration.

Basically, it is simpler to remember that any item that is not a good is a supply of services, so that nothing escapes. For instance, the sale of a racehorse is a supply of a taxable good, but the sale of a share in a syndicated racehorse would be the supply of a service. If all the shares were sold then, in essence, the horse is sold and that becomes a supply of goods. Either way, VAT is payable.[7]

Some countries have preferred to introduce a VAT on goods and leave the extension of the tax to services until later (for example, Brazil, Ecuador, and Indonesia). There are at least four powerful reasons to ensure that the VAT includes services from the start. First, the contribution of the sector to gross national product is sizable and grows as the economy grows. Consequently, it may have a fairly large revenue potential. Second, failure to tax services distorts consumer choices, encouraging spending on services at the expense of goods and saving. Third, untaxed services mean traders are unable to claim VAT on their service inputs. This causes cascading, distorts choice, and encourages businesses to develop in-house services, creating further distortions. Fourth, as most of the services that are likely to become taxable are positively correlated with the expenditure of high-income households, subjecting them to taxation may improve equity.

The question remains, however, whether it is better to include services under a VAT or to use selective taxation (special excises) instead. Both approaches have been used. It has been argued that inclusion of services under the VAT is greatly preferable to the use of a separate tax or taxes on services to avoid multiple taxation, which arises from the nondeductibility of service taxes on purchases by business firms and, at the same time, the application of VAT to purchases by service firms. Although true, the importance of the argument needs to be qualified. If the service is one that by its own nature is usually rendered to a final consumer, application of a selective tax at the time the service is rendered gives rise to multiple taxation only to the extent that its price includes elements of VAT paid by the service firm on its purchases. If, on the other hand, the service is normally rendered to a business, the argument carries more weight. The solution is not easy, however, because many of the services rendered to businesses are in the hands of hard-to-reach taxpayers—commercial transport may be a good example—and to include them in the VAT net would greatly complicate the task of administration. Perhaps, one option would be to allow them to register if they wished to do so.

There seems to be a case, therefore, to approach the question of the taxation of services on the basis of who the main users are. If the main

[7]The actual time when VAT becomes payable can allow for some discretion on the part of both trader and customer. See Bragg and Williams (1984, pp. 218–25).

users are final consumers, it makes little difference whether the government taxes services under the VAT or by selective taxes. The decision will probably have to be taken on the basis of the adequacy of the rate structure of the VAT vis-à-vis each particular service. If the main users are business firms, it might be best not to subject the service to any tax.[8] The value added by the service firm will eventually be taxable when it becomes part of the price of the goods produced by the user of the service.

An excellent presentation of examples of supply, value, and consideration in New Zealand is shown as Table 17-1.

Imports and Exports

The valuation treatment of the sale or purchase of goods across international boundaries is fairly straightforward and is dealt with below. This is followed by a rather longer discussion on the treatment of internationally provided services. Finally, a few special cases are mentioned, such as purchases by tourists, goods imported by a final consumer, and free zones.

The Valuation of Imports and Exports

The VAT is levied on imported goods at a value including:

- The customs value of the goods.
- Customs duty and any other tax payable at import.
- The cost of transport and insurance to the country.
- Any fees or levies on imports.
- Any excise duty levied.

The customs value is usually based on a price that should reflect an arm's length transaction. Where the relation between the seller and the importer creates doubt about the value placed on the goods, the customs use a valuation code to establish a value that reflects an arm's length value.

Some countries levy export taxes and, reflecting the treatment of

---

[8]The exemption may not be advisable, however, for services that contain substantial elements of taxed inputs. It would be unfair to the services vendor and would encourage its substitution by the user. For instance, advertising pays VAT on its purchases of materials. If these were sufficiently substantial, it might pay clients to produce their own advertising in-house and claim the credit for the VAT paid on the advertising inputs.

imports, the value for zero rating should include the value of the goods f.o.b. and any export taxes or fees.

Treatment of Goods

The country of origin, under all existing VATs, treats exports as zero-rated supplies so that the goods are exported free of VAT. The destination country charges the goods at the VAT rate appropriate to similar domestic goods, so that equal treatment with internal trade is assured.

This simple statement is open to some caveats. Not all VAT is necessarily refunded on the zero-rated export; if some of the inputs are produced by exempt suppliers (for example, financial institutions, agriculture), then the VAT charge on the inputs of those exempt suppliers is not recovered by the VAT refund on export.

Again, when the good is imported, the VAT levied is not necessarily levied at a point of *sale*. The charge is not a VAT payment in the usual way, but is a charge on the physical importation of the goods. Many developed countries use a "postponed accounting system," whereby importers do not pay the charge on the physical importation, but only when they make their first VAT return following the importation. This, of course, has important implications for company liquidity. When the United Kingdom abolished the postponed accounting system in October 1984, firms that had enjoyed up to 11 weeks tax-free inventories suddenly found themselves liable for a payment that netted the authorities some £1.2 billion in a once and for all windfall. Of course, this revenue gain can only be enjoyed by countries that have initially decided not to levy VAT when the goods physically enter the country.

In developing countries, sometimes over 50 percent of the total VAT revenue is derived from imports. Control is better at the ports, customs officials levy the VAT at the same time as other formalities are completed, and goods are not physically released until the tax is paid. There is little that concentrates the trader's mind on settling his obligations promptly as much as the knowledge that his goods are in bond (and liable to penal storage charges if left there unduly long).

It is possible to abolish the frontier VAT on transactions within a customs union. After all, if a customs union succeeds in abolishing customs frontiers, it seems rather redundant to keep the customs officials purely for the sake of VAT. It would be much better to allow goods to be imported and for the accounts of the importer and the exporter to be settled through a central clearing agency. This is theoretically feasible and is indeed EC policy to be introduced by 1992 (see Chapter 8).

Treatment of Internationally Provided Services

The intention is to treat internationally provided services in such a way so that the end result is the same as that achieved for the taxation of internationally traded goods. However, there are difficulties.[9]

If it is difficult to define the place of supply of a service domestically (see the earlier discussion), it is even more difficult internationally. Basically, there are two options; first, where the supply is received and, second, where the supply is performed.

Under the first category, the treatment is parallel to that of the supply of goods. It is a commonsense view that it is the trader enjoying the use of the service that pays the VAT at the rate appropriate to his own country. The supplier of the service (the exporter) is allowed to claim as an offset to his zero tax liability on his export service earning any VAT paid on his inputs (providing his service would have been taxable if supplied domestically). If the service performed is exempt in the exporting country, no VAT can be recovered on inputs. However, there is an important exception to this in the EC when financial and insurance services are provided to those outside the EC; to prevent these important EC services being at an international disadvantage, they are allowed to claim VAT paid on inputs needed to provide the overseas service. As might be imagined, this can be a tricky calculation for a large financial center.

The other option is to tax services where they are performed. This is different from the previous category because a banker, an architect, or a consultant might well perform the services sitting in his home country, but it is the customer that enjoys them. That is, the supply of the service and the enjoyment of it can be separated. Where this is not necessarily possible, for example, with actors, sports players, lectures, and transport, then the VAT is levied wherever the service is performed (and their agents are usually liable for the VAT payment, as is the case in New Zealand). The reasoning is that such a service is likely to be in direct competition with locally provided services and should be taxed the same way.

All services are expected to fall into one or the other category, but an underlying rule that ought to be covered by legislation is that any

[9]For an interesting discussion, see Campbell (1986, pp. 4–10).

service that is not covered by these two categories is still taxable in the suppliers' country.

Internationally, it is difficult to identify the trader responsible for payment of the VAT. In both the import and export of goods and services, it is important to define the taxable person and this often revolves around the definition of permanent residence.[10] Some countries (for example, the Federal Republic of Germany) deem a foreign taxable person to be established if traders have a residence, a registered office, a place of effective management, a branch registered with the trade registry, or an affiliated company forming part of a group; on the other hand, France uses no concept of a permanent residence for VAT. The foreign taxable person in France is considered to be liable to VAT when he sells goods in France or performs a service in France.

Under the "reverse charging rule," some VAT systems require the customer enjoying the service supplied by a foreign trader to pay the VAT. As the VAT paid in this way can be used as a credit against any VAT liability, the tax actually falls on only unregistered persons, and on partly and wholly exempt traders. It would seem preferable to cut out the reverse charging rule (and all the paperwork created by it) and simply require only exempt, partly exempt, or unregistered persons liable to pay the tax.

Possible Distortions

As services are flexible, transitory, and difficult to record or check, distortions are bound to occur. Some examples might show this.

(1) An international telephone link allows a customer in the "importing country" to enjoy the information services of a computer data bank in another country. The fee for the service might be collected by a subsidiary in a third, non-VAT country (for example, an offshore tax haven). In this case the supplier has operated a passive deal in accessing the data bank and unless the telephone calls are checked, the accounts will show the charge as an export service to the tax haven. The customer will have enjoyed the services in another VAT-liable country, but there will be no payment to levy VAT on as the parent company is debited through the tax haven. There is no doubt that the service has been provided and enjoyed in two VAT-liable countries, but no tax is collected.

---

[10]For a detailed consideration of this subject, see Chesnais (1984, pp. 3–4).

(2) A lawyer sells advice to a client abroad, who is not registered for VAT. The VAT is not collected under the category of supplied where received (because it would be too difficult to tax the final customer), but the lawyer pays VAT on his inputs and is unable to zero rate his fee for advice made abroad. This could distort trade because "exporters" of legal advice are not competing on a level field; the purchaser could choose to buy advice from the country with the lowest VAT or from a country with no sales tax on legal advice at all.

(3) A bank lends money to a customer in another VAT-liable country. The service is exempt in both countries. However, a distortion is possible because it would be even more advantageous for the bank to lend to a non-VAT country and obtain the advantage of being able to offset some of the VAT on bank supplies (purchase of capital, equipment, office supplies, and so on) against the zero-rated service. As one commentator noted, "It is a deliberate feature of the system that it should encourage the 'export' of services from the EC, but when the 'service' in question is the provision of capital, the desirability of this policy may be debatable."[11]

Some Special Cases

TREATMENT OF TOURISTS

Sales to tourists of goods they do not consume in the country, but actually take out of the country, are clearly exports. When the tourist returns home, if his country uses a VAT, he should have to pay VAT on his foreign purchase at the rate appropriate to the similar domestic good. Most VAT systems legislate for some treatment to reflect this. In theory, any purchase that can be produced at the point of exit and can be proved to have been bought domestically should be allowed a refund. The crucial requirements are, first, that there should be documentary proof of purchase and tax payment and, second, proof that the good has been exported.

In some more cumbersome schemes, retailers must fill out special invoices showing the tax paid and the passport number (and probable date of exit) of the purchaser. The purchaser must physically present the goods to customs officials when leaving the country. These officials then tell the retailer the good has been exported and the retailer refunds the tax to the foreign (home) address of the purchaser.

---

[11]Campbell (1986, p. 10).

Clearly, for small sales, the cost of compliance is simply not worth it. Some countries specify a minimum amount the purchase must exceed before refunds will be given, but most accept a simpler method or, indeed, accept that there will be substantial evasion.

A simpler method is for the customs officials to accept a foreign credit card receipt as proof of purchase and tax liability, or to allow the repayment to be made by a credit to the customer's foreign credit card account. This reduces the amount of unnecessary paperwork and uses the credit card electronic network to achieve the refunds. What happens in some countries is that retailers simply sell the goods VAT free, make no return, and claim the input credit. This is a perfectly efficient way to achieve informally the same end as zero rating; what it does create is the temptation to make nontourist sales VAT free as well. In other countries, selected stores are designated as "mini duty-free zones" and sales to foreigners are VAT free. Of course, policing such stores is really impractical.

Indeed, it is the problem of policing the tourist purchases that leads to the cumbersome method described above. Basically, it seems desirable to encourage tourists to buy goods for export and, if at all possible, to use the credit card mechanism. It is also reasonable to allow verification that goods have been exported to be performed by customs officials at the point of importation; this gets around the trouble of carrying purchases instead of putting them in with the baggage.

TEMPORARY IMPORTATION

Tourists often move from country to country accumulating purchases as they go. They are a casual example of temporary importation, because, of course, their accumulated purchases are all expected to be, finally, exported to their home country.

However, there are more important temporary imports.[12] Suppliers of services may need to import equipment to carry out their professional duties, salesmen import samples, traders import goods that they hope to sell (for example, aircraft), but must re-export when disappointed. People running conventions and international fairs import large quantities of specialized display equipment, and so on. Of

---

[12]And some, perhaps, not important commercially, but crucial to the individual; provision has been made specifically in some European VATs that the tax paid on an engagement ring sent by a person resident abroad to his fiancée may be refunded if the ring is re-exported when the owner can prove movement to a residence abroad. See "Value Added Tax," *Accountancy* (1985, p. 32).

course, much temporary importation involves transport—trucks, automobiles, ships, and buses.

Whatever legislation is crafted,[13] it should be "uniform and wide-ranging" and allow goods to be temporarily imported "without undue formality."[14] While those sentiments refer to the EC, they seem sensible for a wider application. The important points are that the goods should be identifiable and their use verified, security (in cash, guarantees, or securities) may be called for, and should the goods be directed for use in the owner's own country, the appropriate tax will be levied.

Another example of temporary importation is where a special dispensation is made for large and regular imports of raw materials for inclusion in the manufacture of exports. Rather than charge VAT on the imports and refund the VAT on export (in effect requiring an interest-free loan to the government), the legislation allows traders, on proof that they conduct a regular and substantial export trade, to import goods charged to VAT in the usual way, but with the payment of VAT suspended for, say, three months (as in Korea). Taxpayers must keep full records of quantities and values of goods imported, purchased on the home market, factory production, and export sales. Strict control should be exercised by frequent inspections of records and factory premises. Within a specific time after importation, the trader must deliver a return showing how the raw materials were used. If, in practice, it turns out that the value of export trade is too small or irregular, the license or permission to run a system of suspension can be revoked.

INTERNATIONAL PASSENGER TRANSPORT

The purchase of a ticket to leave the country constitutes the purchase of a service and should be liable to VAT. Unfortunately, this causes distortions as clearly it pays to buy a (taxed) one-way ticket out and buy the return ticket in some untaxed country visited during the trip. Such potential distortions have persuaded many countries to exempt international transport from VAT. Some countries, such as the United Kingdom, have zero rated international passenger and freight transport, thereby putting the provision of these services in a favorable position vis-à-vis others that levy VAT. Nevertheless, it still is reasonable to tax such services and it is difficult to argue that persons able to travel internationally should be favored compared to those

[13]In the EC, it is the Seventeenth Council Directive.
[14]European Community, "Draft VAT Directive on Temporary Importation of Goods," reproduced in *Intertax* (March 1985, pp. 74–75).

traveling domestically or, indeed, to those enjoying other services such as hotels and restaurants.

FREE ZONES

Many countries establish free zones in which goods may be imported or exported without payment of customs duties or VAT. Such zones are supposed to be enclosed areas that can be patrolled and where all goods and persons pass through frontier posts to get into the normal domestic market. Such zones are not confined to developing countries. One of the earliest is in Ireland (Shannon), and in 1984 the United Kingdom established six such free zones. However, the danger is that the goods in the free zones may get sold on the domestic market without bearing domestic taxes, either customs duties or VAT. Basically, the VAT is levied at the "frontier" of the zone exactly as would occur on a usual international frontier. The problem is to police such flows and the more numerous such zones, the more difficult it is to prevent the erosion of revenue.

Free zones are popular in many developing countries. One of the main problems is the proliferation of such zones, often to the point where single factories or even shops are given free-zone status. Of course, it is impossible to police such single establishments and reliance has to be put on the integrity of the traders and their record keeping. Many countries find it difficult to police their free zones for customs duties, let alone the VAT. The real message is to restrict such zones to areas that have boundaries that can be patrolled and frontier ports that can be manned in the normal way.

Table 17-1 also includes other special cases, for instance, hotels and rest houses (examples 18 and 19), progress payments (example 23), government grants and subsidies (example 24), and insurance (example 28, a special case unique to New Zealand; see Chapter 5, section on "Financial Services").

CHAPTER 18

Concluding Remarks

In general, no field of taxation has seen so much nonsensical discussion than the value-added tax.
— JOHN F. DUE, *Hearings Before the Joint Economic Committee*,
U.S. Congress (92nd Congress, 2nd Session,
March 21, 1972), p. 19

The economic and technological changes of the second half of the century . . . have made VAT the quintessential modern tax.
— "VAT Takes the Strain," *Financial Times* (London),
February 15, 1988, p. 44

In its centennial review, *The Financial Times* referred to VAT as the quintessential modern tax and anticipated that if the trend toward higher VAT rates and fewer exemptions continues, the VAT will supplant the income tax as the most important single source of revenue for several governments by the end of the century. It is this fashionable tax this book has tried to review, warts and all. It may have been of interest to those already grappling with the VAT and it should be useful to those (politicians, administrators, or academics) thinking about a country adopting a VAT. A brief review of some of the highlights follows.

Part I: VAT Structure

Chapter 1 showed that the particular form of VAT that evolved in Europe had a profound influence on the countries that subsequently adopted VAT. All use the European invoice or credit method of levying VAT despite quite extensive debates about the alternatives. The desire to have at least the option (even if not exercised) to levy more than one positive rate of VAT is a powerful inducement to use the invoice method. This method also straightforwardly attaches the tax liability to the transaction and creates a good audit trail.

However, it is quite clear that some might see an alternative form of VAT—for example, the business transfer tax or the "X tax"—that required the use of only a single rate as a significant advantage in itself. Once enacted, the authorities would find it difficult, if not impossible, to give in to the normal inclination of politicians to pander to sectional interests by adjusting differential rates and creating numerous exemptions.

Countries introduce the VAT because of dissatisfaction with their existing sales taxes (cascading turnover taxes, manufacturer and wholesale taxes, or insecure retail sales taxes), because a customs union needs border taxes abolished, or because a buoyant source of new revenue is needed. In Europe, Latin America, and the Caribbean the VAT extends, usually, through the retail stage. In Africa the tax has tended to evolve in a way similar to the original French VAT; at first applied to only a limited number of manufacturers, then others, gradually extended (for example, Senegal). It is perhaps noteworthy how Middle Eastern countries do not adopt general sales taxes, least of all VAT. (In this region only Israel has a VAT.)

More interesting is why countries have not adopted a VAT despite (sometimes prolonged) discussion. A review of the debates in the United States, Australia, Canada, Japan, and Iceland indicated that fears about regressivity, possible high administrative costs, potential evasion, high compliance costs, and the effects on inflation, all made countries wary of the VAT. In addition, some saw the buoyant revenue potential of VAT not as an advantage but permitting the public sector to grow larger. It is true that in many developing countries the VAT has enabled indirect tax revenues to be at least half as high again as the sales taxes replaced. However, other evidence suggests that the causation is reversed. Countries with large public expenditures look around for a buoyant revenue source and VAT becomes that fountain. While VAT is not necessarily a "money machine," it does finance those who have already decided to spend (as also discussed in Chapter 11). Finally, it was shown how federal governments have difficulty in reconciling a new federal VAT with existing state and local sales taxes.

The highest standard rate of VAT (25 percent) is levied in Côte d'Ivoire, Ireland, and Niger. The highest rate of all is levied in Senegal (50 percent). Many countries apply a reduced rate to food of 5 percent or 6 percent. Some, for instance, the United Kingdom, exempt food entirely by using a zero rate. The experience of changing rates has been one way—upward, and standard rates are commonly between 15 percent and 25 percent. Overall, the basic message of Chapter 2 was simple: the fewer VAT rates used the better, and these should be levied on full, unadjusted prices, inclusive of customs duties, import fees and charges, and excises.

Similarly, the general message of Chapters 3, 4, and 5 on exemptions and zero ratings was also straightforward. Adopt a VAT with as wide a base as is practical and resist arguments for special cases and exemptions. The New Zealand VAT is frequently quoted as an excellent example of a base that includes food, new housing, public utilities, all clothing, government purchases and sales, leasing, and even some financial services such as life insurance; the New Zealand authorities resisted the arguments for zero rating or exemptions on grounds of regressivity, "merit," or special pleading. As a result, they got a clean, efficient, no-nonsense VAT that won high marks in terms of introduction and administration and, more interestingly, from the public and traders in terms of acceptability. Services should be taxed. Even in developing countries income elastic services such as electricity, telecommunications, gasoline, garage repairs, restaurants, hotels, and barber and beauty shops should be taxed. Although financial services should be taxed (why tax food and not banks?), the "bundle" of services they provide are difficult to disentangle and easy to drive offshore.

As discussed in Chapter 6, special schemes for small traders should not be looked upon as a regrettable departure from the principles of VAT but rather as being so obviously necessary as to be intrinsic to any VAT system. Such schemes help administrators by removing large numbers of traders from the register and hence saving administrative costs. They help the trader by saving him from the compliance costs of dealing with the tax authorities. A generous threshold based on turnover is recommended with little or no reliance on a *forfait*; cash accounting should be allowed, but small traders should be encouraged to file returns as frequently as the usual VAT taxpayer.

A farmer is a special sort of small trader. In Chapter 7 it was explained how in developed countries, for the purposes of the VAT, the farmer may be treated the same as any other business. If farmers' sales are small, they will be exempt under the small business exemptions. Over the limit, they can register for VAT as full taxpayers. If this is considered impractical, then the method used in many developing countries (especially in Latin America) can be adopted; principal farm inputs, such as seeds, fertilizer, and insecticides, can be zero rated. The third option is to apply the rough justice of the global credit offset as is done in most EC countries.

Some federal governments levy a VAT (Argentina, Brazil, the Federal Republic of Germany, and Mexico) but some of those considering a VAT (Canada and the United States) find the relationship between a federal VAT and state and local sales taxes to be one of the most difficult issues. Chapter 8 looked at the VAT in federal systems and considered the options. The simplest solution is to give the administration and collection of VAT either to the states or to the federal government and then use a formula to share the revenue between the central government and the states. If this is unacceptable because of the loss of fiscal autonomy, then a federal VAT might have a state VAT "piggybacked" on it. This, of course, is more complex for both traders and administrators. The Canadian suggestion of an accounts-based VAT that would enable the provinces to levy their own varieties of rates is an interesting possibility but it would be even more difficult to operate in the United States with 50 states (as opposed to 11 provinces).

The VAT is introduced into an already existing tax structure. It may supplement existing taxes or replace old taxes, but the smooth changeover requires a careful appreciation of the transitional problems. Chapter 9 emphasized the need to ensure early registration of VAT taxpayers, the importance of educational visits to traders, and the importance of adequate compensation for taxes paid on stocks. As the usual VAT ensures that all capital goods are free of tax, some prior planning is needed if existing taxes on capital are not to cause a bunching of capital goods orders.

Part II: Economic Aspects and Consequences

Most governments and the public anticipate with trepidation the effect on prices of introducing a VAT. However, the evidence (Chapter 10) shows that in most countries the introduction of VAT, or a change in VAT rates, is not inflationary; the change might lead to a once and for all shift in prices, but not to an acceleration of price changes.

The most trenchant case against VAT is that it is regressive. The evidence shows (Chapter 11) that a broad-based VAT is likely to be regressive and that making it progressive by extensive use of the zero rate (for example, the United Kingdom) is undesirable on administrative and revenue grounds. Moreover, such use of zero rating does not ensure that the underprivileged groups who are supposed to be helped actually are helped. As an Irish report points out, tax revenues from applying the VAT to expenditures exempted on grounds of regressivity would raise a sum far in excess of that needed to compensate the poor for the diminution of their household consumption due to VAT. Given that exemptions, zero rating, and multiple rates are inefficient ways to reduce the potential regressivity of VAT, can low-income households be compensated? New Zealand used a wage supplement and changes in social security to ensure a compensation to low-income families following the VAT introduction. Suggestions for progressive VAT rates on payrolls under the "X tax" might achieve something similar. But the crucial problem remains as to whether or not compensation can reach those with small rural incomes, the urban informal sector poor, or the old, if there is no or only a rudimentary social security system. These problems become even more important in developing countries where such groups are likely to be large and all the more difficult to reach and compensate.

A similar argument holds when, in developed economies, the potential regressiveness of a VAT may be offset by strongly progressive income, capital gains, and wealth taxes, but in developing countries such progressive taxes, even though draconian in legislation, may be paper tigers in application. Therefore, the presumed correction to the VAT's regressiveness through progressive direct taxation may not take place.

The VAT is an efficient and neutral tax (Chapter 10) and does not distort savings and investment behavior. Any favorable effect of VAT on foreign trade is likely to be small and temporary; usually arguments in favor of VAT on these grounds exaggerate its virtues.

Finally, VAT is not meant to be used as a weapon for short-term demand management and fine tuning. It is designed to be neutral and to build in nonneutrality erodes the basic virtues of the tax.

Part III: Administration and Compliance

As quoted at the beginning of Chapter 12, in developing countries tax administration frequently *is* tax policy. Indeed, in most countries the crucial importance of the effectiveness of tax administration is too often overlooked when ambitious statements are made about efficiency, equality, neutrality, and effects of alternative taxes on savings, work effort, and risk taking. Tax administration is often waved to one side in academic discussions, but Chapters 12 to 15 try to emphasize its importance. Although some governments run their VAT through the customs and excise department (for example, Denmark, Israel, and the United Kingdom), it is usually better to give the responsibility for VAT to the income tax authorities. Each country has to evaluate its own

VALUE-ADDED TAX: PRACTICE AND PROBLEMS

preferences whether or not to centralize the VAT administration, and the arguments were reviewed in Chapter 12.

Staffing is affected by decisions on the threshold for exemptions, goods and services taxed or exempted, the inclusion or exclusion of the agricultural sector, the treatment of groups of companies, the collection of VAT by other agencies such as customs, the staff transferred from taxes replaced, the frequency of VAT returns, the number of VAT rates, the extent of computerization, and the quality and standard of administration desired. Ratios of staff to registered traders can vary from 1:21 up to 1:726 or, as suggested for the United States, 1:1,000. Chapter 12 examined staffing both by assessing the numbers of staff at different functional levels and by comparing the figures derived to the broad staffing ratios.

Chapter 12 also outlined ways of planning staff changes during the transition to a VAT and the different ways planning committees could be organized. The costs of administering a VAT should be 1 percent to 2 percent of revenue; of course, the lower the rate of VAT, the higher are likely to be the costs as ratio to revenue. Given the likely complexity of changing to a VAT, the costs can only be justified if the VAT is a major revenue source, and this suggests a standard rate of 10 percent and above. Chapter 12 also indicated that 18–24 months are needed to prepare and introduce a VAT. The experience of countries as diverse as Belgium, Greece, Hungary, Korea, Mexico, and Portugal suggests the need for gradual but sustained administrative effort to introduce a VAT.

The importance of the VAT register of taxpayers was emphasized in Chapter 13. The register must be comprehensive and must be kept up to date (which involves a large amount of "churning," that is, registering and deregistering taxpayers).

The introduction of a VAT can be used as the justification for a major overhaul of tax identification numbers (TINs). These numbers are crucial for computer-held records and for audit. Similarly, the invoice is the crucial control document for the usual credit-method VAT. Some developing countries have tried to standardize the form the invoice should take, while some other countries dictate the serial numbers, but most allow the invoices to take any form the trader wishes, as long as it contains all the information required for the VAT. Chapter 13 described the most ambitious attempts to cross-check invoices (Korea) and the means countries have used to try to check on the weakest link in the chain—the retail sale. However, basically, VAT is a self-assessed tax, and hence the control of VAT payments and refunds (where revenue is most at risk) and audit, as discussed in Chapter 13, is important.

Much has been made of the self-checking mechanism of VAT but, of course, VAT is evaded, as the discussion of 15 different methods of evasion in Chapter 14 showed. At the same time, the public and courts in most countries appear to view tax evasion in a different light to most other crimes. Rightly or wrongly, it makes sense for the VAT authorities to rely on sanctions other than criminal prosecution. Financial penalties should be, as far as possible, automatic.

The development of powerful, versatile, economic, and most important of all, reliable personal computers and their software packages has revolutionized tax administration, for both officials and traders, especially in developing countries. Chapter 15 discussed the options, planning, potential outputs, systems design, personnel, and training needed to use computers in administering a VAT. Although some VAT officers caution about relying too much on computers, the tide is one way and computers have a central role in administering VAT.

A VAT depends for its success on the taxpayer's willing compliance as much as (indeed probably more than) on efficient administration. Chapter 16 dealt with this often neglected topic. Traders must anticipate their obligations under VAT and take decisions involving their pricing, margins, and bookkeeping. They must also cope with the visits of VAT officials. All this has a cost. The chapter also reviewed the debate on the trader's compliance costs and, while it is difficult to put a monetary value on such costs, clearly they exist; VAT administrators are well advised to keep them constantly in mind and do as much as possible to mitigate them.

The VAT, like any tax, is based on an Act that ought to include precise definitions; Chapter 17 looked at the possible definitions about the taxpayer, his business, the place and time of supply, the value of goods and services, and the treatment of exports and imports. There are, of course, numerous detailed legal debates in every country about these matters but the intent of this chapter was to give the flavor of the debate on some of the more important definitional issues.

This book started out to try to illustrate how, using one tax as an example, practical considerations influence the form, shape, and structure of a tax; how theory influences the choice of particular forms of tax, but also how important the practical considerations of both tax officials and taxpayers are in modifying tax structures. If the text has weighed too heavily on the side of practice, perhaps that is because practical considerations do dominate the real world of taxation.

One reader of the manuscript of this book wrote that it could become the Baedeker of VAT. A memory the author has of using a Baedeker was in Capri, where the guidebook informed the visitor that the phosphorescence in the Blue Grotto could be seen by throwing a small coin to a local boy who would dive into the water; the same effect, the book continued, could be achieved more cheaply by trailing one's hand through the water. This illustrates the virtues of Baedeker; not only does it tell the reader what is important, it also discusses different ways to achieve results, and then recommends efficiency and economy. If this book can even remind a reader of Baedeker, it will have been worth the effort.

APPENDICES

An Example of a Value-Added Tax Return Form

Value Added Tax Return

For the period

to

Due to reach the VAT Central Unit by These dates must not be altered.

H M Customs and Excise

For Official Use

Registration No   **Period**

Before you fill in this form please read the notes on the other side. You must complete all boxes — writing "none" where necessary. If you need to show an exact amount of pounds, please write "00" in the pence column. Don't put a dash or leave the column blank. Please write clearly in ink. You must ensure that the completed form and any VAT payable are received no later than the due date by the Controller, VAT Central Unit, H M Customs and Excise, 21 Victoria Avenue, SOUTHEND-ON-SEA X

An envelope is enclosed for your use.

SPECIMEN COPY

FOR OFFICIAL USE

		For Official Use	£	p
VAT DUE in this period on OUTPUTS (sales, etc), certain postal imports and services received from abroad	1			
Underdeclarations of VAT made on previous returns (but not those notified in writing by Customs and Excise)	2			
TOTAL VAT DUE (box 1 + box 2)	3			
VAT DEDUCTIBLE in this period on INPUTS (purchases, etc)	4			
Overdeclarations of VAT made on previous returns (but not those notified in writing by Customs and Excise)	5			
TOTAL VAT DEDUCTIBLE (box 4 + box 5)	6			
NET VAT PAYABLE OR REPAYABLE (Difference between boxes 3 and 6)	7			

Please tick only ONE of these boxes:

box 3 greater than box 6   payment by credit transfer ☐   payment enclosed ☐

box 6 greater than box 3   repayment due ☐

How to pay the VAT due

Cross all cheques and postal orders "A/C Payee only" and make them payable to "H M Customs and Excise". Make credit transfers through account 3078027 at National Girobank or 10-70-50 52055000 for Bank Giros and keep your payment slip. You can order pre-printed booklets of credit transfer slips from your local VAT office. In your own interest do not send notes, coins, or uncrossed postal orders through the post. **Please write your VAT registration number on the back of all cheques and credit transfer slips.**

| Value of Outputs (excluding any VAT) | 8 | | 00 |
| Value of Inputs (excluding any VAT) | 9 | | 00 |

Please tick box(es) if the statement(s) apply:

box 5 includes bad debt relief ☐   box 8 includes exempt outputs ☐   box 8 includes exports ☐

Retail schemes If you have used any of the schemes in the period covered by this return please tick the box(es) to show all the schemes used.

☐ A ☐ B ☐ C ☐ D ☐ E ☐ F ☐ G ☐ H ☐ J

Remember, you could be liable to a financial penalty if your return and all the VAT payable are not received by the due date.
DECLARATION by the signatory to be completed by or on behalf of the person named above.

I, ... declare that the
(full name of signatory in BLOCK LETTERS)
information given above is true and complete.

Signed .... Date.. 19......
*(Proprietor, partner, director, secretary, responsible officer, committee member of club or association, duly authorised person)   *Delete as necessary

FOR OFFICIAL USE

VAT 100   F3790 (October 1987)

NOTES

These notes and the pamphlet, *Filling in your VAT return,* will help you to fill in this form. You may also need to refer to other VAT notices and leaflets. If you are using the cash accounting scheme, remember that the amounts of VAT due and deductible are based on payments received and made, **not** on invoices.

If you need help or advice, or any of the answers overleaf gives a negative figure, please contact your local VAT office quoting your VAT registration number.

Box 1 You must show the VAT due on all goods and services you supplied in this period. This is your *output* tax.

If you use a retail scheme the *How to work* pamphlet for your scheme will help you work out the output tax due.

Remember to include VAT due on:

- goods taken for private use
- gifts and loans of goods
- sales to staff
- sales of business assets
- imported services listed in *The VAT guide,* Appendix G
- postal imports — other than Datapost — with a value of £1300 or less.

Remember to subtract any VAT credited to your customers.

Box 2 If any of your previous returns showed too little VAT payable by you or too much VAT repayable to you, show the amount here — but leave out:

- adjustments notified in writing by Customs and Excise
- VAT declared on a previous return which you have not paid in full.

Box 4 You must show the amount of VAT deductible on any business purchases you have made, including imported goods and services and goods removed from bonded warehouse. This is your *input* tax.

If this is your first return include any VAT you can reclaim on goods and services received before registration (see *The VAT guide,* paragraph 38).

Exclude any VAT on:

- goods and services not supplied for the use of your business
- business entertainment (except of overseas customers)
- motor cars
- second-hand goods which have been sold to you under one of the VAT second-hand schemes.

If you are a builder see VAT Leaflet, *Construction industry,* about non-deductible input tax on fixtures and fittings.

Remember to subtract any VAT credited by your suppliers.

If you have exempt outputs this may affect the amount of input tax you can reclaim (see *The VAT guide,* paragraph 35).

Box 5 If any of your previous returns showed too much VAT payable by you or too little VAT repayable to you show the amount here.

Include:

- any VAT you are claiming back as bad debt relief under the conditions set out in the VAT Leaflet, *Relief from VAT on bad debts,* and tick the box on the front of this form.

Exclude:

- adjustments notified in writing by Customs and Excise
- repayments of VAT claimed on a previous return but not yet received from Customs and Excise
- assessments already paid in this or other periods.

Box 7 If the amount to be entered is under £1 you must still fill in this form and send it to the VAT Central Unit. You need not send any payment, nor will any repayment be made to you.

Boxes 8 and 9 Show your total outputs in box 8. Include zero-rated sales, exports, exempt income such as rents, and other business income. Leave out the VAT. If exports or exempt outputs are included please tick the appropriate box(es) on the front of this form.

Show your total inputs in box 9. Include imports and other business expenses. Leave out the VAT.

For both boxes 8 and 9 you should show net figures after deducting any credits. Do not deduct any cash discounts. If your accounts are net of cash discounts you should add back a reasonable amount for any discounts given or received.

Some income and expenses must be left out of boxes 8 and 9. There are two ways to work these boxes out — Basis A and Basis B. Use the same basis for both boxes. Whichever basis you use always leave out:

- VAT
- wages and salaries
- PAYE and National Insurance contributions
- money put into or taken out of the business
- loans, dividends, grants, gifts of money
- compensation payments or insurance claims
- Stock Exchange dealings.

If you use Basis A also leave out:

Box 8

- sales of cars on which you paid no VAT (see *The VAT guide,* Appendix C, paragraph 8)
- exempt outputs excluded from any partial exemption calculation.

Box 9

- exempt purchases
- MOT fees and vehicle licence duty
- local authority rates
- purchases on which you cannot reclaim input tax (see *The VAT guide,* paragraph 33).

If you decide to use Basis B check if either or both of your outputs or inputs are above £50,000 on average (or £20,000 if you make monthly returns). If they are you must tell Customs and Excise by attaching a letter to the first VAT return that you make using Basis B, quoting "reference 2B/Basis B".

If you later decide to change to Basis A, you must inform Customs and Excise in the same way.

Remember, you must tell your local VAT office about any changes in your business circumstances. You will find details in *The VAT guide,* Section XI.

Printed in the U.K. for H.M.S.O. 9/87 Dd 8055731 C 75000 38806 G 1373

APPENDIX **II**

Chronological Schedule of Work to Be Done to Introduce a VAT in About Eighteen Months

The following timetable sets out broad guidelines for the work that needs to be done month by month starting July 1988 to introduce a VAT by, say, January 1, 1990, and enforce it effectively thereafter. It might be intended as an aide-mémoire for the head of the VAT committee and for the heads of the various subcommittees preparing the VAT. Progress should be monitored regularly to identify any failure that could jeopardize the planning or the proper implementation of the VAT on the target date. It has to be pointed out that while the list may appear reasonably comprehensive, there will inevitably still be many unrecorded auxiliary activities to which attention has to be given if the VAT is to be implemented successfully and on time.

Month	*Tasks*
By end-1988	1. Settle policy proposals on the scope and the structure of the VAT, including a cost-benefit analysis, and on transitional measures, and obtain the relevant ministerial approval with regard to policy, the funding plan, and so on.
	2. Training subcommittee prepares training plan, identifies training courses and orientation seminars for executives and managers, selects training staff, and identifies the need for other training resources, such as office space, photocopiers, and secretarial support.
	3. Design and present an orientation seminar on the basic principles of VAT for executives and managers at the revenue, customs, and excise departments.

409

4. Prepare a course for training all supervisors and operating personnel concerned with the VAT in the revenue and customs departments on the basic principles of VAT operation.

5. Design VAT return form, VAT payment form, and application form for VAT registration.

6. Within the revenue department, determine the administrative framework of the VAT, such as detailed procedures for the registration of taxpayers, processing of VAT returns, audit for VAT, and collection procedures.

7. Start discussion on the extent of computer support in VAT administration and the system's design.

8. Identify the resource needs for implementation of the VAT, with particular attention to funding and the filling of outstanding vacancies.

9. Legal subcommittee starts discussion on VAT and drafts laws and basic regulations.

10. Make final decisions, both within the revenue department and with the customs department, on registration procedures and the incorporation of VAT registration information in the tax master file.

11. Discuss with the customs department the role of customs in the enforcement of the VAT.

12. Decide on computer involvement and consequently determine the needs for changes in existing programs and/or the development of new programs.

13. Determine the broad setup of the administrative system for VAT and examine possible consequences for the organization of the revenue department.

14. Draft a simple VAT information booklet for press and public use, for distribution in February 1989.

15. Produce a trial list of potential VAT taxpayers based on the information available in:

- The revenue department's computer system (data on business tax and income tax).
- The customs department (exporters and importers).
- Local manual listings, knowledge and surveys, including press advertisements and telephone directories.

16. Make a preliminary estimate of staff required in each office to administer the VAT at the beginning of each month as registration, educational visits, collection, enforcement, and verification progress. The estimate should be based on the numbers of likely taxpayers on the list at 15 above.

17. Begin preparation of a staff manual on the VAT legislation and procedures.

18. Draft staff manual on VAT registration procedures.

19. Start preparations for extensive publicity campaign to be held from May 1989, including the production of publicity literature.

January 1989

1. Review all actions to date and monitor progress to identify delays.

2. Complete preliminary draft of the VAT law for full committee review.

3. Give course on VAT principles to relevant supervisors and operating personnel.

4. Design forms for VAT administration.

5. Design general audit policy for VAT.

6. Work out curriculum for VAT auditors' training, determine content of manuals for that training, and select instructors.

7. Establish VAT units in each regional, provincial, district, and area offices.

February 1989

1. Complete drafting of VAT law and submit draft for government approval.

2. Conduct first media campaign to inform the

public about the main features of the VAT (including distribution of booklet prepared in 1987).

3. Assess requirements for informational material, printing forms, etc., for public and official use.

4. Draft basic regulations.

5. Hold talks with banks (if included in collection design) regarding collection procedures.

6. Draft manuals for VAT auditors' training.

March 1989

1. Submit final law and proposed regulations to parliament.

2. Assess needs for and order office supplies and equipment (for a simple example, rubber stamps).

3. Design and print forms for staff use on educational and verification visits and for interoffice use.

4. Continue drafting manuals for VAT auditors' training.

April 1989

1. Select participants for VAT auditors' training and complete preparation of the actual organization of the training.

2. Design curriculum and manuals for the training of officials who will be receiving and processing VAT returns and payments.

3. Set up telephone information service, where the public and traders can get information about any issues related to VAT.

4. Design and draft a staff manual on educational visits.

5. Draft a VAT guide for businesses for issue with registration certificates.

6. Monitor progress, in the revenue department, in collection offices, and in the customs and excise departments, to identify bottlenecks.

May 1989

1. Hold discussions with trade and professional

organizations about various issues regarding VAT administration.

2. Complete drafting basic regulations and submit for government/ministerial approval.

3. Start discussions on and drafting of more detailed regulations for implementation of basic regulations.

June 1989

1. Publish the VAT law and the basic regulations.

2. Start large-scale publicity campaign for the VAT, emphasizing the registration requirements and procedures.

3. Commence lectures and seminars with trade and professional organizations to present details of the intended VAT procedures.

4. Distribute to the local offices blank application forms for registration, for issue on request.

5. Start VAT auditors' training.

July 1989

1. Send out VAT registration forms with letters (and attached information booklet) to those identified in November 1987 as likely taxpayers for VAT, telling them that they will be considered full VAT taxpayers unless they provide evidence to the contrary within, say, three weeks.

2. Visit interested persons who have requested such a visit to resolve particular VAT problems.

3. Review progress in preparation of computer programming.

4. Agree with banks on procedures for receiving returns and VAT payments and for communications with the revenue department offices.

5. Design claim forms for stock relief.

6. Prepare organization of educational visits.

August 1989

1. Assign VAT prefix to TINs of taxpayers who returned their registration forms and to other taxpayers based on customs and excise

information and available data on taxpayers who failed to return their registration forms.

2. Send registration certificates to taxpayers defined in (1), accompanied by a batch of payment vouchers and related instructions on monthly payments.

3. Start educational visits to the premises of already registered taxpayers.

4. Commence a publicity campaign designed to get those not yet registered to do so between September 1 and October 31.

5. Monitor progress in all fields and advise the Minister if delays would be thought to be crucial with regard to the introduction date of January 1, 1989.

September 1989

1. Enter data from application forms of voluntary registrants.

2. Print certificates of registration and mail to voluntary registrants, with payment vouchers and instructions.

3. Complete and publish more detailed VAT regulations.

4. Design procedures for processing claims for stock relief.

October 1989

1. Continue registration procedures from September.

2. Continue training staff.

3. Test adapted and newly designed computer programs for processing payment forms and incoming returns; test on-line retrieval of VAT taxpayer master file data.

4. Design criteria for VAT audit selection.

5. Conduct publicity campaign about the effect of VAT on prices, asking the public's collaboration to help contain that effect.

6. Distribute claim forms for stock relief to the relevant offices and give them instructions about the reception and processing of stock relief claims.

November 1989

1. Continue registration procedures from September and October.
2. Line-up computerized VAT on-line retrieval system and print alphabetical and numeric lists of registered taxpayers for distribution to the relevant regional, provincial, and area offices for backup purposes.
3. Monitor progress of educational visits and consider action to deal with any problems.
4. Continue educational/canvass visits.
5. Check that revised customs entry forms that accommodate the TIN prefix are available for use from January 1, 1990.

December 1989

1. Evaluate progress of registration and consider emergency publicity campaign to increase voluntary compliance by those liable.
2. Train office staff to deal specifically with questions on VAT returns, on validation of manually entered names and addresses on forms, and on stock relief regulations.
3. Continue educational/canvass visits.
4. Publicize stock relief facility and final date for claims.
5. Issue forms for stock relief on request.
6. Publicize the changes in customs entry forms effective from January 1, 1990.

January 1990
(VAT starts)

1. Conduct publicity campaign to emphasize need for invoicing and bookkeeping to enable returns to be completed properly.
2. Revive publicity campaign about the effect of the VAT on prices (see October 1989).
3. Continue educational visits to newly registered taxpayers and the registration drive.
4. Receive and process stock relief claims and issue credit vouchers.
5. Distribute blank computer-printed payment forms and address labels for payment in February (if there is a monthly payment requirement).

February 1990

1. Continue educational visits and the registration drive.

2. Initiate publicity to encourage timely filing of returns.

3. Complete the data-entry of incoming VAT returns.

4. Reconcile receipts from banks and other collection points with batches of returns received and resolve any differences.

March 1990

1. Send reminder letters to those registered who failed to file their first return or make their first payment by February 28.

2. Issue (via computer) fines for late filing or payment to those who do not react to the reminders.

Bibliography

Aaron, Henry J., "Introduction and Summary," in *The Value-Added Tax: Lessons from Europe*, ed. by Henry J. Aaron (Washington: Brookings Institution, 1981).

_____, "The Impact of a Value-Added Tax on U.S. Competitiveness," in *The Consumption Tax: A Better Alternative?* ed. by Charls E. Walker and Mark A. Bloomfield (Cambridge, Massachusetts: Ballinger Publishing Company, 1987).

_____, "The Political Economy of a Value-Added Tax in the United States," *Tax Notes*, Tax Analysts (Arlington, Virginia), Vol. 38 (March 7, 1988), pp. 1111–16.

Alverson, Terree, "Does the Value-Added Tax Contribute to Increased Government Spending and Taxation?" *Economic Outlook*, Chamber of Commerce of the United States (Washington), April/May 1986, pp. 12–16.

Andersson, Krister, "Sweden," in *Comparative Tax Systems: Europe, Canada, and Japan*, ed. by Joseph A. Pechman (Arlington, Virginia: Tax Analysts, 1987).

"Argentina: Amendments to the Value Added Tax Act," *CIAT Newsletter*, Inter-American Center of Tax Administrators (Panama), Vol. 4, January/February 1987.

"Auditing Guideline: Computer Assisted Audit Techniques," *Accountancy* (London), Vol. 93 (February 1982), p. 117.

Australia, *Reform of the Australian Tax System: Draft White Paper* (Canberra: Government Publishing Service, 1985).

Bakker, Carl, and Phil Chronican, *Financial Service and the GST: A Discussion Paper* (Wellington, New Zealand: Institute of Policy Studies, Victoria University Press, 1985).

Ballard, Charles L., John B. Shoven, and John Whalley, *The Welfare Cost of Distortions in the United States Tax System: A General Equilibrium Approach*, NBER Working Paper No. 1043 (Cambridge, Massachusetts: National Bureau of Economic Research, December 1982).

_____, "General Equilibrium Computations of the Marginal Welfare Costs of Taxes in the United States," *American Economic Review* (Nashville, Tennessee), Vol. 75 (March 1985), pp. 128–38.

Ballard, Charles L., John Karl Scholz, and John B. Shoven, "The Value-Added Tax: A General Equilibrium Look at Its Efficiency and Incidence," in *The Effects of Taxation on Capital Accumulation*, ed. by Martin Feldstein (Chicago: University of Chicago Press, 1987).

417

Bannock, Graham, *VAT and Small Business: European Experience and Implications for North America* (Willowdale, Ontario: Canadian Federation of Independent Business; Washington: National Federation of Independent Business, 1986).

Barham, Vicky, S.N. Poddar, and John Whalley, "The Tax Treatment of Insurance Under a Consumption Type, Destination Basis VAT," *National Tax Journal* (Columbus, Ohio), Vol. 40 (June 1987), pp. 171–82.

Barman, Kiran, and Usha Bisonoi, "Value Added Tax as an Alternative to Corporation Tax," *Economic Affairs* (Calcutta), Vol. 28 (October/December 1983), pp. 860–65.

Barnard, James, "A Matter of Enforcement," *Portcullis*, H.M. Customs and Excise (London), February 1976.

"Belgium: Income Tax Changes Ahead," *World Tax Report* (London), May 1987, p. 9.

Bertram, David, and Stephen Edwards, *Comprehensive Aspects of Taxation*, 1984–85 Edition, Part 1 (London, New York: Holt, Rinehart and Winston, 1984).

Bird, Richard M., "A New Look at Indirect Taxation in Developing Countries," *World Development* (Oxford), Vol. 15 (September 1987), pp. 1151–61.

Bloomfield, Mark A., "Commentary," in Charles E. McLure, Jr., *The Value-Added Tax: Key to Deficit Reduction?* (Washington: American Enterprise Institute for Public Policy Research, 1987).

Bradford, David F., "On the Incidence of Consumption Taxes," in *The Consumption Tax: A Better Alternative?* ed. by Charls E. Walker and Mark A. Bloomfield (Cambridge, Massachusetts: Ballinger Publishing Company, 1987).

Bragg, Richard J., and David W. Williams, "VAT Increases and Contracts," *British Tax Review* (London), July–August 1984, No. 4, pp. 214–26.

Brecher, Stephen M., Donald W. Moore, Michael M. Hoyle, and Peter G.B. Trasker, *The Economic Impact of the Introduction of VAT* (Morristown, New Jersey: Financial Executives Research Foundation, 1982).

Browning, Edgar K., "The Burden of Taxation," *Journal of Political Economy* (Chicago), Vol. 86 (August 1978), pp. 649–71.

————, and William R. Johnson, *The Distribution of the Tax Burden* (Washington: American Enterprise Institute for Public Policy Research, 1979).

Buckett, Alan, *VAT Enforcement and Appeals Manual* (London: Butterworths, 1986).

Campbell, Colin, "The International Aspects of a Cross-Border Tax System," *International Tax Report* (London), September 1986, pp. 1–10.

Canada, *Tax Reform 1987: Sales Tax Reform* (Ottawa: Department of Finance, June 18, 1987).

————, *Tax Reform 1987: The White Paper* (Ottawa: Department of Finance, June 18, 1987).

Casanegra de Jantscher, Milka, "Problems of Administering a Value-Added Tax in Developing Countries," IMF Working Paper WP/86/15 (unpublished; Washington: International Monetary Fund, December 18, 1986).

————, "Problems in Administering a Consumption Tax," in *The Consumption Tax: A Better Alternative?* ed. by Charls E. Walker and Mark A. Bloomfield (Cambridge, Massachusetts: Ballinger Publishing Company, 1987).

Castellucci, Laura, "Italy," in *Comparative Tax Systems: Europe, Canada, and Japan,* ed. by Joseph A. Pechman (Arlington, Virginia: Tax Analysts, 1987).

Centro Interamericano de Administradores Tributarios (Inter-American Center of Tax Administrators), *Summary of Value Added Tax in CIAT Member Countries in the Americas* (Panama: CIAT, February 1988).

————, and Instituto de Estudios Fiscales, Ministerio de Economía y Hacienda de España, *Revista de Administración Tributaria: La Estructura y Administración del Impuesto sobre el Valor Agregado (Tax Administration Review: Structure and Administration of Value Added Tax),* January 1988, No. 4 (Panama: CIAT).

Chakravarty, A., "The Idea Behind Modvat," *Capital* (Calcutta), Vol. 196 (June 1–14), pp. 41–43.

Chesnais, Bernard, "Application of Value Added Tax to Cross-Border Transactions and International Services," *Tax Planning International Review* (London), Vol. 11 (August 1984), pp. 3–8.

"Chile," in International Bureau of Fiscal Documentation, *Taxation in Latin America,* Vol. 1, Supplement No. 65 (Amsterdam), December 1986.

Choi, Kwang, *Value-Added Taxation: Experiences and Lessons of Korea,* Working Paper 84-06 (Seoul: Korea Development Institute, March 1984).

Cnossen, Sijbren, "What Kind of Sales Tax? Critique of a Government Discussion Paper," *Canadian Tax Journal* (Toronto), Vol. 23, No. 6 (November–December 1975), pp. 505–19.

————, "Dutch Experience with the Value-Added Tax," *Finanzarchiv* (Tübingen), Vol. 39, No. 2 (1981), pp. 223–54.

————, "What Rate Structure for a Value-Added Tax," *National Tax Journal* (Columbus, Ohio), Vol. 35 (June 1982), pp. 205–14.

————, "Sales Taxation: An International Perspective," in *Taxation Issues for the 1980's,* ed. by John G. Head (Sydney: Australian Tax Research Foundation, 1983).

———— (1986a), "Interjurisdictional Coordination of Sales Taxes," paper presented at World Bank Conference on Value Added Taxation in Developing Countries, Washington, April 21–23, 1986; forthcoming in *Value Added Taxation in Developing Countries,* ed. by Malcolm Gillis, Carl S. Shoup, and Gerardo P. Sicat (World Bank).

———— (1986b), "Tax Harmonization in the European Community," *Bulletin for International Fiscal Documentation*, International Bureau of Fiscal Documentation (Amsterdam), Vol. 40 (December 1986), pp. 545–63.

———— (1987a), *Tax Coordination in the European Community* (Deventer, Netherlands: Kluwer Law and Taxation Publishers, 1987).

———— (1987b), "The Technical Superiority of VAT over RST," *Australian Tax Forum* (Clayton, Victoria), Vol. 4, No. 4 (1987), pp. 419–64.

———— (1987c), "VAT and RST: A Comparison," *Canadian Tax Journal* (Toronto), Vol. 37 (May/June 1987), pp. 573–615.

————, and Carl S. Shoup, "Coordination of Value-Added Taxes," in *Tax Coordination in the European Community*, ed. by Sijbren Cnossen (Deventer, Netherlands: Kluwer Law and Taxation Publishers, 1987).

"Congressional Reports: Estimated Revenue Effects of Options to Raise Revenue," *Tax Notes*, Tax Analysts (Arlington, Virginia), Vol. 36 (July 6, 1987), pp. 87–91.

Dekker, W., "EC: Five-Year Plan on European Integration," *Intertax* (Deventer, Netherlands), No. 5 (May 1985), pp. 121–23.

Dengel, Annette, "Federal Republic of Germany," in *Comparative Tax Systems: Europe, Canada, and Japan*, ed. by Joseph A. Pechman (Arlington, Virginia: Tax Analysts, 1987).

de Vries, Edo, "Back VAT," *British Tax Review* (London), No. 4 (July–August 1985), pp. 204–13.

Dickson, Ian, "Blanket Approach Costs to Acceptable," *National Business Review* (Wellington, New Zealand), May 6, 1985.

Dodd, Michael, "New Zealand: Planning for Goods and Services Tax," *Tax Planning International Review* (London), Vol. 13 (January 1986), pp. 24–25.

Douglas, Roger, *Statement on Taxation and Benefit Reform 1985* (Wellington, New Zealand, 1985).

————, *Toward Prosperity* (Auckland, New Zealand: David Bateman, 1987).

Due, John F. (1983a), "The Experience of Zimbabwe with a Retail Sales Tax," *Bulletin for International Fiscal Documentation*, International Bureau of Fiscal Documentation (Amsterdam), Vol. 37 (February 1983), pp. 51–58.

———— (1983b), "The Retail Sales Tax: The United States Experience," in *Comparative Tax Studies: Essays in Honor of Richard Goode*, ed. by Sijbren Cnossen (Amsterdam: North-Holland Publishing Co., 1983).

————, "The Exclusion of Small Firms from Sales and Related Taxes," *Public Finance* (The Hague), Vol. 39, No. 2 (1984), pp. 202–12.

————, "Trends in Sales Tax Audit Selection Since 1960," *National Tax Journal* (Columbus, Ohio), Vol. 38 (June 1985), pp. 235–40.

———— (1986a), "The Choice Between a Value-Added Tax and a Retail Sales Tax," in *Report of Proceedings of the Thirty-Seventh Tax Conference*, Canadian

Tax Foundation, November 18–20, 1985 (Toronto: Canadian Tax Foundation, 1986).

——— (1986b), "The Implications for Australia of the Experience in the United States, Canada and Other Countries with Retail Sales Tax," in *Changing the Tax Mix: Papers Presented at a Conference Organised by the Centre of Policy Studies, Monash University*, ed. by John G. Head (Sydney: Australian Tax Research Foundation, 1986).

———, *Indirect Taxation in Developing Economies* (Baltimore: Johns Hopkins University Press, rev. ed., 1988).

———, and Ulla Brems, *The Controversial Norwegian Value Added Tax*, BEBR Faculty Working Paper No. 1245 (Urbana-Champaign, Illinois: College of Commerce and Business Administration, University of Illinois, April 1986).

"EC: VAT," *World Tax Report* (London), December 1987, pp. 12–13.

Edwards, J.S.S., and C.P. Mayer, *Issues in Bank Taxation* (London: Institute for Fiscal Studies).

"European Communities: Harmonization of VAT," *European Taxation*, International Bureau of Fiscal Documentation (Amsterdam), Vol. 25 (May 1985), pp. 140–43.

European Community, Amended Proposed Seventh Directive on the Harmonization of the Laws of the Member States Relating to Turnover Taxes—Common System of Value Added Tax to Be Applied to Works of Art, Collectors' Items, Antiques and Used Goods, Submitted by the Commission to the Council on January 11, 1978 (Brussels).

———, Commission of the European Economic Community, *The EEC Reports on Tax Harmonization: The Report of the Fiscal and Financial Committee*, 1958 (Neumark Report) and the *Reports of the Sub-Groups A, B and C*, an unofficial translation by H. Thurston (Amsterdam: International Bureau of Fiscal Documentation, 1963).

———, *Completing the Internal Market—The Introduction of a VAT Clearing Mechanism for Intra-Community Sales*, COM(87)323 final/2 (Brussels, August 25, 1987), reproduced in *Intertax* (Deventer, Netherlands), January 1988, pp. 19–26.

———, *Completion of the Internal Market: Approximation of Indirect Tax Rates and Harmonization of Indirect Tax Structure*, COM(87)320 final (Brussels, August 5, 1987).

———, "Draft VAT Directive on Temporary Importation of Goods," reproduced in *Intertax* (Deventer, Netherlands), March 1985, pp. 74–75.

———, Eighth Council Directive of December 6, 1979 on the Harmonization of the Laws of the Member States Relating to Turnover Taxes—Arrangements for the Refund of Value Added Tax to Taxable Persons Not Established in the Territory of the Country, 79/1072/EEC (Brussels); *Official Journal*, No. L331, December 27, 1979, p. 11.

————, "First Report from the Commission to the Council on the Application of the Common System of Value Added Tax, Submitted in Accordance with Article 34 of the Sixth Council Directive (77/388/EEC) of May 17, 1977," COM(83)426 final (Brussels, September 14, 1983), reproduced in *Intertax* (Deventer, Netherlands), Part I in January 1984, pp. 17–33, Part II in February 1984, pp. 62–76, and Part III in March 1984, pp. 95–123.

————, "Further Harmonization of VAT," Report from the Commission to the Council on the Transitional Provisions Applicable Under the Common System of VAT, Submitted in Accordance with Article 28 of the Sixth Council Directive of May 17, 1977, COM(82)885 final (Brussels, January 17, 1983), reproduced in *Intertax* (Deventer, Netherlands), April 1983, pp. 137–52.

————, "Proposal for a Council Directive Amending Directive 77/388/EEC on the Harmonization of the Laws of the Member States Relating to Turnover Taxes in Respect of the Common Value Added Tax Scheme Applicable to Small and Medium-Sized Businesses," COM(86)444 final (Brussels, October 9, 1986); *Official Journal*, No. C272, October 28, 1986, p. 12.

————, "Proposal for a Fourteenth Council Directive on the Harmonization of the Laws of the Member States Relating to Turnover Taxes—Deferred Payment of the Tax Payable on Importation by Taxable Persons," submitted by the Commission to the Council on July 19, 1982.

————, "Proposed Standstill on VAT and Excise Duties," reproduced in *Intertax* (Deventer, Netherlands), February 1986, pp. 45–47.

————, *Report on Behalf of the Committee on Economic and Monetary Affairs and Industrial Policy on the Removal of Tax Barriers Within the European Community* (Rapporteur: K. de Gucht), European Parliament Session Documents (Series A, Document A2-63/87, Brussels, May 22, 1987).

————, Second Council Directive of April 11, 1967 on the Harmonization of Legislation of Member States Concerning Turnover Taxes—Structure and Procedures for Application of the Common System of Value Added Tax, 67/228/EEC (Brussels); English text in the Special Edition 1967 of the *Official Journal*, November 1972, p. 16.

————, Seventeenth Council Directive of July 16, 1985 on the Harmonization of the Laws of the Member States Relating to Turnover Taxes—Exemption from Value Added Tax on the Temporary Importation of Goods Other Than Means of Transport, 85/362/EEC (Brussels); *Official Journal*, No. L192, July 24, 1985, p. 20.

————, Sixth Council Directive of May 17, 1977 on the Harmonization of the Laws of the Member States Relating to Turnover Taxes—Common System of Value Added Tax: Uniform Basis of Assessment, 77/388/EEC (Brussels); *Official Journal*, No. L145, June 13, 1977.

————, Tenth Council Directive of July 31, 1984 on the Harmonization of the Laws of the Member States Relating to Turnover Taxes, Amending Directive 77/388/EEC—Application of Value Added Tax to the Hiring

Out of Movable Tangible Property, 84/386/EEC (Brussels); *Official Journal*, No. L208, August 3, 1984, p. 58.

―――, Twentieth Council Directive of July 16, 1985 on the Harmonization of the Laws of the Member States Relating to Turnover Taxes—Common System of Value Added Tax: Derogation in Connection with the Special Aids Granted to Certain Farmers to Compensate for the Dismantlement of Monetary Compensatory Amounts Applying to Certain Agricultural Products, 85/361/EEC (Brussels); *Official Journal,* No. L192, July 24, 1985, p. 18.

―――, "VAT on Goods and Services Supplied by Craftsmen in the Applied Arts Sector," Written Question No. 213/83 by Luc Beyer de Ryke, reproduced in *Intertax* (Deventer, Netherlands), February 1984, pp. 79–80.

―――, "VAT on Works of Art—Belgium—Common EEC System," Written Question No. 1891/83 by Luc Beyer de Ryke, reproduced in *Intertax* (Deventer, Netherlands), September 1984, p. 354.

"Exemption of Welfare Supplies by Charities and Public Bodies," *Accountancy* (London), Vol. 97 (February 1986), p. 35.

Ferron, Mark J., "Excise Taxation: Theory and Practice in Developed and Developing Countries" (unpublished; International Monetary Fund, March 14, 1984); a modified version of the paper under the title "Issues in Excise Taxation" was published in *Fiscal Issues in South-East Asia*, ed. by Parthasarathi Shome (Singapore: Oxford University Press, 1986).

France, Conseil des Impôts, *Sixième Rapport au Président de la République Relatif à la T.V.A.*, Année 1982 (Paris, 1983).

Frenkel, Jacob A., and Assaf Razin, "Budget Deficits Under Alternative Tax Systems: International Effects," *Staff Papers*, International Monetary Fund (Washington), Vol. 35 (June 1988), pp. 297–315.

Galvin, Charles O., "It's VAT Time Again," *Tax Notes*, Tax Analysts (Arlington, Virginia), Vol. 21 (October 24, 1983), pp. 275–81.

García Azcárate, Tomas, "El impuesto sobre el valor añadido y la agricultura española: unos primeros resultados," *Hacienda Pública Española*, No. 99, Ministerio de Economía y Hacienda, Instituto de Estudios Fiscales (Madrid, 1986).

Gillis, Malcolm, "Worldwide Experience in Sales Taxation: Lessons for North America," *Policy Sciences* (Dordrecht, Netherlands), Vol. 19, No. 2 (1986), pp. 125–42.

Goode, Richard, *The Individual Income Tax* (Washington: Brookings Institution, rev. ed., 1976).

Goodwin, Michael, "VAT Compliance Costs to the Independent Retailers," *Accountancy* (London), Vol. 97 (September 1976), pp. 48–60.

Gordon, Leon, "Abolishing Fiscal Frontiers in the EEC," *Tax Planning International Review* (London), Vol. 15 (March 1988), pp. 3–8.

Gravelle, Jane G., "Assessing a Value-Added Tax: Efficiency and Equity," *Tax*

Notes, Tax Analysts (Arlington, Virginia), Vol. 38 (March 7, 1988), pp. 1117–23.

"Greece: VAT," *World Tax Report* (London), October 1987, pp. 11–13.

Greene, Leonard M., and Bette K. Fishbein, "The VAT Alternative," in *Examination of Basic Weaknesses of Income as the Major Federal Tax Base*, ed. by Richard W. Lindholm (New York: Praeger Publishers, 1986).

Guerard, Michèle, "The Brazilian State Value-Added Tax," *Staff Papers*, International Monetary Fund (Washington), Vol. 20 (March 1973), pp. 118–69.

Habibi, Noureddine, "L'introduction de la TVA au Maroc soulève une polémique," *Le Journal de l'Economie Africaine* (Paris), June 12, 1986, pp. 57–59.

Haig, Robert M., "The Cost to Business Concerns of Compliance with Tax Laws," *Management Review* (New York), Vol. 24 (November 1935), pp. 323–33.

Hall, Robert E., and Alvin Rabushka, *The Flat Tax* (Stanford, California: Hoover Institution Press, 1985).

Han, Seung Soo, "The Value Added Tax in Korea," paper presented at World Bank Conference on Value Added Taxation in Developing Countries, Washington, April 21–23, 1986; forthcoming in *Value Added Taxation in Developing Countries*, ed. by Malcolm Gillis, Carl S. Shoup, and Gerardo P. Sicat (World Bank).

Heian, Betty C., and Terry D. Monson, "Value-Added Taxation in the Côte d'Ivoire," paper presented at World Bank Conference on Value Added Taxation in Developing Countries, Washington, April 21–23, 1986; forthcoming in *Value Added Taxation in Developing Countries*, ed. by Malcolm Gillis, Carl S. Shoup, and Gerardo P. Sicat (World Bank).

Heller, Peter S., "Testing the Impact of Value-Added and Global Income Tax Reforms on Korean Tax Incidence in 1976: An Input-Output and Sensitivity Analysis," *Staff Papers*, International Monetary Fund (Washington), Vol. 28 (June 1981), pp. 375–410.

Hemming, Richard, and John A. Kay, "The United Kingdom," in *The Value-Added Tax: Lessons from Europe*, ed. by Henry J. Aaron (Washington: Brookings Institution, 1981).

Herschel, Federico J., "Tax Evasion and Its Measurement in Developing Countries," *Public Finance* (The Hague), Vol. 33, No. 3 (1978), pp. 232–68.

Hicks, Alistair, "VAT and the Arts," *The Spectator* (London), January 10, 1987, p. 29.

Holland, J.C., "The Nature of VAT," *Bulletin for International Fiscal Documentation*, International Bureau of Fiscal Documentation (Amsterdam), Vol. 41 (January 1987), pp. 23–28.

Hufbauer, Gary, "The Consumption Tax and International Competitiveness," in *The Consumption Tax: A Better Alternative?* ed. by Charls E. Walker and Mark A. Bloomfield (Cambridge, Massachusetts: Ballinger Publishing Company, 1987).

Ireland, *Budget, 1985*, Financial Statement of the Minister of Finance, January 30, 1985 (Dublin: Stationery Office, 1985).

———, Central Bank, *Quarterly Bulletin*, "Submission to Commission on Taxation" (Dublin), Winter 1980, pp. 43–72.

———, Commission on Taxation, *Third Report of the Commission on Taxation: Indirect Taxation* (Dublin: Stationery Office, June 1984).

———, Commission on Taxation, *Fifth Report of the Commission on Taxation: Tax Administration* (Dublin: Stationery Office, October 1985).

———, Revenue Commissioners, *Guide to the Value Added Tax* (Dublin, 1972).

"Italy: Tightening the Fiscal Belt," *World Tax Report* (London), October 1987, p. 8.

Jap, Kim Siong, "The Value-Added Tax Law in Force," *Bulletin for International Fiscal Documentation*, International Bureau of Fiscal Documentation (Amsterdam), Vol. 40 (July 1986), pp. 315–18.

"Japan: Sales Tax," *World Tax Report* (London), March 1987, pp. 13–14.

Jenkins, Glenn, "The Evolution of Sales Tax Reform in Canada," in *Policy Forum on the Business Transfer Tax*, ed. by Robin W. Boadway and Jack M. Mintz (Kingston, Ontario: John Deutsch Institute for the Study of Economic Policy, Queens University, 1986).

Johnstone, Dorothy, *A Tax Shall be Charged* (London: H.M. Stationery Office, 1975).

Lee, Catherine, Mark Pearson, and Stephen Smith, *Fiscal Harmonization: An Analysis of the European Commission's Proposals* (London: Institute for Fiscal Studies, 1988).

Lienard, Jean-Louis, Kenneth C. Messere, and Jeffrey Owens, "France," in *Comparative Tax Systems: Europe, Canada, and Japan*, ed. by Joseph A. Pechman (Arlington, Virginia: Tax Analysts, 1987).

Lindholm, Richard W., *A New Federal Tax System* (New York: Praeger Publishers, 1984).

Longo, Carlos A., "Indirect Tax Harmonization: The Case of LAIA?" *Bulletin for International Fiscal Documentation*, International Bureau of Fiscal Documentation (Amsterdam), Vol. 35 (December 1981), pp. 533–43.

Lukács, József, "Hungary: The Introduction of VAT in 1988," *Bulletin for International Fiscal Documentation*, International Bureau of Fiscal Documentation (Amsterdam), Vol. 41 (October 1987), pp. 446–51.

Makino, Yo, "LDP Passes Sweeping Tax Reform," *Japan Economic Journal* (Tokyo), Vol. 24 (December 1986), pp. 1 and 4.

Matthews, Milton P., *A Measurement of the Cost of Collecting Sales Tax Monies in*

Selected Retail Stores (Salt Lake City, Utah: Bureau of Economic and Business Research, University of Utah, 1957).

McLure, Charles E., Jr., "Merit Wants: A Normatively Empty Box," *Finanzarchiv* (Tübingen), Vol. 27 (June 1968), pp. 474–83.

——, "The TVA and Fiscal Federalism," in U.S. Congress, *The Value-Added Tax: Hearings Before the Joint Economic Committee*, 92nd Congress, 2nd Session, March 21–24, 1972 (Washington: Government Printing Office, 1972).

——, "A Federal Tax on Value Added: U.S. View," *Proceedings of the Sixty-Sixth Annual Conference on Taxation*, National Tax Association—Tax Institute of America, Toronto, September 9–13, 1973 (Columbus, Ohio, 1974), pp. 84–103.

—— (1980a), "State and Federal Relations in the Taxation of Value Added," *Journal of Corporation Law* (Iowa City, Iowa), Vol. 6, No. 1 (Fall 1980), pp. 127–39.

—— (1980b), "The Tax Restructuring Act of 1979: Time for an American Value-Added Tax?" *Public Policy* (Cambridge, Massachusetts), Vol. 28 (Summer 1980), pp. 301–22.

——, "VAT Versus the Payroll Tax," in *Social Security Financing*, ed. by Felicity Skidmore (Cambridge, Massachusetts: MIT Press, 1981).

—— (1987a), *State and Local Implications of a Federal Value Added Tax* (Washington: Academy for State and Local Government, 1987).

—— (1987b), *The Value-Added Tax: Key to Deficit Reduction?* (Washington: American Enterprise Institute for Public Policy Research, 1987).

Meyer, Carrie, and John F. Due, "Dominican Republic: Value Added Tax," *Bulletin for International Fiscal Documentation*, International Bureau of Fiscal Documentation (Amsterdam), Vol. 42 (January 1988), pp. 13–16.

Miles, Colin, *VAT and Imports & Exports* (Bicester, Oxfordshire: CCH Editions Limited, 1987).

Morgan, David R., "An Agenda for Tax Reform," in *Changing the Tax Mix: Papers Presented at a Conference Organised by the Centre of Policy Studies, Monash University*, ed. by John G. Head (Sydney: Australian Tax Research Foundation, 1986).

Murray, Russell G., "Value Added Credits: Will They Work?" *Tax Notes*, Taxation with Representation Fund (Arlington, Virginia), Vol. 8 (February 5, 1979), pp. 139–40.

Musgrave, Richard A., "Effects of Business Taxes on International Commodity Flows," in *Public Finance in a Democratic Society: Collected Papers of Richard A. Musgrave*, Vol. I: Social Goods, Taxation and Fiscal Policy (New York: New York University Press, 1986).

Mutén, Leif, Comment on "Sweden," in *World Tax Reform: A Progress Report*, ed. by Joseph A. Pechman (Washington: Brookings Institution, 1988).

Nellor, David, "The Effect of the Value-Added Tax on the Tax Ratio," IMF

Working Paper WP/87/47 (unpublished; Washington: International Monetary Fund, July 9, 1987).

Nelson, Robert H., "The Economics Profession and the Making of Public Policy," *Journal of Economic Literature* (Nashville, Tennessee), Vol. 25 (March 1987), pp. 49–91.

New Zealand, *An Act to Amend The Goods and Services Tax Act 1985* (Wellington: Government Printer, March 24, 1988).

———, GST Coordinating Office, *Bloodstock and Racing Industry* & *GST* (Wellington).

———, GST Coordinating Office, *Clubs, Charities and Associations* & *GST* (Wellington: Government Printer, 1986).

———, GST Coordinating Office, *The Fire and General Insurance Industry* & *GST* (Wellington: Government Printer, April 1986).

———, GST Coordinating Office, *Pricing* & *GST* (Wellington).

———, GST Coordinating Office, *Understanding GST: A Guide to the Legislation* (Wellington: Government Printer, 1986).

———, GST Coordinating Office, *Working with GST* (Wellington: Government Printer, 1985).

———, Inland Revenue, *GST Guide* (Wellington: Government Printer, June 1986).

———, Inland Revenue, *Goods and Services Tax: Supplement to the GST Guide* (Wellington: Government Printer, 1986).

———, *Report of the Advisory Panel on Goods and Services Tax to the Minister of Finance* (Wellington: Government Printer, June 1985).

Oldman, Oliver, and LaVerne Woods, "Would a Value-Added Tax System Relieve Tax Compliance Problems?" in *Income Tax Compliance*, a Report of the American Bar Association Taxation Conference (Reston, Virginia, March 16–19, 1983).

Organization for Economic Cooperation and Development, *Revenue Statistics of OECD Member Countries, 1965–1985* (Paris: OECD, 1986).

Parkinson, Dennis A., *Value Added Tax in the EEC* (London: Graham & Trotman, 1981).

Peacock, Alan, and Francesco Forte, eds., *The Political Economy of Taxation* (Oxford: Basil Blackwell, 1981).

Pechman, Joseph A., ed., *Comparative Tax Systems: Europe, Canada, and Japan* (Arlington, Virginia: Tax Analysts, 1987).

———, *World Tax Reform: A Progress Report* (Washington: Brookings Institution, 1988).

Perry, Guillermo, and Alba Lucia Orozco de Triana, "The Vat in Colombia: Structure and Administration," paper presented at World Bank Conference on Value Added Taxation in Developing Countries, Washington, April 21–23, 1986; forthcoming in *Value Added Taxation in Developing*

Countries, ed. by Malcolm Gillis, Carl S. Shoup, and Gerardo P. Sicat (World Bank).

Philippines, Department of Finance, National Tax Research Center, "Adopting a Value-Added Tax, Amending for this Purpose Certain Provisions of the National Internal Revenue Code, and for Other Purposes," *Tax Monthly* (Manila), Vol. 28 (August 1987), pp. 11–21.

———, "Highlights of the APTIRC Seminar Workshop on Value-Added Taxation in Asia," *Tax Monthly* (Manila), Vol. 29 (June 1988), pp. 1–9.

Pink, Geoffrey C., *Tax Aspects of Commodity and Financial Future Transactions* (London: Butterworths, 1985).

Poddar, Satya, "Value-Added Tax at the State Level," paper presented at World Bank Conference on Value Added Taxation in Developing Countries, Washington, April 21–23, 1986; forthcoming in *Value Added Taxation in Developing Countries*, ed. by Malcolm Gillis, Carl S. Shoup, and Gerardo P. Sicat (World Bank).

Pohmer, Dieter, "Germany," in *The Value-Added Tax: Lessons from Europe*, ed. by Henry J. Aaron (Washington: Brookings Institution, 1981).

Porras, Fernando A., "Value Added Sales Tax (ITBM) in Panama," technical paper presented at XIII CIAT General Assembly (Quito, Ecuador: Centro Interamericano de Administradores Tributarios, 1979).

Portugal, Comissão do IVA, *O Impacto do IVA na Economia Portuguesa* (Lisbon: Imprensa Nacional, 1984).

"Portugal: Effects of VAT," *World Tax Report* (London), February 1986, p. 9.

"Portugal: Taxation 1987," in *European Taxation*, International Bureau of Fiscal Documentation (Amsterdam), Vol. 27, No. 8 (August 1987), pp. 264–70.

Prebble, John, "Tax Reform in New Zealand," *Asian-Pacific Tax and Investment Bulletin* (Singapore), Vol. 5, No. 1 (January 1987), pp. 1–21.

Price Waterhouse, *Information Guide: Value Added Tax*, Supplement (New York, April 1980).

———, "New Zealand: The Introduction of Goods and Services Tax," *Asian-Pacific Tax and Investment Bulletin* (Singapore), Vol. 4 (August 1986), pp. 299–311.

Rayney, Peter, "VAT and the Property Developer," *Accountancy* (London), Vol. 98 (October 1987), pp. 80–82.

Robinson, Bill, ed., *Options for 1988: The Green Budget* (London: Institute for Fiscal Studies, 1988).

Roth, William V., Jr., *The Business Transfer Tax Act of 1985* (S.1102, 99th Congress, 1st Session, Washington, May 8, 1985).

———, "The Roth Reforms," speech to the National Press Club, Washington, February 20, 1986.

Sampson, Anthony A., "The Shift to Indirect Taxation in a Unionized Economy," *Bulletin of Economic Research* (Leeds), Vol. 38 (January 1986), pp. 87–91.

Sandford, Cedric, *Value-Added Tax—U.K. Experience: Lessons for Australia*, Occasional Paper No. 22 (Canberra: Centre for Research on Federal Financial Relations, Australian National University, 1981).

———, "The Costs of Paying Tax," *Accountancy* (London), Vol. 97 (June 1986), pp. 108–11.

———, Michael R. Goodwin, Peter J.W. Hardwick, and M.I. Butterworth, *Costs and Benefits of VAT* (London: Heinemann Educational Books, 1981).

Schenone, Osvaldo, "Notas sobre la Aplicación del Impuesto al Valor Agregado en la Argentina," *Desarrollo Económico* (Buenos Aires), Vol. 21, No. 81 (April–June 1981), pp. 97–108.

Shoup, Carl S., "Taxation in France," *National Tax Journal* (Columbus, Ohio), Vol. 8 (December 1955), pp. 325–44.

———, "Factors Bearing on an Assumed Choice Between a Federal Retail-Sales Tax and a Federal Value-Added Tax," in *Broad-Based Taxes: New Options and Sources*, ed. by Richard A. Musgrave (Baltimore: Johns Hopkins University Press, 1973).

Sinclair, P.J.N., review of *The Value-Added Tax: Lessons from Europe*, ed. by Henry J. Aaron (Washington: Brookings Institution, 1981), in *Public Finance Quarterly* (Beverly Hills, California), Vol. 11 (July 1983), pp. 380–84.

Smith, Stephen, "Tax Enforcement and the Black Economy: Cost-Effectiveness and Compliance," *Public Money* (London), Vol. 6 (December 1986), pp. 25–28.

Software Digest Ratings Newsletter (Philadelphia, Pennsylvania), Vol. 3 (July 1986).

Somerville, Ian, and John Arnold, *VAT Survival: Penalty . . . or Peace of Mind . . .* (London: Deloitte, Haskins, & Sells, 1985).

South Africa, *Report of the Commission of Inquiry into the Tax Structure of the Republic of South Africa* (Margo Commission) (Pretoria: Government Printer, 1987).

Stephens, Robert J., "Tax Reform in New Zealand," *Australian Tax Forum* (Clayton, Victoria), Vol. 4, No. 3 (1987), pp. 327–46.

Stockfisch, J.A., "Value-Added Taxes and the Size of Government: Some Evidence," *National Tax Journal* (Columbus, Ohio), Vol. 38 (December 1985), pp. 547–52.

Strachan, Valerie, "VAT in the U.K.: The Tax Collector's View," in *The Political Economy of Taxation*, ed. by Alan Peacock and Francesco Forte (Oxford: Basil Blackwell, 1981).

Tait, Alan A., *Value Added Tax* (London: McGraw-Hill, 1972).

——, "Is the Introduction of a Value-Added Tax Inflationary?" *Finance & Development* (Washington), Vol. 18 (June 1981), pp. 38–42.

——, "The Value-Added Tax: Revenue, Inflation, and the Foreign Trade Balance," paper presented at World Bank Conference on Value Added Taxation in Developing Countries, Washington, April 21–23, 1986; forthcoming in *Value Added Taxation in Developing Countries*, ed. by Malcolm Gillis, Carl S. Shoup, and Gerardo P. Sicat (World Bank).

Tanzi, Vito, "Taxation and Price Stabilization," in *Comparative Tax Studies: Essays in Honor of Richard Goode*, ed. by Sijbren Cnossen (Amsterdam: North-Holland, 1983).

Tielemans, P.P.S.C., "Towards a European Community Without Borders: Utopia or Reality?" *European Taxation*, International Bureau of Fiscal Documentation (Amsterdam), Vol. 27 (July 1987), pp. 207–12.

Topham, Neville, "A Reappraisal and Recalculation of the Marginal Cost of Public Funds," *Public Finance* (The Hague), Vol. 39, No. 3 (1984), pp. 394–405.

"TPI Country Survey—Canada: Sales Tax Reform," in *Tax Planning International Review* (London), Vol. 14 (December 1987), pp. 25–27.

"Treatment of Donations to Charities: Live Aid," *Accountancy* (London), Vol. 96 (September 1985), p. 22.

Ture, Norman B., Prepared Statement in U.S. Congress, *The Value-Added Tax: Hearings Before the Joint Economic Committee*, 92nd Congress, 2nd Session, March 21–24, 1972 (Washington: Government Printing Office, 1972).

Turnier, William J., "Designing an Efficient Value Added Tax," *Tax Law Review* (New York), Vol. 39, No. 4 (Summer 1984), pp. 435–72.

United Kingdom, Board of Inland Revenue, *Report for the Year Ended 31st December 1985*, Cmnd. 9831 (London: H.M. Stationery Office, July 1986).

——, Commissioners of H.M. Customs and Excise, *Review of Value Added Tax*, Cmnd. 7415 (London: H.M. Stationery Office, 1978).

——, Commissioners of H.M. Customs and Excise, *76th Report of the Commissioners of Her Majesty's Customs and Excise for the Year Ended 31 March 1985*, Cmnd. 9655 (London: H.M. Stationery Office, December 1985).

——, Commissioners of H.M. Customs and Excise, *Report for the Year Ended 31 March 1986*, Cm. 5 (London: H.M. Stationery Office, November 1986).

——, Committee on Enforcement Powers of the Revenue Departments (Keith Committee), *Report*, Vols. 1 and 2, Cmnd. 8822 (London: H.M. Stationery Office, 1983).

——, Department of Trade and Industry, *Burdens on Business* (London: H.M. Stationery Office, 1985).

——, H.M. Customs and Excise, *Value Added Tax: Second-Hand Works of Art, Antiques and Scientific Collections*, Notice No. 712 (London, February 1973).

————, H.M. Customs and Excise, *Value Added Tax: Construction Industry*, Notice No. 708 (London, 1975).

————, H.M. Customs and Excise, *Value Added Tax: Construction Industry: Alterations & Repairs & Maintenance*, Notice No. 715 (London, August 1975).

————, H.M. Customs and Excise, *Value Added Tax: Young Children's Footwear and Clothing*, Notice No. 714 (London, revised September 1986).

————, *Report of the Committee on Turnover Taxation* (Richardson Committee), Cmnd. 2300 (London: H.M. Stationery Office, 1964).

United States, Congress, *The Value-Added Tax: Hearings Before the Joint Economic Committee*, 92nd Congress, 2nd Session, March 21–24, 1972 (Washington: Government Printing Office, 1972).

————, Congress, *Tax Reform and Deficit Reduction: Hearings Before the Committee on Ways and Means*, 98th Congress, 2nd Session, September 25–27, 1984 (Washington: Government Printing Office, 1984).

————, Department of the Treasury, *Tax Reform for Fairness, Simplicity, and Economic Growth: The Treasury Department Report to the President*, Vol. 1: Overview, Vol. 2: General Explanation, and Vol. 3: Value-Added Tax (Washington: Office of the Secretary, Department of the Treasury, November 1984).

————, General Acounting Office, *Tax Policy: Choosing Among Consumption Taxes* (Washington: General Accounting Office, 1986).

"Value Added Tax," in *Accountancy* (London), Vol. 96 (July 1985), p. 32.

"Value Added Tax," in *Accountancy* (London), Vol. 97 (February 1986), p. 35.

"Value Added Tax: Finance Act 1985—Keith Committee Proposals," *Accountancy* (London), Vol. 96 (October 1985), pp. 36–37.

"VAT: Avoidance Methods on Management Charges," *International Tax Report* (London), October 1985, p. 10.

"A VAT Spat in Greece," *Newsweek* (New York), June 1987, p. 37.

Walker, Charls E., and Mark A. Bloomfield, eds., *The Consumption Tax: A Better Alternative?* papers presented at a conference sponsored by the American Council for Capital Formation—Center for Policy Research, 1986 (Cambridge, Massachusetts: Ballinger Publishing Company, 1987).

Walters, Alan, *Britain's Economic Renaisssance: Margaret Thatcher's Reforms, 1979–1984* (New York: Oxford University Press, 1986).

Waugh, Auberon, "A Call to the Youth of England Now Abed," *The Spectator* (London), September 6, 1986, p. 8.

Wheatcroft, G.S.A., and J.F. Avery Jones, eds., *Encyclopedia of Value Added Tax*, Vol. 2 (London: Sweet & Maxwell).

White, Brenda, "A Tax on Knowledge," *Journal of Information Science: Principles and Practice* (Amsterdam), Vol. 10, No. 1 (1985), pp. 29–37.

Yocum, James C., *Retailers' Costs of Sales Tax Collection in Ohio*, Bureau of

Business Research Monograph No. 100 (Columbus, Ohio: Bureau of Business Research, College of Commerce and Administration, Ohio State University, 1961).

Index

Letters are used as follows: c for chart, n for footnote, and t for table

Kay, John A., 16n, 44n, 212n, 216n, 221n, 417
Kenya: single-stage VAT, 7
Korea: administration, 243, 249, 250, 402; compensation to exporters, 224; computerization, 250, 328; consumption tax, 16; cross-checking by computer, 281, 282t, 284; exemptions, 52t, 67, 89; evasion, cross-checking for, 304; financial transactions, 98, 99; first VAT in Asia, 204–205; introduction of VAT: effect on prices, 194t, 211t, price change forecasts, 192, 198–99, price freeze, 199, publicity for, 173, test runs, 174–75, transitional measures, 184t; invoices, control of, 281, 282t, 284; leasing houses and land, 89; penalties for evasion, 307t; policies, 204–205; prices, 192, 194t, 198–99, 204–205, 211t; rates, 40t, 41, 98, 205, 249: by industry, 119t, for small traders, 119; refunds of tax on stocks, 178; regressivity, 216; retailers, cash registers for, 283; revenue, 10t, 26t, 28t; sales tax on manufacturing, 8; secondhand goods taxable, 103; small businesses: compliance costs, 117, special schemes for, 111, 136–37, treatment of, 124t, 136–37; substitution for other taxes, 10t, 16, 24, 204–205; temporary imports, 395; transport, passenger, 67; taxpayers as percent of population, 272t; zero rating, 52t, 53

Land, 63–65, 80–82
Latin America: administration, 234, 243, 247, 248, 326; adoption of VAT, 20, 20n; agriculture, 148t, 151; Andean Pact, 20; exemptions: of agricultural inputs, 53, of leasing immovable property, 89, of smallest businesses, 118; farmers, treatment of, 151; financial transactions, stamp taxes on, 98; harmonization, 20; invoices issued to final consumer, 356; Latin American Integration Association (LAIA), 20; noncompliance of traders, results of, 139–40; rates, 46, 148t; retail stage: exemption of smallest traders, 118, extension through, 399, simpli-

fied invoices for, 386, small traders, 110; secondhand goods taxable, 103; small businesses, 110, 118, 124t; zero rating, 54 (see also Western Hemisphere)
Leasing, 52t, 84t, 87–92: agents, 90–92; goods, 90–92; hotel accommodations, 88–90; housing, rental, 52t; immovable property, 84t, 87–90
Lee, Catherine, 161n, 417
Liability, 365–96: business tests, 368–70; calculation of sales by small retailers, 167, 385–86; credit sales, 385–86; debatable cases, 370–71; goods and services: international, 376t, 389–96, supply of, 371–73; 386–89; groups of companies, 367–68; invoices, role of, 385–86; partnerships, 366–67; taxable activity, 368–71: tests for, 368–70; taxable persons, 365–66: clubs as, 367; time of supply provisions, 373, 376t; traders or businesses, 371 (see also Control, Enforcement, and Penalties)
Lienard, Jean-Louis, 216n, 417
Lindholm, Richard W., 32t, 32t(n), 33, 33n, 417
Longo, Carlos A., 20n, 417
Lukács, József, 25n, 417
Luxembourg: administration, 146n, 239t; agriculture, 148t; buildings, 63t; craftsmen's trade, rates on, 105; cultural activities, 75t; exemptions, 52t, 130; goods and services tax, 23t: excised goods, 46t; introduction of VAT: effect on prices, 194t, 211t, transitional measures, 184t; leasing immovable property, 84t; rates, 40t, 67, 72, 91, 105: special, 75t; revenue, 10t, 26t, 28t, 161t; sales tax, single-stage, 15; secondhand automobiles, 104; small businesses, 124t, 130, 131; substitution for other taxes, 10t, 22; transport tax, 69

Madagascar: exemptions, 52t; forfait system for small traders, 120–21, 120n; introduction of VAT: effect on prices, 194t, 211t; rates, 40t; revenue, 10t, 26t, 28t; small businesses, 124t; substitution for other taxes, 10t